STRANGERS TO THAT LAND

Ulster Editions and Monographs

General Editors

Elizabeth McIntyre

John McVeagh

Robert Welch

ULSTER EDITIONS AND MONOGRAPHS

ISSN 0954–3392

1 *Joyce Cary Remembered*. Compiled and edited by Barbara Fisher
2 *Swift's Irish Pamphlets — An Introductory Selection.* Edited by Joseph McMinn
3 *Charles Lever: New Evaluations*. Edited by Tony Bareham
4 *The Achievement of Brian Friel.* Edited by Alan Peacock
5 *Strangers to that Land: British Perceptions of Ireland from the Reformation to the Famine.* Edited by Andrew Hadfield and John McVeagh

STRANGERS TO THAT LAND

British Perceptions of Ireland from the Reformation to the Famine

edited by

Andrew Hadfield and John McVeagh

Ulster Editions and Monographs 5

COLIN SMYTHE
Gerrards Cross, 1994

First published in 1994 by Colin Smythe Limited,
Gerrards Cross, Buckinghamshire

British Library Cataloguing-in-Publication Data

A catalogue record of this book is available
from the British Library

ISBN 0–86140–350–9

Produced in Great Britain
Printed and bound by TJ Press (Padstow) Ltd., Cornwall

A country so remote from the rest of the world, and lying at its furthest extremity, forming, as it were, another world . . .
(Giraldus Cambrensis, 1188)

Now it is no wonder if those that were but Strangers to that Land should not (at first sight) understand the compleat interest thereof . . .
(Vincent Gookin, 1655)

Ireland really is my problem; the breaking point of the huge suppuration which all British and all European society now is.
(Thomas Carlyle, 1849)

In memory of Reginald Hadfield
1904–1992

CONTENTS

List of Illustrations xi

Acknowledgements xii

Preface 1

Introduction 3

PART ONE: 1540–1660 edited by Andrew Hadfield

1. Giraldus Cambrensis and English Writing about Ireland 25
2. John Bale and the Reformation in Ireland 30
3. The Nature of the Irish 36
4. Three Travellers' Observations of Irish Life 53
5. Land and Landscape 63
6. Irish Society 73
7. Hugh O'Neill, Second Earl of Tyrone (1540–1616) 88
8. War and Rebellion 97
9. Colonization 108
10. The Rebellion of 1641 115
11. The Transplantation to Connaught, 1655–9 123

PART TWO: 1660–1850 edited by John McVeagh

12. Passage and Travel 134
13. The Sense of Difference 148
14. From War to Union 160
15. Irish Life and Customs 187

16. Irish Towns 219
17. Picturesque and Romantic Ireland 238
18. Poverty and Famine 251

Notes 266

Bibliography 298

Index 306

LIST OF ILLUSTRATIONS

John Derricke, 'The triumphant return of the English soldiers', 1581
John Derricke, 'The flight of the Irish', 1581
Map of Ireland, 1611
Map of Limerick, 1617
Map of the Battle of Kinsale, 1617
Map of Londonderry, 1629
Prospect of Bleeding Ireland's Miseries, 1647
Ross Castle, 1746
Dunluce Castle, 1746
Map of Ireland, 1776
Mayo mud cabin, 1836
Mayo stone cabin, 1836
Hovel at the Reek, 1836
Better Irish cottage, 1836
Better Connaught cabin, 1836
A village in the west of Ireland, 1859
Contrasting fashions, 1859
Bog village, Roscommon, [1881]
Deserted wharves, Westport, [1881]

ACKNOWLEDGEMENTS

The editors gratefully acknowledge a grant made by the University of Ulster Academic Publications Committee towards the publication costs of this book, which appears as volume 5 in the series *Ulster Editions and Monographs.* Andrew Hadfield wishes to thank the British Academy for the award of a post-doctoral research fellowship which made his contribution to the book possible and John McVeagh wishes to thank the British Academy and the University of Ulster for research grants which enabled him to consult much of the travel literature discussed.

Acknowledgements are due to the Royal Irish Academy for permission to quote the Giraldus extracts from the *Expugnatio*; Van Gorcum for permission to quote the Campion passage; David Beers Quinn for the two extracts quoted from 'A Discourse of Ireland'(c. 1599); Oxford University Press for permission to quote from W. L. Renwick's edition of Edmund Spenser's *A View of the Present State of Ireland* (Oxford, 1970); Lawrence and Wishart for permission to quote two extracts from *Cobbett in Ireland: A Warning to England*, edited by Denis Knight; David Duff, editor of *Victorian Travels*, and Frederick Muller, publisher, for a passage describing Queen Victoria's impressions of Cork; and the estate of Edward MacLysaght for permission to quote two passages from John Dunton, first published in his *Irish Life in the Seventeenth Century*.

The comments of many colleagues on early drafts of the project helped the editors to correct numerous errors and stylistic infelicities. Thanks go out to Paul Hammond, Michael Brennan, Lesley Johnson, Angela Keane, Stephen Steger-Hoey, Seamus MacMathuna, Nick Furbank, and Bob Welch. To Bob Hunter particular acknowledgement is due: his suggestions made the introduction better.

PREFACE

The aim of this book is to provide the reader with a series of representations of Ireland made by British, predominantly English, men and women from the sixteenth to the nineteenth centuries and a historical context as a guide, or starting point for further research into the subject. It has been our general principle that passages included should not be too brief. Readers, we judged, were not to be simply confronted with a mass of statements which could have been made either directly as quotations or paraphrased in a secondary, critical work. It was also important, we felt, to preserve (where possible) the narrative continuity of a historical or descriptive work. For the same reasons we have tried to keep explanatory notes short, and to outline the context in which pieces were written without overtly guiding interpretation. We hope we have performed the tricky juggling act of making available writing that is both representative and interesting, and of clarifying its significance without smothering it in critical verbiage of our own.

Texts and extracts selected for inclusion here have been limited to first hand descriptions of Ireland written by native English, Scottish and Welsh writers. To some degree, obviously, this principle has constrained our choice. A good deal of important writing on Ireland by Richard Stanihurst, Sir John Temple, Gerard Boate, Henry Jones, Lawrence Eachard, Vallancey, J. W. Croker, Matthew Arnold, and others, has been excluded, either because the authors in question did not actually visit Ireland, or because they were not first generation immigrants. This decision, it is true, may be termed arbitrary as 'ways of seeing' can never be distinguished purely on the basis of the observation (or the lack of it) of primary phenomena; national identities are anyhow problematic (see below, pp. 3 ff). What the selection highlights is that those who came to Ireland with a clear sense of their own Englishness, Britishness, Scottishness, national or civil character, were forced to confront a shocking cultural difference which either reinforced their oppositionally defined sense of subjectivity or jolted their confidence in that assumed identity. They may not have observed (or written) Ireland in an *absolutely* different way from those who stayed at home, as Karen Kuppermann claims was the case with the attitudes of the settlers in the Virginian colonies towards the North American Indians.[1] Nevertheless, many had to come to terms with the revelation of Edmund Spenser's Eudoxus, who exclaimed, 'Lord, how quickly doth that country alter men's natures!'[2]

1 K. O. Kupperman, *Settling with the Indians: the meeting of English and Indian cultures in America, 1580–1640* (Totowa, N. J.: Rowan and Littlefield, 1980).

2 Spenser, E., *A View of the Present State of Ireland*, ed. by W. L. Renwick (Oxford: Clarendon Press, 1970) p. 151.

INTRODUCTION

A serious problem presents itself when one is dealing with units like nations which become distinct only in the long term. It is dangerous to assume that political identities are stable phenomena, that 'national characters' exist before they can be represented. To put it another way, one might say that the logic of tracing the historical narrative of nationhood becomes circular when it is that narrative itself which serves to produce what is to be described. Only when the object in question (here, Ireland; or, rather, Ireland as a part of Britain) can be identified do its emergence and origins become clear. As Geoffrey Bennington has argued, the 'post' always comes first, in the sense that a nation has to have an identity before it can have a history, which, paradoxically, provides the identity.[1] The logic we are talking about is grammatical, that of the future perfect tense.[2]

Nations, in Benedict Anderson's phrase, are 'imagined communities', which are believed to exisit in 'homogenous empty time'.[3] In this collection it is an axiomatic starting point that the 'imagined communities' of Britain, England or Ireland did not remain as simple and stable entities in the three centuries under review. The relationship(s) between them changed as different groups, different classes with different senses of identity and purpose presumed to speak for Ireland. All this makes the question of representation — its authority and authenticity — a difficult and complex one; a confused and contradictory field is opened up. The problem is, of course, not simply a 'dead', historical question,[4] as nations never become fixed lines or indelible colours on a map.[5] One might refer to the attempts made at defining that hybrid cultural product, Anglo-Irish literature; at once the result of a historical interaction, yet needing to efface a socio-political origin and existence to validate itself as an essential form. Who can speak for Ireland? Who can presume to write Ireland down?

The *indigenous* literature of Ireland in English is generally known as Anglo-Irish literature. It is the result of the intermixture of two cultures, Irish and English. . . . There is a parallel between Anglo-Irish literature and American literature. Both are modern literatures in English which, after passing through a colonial phase, acquired a *distinctive national quality* and at their best achieved those qualities which commend *international recognition.*[6]

What first began to be written in Ireland, and *on behalf of Ireland*, in the English tongue cannot properly be called Irish literature. . . . It was never in [Swift's power] . . . to make a song that would 'rise in the heart' in a man or in a people; and that, after all, is the true mark of a national literature.[7]

[Anglo-Irish literature] has been called writing in English by Irish authors, and that is a reasonably broad working definition of it. . . . The need to justify removing Irish writing in English from histories of English literature in order to see it in its own terms as a *continuous activity*, a *development* of a particular literature, is now less pressing since the idea of separate *Irish political identity* has become accepted.[8] [Emphases all ours]

The nation serves to authenticate the literature written, and is then, in a circular double-bind, itself written by the literature.[9] Outside of appeals to a universal standard of literary excellence, is the argument any more sophisticated than the blunt assertion made by Thomas McDonagh, the martyr of 1916 and, ironically, the author of substantial work on English as well as Irish literature? McDonagh had stated that

Anglo-Irish literature is applied very rarely to the meagre writings of the planters; it is worth having as a term only to apply to the literature produced by the English-speaking Irish, and by these in general only when writing in Ireland and for the Irish people[10]

The same could be said of many contemporary political positions, where speaking for the nation's true form is the key to strategy and action. Bishop and Mallie describe the creation of one major modern force in Ireland — the Provisional I.R.A. — at a meeting in a small town in the Irish midlands in 1969:

Their first act was to repudiate the proposals passed at the earlier Convention and to reaffirm their allegiance to 'the thirty-two County Irish Republic proclaimed at Easter 1916, established by Dial Eireann in 1919, overthrown by force of arms in 1922 and suppressed to this day by the British-imposed Six County and Twenty-six County partitionist states'.[11]

In a sense we are still inside the logic of the future perfect: a 'real' Ireland, strangled at birth, which will eventually be re-born, like the once and future king in British mythology.[12] W. J. McCormack criticized the influential *Crane Bag* journal for a similarly dangerous Platonic Utopianism when its editorial advocated the 'fifth province' argument:

Long, long ago, some people thought that the four provinces of Ireland 'met at the Stone of Divisions on the Hill of Uisneach', thus positioning a fifth not unlike Euclid's definition of a point: 'others say that the fifth province was Meath (Mide), "the middle", though they disagree about the location'. Anyway the purpose of *The Crane Bag* is to promote the excavation of such unactualized places within the reader, which is the work of constituting the fifth province.

McCormack's point is that for a journal keen to explore and discuss the cultural politics of contemporary Ireland, and to do so with 'an indiscriminate eclecticism' broad enough to include the now familiar 'tribalist' arguments of Conor Cruise O'Brien, to pretend that its forum is beyond the political or the national (Anderson's 'homogenous empty time'?) is not only bad logic but hypocrisy.[13]

Those within Ireland who deny the validity of such national authorities proclaim their difference through an appeal to a separate history which affirms that separate identity. The most common manifestation of this is an equation of Protestantism with the territory of Ulster. Appealing for 'a full scale war against Republican terrorists' at the Ballycastle march on July 12, 1988, James McClure, Past Imperial Master of the Independent Orangemen, predicted that

After the battle is over and the victory is won, there is no doubt that much of the country will lie in ruins but from the ashes, the Sons of the Reformation will build a greater and better Ulster, an Ulster that will be a proud place to bring up our children and our children's children.[14]

Wallis, Bruce and Taylor have argued that

Among Catholics [in Northern Ireland], national identity has become so secure, so taken for granted, that it can to some degree be separated from its religious base. Nationalism and Catholicism are separable. . . . It is an irony of Ulster that while overt commitment to religion is weaker among Protestants, their ideological position is ultimately much less readily secularised . . . there is nowhere else to go. No identity beyond evangelical Protestantism is secure.[15]

As McClure's comments illustrate, the logic of such an 'ethnic' identity is not of a different order to a 'national' one.[16] In any case, there are those who do accept what is commonly termed the 'two nations' thesis,[17] one form of this being the geneaology of the Cruthain:

The Cruthain simply means the ancient British people . . . People are convinced that the bulk of the Protestants came here in the 17th Century as planters. The Protestants themselves are convinced of that, most of them don't go beyond that, they haven't looked at their historical background, where they came from . . . Before the 17th Century the Scots-Irish were here although there were no Catholics and Protestants. The Prods always think that their history only started in the 17th Century.[18]

Recent English reactions, the product of a comfortable insulation from their own nation's historical involvement in the formation of modern Ireland, have, more often than not, been a mixture of disgust and bemusement:

'Christ', he said, calling for a large Scotch, 'what a bloody awful country'.[19]

South Armagh, still light years away from civilization, still living in the dark ages, where barbarity and cruelty are the prime factors of a successful life. . . . It is so unfair that all this beauty should be wasted on these people.[20]

WHAT DO WE WANT for Northern Ireland, that wretched, God-stricken back alley of Europe where they shoot people's kneecaps?[21] [our emphasis]

The use of the first person plural pronoun brings us back to the fundamental problem: who speaks and for whom?

There is a literary as well as a political-historical issue at stake; one with a direct bearing on the present volume. Much of what is dealt with here could be classified as topographical or ethnic description, of all forms of writing perhaps the least politically neutral, in the sense that it subordinates itself so easily to the imperialistic impulse. Mary Louise Pratt underlines this aspect of the politics of style when she notes the nineteenth century explorer John Barrow in southern Africa, 'seeing' the continent's face unfolding before him as he travels: Barrow's actual journey depended on the inhabitants of the region contributing to his enterprise in large numbers but he describes a landscape emptied of human presence, inviting the inevitable takeover.[22] Writing of Locke's *Two Treatises of Government*, a prime colonial text, Homi BhaBha points to an 'indeterminacy' at the centre of the text which is both structural and thematic. The book splits in two, like its definitions. As BhaBha points out, 'slave', for Locke, means proper ownership in colonial Carolina, but unacceptable tyranny in the state of nature — or in England.[23] Seeking to control these opposed significations which threaten to rupture the discourse, the writer produces two narratives, not one. Similar disjunctions are a familiar feature in much Anglo-Irish writing. Thus in *A Modest Proposal* Jonathan Swift explodes in sudden rage as if hating the ironic restraint under which he has written, then resumes the original stance, and closes.[24]

ii

Looking back to the start of the period covered in this book (often termed the 'early modern', that is from roughly 1500 to 1700), one finds the same conflict of identities, traditions and communities, something which has been at the centre of the analytical concern of many modern Irish historians. Groups that have been identified are the native (Gaelic) Irish, the 'Old' English and the 'New' English, who are not to be lumped together with the English government in London, but have their own, separate voices.[25] Crucial to the debate amongst historians of sixteenth century Ireland are two related questions. From when can the Anglo-Irish tradition be dated? Which group, 'Old' or 'New' English (or both, at different times), can be called the 'Anglo-Irish'?[26]

Unfortunately, these are matters beyond the strict concerns of this volume. But it must not be assumed that British/English responses to Ireland, even if they could be separated from such attempts to establish a recognisable selfhood, have any less fluid a history. The most significant and influential representations of Ireland and the Irish in the early modern period date back to the conquest of Henry II (see below, p. 9). Giraldus Cambrensis's two books, the *Topographia Hibernica* (*The History and Topography of Ireland*) and the *Expugnatio Hibernica* (*The Conquest of Ireland*) were acknowledged on both sides of the Irish Sea to be the founding texts for the discourse of English writing about Ireland. Thus, John Hooker, who translated the *Expugnatio* and then continued the history of Ireland up to 1586 in his contribution to Holinshed's *Chronicles*, berated the failure of earlier historians to record their debt to the Anglo-Norman author:

> In this they were much to be blamed, that all of them were beholding unto Giraldus, and not one of them would yield that courtesy either to publish his history, or, using the same, to acknowledge it. For some misliking both method and phrase, framed it in a more lofty style, and under that colour have attributed unto themselves the honor and fruits of another man's doing.[27]

Similarly, Geoffrey Keating, himself of Anglo-Norman descent, but writing in Irish in the early seventeenth century (labelling him, in the term used by Giraldus,[28] a 'degenerate'), made it quite clear from the start of his History of Ireland whom his work was intended to combat:

> We shall set down here a few lines of the lies of the new foreigners[29] who have written concerning Ireland, following Cambrensis; and shall make a

beginning by refuting Cambrensis himself . . . because it is Cambrensis who is as the bull to the herd for them for writing the false history of Ireland, wherefore they had no choice of guide.[30]

Given that Keating's assumed Irishness goes against the grain of his genealogical origin, it has to be asked, concomitantly, how English was Giraldus, whose texts served, according to Keating, to obliterate the historically defined identity he [Keating] wished to defend in the name of a different, but hegemonic[31] identity which appealed to another history to validate itself? Michael Richter has shown that Giraldus did ally himself to the interests of the crown when he travelled to Ireland with Prince John's expedition in 1185, where he saw what he was later to transform into his two crucially important works. However, later on still he came to perceive himself as more Welsh than English, hence the soubriquet, Cambrensis, which, in fact, post-dates these books.[32] On the other hand, as Richter has argued elsewhere, the invaders and colonists who went to Ireland in the twelfth century tended to see themselves as English (and were called 'English' by the Irish) rather than Anglo-Norman.[33] But, again, to assume that Giraldus was an ironic aberration is to miss the point because an English identity, like the Irish counterpart with which it was (and is still) engaged in a dialectical interaction, is not static. Identities depend on difference for their articulation. Richter argues that just because we choose to adopt the labels 'English' and 'Irish' does not mean that we are committed to a belief that these terms always described the same reality:

[T]his much is clear in any case: Tudor and Stuart policies towards Ireland – massive military enterprises from England and plantation of Ireland – marked a new departure. There was little continuity from the time of the battered Pale.[34]

In terms of a history of structural transformation, of shifts of continuity and discontinuity, Henry VIII's declaration through an act of parliament in 1541 that he was no longer lord, but king of Ireland, could be seen as the most significant fulcrum.

The importance of this event has been recognised by many historians looking from the other side of the medieval/modern divide, among them Stephen Ellis who has described the new constitutional position of the Irish in the following terms:

Instead of the island's effective partition — the political structures, customs and law of the Gaelic parts unrecognised in the lordship and vice versa — there should be a new kingdom embracing the whole island and all its institutions, and with the Gaelic population enjoying full constitutional rights under the crown as did the Old English.[35]

Before this change it was, of course, feasible, indeed common, to argue that the whole of Ireland should come under the crown's control, as the author of 'The State of Ireland and the plan for its reformation' (c1515) had done;[36] but, after, it was no longer possible to separate rigidly English and Irish subjects as two distinct groups each with a different status. The Gaelic Irish and 'degenerate' English were held to be subjects of the crown, de facto as well as de jure; the late Medieval distinctions between a 'land of peace' and 'a land of war' with the marcher borders in between could no longer be made.[37] Ireland, as defined from across the water, had become a separate kingdom under the sovereignty of the English king and its people his subjects:

> As long as the jurisdictional area over which the king claimed authority was referred to as the lordship of Ireland it was being implied that only those within this designated area were the king's subjects, and that those outside that jurisdiction had no recourse to the protection of the crown in the event of their being attacked. This reality was admitted by Old English and Gaelic Irish alike as the implication of the change in title which made it clear that all within the newly defined kingdom of Ireland were subjects of the king and would be entitled to the protection of his law if they acknowledged him as their sovereign.[38]

This is only one side of the coin; the act also increased the theoretical power of the king to demand obedience and loyalty from his subjects. As 'king in parliament'[39] he was virtually an absolute monarch; Henry II's right to intervene in Ireland had been based upon the Papal grant of the Laudabiliter, given to him, unsurprisingly, by the only Englishman to become Pope, Adrian IV, in 1155–6.[40] English claims on Ireland were supplemented by a belief in earlier English/British conquests and Irish submissions which assumed greater importance after Henry VIII's break with Rome,[41] but, until then, England's territorial domination supposedly depended upon a religious and civilizing mission to reclaim the Irish church and people for European Christendom.[42]

The constitutional transformation signalled a consequent need and desire to bring the whole of Ireland to heel via assimilation and conquest, to make a political abstraction into a governmental reality; hence the plans of Finglas and Skeffington in the 1530s (as preparation for the act), and St. Leger's policy of 'Surrender and Regrant', designed to buy the loyalty of the Gaelic lords, which was launched in the following decade.[43] This political metamorphosis cannot be separated from the religious revolution known as the Reformation. The English now distinguished themselves from both the Gaelic Irish and the 'Old' English by virtue of their Protestantism.

A conflict of competing colonial groups was added to that of native versus invaders. At one level the struggle for power became more complex and ideological; at another, it stayed the same: '[t]he religious difference *reinforced* at every point older conflicts of a political or cultural nature' (our emphasis).[44] A recognition of the significance of recent events may have led to the disastrous revolt of 'Silken Thomas', the tenth Earl of Kildare, in 1534, which he tried to elevate from a local, factional struggle to a crusade in defence of a beleagured Catholicism (something which was to characterize Irish resistance to English advances from now on).[45] This signalled the end of the power of the Geraldines of Kildare, who had been the most significant Irish dynasty used by the English crown for nearly a hundred years. Henceforth it became the policy to rule through an English-born appointee.[46]

iii

Henry's death in 1547 led to the confused and conflicting years of the mid-Tudor polity.[47] First came Edward VI's attempt to impose a more radical version of the Reformation on the Irish, with the removal of all elements of ritual from church services and an insistence on the use of English rather than Latin. This, some historians have argued, guaranteed its inevitable failure and served merely to foster a coherent bond of Counter-Reformation belief (and 'Irishness') among its opponents.[48] He was followed by Mary (1553–8), who reinstated Catholicism. Although Mary's accession was apparently celebrated by many Irish Catholics (see Bale below, chapter 2), she continued to work within the framework of political legitimacy laid down by her father and ruled Ireland as a Tudor sovereign independently from the Papal authority to which she adhered.[49] In Ireland, as in England, there was to be no re-establishment of the religious orders; nor was there to be tolerance of Gaelic lifestyles and culture. In Leix and Offaly, the first colonies of English settlers were created and they were renamed King's and Queen's Counties.[50]

The long reign of Elizabeth marks the watershed in Tudor policies, as well as the end of the dynasty. By the time of her death, the last and most serious threat to English rule, the Nine Years' War, had been (effectively) won with the victory at Kinsale in 1601 and with the surrender of Hugh (the great) O'Neill — the Earl of Tyrone, to give him his English title. O'Neill's surrender came a week after Elizabeth's death (1603), of which he had been deliberately kept ignorant.[51] Yet it would be wholly inaccurate to see Mountjoy's triumph as the inevitable and logical outcome of a superior, confident and aggressive culture imposing its will on a backward society.[52] Elizabeth came to the throne at a time of chaos in Ireland, with the efforts of Sussex and Sir Henry Sidney to subdue Shane O'Neill only succeeding when he over-reached himself in attempting to balance between the Ulster Scots, the MacDonnells, and the crown forces. He was killed as he tried to strike a deal with the former, his traditional foes,[53] suggesting that Ulster was the scene of a conflict between three, rather than two, kingdoms.[54] A period of relative calm preceded the outbreak of the FitzMaurice/Desmond rebellion, concentrated in Munster, which lasted from 1575 to 1583. The threat of Spanish invasion heightened defensive preparations in 1588; indeed the fear of Spain using Ireland as a base to invade England and dominate Europe never really diminished in the later Elizabethan years.[55] The prospect of losing Ireland was a constant preoccupation of the crown which had to be balanced against its need not to cause financial difficulties through serious overspending.[56] Many of the treatises composed, from the anonymous plan of 1515 and Finglas's *Breviat* onwards, promise not only an end to disloyalty and rebellion in Ireland, but the start of a profit to the Exchequer.[57]

Whatever the difficulties encountered by English officialdom, the early years of Jacobean Ireland saw both the departure of the most influential Gaelic leaders to mainland Europe — the flight of the Earls, an event of symbolic if not political importance, as the sign of the end of an Irish inheritance now pushed underground[58] — and the establishment of the modern political divisions of Ireland. Now a predominantly Protestant North-East became separated from the main Catholic body of the country.[59] However, there is significant disagreement among historians as to how this assertion of control had been achieved; whether there was a programmatic Elizabethan policy of colonization and confiscation, or a more pragmmatic approach to events with the ultimate goal of establishing English constitutional rule in Ireland.[60] Actions may or may not have been planned in advance. But the reality of military conquest, the setting up of colonies and the transfer of land ownership from Catholic to Protestant is not to be denied and becomes evident in the texts cited and discussed below.

Jacobean Ireland is perhaps most notable for the extent of the plantation that took place, which created the divide referred to above. Earlier schemes had been both planned and carried out not only by Mary, but also, in the 1570's by Walter Devereux, the first Earl of Essex, and Sir Thomas Smith in eastern Ulster. Neither could be termed a success. After the rebellion of FitzMaurice, plantation was attempted in Munster on a larger scale, whose more dispersed model was to prove its undoing.[61] Only under James was Irish resistence feeble enough for success to be a strong possibility in the long term.

Plantation as a policy varied in its aims. Was it to help 'Anglicize' and 'civilize' the natives by having the English mixed with them, or to remove (transplant) them and replace them with colonies of loyal English and lowland Scots? At any rate, a useful side-effect of the latter method in Ulster was the securement of a Protestant majority in the Irish parliament.[62] The two manifestations of colonisation had been apparent in the plans of Smith, who never actually set foot in Ireland, having been posted off as ambassador to France when on the point of leading an expedition.[63] His early programme had envisaged the mutual co-existence of colonists and natives, but after the murder of his son in October 1573 his second set of proposals demanded that separate fortified garrison towns be erected.[64] Such vacillations were to haunt the Ulster plantation, as was the constant pressure of finance. Money considerations forced the scheme in part upon the reluctant London companies as a private venture; the same considerations may not have prevented it from spreading wider than it did.[65] Again, pressures came from many directions and Ireland remained more resistant to manipulation than those who wished to recast it in their own image might have hoped.[66]

The great trauma of the mid-seventeenth century for both the English in Ireland and those safely at home was the rebellion of 1641. Before this event it had been assumed by many English colonists, officials and observers that Ireland had, at last, been 'pacified' (to anticipate Gladstone's term) and that reconciliation between the two islands could take place.[67] Sir James Ware, for example, when publishing Edmund Spenser's *View of the Present State of Ireland* for the first time in 1633,[68] argued that had Spenser been writing for the 1630s rather than the 1590s, when it had seemed as if the recalcitrant Irish would never be defeated and a Spanish invasion to compensate for the failure of the Armada had appeared imminent, he would have tempered his more extreme pronouncements. Ware obligingly performed the act for him.[69] The 'discovery' of Sir John Davies's *A Discovery of the True Causes* why Ireland was never entirely subdued (1612), one of the most important Jacobean works on Ireland, was that Ireland had been troubled for far longer than it need have been because English law had never been properly spread to the native Irish, thus perpetuating the division of the island into a land of war and a land of peace. The Elizabethan conquest provided the opportunity to make good this perceived lack, end violence and ensure, he hoped, Irish loyalty.[70] The outraged sense of betrayal on the part of the English and Irish Protestants could almost be seen as comic were it not for the reality of the bloodshed (on both sides) and its consequences.[71] There followed a prolonged war between strange mixtures of heterogeneous groups; firstly, the 'Old' English and native Irish (the Confederates) against an unhappy union of Royalist Irish Protestants and Royalist troops under the Duke of Ormond. Ormond's forces eventually surrendered to parliamentary troops led by General Jones, who then took the fight to the Confederates. 'By 1648, indeed, a bewildering number of hands were in the game';[72] Ormond, backed by Charles, formed an alliance with his previous enemies. Cromwell invaded Ireland in 1649, returning to England a year later after brutally ending the war and carrying out the notorious massacres at Drogheda and Wexford; to this dark triumph Marvell's famous Ode might have seemed a suitably ambiguous tribute.[73] Many of the arguments over the nature and merits of colonization and plantation were once more repeated with the proposed scheme of transplanting the 'guilty' rebel Irish to Connaught (1653). Like earlier plantation schemes, this was only partially achieved, mainly because of its inherent impracticalities.[74] (See below, p. 123.) Nevertheless, from now on land increasingly came into Protestant ownership. Before 1641 most landlords had been Catholic; after 1652 most were Protestant, as mass confiscations placed two-thirds of Ireland at the disposal of the victorious English newcomers.[75]

The Rebellion of 1641 can clearly be seen, from the perspective of the 'long duration',[76] as the product of many years of oppression, exploitation and brutality. But the uprising must also be examined in terms of its immediate, specific context; considered in this way, it reveals the unstable nature of forces on either side of the religious/national divide. As Conrad Russell has argued, it took the draconian policies of Wentworth and his insensitivity to the different demands and desires of the numerous groups in Ireland to provoke the 'Old' and 'New' English to unite in the 1640 parliament and have him impeached and subsequently executed. Russell's statement, 'Strafford, it seemed, was the only Englishman ever to break down the religious divide in Irish politics'[77] shows his keen sense of historical irony, as this union was to precipitate the very event which polarised Irish of both faiths. The 'Old' English soon grew to feel, after the demands of 'the Graces' to ensure their protection were not met,[78] that their long-term interest lay with the Gaelic Irish, their co-religionists, rather than the Protestant 'New' English. Again, the impossibility of separating Irish and English history is demonstrated and Russell has argued for an approach to the (English) Civil War based on an awareness of the British context of events (which, of course, also includes Scotland). In 1641, the key group, the 'Old' English, who were the 'pigs in the middle of Irish politics', began to see that it was no longer possible to be 'a gentleman first, and a Catholic second':

> The Earl of Ormonde . . . commented that he was the first Englishman to be treated as if he were Irish. He was not the last: in 1641, one of the rebels marked the great watershed in Irish history by describing them [the Old English] as the 'new Irish'.[79]

What of the Protestants? While the most important development of the seventeenth century and certainly of Restoration Ireland was the emergence of Protestant Ireland, linked with England, T. C. Barnard has recently argued that to look at Protestantism in Ireland as a monolithic entity is to oversimplify and confuse the issue. Barnard demands that historians look beyond the literature and polemic of the Anglo-Irish gentry to the mass of the ordinary people below, claiming that it is dangerous to lump 'English colonist, Anglo-Irish and Irish Protestant together' as synonyms, because

> By the mid-seventeenth century, if not before, Irish Protestant society was splintered and disunited to a degree which not even shared religion and privileges could hide, and would remain so.[80]

Barnard, as some of the more astute modern commentators on Irish affairs have done,[81] has insisted that the reality of class difference and conflict be placed at the centre of an analysis of (national) identity: perhaps we should not think so much in terms of simple blocks as of 'historic blocs', concatenations of interest groups and forces which combine to fabricate a composite, compromised (and therefore, by no means secure) identity.[82] The problem is not that it is impossible, ipso facto, to describe a Protestant identity in seventeenth century Ireland, but that before and after 1641, such an identity was characterised by difference and so tended to vary with historical circumstance. The key question which had to be asked, was: what is Ireland?

> Protestant settlers . . . imagined their worlds in Ireland sometimes as a neglected and exploited colony, a proud kingdom or a thriving province, or sometimes as a special quarter of the Christian commonwealth.[83]

Some, like Richard Lawrence, were heavily influenced by the militantly Calvinist rhetoric of Sir John Temple's *The Irish Rebellion*, which blamed the catastrophe on a moral laxness of the English government in Ireland in the 1630s when Irish and British were not rigidly separated, but looked forward to a time when such sins would be put right and God's chosen people would triumph. 'One reason for the lasting and corrosive effect of the book was its ability to counter the sense of isolation and even abandonment among Irish Protestants'.[84] Others, like Vincent Gookin (from whose writings the present book takes its title), had exhibited a more profound sense of historical change and argued that the situation of the 1650s was no longer that of the 1630s; the Catholics having been thoroughly conquered and dispossessed, Protestant society could easily accommodate them (see below, p. 123). Many moved between these two positions, just as they could move between an Englishness and an Irishness. The question was given a crucial added impetus in 1641 as it had been exactly a hundred years earlier, but it can obviously be dated back to the first easily recognisable linkage of the histories of England and Ireland, the Laudabiliter.

iv

The seventeenth century can be seen as a watershed in the history of British perceptions of Ireland. Despite the turbulent history of that century, when the united Britain achieved by the accession of James I threatened to fragment during the Civil War, the Interregnum or the Exclusion Crisis, there was apparent in 1700 a greater sense of centralized control under the rule of Westminster than had existed in 1600.[85] Under such stable conditions it was possible for what we now know as 'travel writing' to develop within the British Isles as opposed to remaining centred mainly on Europe (see below pp. 20–21). But even after 1700 Ireland could still appear to topographers a peculiar and dubious part of the new Britain. Arthur Young in 1776 did visit Ireland; Defoe in the 1720s, touring through 'the whole Island of Great Britain', did not.[86]

In fact, much early English writing on Ireland invoked a world rather than a European context, aligning the land and its people with barbarous countries far removed from civil life. The outlook resurfaces in later periods, sometimes in modified form as when eighteenth century visitors weigh Irish against Spanish or Italian poverty, at other times peculiarly unchanged as when Carlyle and Thackeray compare Ireland with Dahomey and the Hottentots.

(See below, chapter 17). Margaret Hodgen remarks that European travellers into strange lands during the Renaissance reported what they saw, but often this meant what earlier reports had conditioned them to expect to see. To observe giant footprints meant they were in the vicinity of giant men, to see cave dwellers was to see troglodytes. Thus travellers reported signs of cannibalism (though no first hand description of cannibal practice has ever come to light) and also 'images of semihuman monsters, evidence of beast-men, with whom to some observers the savages seemed to correspond'.[87] The Renaissance debate over the relationship between civilised and uncivilised peoples was no academic logomachy. As has been pointed out above, it was an earnest issue with practical implications for land and power. A century after Spenser the Cromwellian William Petty, maker of the Down Survey, argued in his *Scale of Creatures* (1676–77) that 'there were multiple kinds of men, each with his rightful place in the natural order but inferior to European man'.[88] The connection between Petty's anthropological theory and his Irish work, whose purpose was to re-allocate the land to the colonisers, does not need forcing. As the 'English' (the term should include Scottish adventurers, French Huguenot refugees, Dutch Protestants and others) tightened their grip on Ireland after 1540, and particularly after 1641, discriminatory formulations in travel and other discourse kept pace with political events and enabled the colonising process by 'othering' the land and its people. D. W. Hayton has pointed out how closely the stereotyping of Irish people in English literature after 1660 mirrors changes in the political relations between the two countries.[89] Apart from its people, Ireland is portrayed as a fairyland, a bogland, a wasteland, a land of potential wealth neglected by its inhabitants, a land asking to be taken over. These patterns of imagery in topographical writing can begin to function as ways of seeing, in that, once established and accepted, the literary conventions provide a framework and a set of concepts for later travellers, helping them to make sense of what they observe when they encounter Ireland for the first time.

But whilst solutions to England's 'Irish problem' might have been as simple as they were brutal, they were not applied in any consistent way. Perhaps the Cromwellian and Williamite 'settlements' might have worked if really imposed, in the sense that to wipe out the Irish population east of Connaught should have forestalled rebellion, but the English decision (as in 1607) that only proprietors should be uprooted meant that an alien majority was left surrounding the planters and landholders who were granted their precarious tenure, and this was to destabilise the confidence of the ascendancy class for centuries. Travellers' accounts in the seventeenth century, reacting to war and the uncertain tenure of property, stress Ireland's savagery, poverty, disaffection and foreignness, or, in a more purposeful mode, they merely measure out the acres. The major genres are the economic-analytical and the racialist-comic. Examples of the first are Petty's and Clarendon's writing, and Gookin's *Great Case of Transplantation* (1655) and even the *Civil Survey* (1654–56) could be included. As the varied aims behind such writings will show, expropriation was a charged and divisive issue, not a uniform policy.[90] Satire may be illustrated in J. Farewell's *The Irish Hudibras* (1689), partly reprinted below (chapter 15). Even plantation propaganda, though it usually involved abusing the Irish, was a complicated rather than simple genre since it was written in praise of Ireland; otherwise the propaganda could not have worked. The mode turns up surprises, as in Luke Gernon's *Description* (1620) of the Irishman not as a wild beast but as a prompt, pleasing, decently dressed human being.[91] Nor is all avowed anti-Irish writing of the period to be read at its face value; it may be generic satire rather than specific description. Hibernophobia forms part of a generalised xenophobia. A poem like Marvell's *Character of Holland* (to take a different example of xenophobic writing from the same period) may represent its author's views; more likely it aspires to witty intensity.[92] Such verse, which may invoke Juvenal's authority for its savagery of tone, sets out to appear as hostile as possible and sometimes cultivates a rough style in order to suggest its author's uncontrollable anger.[93] To interpret it literally would be to misread the signs.

Militarised Ireland attracted the greatest attention in seventeenth century English writing, from Thomas Gainsford's *History of Tyrone* (1619) near the beginning of the century, to John Stevens, a Jacobite participant in the Williamite war near its end. Manuscript diaries, many of them anonymous, supply further coverage of the subject. In spite of the danger, Ireland could still attract individual travellers like the antiquarian Thomas Dineley, whose *Observations* (1681) portray ordinary town and country life in Ireland between two wars.[94] A regular theme in this writing is the shock of the actual. When John Dunton travelled from Dublin to Connemara in 1698 he replaced the mean opinion which had 'prepossessed' him with a more positive response,[95] perhaps touching up his descriptions for effect as travellers have been known to do.

James II's parliament in 1689 overturned (on paper) the Protestant confiscations of the 1650s by repealing two thousand landlords' rights at a stroke. But the would-be recoverers were themselves re-expropriated when the loss of Athlone, Limerick and Galway in 1691 forced the Irish Jacobites to capitulate and enabled King William to implement a further land confiscation. Within a century, therefore, three annexations or re-annexations of territory had taken place, and two Irish landowning populations had been dispossessed. Who reallly owned the country? Who were its true rulers? And the people below politics: who spoke for them? Petty calculated near the end of the century that colonists held three quarters of the land of Ireland but constituted three elevenths of her population.[96] These imposed conquerors would make bad landlords. Constantia Maxwell attributed to the settlement the cleavage between landlord and tenant which was to plague Ireland for the next two hundred years.[97] Ireland was defined in 1691 and thereafter as a Protestant nation. J. C. Beckett points out that, despite the obvious similarity between 1691 and 1603, a major difference was the existence of an administrative structure in 1691 which took immediate action to solidify the conquest. The penal laws enacted from 1695 onwards reduced to vanishing point the political existence of the Catholic, Irish-speaking majority.[98]

The legal policy of strangling a people was relaxed with the years, and would face sharp challenges after 1800. But in their time of peaceful power the overlords of eighteenth century Ireland continued to deny one nationhood in order to assert another. War as such being over, they consolidated by cultural means, invoking the ideology of improvement to extend the English hegemony. They built palatial dwellings in parks the size of small kingdoms laid out, under the pacific Hanoverians, 'for show rather than for defence'.[99] They may not have been fortified, but not even the old castles can have exerted greater domination than these new mansions, sharply set off, however, in the ruin-littered countryside by evidences of a previous order and by the ubiquitous poverty. Travellers noted the contrast, but not its symbolism, and no writer of the period probes the irony — how should they? — of Molyneux and Swift, Berkeley and Grattan fighting for what they defined as Ireland's freedom while neglecting the 'Hidden' Ireland and lamenting the deplorable Ireland all too visible from their stately windows. R. F. Foster has written on the 'baulked sense of differentiation and nationality' which characterises the ruling culture of this period,[100] but this, in fact, is less an eighteenth-century phenomenon than a leitmotif of Irish history. In 1782 the new-made rulers of 'Ireland' wrested a short-lived parliamentary independence from Britain only to find themselves shouldered off stage after the quelling of the tumult of the 1790s. While Ascendancy orators and politicians pursued their dream of national independence, large numbers of the ordinary inhabitants of Ireland, unrepresented in politics, lived hand to mouth throughout the century, increasing their misery by alcohol dependence (as travellers frequently noted) and by population growth. The closing decade, in E. M. Johnston's words, saw 'the unsolved problems of the century' coming home: these were, the power of the Ascendancy, the structure of government, the separation of the Catholic majority.[101] But though the problems came home, they were not solved. The 1800 Union between England and Ireland ended Anglo-Ireland's era of absolute power but was politically even more ambiguous than Scotland's Union with England had been almost a century before. England, now Britain, was being united, but with whom, and for whom? The 'injured lady' of Ireland, as Swift had called her — meaning Anglo-Ireland — was married at last, but had she any greater cause than before to celebrate her condition?

Eighteenth century English visitors saw in Ireland a country no longer requiring to be tamed but waiting to be exploited — in the modern jargon, an 'underdeveloped' country (meaning foreign and subject). The perception was not new. Travellers deplore a generally neglected or ruined environment while singling out for praise a neat new town or a patch of improved landscape (which meant landscape resembling England). In the second half of the century travellers found the wilderness itself picturesque, while admiring the civility of Dublin and of the country houses of their friends, and contradistinguishing the latter from the barbaric-exotic culture of indigenous Ireland, now overlaid but not lost to sight. They seek in Ireland, that is to say, an alternative if lesser England; yet recognise the essential difference of the geography and culture. Travel at this period was also moving towards tourism. Certain celebrated beauty spots in Wicklow, Antrim, Kerry and Killarney began to form a fashionable visitors' circuit, the cult of which some commentators (like Samuel Johnson[102]) found annoying, and which the Victorians would turn sentimental. Relics of an older mode of writing survive in the eccentric travel satire of *The Comical Pilgrim* (1722; once attributed to Defoe), but plain Augustan description soon carried all before it. Addison as a Whig administrator in the Dublin Parliament reflects the new outlook, steering the penal laws through Parliament and taking his recreation at the Curragh — 'our Irish New Market'.[103]

Addison, to judge from his Irish letters, did not want to involve himself with Irish life. His attitude, showing no trace of an attachment to land or people, exemplifies the unfriendly, colonial English character. Still less affectionate towards Ireland (though exceedingly concerned with the welfare of the Irish people) was the missionary John Wesley, who visited Ireland twenty-one times, and recorded each visit in his journal. Wesley hardly ever strikes an appreciative note. He saw in Irish scenery only a reminder that heaven was more attractive. The Irish people he dismissed as degenerates.

I can easily believe that the Irish were originally Tartars or Scythians, though calling at Spain in their way; but not that they were a jot less barbarous than their descendants in Scotland; or that ever they were a civilized nation till they were civilized by the English; much less that Ireland was, in the seventh or eighth century, the grand seat of learning — that it had many famous colleges, in one of which only, Armagh, there were seven thousand students. All this, with St. Patrick's converting thirty thousand at one sermon, I rank with the history of 'Bel and the Dragon.'[104]

Other travellers could be friendlier, like the anonymous author (or authors) of *A Tour Through Ireland by Two English Gentlemen* (1788) or the indefatigably inquisitive Richard Pococke, digging out the secrets of far Cork, Kerry, Mayo and Donegal in the 1740s and 1750s. Richard Twiss rejected English prejudices about drink, gaming and Irish bulls, but his prickly manner annoyed Ireland in its turn. A chamber pot sold in Dublin after his visit bore the legend: 'Come let us piss/On Mr Twiss'.[105] Philip Luckombe's declaration (1779) that Ireland ought to be known 'next to Great Britian'[106] may indicate the beginning of the decline of the grand tour of Europe. If one writer brings together the economic, aesthetic and political issues touched on by individual eighteenth-century travellers, it is perhaps Arthur Young in 1775–8. Young praises with equal enthusiasm agricultural improvement and beautiful scenery, and in spite of his upper-class connections remains sympathetic to people of common life. Perhaps the stereotype of the passionate Celt influences Young's portrayal of the Irish cottier,[107] but English travellers generally, as the century closed, were turning their attention to the life of the oridinary Irish people.

Travel in Ireland was becoming more carefully and systematically planned. G. Taylor and A. Skinner's *Maps of the Roads of Ireland* (1778), an influential volume, signals the trend. *The Compleat Irish Traveller* (1778) provided a gazetteer of distances and landmarks, with descriptions and travelling advice. J. Dodd's *The Travellers'*

Director through Ireland (Dublin 1801), J. Pigot's *Commercial Directory of Ireland* (London 1820), and other travel handbooks built on these forerunners. Eccentric journeys, like the one recorded in Samuel Derrick's *Letters* (Dublin 1767), still took place and unambitious individual travelling continued, as described in Plumptre's *Narrative of a Residence* (1817), T. Reid's *Travels in Ireland* (1823) and J. B. Trotter's *Walks through Ireland* (1819).

The traveller Sir John Carr's optimism about Ireland, to whom Grattan's lifetime had seemed 'a new Aurora',[108] could hardly have proved more short-lived. Peace was shattered by a revolutionary uprising, and revolution was followed by the Union, whose inauguration the fifteen-year-old De Quincey witnessed. (See below, Chapter 14). For De Quincey the Union offered a sordid parallel to the extinction of the Venetian republic. In Britain Union with Ireland was seen as a military necessity, but though it closed the back door against Napoleon it failed to merge the British and the Irish. Temporary economic expansion ground to a halt after the Napoleonic war, and then depression combined with population growth steadily worsened the conditions of Irish life. O'Connell's demands for Catholic emancipation and Repeal introduced a different nationalism from that of the aristocratic volunteers and United Irishmen of the preceding century. O'Connell spoke for dispossessed Ireland — the Ireland of the Catholic clergy and of the peasants. Therefore Protestant Britain found him disgusting. Carlyle dismissed O'Connell as 'the Demosthenes of blarney'.[109] But in the 1840s an Irish challenge was also mounted against O'Connell by the Young Irelanders, a Protestant middle class group with whom he disputed over the 1845 Queen's Colleges of Belfast, Cork and Galway; O'Connell's stance demonstrating his clericalism. When the Famine transformed Irish life it overshadowed this quarrel, and also forced a revision of the British policy of laissez-faire, as the government intervened to try to support three million starving people. From the Famine onwards the landlords' influence declined. Famine too killed the organized movement for repeal, and forty years later, when Parnell demanded home rule for Ireland, but failed to get it, a more violent revolutionary movement came to the fore. A fact of significance was that Ulster, not being so potato-dependent, suffered less severely in the Famine than the rest of Ireland. As industry then expanded in northern Ireland the gap widened between north and south, breeding future trouble.

All of which would seem to mark the Famine as another watershed, suggesting it to be a terminus for the present volume. J. C. Beckett comments that, politically speaking, Ireland after the

1840s fell into the background of English consciousness.[110] Irish affairs, he argues, were upstaged by the Crimea, the Indian mutiny, the fight for a united Italy and the American civil war. But even in the background Ireland was to encounter the same complex of attitudes as before. Britain in these years supported self-determination in Greece, Serbia, Italy, Hungary and Poland and accepted it as reasonable in Australia, South Africa and Canada, yet remained firm against Irish home rule. Ireland was a valuable market and food source for England, but, as Beckett points out, fundamentally, the English were driven by the irrational determination to maintain 'national' territory and to keep down recalcitrant groups.

By the time of the Famine English travel writing often strikes an apocalyptic note, gazing into Ireland as into the abyss. Class conflict, or, more frequently in an Irish context, religious and nationalist antagonism, radicalises and fractures the surface of a discourse which had seemed confident and certain of its status in the late Eighteenth Century. The taste for Irish travel may have received a boost from Napoleon's closing of the Continent. Wordsworth and Scott toured Ireland; Shelley and Keats made briefer visits. Keats could not stand what he saw in Dublin in 1818 and returned home early, giving as his reason the unbearable sight of the extreme degradation of the Irish poor. It was to be the main burden of Irish travel writing for the next half century. Nevertheless, rhapsodies over Killarney, the Giant's Causeway, Kerry or Donegal did not disappear before these deepening portrayals of human suffering. The two themes, strangely, interweaving as if each is feeding the other, reached a peak in the Famine years of the 1840s and 1850s. Patricia Hodgart points out that for Shelley, as for Keats, the experience of Ireland was formative. It constituted 'probably his first sight of real distress and hopeless ignorance'.[111] There was, perhaps, a distinctly Romantic experience of Ireland, despite Wordsworth's reactionary pronouncements.[112] Scott had visited Ireland in 1815 and describes Wicklow and elsewhere in 'Pat land' in his letters and journal.[113] Later in the century Arnold was to see in Irish history the cultural degradation of a nation.[114]

English writers reacted to the relentless downturn in Irish economic life after 1815, and to its social consequences — increased beggary and squalor — in a variety of ways. The experience fuelled Cobbett's rage against Anglo-Irish exploitation, and therefore against English class tyranny. Cobbett's first visit, as Denis Knight points out,[115] took place in 1834; well after the Romantics (See below, chapter 18). His accounts, more politically radical than anything written before, could be said to follow on from Keats.

The description of a Kilkenny horse fair with two thousand animals in fine condition and a crowd of human beings all hungry and cold invites us, looking forward, to link Cobbett with Carlyle, and, looking backward, to link him with Swift, whose Yahoos seem to be in his mind here. Cobbett wrote much on Ireland, but always did so with an eye fixed on the English working class; this, he judged, would be next on the exploiters' list. It was this kind of prescience, no doubt, which Karl Marx had in mind when he recommended his daughter Eleanor should read Cobbett on Ireland. In a speech in 1869 Marx commented that Cobbett's reply to Castlereagh on Ireland was the same as his own reply to Gladstone.[116]

The facts described by Cobbett and others, if not Cobbett's political judgement, become a commonplace of nineteenth-century English travellers' descriptions of Irish life. As mentioned above, another is the poetry of the Irish countryside, descriptions of which, in the hands of some mid-Victorian travellers, recall Ruskin's definition of the picturesque: indifference to misery.[117] One impulse behind Carlyle's 1849 *Reminiscences*, a bitter reaction to a bitter land, which still retains its power to puzzle and antagonise the reader, is his wish to knock this sentimental trend on the head. Ireland horrified Carlyle; it was 'like a drunk country fallen down to sleep amid the mud'.[118] Carlyle attempts to provoke anger, but given the Irish scene in the Famine years anger is a serious emotion, whereas weeping over Innisfallen is not. Thackeray, writing a few years before Carlyle, is less easy to pin down. He too debunks the clichés of travel writing as much as he describes Ireland. A Thackeray theme is the untidiness of the country — untidiness, but not hellishness. He advises the Irish to acquire a broom and soap and water and clean themselves up.[119] For Thackeray hell does not seem to exist; perhaps his difference from Carlyle could not be better illustrated. A. P. Curtis has described a third Victorian commonplace in the simian Irishman,[120] a favourite cartoon in English newspapers of the Repeal years: an old stereotype taking on new energy in Fenian Ireland. But this is armchair satire written in London; little of it occurs in topographical description composed at first hand. Meanwhile plans to methodise the knowledge of Ireland proceeded, as in the establishment of the Ordnance Survey.[121]

Friedrich Engels summarises for us. Turning to a commonplace of travel literature, England's difference from Ireland, he advances the psycho-historical observation that Ireland's character has been deformed by its colonial condition. Physically, Engels explains,[122]

Ireland's characteristics as seen by the visitor from England are not architectural remains but architectural ruins: first of all churches, then after 1100 churches and castles, then after 1800 peasants' houses. Of the last, he says, so many exist in the Galway region that the land thereabouts appears 'an utter desert'.[123] Like the land they were living in, the inhabitants of Ireland also appeared to Engels as a ruined people, and by this he means not just that the Irish poor were starving but that the whole population of Ireland suffered from a psychological destitution which was the legacy of its centuries-old colonial history. Impoverishment, he notes, also characterises the aristocracy. They inhabit country seats in fine parks surrounded by waste land and pass their time in endless dread of bankruptcy. And the ordinary people? Their history has made them feel 'no longer at home in their own country'.[124] Engels, of course, when he made his Irish journey, was not an English traveller but a foreigner who had decided to make his home in Britain, had become extremely well informed in Irish history, and was engaged on a brief research-holiday in the country. His standpoint reflects this difference. Unlike the English travellers with whom this volume is chiefly concerned, Engels perceives the Irish-British relationship from Ireland's side. And for him there is nobody — coloniser any more than colonised — who can claim a true home in Ireland any more.

1. GIRALDUS CAMBRENSIS AND ENGLISH WRITING ABOUT IRELAND

Although the writing included in this book is that of English eyewitnesses, it would be wrong to present this material as if it occurred in vacuo because 'observers of anything culturally unfamiliar . . . had to be able to classify before they could properly see'; that is, 'they had no alternative but to appeal to a system which was already in use'.[1] Giraldus's representations of Irish characteristics and culture were the most widely circulated pre-Renaissance accounts available to Tudor and Stuart readers (see Introduction, p. 7) and it is remarkable how frequently the topics and features he considered to be recognisably Irish are followed by those who claimed the authority of writing from experience. Of course, other, usually ancient (classical) works are often cited in histories and descriptive accounts, for example Solinus, Strabo, Diodorus Sicilius, Tacitus, Julius Caesar, Hector Boethius, Buchanan, and others;[2] but it is Giraldus who, acknowledged or unacknowledged, provides the key material.

Included here are extracts from both Giraldus's works on Ireland, the *Topographia Hibernica* (1188) and the *Expugnatio Hibernica* (1189). They illustrate the conception Giraldus had of the nature of the Irish, as well as the English crown's five-fold claim to Ireland, which, minus the papal grant (the fifth right), was to be vigorously re-asserted after the Reformation. Of particular interest is Giraldus's observation of cultural change, 'degeneration', and his explanation for it, something that was to obsess and trouble later writers keen to conquer and transform Ireland into a duplicate of a supposedly loyal English kingdom.[3]

From *Expugnatio Hibernica* (1189), Bk. 2, Ch. 6: 'The Five-fold Right [of the English King Over Ireland]':[4]

Therefore let the envious and thoughtless end their vociferous complaints that the kings of England hold Ireland unlawfully. Let them learn, moreover, that they support their claims by a right of ownership resting on five different counts, two of long standing and three of recent origin, as is revealed in the *Topography.*[5] For the British History bears witness to the fact that when Gurguntius, son of Belinus and king of Britain, was returning in triumph from Dacia, he found the Basque fleet in Orkney, and having provided them with guides, sent them for the first time into Ireland.[6] It also recalls the fact that the kings of Ireland were among the rulers who paid tribute to Arthur, that famous king of Britain, and that Gillomar king of Ireland was present at his court at Caerleon along with other island kings.[7] Besides, the city of Bayonne, which today is included in our province of Gascony, is the chief city of the territory of the Basques from which the Irish originally came.[8] Again, while a man is always free to give up his lawful claims, in our own times all the princes of Ireland, although hitherto not subject to the domination of any overlord, freely bound themselves in submission to Henry II king of England by the firm bonds of their pledged word and oath.[9] For although they may not hesitate to go back on their word within a very short space of time, thanks to that fickleness which comes from their innately unstable temperament, they are not therefore absolved from this bond of their pledged word and oath of fealty. For men are free to make contracts of this sort, but not to break them.

As well as this there is the added weight of the authority of the supreme pontiffs, who have responsibility for all islands by reason of their own peculiar rights, and of the princes and rulers of all Christendom.[10] This should in itself be sufficient to perfect our case and put the finishing touch to it.

2) *The Topography of Ireland* (1188), Ch. 10: 'Of the Character, Customs and Habits of this People':[11]

I have considered it not superfluous to give a short account of the condition of this nation, both bodily and mentally; I mean their state of cultivation, both interior and exterior. This people are not tenderly nursed from their birth, as others are; for besides the rude fare they receive from their parents, which is only just sufficient for their sustenance, as to the rest, almost all is left to nature. They are not placed in cradles, or swathed, nor are their tender limbs either fomented by constant bathings, or adjusted with art. For the midwives make no use of warm water, nor raise their noses, nor depress the face, nor stretch the legs; but nature alone, with very slight aids from art, disposes and adjusts the limbs to which she has given birth, just as she pleases. As if to prove that what she is able to form she does not cease to shape also, she gives growth and proportions to these people, until they arrive at perfect vigour, tall and handsome in person, and with agreeable and ruddy countenances. But although they are richly endowed with the gifts of nature, their want of civilization, shown both in their dress and mental culture, makes them a barbarous people. For they wear but little woollen, and nearly all they use is black, that being the colour of the sheep in this country. Their clothes are also made after a barbarous fashion.

Their custom is to wear small, close-fitting hoods, hanging below the shoulders a cubit's length, and generally made of parti-coloured strips sewn together. Under these, they use woollen rugs instead of cloaks, with breeches and hose of one piece, or hose and breeches joined together, which are usually dyed of some colour. Likewise, in riding, they neither use saddles nor boots, nor spurs, but only carry a rod in their hand, having a crook at the upper end, with which they both urge forward and guide their horses. They use reins which serve the purpose both of a bridle and a bit, and do not prevent the horses from feeding, as they always live on grass. Moreover, they go to battle without armour, considering it a burthen, and esteeming it brave and honourable to fight without it.

But they are armed with three kinds of weapons: namely, short spears, and two darts; in which they follow the customs of the Basclenses (Basques);[12] and they also carry heavy battle-axes of iron, exceedingly well wrought and tempered. These they borrowed from the Norwegians and Ostmen,[13] of whom we shall speak hereafter. But in striking with the battle-axe they use only one hand, instead of both, clasping the haft firmly, and raising it above the head, so as to direct the blow with such force that neither the helmets which protect our heads, nor the platting of the coat of mail which defends the rest of our bodies, can resist the stroke. Thus it has happened, in my own time, that one blow of the axe has cut off a knight's thigh, although it was incased in iron, the thigh and leg falling on one side of his horse, and the body of the dying horseman on the other. When other weapons fail, they hurl stones against the enemy in battle with such quickness and dexterity, that they do more execution than the slingers of any other nation.

The Irish are a rude people, subsisting on the produce of their cattle only, and living themselves like beasts — a people that has not yet departed from the primitive habits of pastoral life. In the common course of things, mankind progresses from the forest to the field, from the field to the town, and to the social condition of citizens; but this nation, holding agricultural labour in contempt, and little coveting the wealth of towns, as well as being exceedingly averse to civil institutions — lead the same life their fathers did in the woods and open pastures, neither willing to abandon their old habits or learn anything new. They, therefore, only make patches of tillage; their pastures are short of herbage; cultivation is very rare, and there is scarcely any land sown. This want of tilled fields arises from the neglect of those who should cultivate them; for there are large tracts which are naturally fertile and productive. The whole habits of the people are contrary to agricultural pursuits, so that the rich glebe is barren for want of husbandmen, the fields demanding labour which is not forthcoming.[14]

Very few sorts of fruit-trees are found in this country, a defect arising not from the nature of the soil, but from want of industry in planting them; for the lazy husbandman does not take the trouble to plant the foreign sorts which would grow very well here. There are four kinds of trees indigenous in Britain which are wanting here. Two of them are fruit-bearing trees, the chestnut and beech; the other two, the *arulus* and the box, though they bear no fruit, are serviceable for making cups and handles. Yews, with their bitter sap, are more frequently to be found in this country than in any other I have visited; but you will see them principally in old cemeteries and sacred places, where they were planted in ancient times by the hands of holy men, to give them what ornament and beauty they could. The forests of Ireland also abound with fir-trees, producing frankincense and incense. There are also veins of various kinds of metals ramifying in the bowels of the earth, which, from the same idle habits, are not worked and turned to account. Even gold, which the people require in large quantities, and still covet in a way that speaks their Spanish origin, is brought here by the merchants who traverse the ocean for the purposes of commerce. They neither employ themselves in the manufacture of flax or wool, or in any kind of trade or mechanical art; but abandoning themselves to idleness, and immersed in sloth, their greatest delight is to be exempt from toil, their richest possession the enjoyment of liberty.

This people, then, is truly barbarous, being not only barbarous in their dress, but suffering their hair and beards (*barbis*) to grow enormously in an uncouth manner, just like the modern fashion recently introduced; indeed, all their habits are barbarisms. But habits are formed by mutual intercourse; and as this people inhabit a country so remote from the rest of the world, and lying at its furthest extremity, forming, as it were, another world, and are thus secluded from civilized nations, they learn nothing, and practise nothing but the barbarism in which they are born and bred, and which sticks to them like a second nature. Whatever natural gifts they possess are excellent, in whatever requires industry they are worthless.

3) *The Topography of Ireland*, Ch. 19: 'How the Irish are very ignorant of the rudiments of the Faith'.

The faith having been planted in the island from the time of St. Patrick, so many ages ago, and propagated almost ever since, it is wonderful that this nation should remain to this day so very ignorant of the rudiments of Christianity.[15] It is indeed a most filthy race, a race sunk in vice, a race more ignorant than all other nations of the first principles of the faith. Hitherto they neither pay tithes nor first fruits;[16] they do not contract marriages, nor shun incestuous connections; they frequent not the church of God with proper reverence. Nay, what is most detestable, and not only contrary to the Gospel, but to every thing that is right, in many parts of Ireland brothers (I will not say marry) seduce and debauch the wives of their brothers deceased, and have incestuous intercourse with them; adhering in this to the letter, and not to the spirit, of the Old Testament; and following the example of men of old in their vices more willingly than in their virtues.

4) *The Topography of Ireland*, from Ch. 24: 'How Newcomers are stained with the same Vices.'

Thus it appears that every one may do just as he pleases; and that the question is not what is right, but what suits his purpose; although nothing is really expedient but what is right. However, the pest of treachery has here grown to such a height — it has so taken root, and long abuse has so succeeded in turning it into a second nature — habits are so formed by mutual intercourse, as he who handles pitch cannot escape its stains — that the evil has acquired great force. A little wormwood, mixed with a large quantity of honey, quickly makes the whole bitter; but if the mixture contains twice as much honey as it does wormwood, the honey fails to sweeten it. Thus, I say, 'evil communications corrupt good manners;' and even strangers who land here from other countries become generally imbued with this national crime, which seems to be innate and very contagious. It either adopts holy places for its purposes, or makes them; for, as the path of pleasure leads easily downwards, and nature readily imitates vice, who will doubt the sacredness of its sanctions who is predisposed and foretaught by so many sacrilegious examples, by so many records of evil deeds, by such frequent forefeitures of oaths, by the want of all obligations to honesty?

2. JOHN BALE AND THE REFORMATION IN IRELAND

Bale, a converted Carmelite monk, became one of the most influential architects of English Reformation thought. His commentary on the Revelation, *The Image of Both Churches,* and his martyrologies of Anne Askew and Sir John Oldcastle were amongst the most widely read works in English in the middle decades of the Sixteenth Century.[1] His outline of providential eschatology helped form both the theology expressed in the notes to the *Geneva Bible* and the historical structure of John Foxe's *Acts and Monuments of the Christian Church,* thus making him instrumental in fostering a national consciousness — that is, a sense of Englishness.[2] Ironically, Bale's major work on Britain, the *Scriptorum Illustrium Majoris Brytanniae Catalogus,* a catalogue of the writings of the authors of Great Britain arranged chronologically with a commentary, was written in exile and in Latin.[3]

His connection with Ireland was brief: he was sent over against his will as bishop of Ossory in December, 1552, after having met Edward VI in August. He fled into exile for the second time[4] when the boy-king died (6 July 1553) and after a series of mishaps and misfortunes recorded in his self-consciously Pauline *Vocacyon of Johan Bale to the Bishopperycke of Ossorie* (1553),[5] arrived in Frankfurt. He returned in triumph to England when Elizabeth became queen in 1559 and died in relative obscurity in 1563.

The extracts included here are all from the *Vocacyon,* the only work of Bale's describing his Irish experiences, which in many ways foreshadows the problems later writers had in dealing with Ireland. Bale's depiction of the Irish strongly resembles that of Giraldus, but Catholicism has replaced 'barbarianism', or heathenism, as a diagnosis of Ireland's culpable divergence from English norms. His animus against the Henrican prayer book and preference for Edward's far more radical version is based on the belief in the need for preaching to the people in the vernacular, their own language, rather than 'Latin momblings', 'howlinge and jabberinge in a *foren* language' [in other words, Latin. My emphasis], an argument clearly rather strained in Ireland where probably more understood the Latin than the English,[6] but accepted by Bale on the grounds that 'If Englande and Irelande be undre one kinge, they are bound to the obedience of one law undre him', something by no means obvious to all students of the constitution.[7] One might ask how Bale's equation of Britain and England ('to saye sumwhat of the Christen Churche of our realme, in those dayes called Britiane, and now named Englande'), contradicted elsewhere in his writings,[8] and his reconstruction of a church history in the text, place the Irish in a legal and religious tradition. For Giraldus the Irish are the fallen on the brink of reconversion; but for Bale have they been permanent exiles? Interesting to note is Bale's reaction to Mary's accession; unable to resist politically, accepting as he did the legality of the ruler as God's regent on earth,[9] he had his morality plays performed in the market square at Kilkenny.[10] These argued the necessity of obedience to the godly Protestant ruler, an act of limited but significant defiance, illustrating the uncomfortably shifting and unstable nature of Bale's existence. Then he fled.

1) First Impressions

Upon the xxi. daye of January we entred into the shippe; I, my wyfe, and one servaunt; and beinge but ii. nyghtes and ii. dayes upon the sea, we arryved most prosperously at Waterforde, in the coldest time of the yeare, so mercifull was the Lorde unto us.

In beholdynge the face and the ordre of that cytie, I see many abhomynable ydolatryes mainteined by the Epicurysh prestes, for their wicked bellies sake. The Communion, or Supper of the Lorde, was there altogyther used lyke a popysh masse, with the olde apysh toyes of Antichrist, in bowynges and beckynges, knelinges and knockinges, the Lordes death, after S. Paule's doctrine, neyther preached nor yet spoken of.[11] There wawled they over the dead, with prodigyouse howlynges and patterynges, as though their sowles had not bene quyeted in Christe and redemed by hys passion, but that they must come after and helpe at a pinche with Requiem Eternam, to delyver them out of helle by their sorrowfull sorceryes. Whan I had beholden these heathenysh behavers, I seyd unto a Senatour of that citye, that I wele perceyved that Christe had there no Bishop, neyther yet the Kynges Majestie of England any faythful officer of the mayer, in suffering so horrible blasphemies.

2) How the death of Edward VI was received in Kilkenny

Upon the assension daye, I preached again at Kilkennie, likewyse on Trinite sondaye, and on S. Peters Daye at midsomer than followinge.

On the xxv daye of July, the prestes were as pleasauntly disposed as might be, and went by heapes from taverne to taverne, to seke the best Rob Davye and aquavite, which are their speciall drinkes there.[12] Thei cawsed all their cuppes to be filled in, with Gaudeamus in dolio,[13] the misterie therof only knowne to them, and, at that time, to none other els.

Which was, that Kynge Edwarde was dead, and that they were in hope to have up their maskynge masses againe . . . For ye must consydre that the prestes are commenly the first that receive suche news. The next day folowinge, a very wicked justice called Thomas Hothe, with the Lorde Mountgarret, restored to the Cathedrall churche, requyrynge to have a communion, in the honour of S. Anne. Marke the blasphemouse blyndnesse and wylfull obstinacye of thys beastly papyst. The prestes made hym answere, That I had forbydden them that celebracion, savynge only upon the Sondayes. As I had, in dede, for the abhomynable ydolatries that I had seane therein. I discharge you (sayeth he) of obedience to your Bishop in this point, and commaunde yow to do as ye have done heretofore, which was, to make of Christes holy communion an ydolatrouse masse, and to suffre it to serve for the dead, cleane contrarye to the Christen use of the same.

Thus was a wicked justice not only a vyolatour of Christes institucion, but also a contempner of his princes earnest commaundement, and a provoker of the people by his ungraciouse example to do the lyke. Thys coulde he do whith other mischefes more, by his longe beynge there by a whole monthe's space, but for murthers, theftes, ydolatryes, and abhominable whoredomes, wherewith all that nacion haboundeth, for that time he sought no redresse, neyther appointed any correction. The prestes thus rejoycing that the Kinge was dead, and that they had bene that daye confirmed in their supersticiouse obstinacie, resorted to the forseyd false justice the same night at supper, to gratifye him with Rob Davye and Aqua vite; for that he had bene so frendly unto them, and that he might styll continue in the same. The next daye after was the Layde Jane Gylforde proclaimed their Quene, with solemnite of processions, bonefyres, and banquettes, the seyd justice, as I was infourmed, sore blamynge me for my absence that daye; for, in dede, I muche doubted that matter.

So sone as it was there rumoured abrode that the kynge was departed from this lyfe, the ruffianess of that wilde nacyon, not only rebelled against the English captaines, as their lewde custome, in suche chaunges, hath bene alwayes, chefly no English deputye beinge within the lande, but also they conspired into the very deathes of so many English men and women, as were left therein alyve: Myndinge, as they than stoughtly boasted it, to have set up a kinge of their owne. And to cause their wilde people to beare the more hate to our nacion, very subtily, but yet falsely, they caused it to be noysed over all, that the younge Earl of Ormonde, and Barnabe, the Barne of Upper Ossorie's sonne, were both slaine in the court at London.

Upon the wylye practise of myschefe, they raged without ordre, in all places, and assaulted the English fortes every where.

And at one of them, by a subtyle trayne, they got out ix of our men, and slew them. [. . .]

On the xx. daye of August, was the ladye marye with us at Kylkennye proclaymed Quene of Englande, Fraunce, and Irelande, with the greatest solempnyte, that there coulde be devysed, of processions, musters and disgysinges, all the noble captaynes and gentilmen there being present. What a-do I had that daye with the prebendaryes and prestes abought wearinge the cope, croser, and myter in procession, it were to muche to write.

I tolde them earnestly, whan they wolde have compelled me thereunto, that I was not Moyses minister but Christes, I desyred them that they would not compell me to his denyall, which is (S. Paule sayth) in the repetinge of Moyses sacramentes and ceremoniall schadowes Gal. v. With that I toke Christes Testament in my hande, and went to the market crosse, the people in great nombre followinge. There toke I the xiii. chap. of S. Paule to the Romanes, declaringe to them brevely, what the autoritie was of the worldly powers and magistrates, what reverence and obedience were due to the same. In the meane tyme, had the prelates goten ii. disgysed prestes, one to beare the myter afore me, and an other the croser, makinge iii. procession pageauntes of one. The yonge men, in the forenone, played a Tragedye of Gods Promyses in the olde lawe at the market crosse, with organe plainges and songes very aptely. In the after none agayne they played a Commedie of sanct Johan Baptiste's Preachinges, of Christe's baptisynge, and of his temptacion in the wildernesse;[14] to the small contentacion of the prestes and other papistes there.

3) On Irish life

Some men peradventure will marvele, that I utteringe matters of Irelande, shulde omitt in this treatise, to write of Coyne and lyverie.[15] Which are so cruell pillages and opressions of the poor commens there, as are no where els in this whole earthe, neither undre wicked Saracene nor yet cruell Turke,[16] besides all prodigiouse kindes of lecherie and other abhominacions therin committed. Thre causes there are, which hath moved me not to expresse them here. One is, for so muche as they pertaine nothinge to the tyttle of this boke, which all concerneth religion. An other is for that the matter is so large, as requireth a muche larger volume. The third cause is, for that I have known ii worthie men, whome, I will not nowe name to have done that thinge so exactly, as noman (I suppose) therein can amende them.[17] But this I will utter brevely, that the Irishe lordes and their undrecaptaines, supportinge the same, are not only companions with theves, as the prophete reporteth, Esa. 1, but also they are their wicked maisters and maintainers. So that they both coupled togyther, the murtherer with his maistre, and the thefe with his maintainer, leyve nothinge undevoured behinde them in that fertile region; no more than ded the devouringe locustes of Egypt, Exo. 10. Anon after their harvestes are ended there, the Kearnes, the Gallowglasses,[18] and the other brechelesse souldiers, with horses and their horsegromes, sumtyme iii waitinge upon one jade, enter into the villages with much crueltie and fearceness, they continue there in great ravine and spoyle, and, whan they go thens, they leave nothinge els behinde them for payment, but lice, lecherie, and intollerable penurie for the yeare after. Yet set the rulers thereupon a very fayre colour, that is for defence of the Englishe pale. I besiche God to sende such protection a shorte ende, and their lordes and Captaines also, if they see it not sone amended. For it is the utter confusion of that lande, and a maintenaunce to all vices.

Thre peoples are in Irelande in these dayes, prestes, lawyers, and kearnes, which will not suffre faythe, truthe and honestye, to dwell there. And all these have but one God their Bellye, and glory in that wicked feate to their shame, whose ende is dampnation, Phil. 3. I speake only of those which are bredde and borne there, and yet not of them all. These for the more part, are sworne bretherne together in myschefe, one to maintaine an others maliciouse cause, by murther previly procured. And, to bringe their conceyved wickednesse to passe, they can do great miracles in this age, by vertue of transubstanciation belyke, for therein are they very conninge. For they can very wittely make, of a tame Irishe, a wilde Irishe for nede, so that they shall serve their turne so wele as though they were of the wilde Irish in dede.

3. THE NATURE OF THE IRISH

How did English people perceive the Irish in the Renaissance? Who, or what, were they? Which features made them distinct from other peoples? Giraldus had described them as a 'gens barbara' (barabarous people), a classification he was also prepared to accord the Welsh;[1] but his analysis seems to imply that this was due to ignorance and that instruction in 'the rudiments of the faith' would remove the gap between them and the civilized.[2] Bale's argument is in many ways an inverted mirror image of Giraldus's; the Irish are ignorant and need to be taught the 'word' of the true faith, which, after the Reformation, demands the use of the vernacular, that is (for Bale) English. This introduces two important new considerations: firstly, the Irish had never received the Reformed religion before, so the (theoretical) continuity between the English and the Irish church was now broken. The difference of the Irish was further highlighted, as, simultaneously, the English right to rule Ireland was correspondingly re-stated and re-formulated (see Introduction, p. 10) and no sacred authority now mediated between the clash of secular powers. A new urgency was given to old questions: what if the Irish disobeyed? What did disobedience imply? Hereditary deficiency, diabolic stubbornness, or was it the product of simple misunderstanding? Secondly, could the Irish vernacular be used to teach the Irish? Or was it an essential part of the Irishness that had to be removed?

It has been argued that English perceptions of the nature of the Irish depended upon the reading of texts describing the peoples found in the Americas so that Ireland formed part of a 'Westward Enterprise' in terms of its representation;[3] alternatively, some historians have claimed that Reformation disputes between 'Protestants' and 'Humanists' as to the primacy of the will or the intellect in determining human action was the real issue at stake.[4] It might equally be argued that both are 'correct' observations, but that such stereotypes were less static phenomena, depending more upon immediate circumstance and history for the precise form of their articulation. Commentators on Irish affairs had a variety of representations they could employ, 'discourses' they could appeal to,[5] to explain what had happened and there is no reason to assume that they need have been consistent in their use of terminology and construction of narrative. The dilemmas which haunted John Bale would not disappear easily. Edmund Campion alleged that education would solve matters, whereas John Derricke, writing only ten years later, claimed that taming wild beasts was easier than converting the 'wild' Irish, so intractable was their nature;[6] William Herbert was quite prepared to teach in Irish, but William Gerard believed that the Irish tongue defined the Irish character; Barnaby Rich argued that Catholicism was the root cause of Irish 'wilfulness' and he condemned English recusants in Ireland as worse than the naturally ignorant 'mere' Irish[7] because they, at least, should have known better, whilst John Hooker's account of the Anglicization of a native Irishman shows that he thought there would always be a residue of Irishness, making converts no better than copies or hybrids.[8] What these positions do indicate is that the play of identity and difference is not easily untangled as a rationally extracted kernel; there is a logic at work behind statements, but it is not always recognisable at the level of the individual's professed faith or in the single work. Perhaps a guide to interpretation is the line taken on cross-cultural transformation ('degeneration'); or, better still, the answer given to the question, what is to be done? William Herbert's response may seem a world away from the advocation of the extermination of the Irish in the anonymous 'Discourse of Ireland' but are they not, once again, mirror images; one for assimilation, one for separation; one detecting a residue of identity beneath the surface, the other seeing only the essence of difference? Are they not, self-evidently, articulated within the same political parameters?

A. ANALYSES

1) Edmund Campion

Campion's *History of Ireland* was hastily assembled in Dublin, probably between August, 1570, and May-June, 1571, where he lived under the protection of James Stanihurst, speaker of the Irish House of Commons, whose son, Richard, he had taught at Oxford. Campion had probably gone to Ireland to escape persecution for his Catholicism, believing the Old English society of Dublin to be a safe haven from the spread of the Reformation, although subsequent events forced him to flee, via England, to Douai. He had been an outstanding scholar at Oxford; after leaving Ireland he became a Jesuit in Rome, returned to England in 1580, was captured and executed in 1581.

Manuscripts of the *History* found their way to England and it was printed in the first edition of Holinshed's *Chronicles* (1586) by Richard Stanihurst and then in Sir James Ware's much used *Ancient Irish Histories* (1633).[9] Campion's stress on the ease with which the Irish could be reformed through spreading the benefits of a Renaissance education possibly owes much to the ethos of the Old English circles in which he moved, as does his depiction of the 'Wild' Irish, whom he was unlikely to have seen in the flesh.[10]

From *Two Bokes of the Histories of Ireland* (1571), Bk. 1, Ch. 5: 'Dispositions of the people':[11]

The people are thus enclyned: religious, francke, amorous, irefull, sufferable of paynes infinite, veary glorious, many sorserers, excellent horsemen, delighted with warres, great almesgevers, passing in hospitalitie. The lewder sorte, bothe clerkes and laye, are sensuall and loose to leacherye above measure. The same being vertuously brede up or refourmed, are suche myrrors of holynes and austeritie that other nations retaine but a shadoe of devotion in comparison of them. As for abstinence and fastynge, which theis daies make so dangerous, this is to them a familiare kinde of chastisment. In whiche vertue and diverse other how farr the best excell, so farr in glotonie and other hatefull crymes the vitious theie are worse than to bad. Theie folowe the deade course to grave with howling and barbarous owtcries, pitifull in apparance, whereof grewe as I suppose the proverbe to weepe Irishe. The uplandishe are lightly abused to beleeve and avouche idle miracles and revelations vaine and childishe. Greedie of praise theie be, and fearfull of dishonour. And to this ende they esteeme theire poetes, who wright Irishe learnedly, and penne therein sonettes heroicall, for the which they are bountefully rewarded; yf not, they sende owt lybells in dispraise, whereof the gentlemen, specially the meere Irishe, stande in greate awe. They love tenderly theire foster children, and bequeathe to them a childes portyon, whereby they nourishe sure frendship, so beneficiall every waie that comonly five hundred kyne and better are geven in reward to wynne an noblemans childe to forster. They are sharpe witted, lovers of learning, capable of any studie whereunto they bende themselves, constant in travaile, aventurous, intractable, kynde hearted, secreate in displeasure.

Hitherto the Irishe of bothe sortes, meere and Englishe, are affected mutche indifferently, save that in theis by good order and breaking the same vertues are farr more pregnant, in those other by licencious and evill custome the same faultes are more extreame and odious. I saie by lycentiousnes and evill custome, for that there is daily triall of good natures among them; howe sone they be reclaymed and to what rare giftes of grace and wisdome they doe and have aspired, againe the veary Englishe of birthe conversant with the brutishe sorte of that people become degenerate in short space, and are quite altered into worst ranke of Irish rooges. Such a force hathe education to make or marre.

2) Sir William Gerard

Gerard, a lawyer and M.P. for Chester, was appointed Lord Chancellor of Ireland in April, 1576, and was, like Campion, connected with the then Lord Deputy, Sir Henry Sidney, under whom he had served in Wales. He was involved in Sidney's attempt to reform the tax of 'cess',[12] the chief grievance of the Palesmen. To this end, he journeyed to court to represent the state of the country to the Privy Council, but his mission ended in failure. Re-appointed to Ireland as a Master of Requests in the summer of 1580, he returned to England owing to illness and died in 1581.

The extracts printed here are from Gerard's 'Notes of his Report to the Privy Council on Ireland, given to Robert Dudley, Earl of Leicester in 1576'. Gerard's belief that 'Sharpe lawes muste woorke the reform' illustrates a confidence that the spread of the English legal system to Ireland would achieve the desired effect. In this he can be said to belong to a 'Reform tradition' in not advocating the need for a complete re-conquest of the country, as later writers, most notably, Edmund Spenser, were to demand.[13]

From Gerard's 'Notes of his Report' (1576):[14]

It is necesarye to understand whoe be the Irishe enymies and howe they annoye the state, and also whoe ar they so termid Englishe rebells, and howe they woorke harme, and then to thinke of the desire to reforme, and whether one lyke and one same course & waye to subdue bothe be to be followed.

The Irishe is knowen by name, speache, habitt, feadinge, order, rule, and conversacion. He accompteth him self cheife in his owne country and (whatsoever he saye or professe) lykethe of noe superior. He mortally hatethe the Englishe. By will he governethe those under him, supplyinge his and their wantes by prayinge and spoylinge of other countryes adjoyninge. Theise lyve as the Irishe lyved in all respectes before the conqueste.

In twoe sortes, theise ar to be dealte with: The one, totallye to conquere theim, and that muste be by force of the swoord, for so were the other of the Irishe subdued before the Englishe were setled: the other waye is by suche pollecye to keepe theim quiett as with smalleste force, and by consequent with least chardge they may be defended from harminge the Englishe. Whiche pollecyes I finde by those recordes from age to age putt in use in that governmente.

The Englishe rebells ar people of our owne nacion,[15] suche whose auncestors and theim selves after the expultion of the Irishe, ever sithence Henrye the secondes tyme, some of longer, some of shorter tyme, have there contynued. Theise Englishe rebells may be devided into twoe kindes: the one, soche as enter into the field in open hostilitie and actuall rebellion agaynste the Prince, comparable to the rebellinge in England. To suppresse those, the swoord muste also be the instrument. Thother sorte of Englishe rebells are suche as refuzinge Englishe nature growe Irishe in soche sorte as (otherwise then in name) not to be discerned from the Irishe.

All the force of the Irishe with all the helpe they had of anye actuall Englishe rebell harmed not (as the recordes verifie) untill this degeneratinge fell, which beganne about the xxxth yeare of the sayd Kinge Edwarde the third his reigne.

The cawsies which move theise recordes to call theim Englishe degenerates apearethe in the same.

Theye (saye theise recordes) speake Irishe, use Irishe habitt, feadinge, rydinge, spendinge, coysheringe,[16] coyninge; they exacte, oppresse, extorte, praye, spoyle, and take pledges and distresses as doe the Irishe. They marrye and foster with the Irishe, and, to conclude, they imbrace rather Irishe braghan lawes[17] then sweete government by justice.

Soche as affirme the swoord muste goe before to subdue theise, greatly erre. For can the swoord teache theim to speake Englishe, to use Englishe apparell, to restrayne theim from Irishe exactions and extortions, and to shonne all the manners & orders of the Irishe. Noe it is the rodd of justice that muste scower out those blottes. For the sword once wente before, and setled their auncestors, and in theim yet resteth this instincte of Englishe nature, generally to feare justice.

[. . .]

I told their Honnors that so long as the Englishe kepte under the government of Englishe lawes they prospered, and when they fell to be Irishe and embraced the Irishe orders, customs and lawes they decayed, so as to restore theim to former Englishe civilitie lawes had from tyme to tyme still bene made restrayninge the Englishe from the Irishe; forbiddinge theim under a payne to foster or marrye with theim or to use or followe anye their Irishe lawes or customs; to use or weare anye their habitt or apparell, to receive or seeke for judgement by anye of their lawes: forbiddinge all captens and marchers to retayne anye Kerne or idell followers, and under payne of deathe to take no prayes.[18]

[. . .]

I sayd to their Honnors all those lawes notwithstandinge the race of the Englishe throughout the pale were in everye forbidden respecte growen more Irishe then before and so the wound greater at this daye then ever before. I sayd if Irishe speache, habit and conditions made the man Irishe, the moste parte of the Englishe were Irishe.

3) John Derricke

Virtually nothing is known of Derricke, who was, again, connected to Sir Henry Sidney, and possibly a friend of his son, Sir Philip, to whom *The Image of Irelande* is dedicated. He may have been the Mr. Derricke employed to make the great seal for Ireland in 1557, in which case the woodcuts extant in some editions might be his work too.

The Image of Irelande, probably written in 1578 and published in 1581, lavishes great praise on Henry Sidney's abilities and may have been an attempt to win him favour at court, where he felt his achievements had been undervalued.[19] Derricke's tract describes the nature of the Irish woodkern, strictly speaking soldiers,[20] but clearly serving metonymically for all the native Irish. Part one shows the woodkern in the context of Irish society and determines what they are, whilst part two describes their habits and customs.[21]

The Image of Irelande (1581); from Part one:[22]

of feathered foules,
there breeds the cheef of all:
A mightie foule, a goodlie birde,
whom men doe Eagle call.
This builde her nast in highest toppe,
of all the Oken tree:
Or in the craftiest place, whereof
in Irelande many bee.
Not in the bounds of Englishe pale,

whiche is a ciuill place:
But in the Deuills Arse, a Peake,
where Rebells moste imbrace.
For as this foule and all the reste,
are wilde by Natures Kinde:
So do thei kepe in wildest nokes
and there men doe them finde.
For like to like the Proverbe saith,
the Leopard with the Beare:
Doth live in midst of desarts rude
and none doeth other feare.
For as the Irishe Karne be wilde,
in manners and in fashion:
So doe these foules enhabite, with
that crooked generation.
Yet when as thei are taken yong,
(though wilde thei be by kinde:)
Entrusted through the fauconers lure,
by triall good I find.
That thei come as twere at becke,
and when as thei doe call:
She scarce will stint on twige or bowe,
till on his fiste she fall.
Thus thei obey their tutors hestes
and doe degenerate:
from wildnesse that belonged to,
their fore possessed state.
But Irishe Karne unlike these foules,
in burthe and high degree:
No chaunglyngs are thei love nowhit,
In civill state to bee.
Thei passe not for ciuilitie,
Nor care for wisdomes lore:
Sinne is their cheef felicitie,
whereof thei have the store.
And if perhappes a little Ape,
be taken from the henne:
And brought from Boggs to champion ground,
such thyngs happe now and then.
Yea though thei were in Courte trained up,
and yeres there lived tenne:
Yet doe thei loke to shaking boggs,
scarce provying honest menne.
And when as thei have wonne the Boggs,
suche vertue hath that grounde:
that they are wurse than wildest Karne,
And more in sinne abounde.

Mikes 4 Trebles + 1 Acc

Mansfield H 6/7 1.85

Lincoln A Ev 2 £50

Peterborough A ~~6~~5-4 2.2 ? 2-

Doncaster A 6-5 2.2

£10 179

£ 81
£ 81
£ 89
£ 96.8

183

From Part two.

Though that the royall soyle,
and fertill Irishe grounde:
With thousande sondrie pleasaunt thynges,
moste nobly doe abounde.
Though that the lande be free,
from vipers generation:
As in the former parte I made,
a perfecte declaration.[23]
Though that the yearth I saie,
be bliste with heauenly thyngs:
And though tis like the fragrant flowre,
in pleasante Maie that springs.
Yet when I did beholde,
those whiche possesse the same:
Their maners lothsome to be told,
as yrksome for to name.
I mervuailede in my mynde,
and thereupon did muse:
To see a Bride it is the Soile,
the Bridegrome is the Karne.

4) John Hooker (1526–1601)

Hooker was born in Exeter and later became chamberlain of the city. He was a staunch Protestant and is mainly notable for his historical writings, among them a history of the rebellion in Exeter in 1549 and his contributions to Holinshed's *Chronicles.* His connection with Ireland dates from 1568, when he went over as a solicitor on behalf of Sir Peter Carew in order to prove his client's claims to vast tracts of land in Munster. He was elected as an M.P. for Athenry to the Irish House of Commons and spoke so vehemently in favour of the Royal prerogative in the 1569 Parliament that the House broke up in confusion in the mêlée that pursued. He died in 1601.

Hooker wrote extensively on Ireland, translating Giraldus's *Expugnatio* and continuing the chronicle of Ireland from the death of Henry VIII up to 1587 for Holinshed's *Chronicles* and also producing a separate life of Sir Peter Carew.[24] The passage cited below is from the second of these works and refers to the capture and execution of Sir James Desmond during the Desmond Rebellion (1578–81), which took place in 1581.[25]

From *The Chronicles of Ireland* in Holinshed's *Chronicles* (1586):[26]

[S]ir Cormac Mac Teige shiriffe of the countie of Corke did notable service upon Sir James of Desmond; which Sir James upon the fourth of August made a roade into Muskroie, and tooke a great preie from the foresaid sir Cormac. Wherupon his brother Donnell assembleth his brothers tenants and countrie and followed the preie, and recovered the same: Sir James, who thought it to be too great a dishonor and reproch to depart with anie thing which he had in hand, withstanding the matter.

Whereupon they fell at hand-fight. In which conflict and fight the said Donnell behaved himself so valiently, and his companie so lustilie stucke to the matter, that the preie was recovered, and Sir James himselfe mortallie wounded and taken prisoner, and all his force, being above a hundred and fiftie persons, were slain and overthrowne. . . [H]e did deliver him unto Sir Warham Sentleger then provost marshall, and to captaine Raleigh; who (according to a commission in like order to them addressed) was examined, indicted, arreigned, and then upon judgement drawen, hanged and quartered: and his bodie being quartered, it was togither with the head set on the towne gates of the citie of Corke, and made the preie of the foules. And thus the pestilent hydra hath lost another of his heads.[27]

This service of this knight was marvellouslie well accepted, and first from the lord justice and councell, and then from hir majestie he received verie freendlie and thankful letters . . . [T]his Sir Cormac, in dutie and obedience to hir majestie and hir lawes, and for his affection to all Englishmen, surpasseth all his own sept & familie, as also all the Irishrie in that land. For albeit a meere Irish gentleman can hardly digest anie Englishman or English government, & whatsoever his outward appearance be, yet his inward affection is corrupt and naught: being not unlike to Jupiters cat, whome though he had transformed into a beautiful ladie, and made hir a noble princesse; yet when she saw the mouse, she could not forbeare to snatch at him; and as the ape, though he be never so richlie attired in purple, yet he will still be an ape.[28] This knight, after he did once yeeld himself to hir majesties obedience, and had professed his loialtie, he ever desired to joine himselfe unto the companie of the Englishmen, and became in time a faithful and freendlie man unto them, lived according to hir majesties lawes; and did so good service at all times when it was requisit and required, as none of that nation did ever the like. And if at anie time he were had in suspicion, he would by some kind of service purge & acquite himselfe, even as he did in this present service in taking of Sir James of Desmond, to his great praise & commendation, and to his acquitall against the reproachfull reports of his adversaries.

5) Barnaby Rich (1540?–1617)

Rich, like his slightly older friend, Thomas Churchyard (see below, p. 98), was a prolific writer of verse, romance and political pamphlets who spent much of his working life as a soldier. Both were vehement Protestants. Rich served in the Dutch Wars until 1573, then went for the first time to Ireland with the first Earl of Essex's expedition to colonize Ulster. After the collapse of the enterprise he served in the military action against the Desmond Rebellion. Rich later became a spy in Ireland, but was forced to seek refuge in England when his lurid descriptions of the corruption and neglect of duties he saw in the Church of Ireland attracted the unwelcome attention of Thomas Jones, Bishop of Meath, and Adam Loftus, the Lord Chancellor, two of the most powerful men in Ireland. He returned to Ireland in 1599 to fight with the second Earl of Essex's army against Tyrone, staying on with Mountjoy's campaign. Rich tried, unsuccessfully, to obtain land on the Ulster Plantation after the Flight of the Earls, and so remained in Dublin until his death in 1617 or 1618, continuing to rail against official corruption, tolerance of recusancy, and Irish abuses in general.[29]

The extracts included here are taken from Rich's longest published tract on Ireland, *A New Description of Ireland* (1610) and a short manuscript book presented to James I in 1615, 'The Anatomy of Ireland', which its editor claimed 'is a document of human interest illustrative of the Tudor informer at work'.[30] Rich's attempts to classify the groups competing in Ireland are fascinating, as are the contradictions between the explanations he offers for the present state of affairs. In places he writes like John Bale fifty years on, employing a theological scale of values and suggesting that Protestant truth will erase national distinctions (although this 'truth' is written and spoken in English); elsewhere, he writes as if the Irish are the 'others' of different discourses, savages or the wilfully damned.[31]

a) *A New Description of Ireland* (1610), from Ch. 4:[32]

To speake now of the Irish more at large, for to them my talke doth especially belong, I say they are behoulding to Nature, that hath framed them comly personages of good proportion, very well limbed, & to speak truly, the English, Scottish and Irish, are easie to be discerned from all the Nations of the world: besides, aswel by the excellency of their complexions, as by the rest of their lineaments, from the crown of the head, to the sole of the foot. And although that in the romote places, the uncivill sort so disfigure themselves with their Glybs, their Trowes,[33] and their misshappen attire, yet they appear to every mans eye to be men of good proportion, of comly stature, and of able body. Now to speak of their dispositions, whereunto thay are adicted and inclined. I say, besides they are rude, uncleanlie, and uncivill, so they are very cruell, bloodie minded, apt and ready to commit any kind of mischiefe. I do not impute this so much to their naturall inclination, as I do to their education, that are trained up in Treason, in Rebellion, in Theft, in Robery, in Superstition, in Idolatry, and nuzeled from their Cradles in the very puddle of Popery.

This is the fruits of the Popes doctrine, that doth preach cruelty, that doth admit of murthers and bloudy executions; by poisoning, stabbing, or by any other maner of practice howsoever: the pope teacheth subjects to resist, to mutinie, and to rebel against their Princes.

From hence it proceedeth, that the Irish have ever beene, and still are, desirous to shake off the English government.

From hence it doth proceed, that the Irish can not endure to love the English, bicause they differ so much in Religion.

From hence it proceedeth, that as they cannot indure to love the English, so they cannot be induced to love anything that doth come from the English: according to the proverbe, love me, and love my dog: so contrariwise, he that hateth me, hateth in like manner all that commeth from me.

From hence it is, that the Irish had rather stil retaine themselves in their sluttishnesse, in their uncleanlinesse, in their rudenesse, and in their inhumane loathsomenes, then they would take any example from the English, either of civility, humanity, or any manner of Decencie.

We see nowe the author of this enmity, is hee that never did other good, where hee had to doe with mens consciences.

There is yet a difference to bee made, of those that do proceed from our malice: and the Irish in this are the more to be pittied, that are no better taught; whose educations, as they are rude, so they are blinded with ignorance, and I thinke for devotions sake, they have made a vow to be ignorant.

But although the vulgar sort, through their dul wits, and their brutish education, cannot conceive what is profitable for themselves, and good for their Countrey, yet there bee some other of that Countrey birth, whose thoughts and mindes being inriched with knowledge and understanding, that have done good in the Country, and whose example hereafter may give light to many others: For I thinke, that if these people did once understand the pretiousnesse of vertue, they would farre exceed us; notwithstanding, our long experience in the Soveraignty of vertue.

b) From 'The Anatomy of Ireland' (1615):

Phylautus: [A]mongst other thyngs that makes me to wondre, me thynkes thys is strange, that the realm of Irelande beynge invyrond wyth Englande, Scotlande Fraunce & Spayne, that hath had such longe & contynuall entrecoursse, trade & traffique, and hath byne so dayly conversant wyth the people of thes natyons, that the cuntry shuld yet so remayne as it dothe, more uncyvyll, more uncleandly, more barbarous and more brutysh in ther costomes & demeanures then in any other parte of the world that is knowne:

Antodonus:[34] the Iryshe are so much inclyned to costome, that they wyll in no wyse gyve place to reason, & the malyce & the hatred they baare to the Englyshe government (whych they have ever spurned at: and are yet desyrous to shaake of) maketh them so to dyspyce the Englyshe, that they dysteyne to learne anythynge from them, be it never so necessary, but had rather conteyne themselves in ther sluttysh and inhumayne loathsomenes, then they would take any example from the Englyshe, eyther of cyvylyte humanyte, or of any other maner of decency:

Phy: why then I perceyve thys savage maner of incyvylyte amongst the Iryshe, it is bred in the bone. they have yt by nature, and so I thynke of ther inhumayne crewelty, that are so apt to rune into rebellyon, & so redy to atempt any other kynde of myschef:

An: they have it no lesse by nature then by nurture, that are trayned uppe in treason in rebellyon. in theft. in robbery. in superstytyon. in Idolatry. and nusseled from ther cradeles in the very puddell of popery: now how educatyon is able to alter, Lycurgus whelpes, hath taught us longe agoe:

Phy: but is ther no meanes left wherby to conforme the Iryshe to the obydyence to ther Prynce!

Ant: the dysceases of Irelande are many. & the sycknes is growne to that contagyon, that it is allmost past cure.

B. SOLUTIONS

1) William Herbert

Herbert was a distant relative of Sir James Croft, Lord Lieutenant of Ireland from 1551–2. Having gained a reputation for learning, especially in alchemy and Neoplatonic arts, he became an undertaker for the Munster Plantation in 1586, finally arriving there in April, 1587. He then became known as a vigorously active colonist and tried to make Kerry and Desmond into a 'Little England'. He was also, as the text below illustrates, a zealous Protestant, but saw the virtue of spreading the word in Irish. His work received praise from Lord Burghley and Sir Francis Walsingham, the very centre of courtly power, and also in Ireland itself, from Meyler Magrath, Archbishop of Cashel. However, the sheriff of Kerry, Edward Denny, criticized his arrogance and claimed that Herbert ruthlessly pillaged the Irish on his estates. He returned to England in 1589 and died in 1593.

The proposals for the reformation of Ireland contained in Herbert's treatises[35] resemble Campion's, which is perhaps a testament to his confidence in the readiness of Munster for drastic change after the Desmond Rebellion had been crushed (Herbert's lands were part of Desmond's estates), as much as anything else. For Herbert, the Irish are pliable enough, if correctly treated, to become loyal English without having to lose their language.[36]

From 'A Description of Munster' (1588):[37]

Touching the inhabitation of this province's waste and desolate parts (through the attainder of sundry accrued unto Her Majesty) and by reason of the calamities of the late wars void of people to manure and occupy the same, as it hath been with great reason thought meet to be performed by gentlemen of good ability and disposition out of England, that by their good example, direction, and industry, both true religion, sincere justice, and perfect civility might be here planted, and hence derived and propagated into the other parts of this realm, so the placing amongst this forward and undisciplined people inhabitants so much differing both in manners, language, and country from them, shall be unto them at the first, (without doubt) and ever without care had, unpleasant and odious, which will easily be acknowledged by any that weigheth the nature of the action together with the disposition of this nation.

The inconveniences that of this in time may grow when they increase both in dislike, number, and ability, may probably be conjectured but hardly measured, unless it be prevented. The prevention of it consisteth in two points whereof neither may be neglected, the bettering and reforming of their wills and dispositions, and the weakening and lessening of their powers and forces.

Their minds and wills are to be bettered principally by instructing them in true religion, the firm foundation of the fear of God, of their loyalty to Her Majesty, and of their love and charity one to another. Secondly, by the sincere and impartial administration of justice, whereby they may repose the safety of their lives, lands, and goods in Her Highness' laws and government. Thirdly, in a courteous demeanour, affability of speech, and care of their well doing, ever expressed towards them by such English gentlemen as shall inhabit and govern amongst them. For the first I have been careful in those parts wherein I am, to have them taught the truth in their natural tongue, to have the Lord's prayer, the Articles of the Creed, the Ten Commandments, translated into the Irish tongue; public prayers in that language, with the administration of the sacraments and other ecclesiastical rites, which in a strange tongue could be to them but altogether unprofitable, and in these things I have hitherunto found great want of a good and godly bishop, but now Mr. Kennam being here placed, a man both learned, godly, and of this country birth, I am in assured hope that by his good example and travail these parts will easily be reformed.

For the second, I have endeavoured what in me hath lain to make them taste the sweetness of Her Majesty's government, by giving every of them the benefit of the law, and thereby redressing all injuries and oppressions offered, that none deal according to his will and rage, but according to right and reason, so that they may find a sufficient protection in Her Majesty's peace.

For the third, together with the two former, I have in such sort inclined and applied myself unto the directions given me by Her most excellent Majesty, that I have drawn upon me the evil will of some of mine English neighbours, of whom I never deserved but well, and whose commodities I have preferred before mine own; only they cannot brook my course, so contrary unto theirs, by the which if it be not redressed I foresee they will make themselves and this action (which they undiscreetly use) odious and hateful unto this people, 'wherehence' very great inconveniences in time may grow, whereby they think to gain much, but without Her Majesty's excessive charge are more like to lose all.

2) 'A Discourse of Ireland', c. 1599.

Nothing at all is known of the author of this treatise, although his familiarity with Ireland and knowledge of economic problems suggests he lived there for some time. The author's aim is to encourage English exploitation of Ireland's natural resources, which marks the pamphlet as part of a distinct genre (see Ch. 5 below). What is notable (and chilling) about the tract is the process of reasoning which enables the writer to 'disappear' the Irish and smooth the island out into a 'West England'; people and land are brutally deracinated. Such writing still has the power to shock, perhaps as much in the 'banality of evil'[38] of its bureaucratic logic as in the drastic nature of its proposition,[39] because this is no more than the reductio ad absurdum of one, often the dominant, English voice. Where Herbert assimilates Irish difference, making it transparent, the author of the 'Discourse' demands that its very opaqueness be a reason for erasing it completely.[40]

How Ireland may be Civilised and wrought unto perfection, &c.

True it is that the malice is so inveterate within Irish heartes, as hardly they can endure their subjection unto the English nation or to mixe or suffer us to participate with them in any interest of their Soile unless we [become] meere Irish with them in Language Apparell and Manners: Which malice they bewray so often as Opportunity serveth of revenge, even upon such English as have otherwise well deserved of them the examples be yet freshe in memory since the Desmondes rebellion and now againe renewed.

The endeavours of her Majesties Progenitors have been greate to reduce this people to Civilitye, in so much as king Richard the second went there in person, and planted manie great English families among them whose names onely remaine English but in Nature digressing are become meere Irish for it is a thing observed in Ireland, and growen to a Proverbe that English in the second generation become Irish but never English. Such power duth Liberty and Custume in evill things gaine over men that the evill overcommeth and corrupteth the good.

Thus the Wisdome of God forsawe in the corruption of mans Nature, when in the planting of the Jewes in the land of Canaan commanded to roote out the auncient people of that Lande least their evill maners should corrupt the Jewes, threatning that the Cananites and the rest of those cursed nations should be as thornes among them if the Jewes obeied not the Counsell of God as in deede it fell out to be so. And as touching the Irish (I speak not of the good, who are to be embraced and cherished) what are they better then Cananites, which contemne God and Relligion observing neither the rites of Baptisme nor Matrimony.

Nevertheless [would] I persuade in no wise anie more to mixe English with the Irish in replanting the Country with English inhabitants, which must be a course necessary to be helde yet I would not the bloud of them should be extinct, but all the race of them to be translated out of Ireland, and English with some Flemmings to be onely planted in their Roomes because the Flemmings is a People of more propinquity to our Nature, and kinde to the English besides of great industry and soone shall induce many Misteries there to the furtherance of the common wealth.

The removing of the Irish maye happily alter their disposition when they Shall be planted in another Soyle. For doubtles in England wee find the Irish servant very faithfull and loving, and generally the people kinde the rather when here there malice can not profit them anye waye. Withall they be heere industrious, and commonly our best Gardiners, fruiterers and keepers of our horses, refusing no labor besides: So that throughout England there will be use made of them as servants, to a very great number. For such as have families in Ireland, the vacant places in every parish throughout the realme of such English families as shall be gone in to Ireland will be sufficient. For considering the populous multitudes in England wherewith every parish is overburthened,[41] one parish with another will willingly spare and set forth without charges to her Majestie at least two families with the men, women and children which may account unto 10 soales. In whose places they will be content to receive five Irish sowles which are also to live upon their labour. Then accounting after 20000[42] parishes in England and the number sent out will be 200000, and the number brought in will be 100000 who with the number of servants besides placed with Masters in England may make up in all 200000. A number besides may remaine in service under English Masters in Ireland not exceeding two in one house. Also the Low Countryes may receive many in exchange of theirs: and these warres with the sword and famine will devour manye. And considering that Ireland is not populous being very thinlye inhabited there will be found more places for them in England then for so many English, as well (after a beginning and impression of so happye a chaunge made in our peoples mindes) be willing to goe thither.

The manner of this proceeding (under correction) may be that as the Soldier gaineth the English inhabitants shall followe, and ever as the Irish shall be received to mercy to send them over into England So shall the country wonne never be regained by the Irish but remaine in quiet possession without disturbance which otherwise shal never be brought to passe.

If then it maye please her Majesty to assume the Landes of Ireland into her handes upon so generall a revolte[43] (excepting such Lande as be holden by the English and true subjects) and these landes to rate after a tenth of all profits Upon the same to be raised, it shall encourage a multitude of able men in England to go out upon their owne charges, and of such as are not of ability to be sent forth at the charges of the parishes, Among which an armie of men may be selected for service well appointed without cost or paye from her Majestie. This will be chearefully performed if the People of England shall be asseured to duell there onely amongest English, and the Irish to be cleare avoided, without which persuasion there be very few that will leave England to duell in Ireland.

Touching the landes of them that have remained true subjects, amongst whom may be many noble men Provision may be made as they may exchange for Landes in England with sufficient contentment And for the providing for all parties her Majestie may give 1.s. in England for gaine of 5.s. in Ireland. Allwaies provided that cleare riddance may be made of the Irish bloud and stirpe there as neare as shall be possible. Whereby her Majestie shall make Ireland profitable unto England or mearely a West England.

Plate 1. 'The triumphant return of the English soldiers', from John Derricke's *Image of Ireland*, 1581.

Plate 2. 'The flight of the Irish', from John Derricke's *Image of Ireland*, 1581.

Plate 3. Map of Ireland, from John Speed's *Theatre of Great Britain*, 1611.

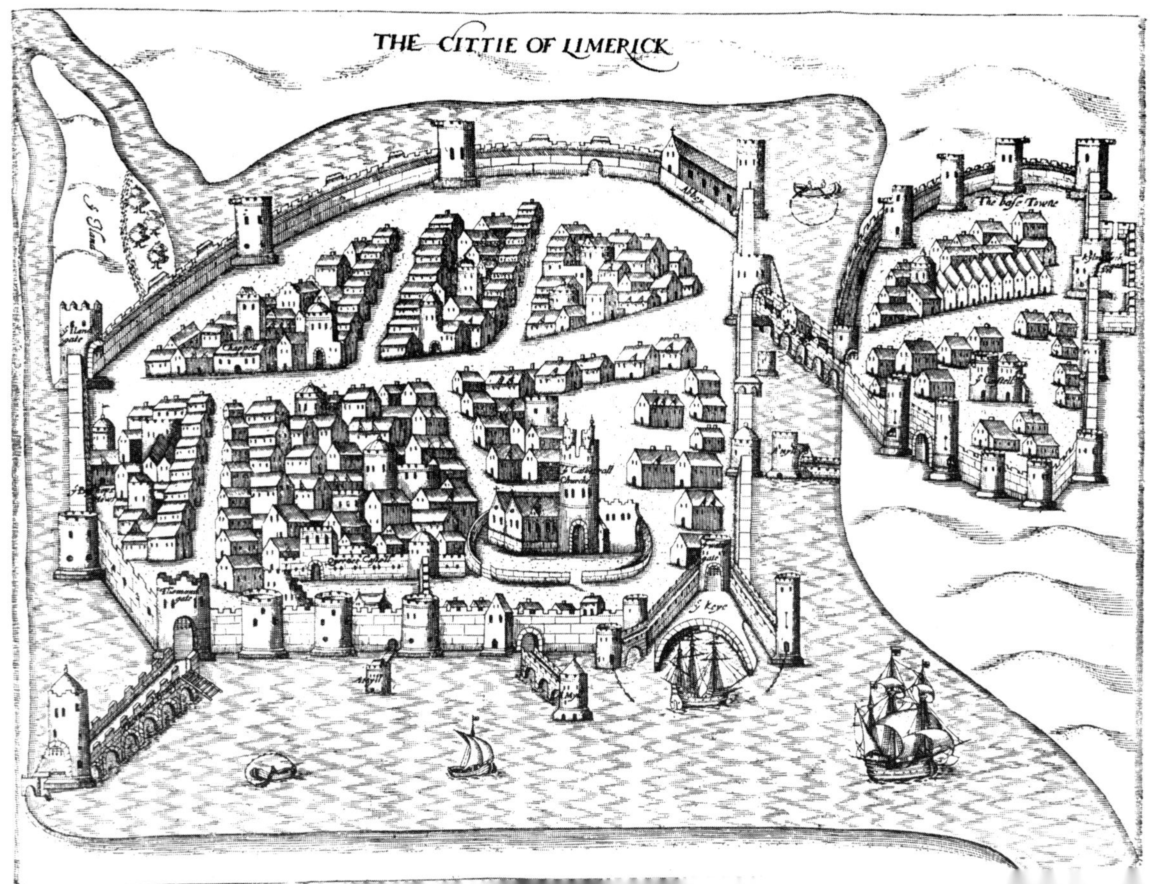
THE CITTIE OF LIMERICK
The base Towne
Abbey
S Keye
S Iland

Plate 5. Map of the Battle of Kinsale, from Fynes Moryson's *An Itinerary*, 1617.

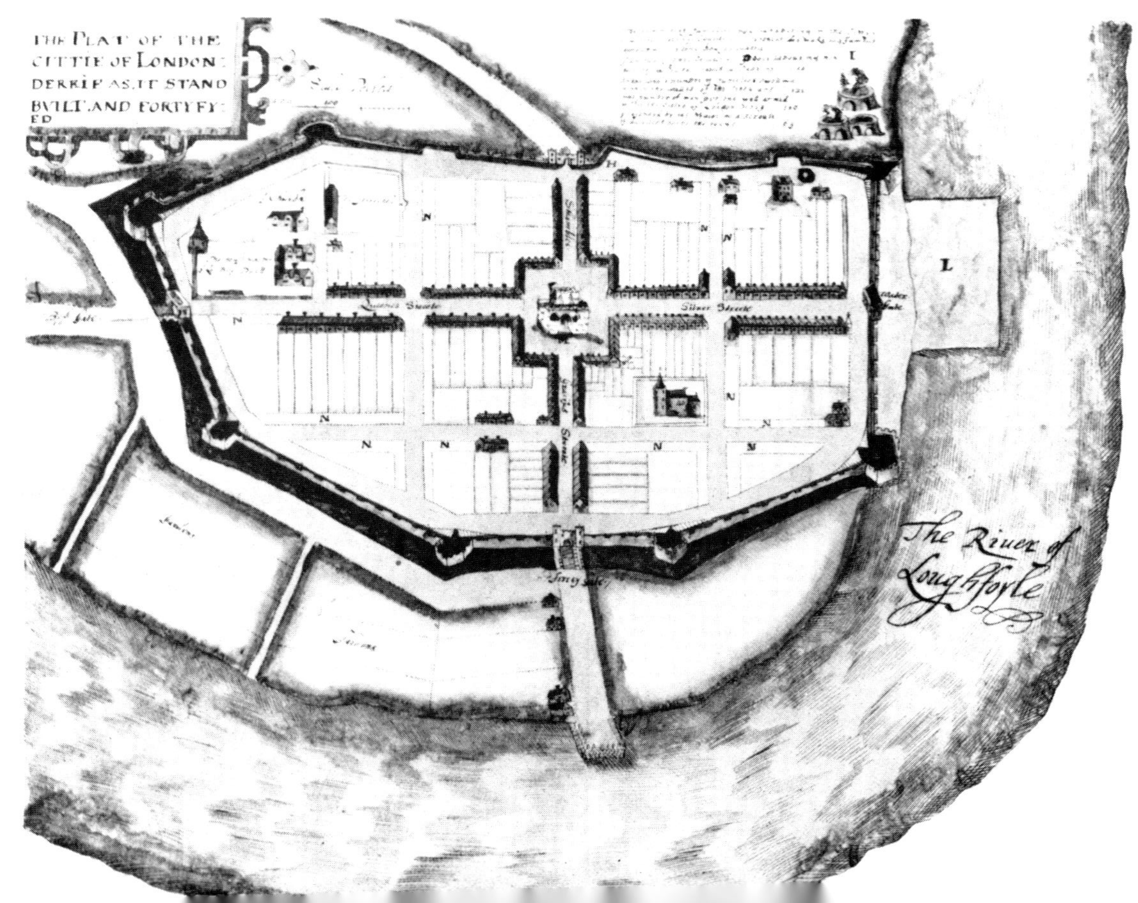
THE PLAT OF THE
CITTIE OF LONDON:
DERRIE AS IT STAND
BVILT AND FORTYFY:
ED
Silver Streete
L
The River of
Loughfoyle

A Prospect of bleeding IRELANDS miseries: Presented in a Brief

Recitement to the eyes and hearts of all her commiserating friends in *England* and *Scotland*, as one maine Motive to move their Christian courage for her assistance, when we consider there hath been at the least two hundred thousand Protestants slain and most inhumanely massacred by the barbarous and blood-thirsty Rebels, putting them to the most cruell kinds of death that they could invent, as you may read by this following Relation. Diligently Collected from the most certain Intelligence.

Recompence unto them double what they have done unto others.

Reader what passages of cruelty thou shalt here peruse thou hast not the least cause to suspect of truth, they being such as by ear evidence have bin made manifestly ue by faithfull Intelligence of eye and eare itnesses.

1. Within the County of Fermanagh eat cruelties have been acted upon the poor nglish Protestants where multitudes of men omen and children have been kill'd in cold lood.

2. In the Castle of Lisgoole there were bove one hundred and fifty men, women, nd children, burnt there when that Castle as set on fire.

3. At the Castle of Moneah about one undred English were slain by the Barbarous Rebels.

4. The Castle of Tullah being yeelded upon composition with promise of fair quarter from the Rebells, but as soon as ever they entred the same they put all to the sword without exception.

5. At Lissenskeah they murthered near one hundred of the Scotch Protestants, which they use in every place as cruelly as the English.

6. One Mr. Middleton they compeld to heare Mass and afterward they caused him his wife and children to be hanged up and murthered.

7. In the Countrys of Armagh and Tirone great and Barbarous cruelties have been exercised.

8. At one place there were carried out at severall times in Troops one thousand Protestants, which were drowned at the bridg of Portnedown, which for that purpose was broke down in the midst.

9. And within the County of Armagh foure thousand Protestants have in severall places been drowned.

10. The Protestants have been driven naked before these Barbarous Butchers in severall companies like sheep appoynted for the slaughter, to the places of execution.

11. And if any faynted or grew weary on the way, they prickt them forward with their sword poynts whereby they killed many on the way.

12. With their Pikes and swords they [illegible] the poor stript Christians into the water [illegible] of the Banks, or Bridges.

13. Those that assay by swiming to save their lives, they shoot or beat out their brains.

14. Sir Phellim Oneal hath proved the cheif actor of these Barborous and bloody massacres.

15. He having caused all the Protestants in Armagh and there abouts under pretence of conducting them murthered of young and old five hundred persons.

16. He caused the Town of Armagh, and Cathedrall Church to be fired which were burnt down.

17. At a town called Killaman, fourty and eight families were Murthered by his direction.

18. In the same town there were twenty too English Protestants Burnt in one house.

19. Within two miles of the same the Rebels murthered of English two hundred Families.

20. They have been so eager at their prey, that they would not suffer the poor Protestants to say their prayers before they murthered them.

21. They have imprisioned some in noysome dungeons of dirt and mire, with bolts on their leggs where they were starved to death by Leasure.

22. At Cassell the Rebels cruelly murthered fifteen English Protestants using the rest most barbarously.

23. They have most Barbarously mangled many Protestants and left them languishing in their payn in the high ways half dead accounting it to favourable to end them of their payn by a suddain death.

24. They have buried many alive both men women and poor harmless infants.

25. At one time at a town called Clownis, they buried seventeen persons which they had half hanged which were heard to send forth Lamentable groans.

26. After they had cruelly wounded some they hung them upon tenter hooks.

27. Others when they had put rops about their necks they dragged through the water.

28. Some they dragged through the woods and Boggs till they dyed.

29. They have put ropes about the necks of many and cast them several times into the water, wherby to cause them to confess where their moneys were.

30. They have hanged up some a small time, and then taken them down again, to make them confess where their money was, which when they told them, then they hanged them outright.

31. When they have stript the Protestants naked, they bid them go look for their God, and bid him cloth them again.

32. They have hung up English by the armes and then hackt them with their swords to try how many blows they would indure before they dyed.

33. Some have had their bellys ript up and so left with their Intrails taken out.

34. They have ript up women big with child, and the young Infants hath falled out, which the Rebells have often given to doggs, and swine to eat or cast into ditches.

35. The Rebells robb'd, stript, and murthered a great company of Protestants in the County of Armagh, some they burnt, some they slew by the sword, and some they hanged, others they starved and put to death more cruelly.

37. They have hanged some by the heels, and then with their skeans cut them in peeces

38. Some young Infants have been found in the feild, Sucking the Brests of their murthered Mothers.

39. A great number of Protestants especially of women and children, they have slasht & mangled in many places of their bodies, and not kill'd outright, but left them wallowing in their blood.

40. Denying to kill them outright, till two or three days after, and then they would dash out their brains with stones.

51. A woman that leapt out of a window to save her self from burning was murthered by the Rebels, and the next morning her child found sucking at her breast which they also murthered.

42. The Rebels stabb'd one Jane Addis, left her sucking child alive by her, & putting the breast into its mouth said suck English bastard, so the child perisht for want, of which Act they bragg'd.

43. Many young Infants have been stifled in vaults and cellers, or starved in caves which have cryed to their mothers rather to send them out to dye by the Rebels then to starve so miserably there.

44. Multitudes of men, women, and children were drowned, cast into ditches, boggs, and turf-pits.

45. Many have been inclosed in their houses which have been set on fire and burnt with their houses to ashes in a most miserable manner, and if any attempted to escape they threw them into the fire again.

46. They have dragg'd out some from their sick beds to the place of execution.

47. In the parish of Loghgall to the river of Toll they forced children to carry their aged parents out of their beds to drown them in that river.

48. They have enforced children to execute their parents, and wives their own husbands by hanging and other ways.

49. The wife of Florence Fitz Patrick was outragious with her husbands souldiers because they brought not the grease of a Protestant woman whom they had cruelly murthered for her to make candls withall.

50. The Irish men some of them detestnot the cruelty of those bloody queans that follow their camp, that cry our spare neither man woman nor child.

51. They have boyld children to death in Cauldrons.

52. They hanged a woman and her daughter in the hair of her own head.

53. In a frosty night they stript a woman big with child which presently after fell in labour, and both child and she dyed at the instant.

54. The Rebels often utter threatnings out to cut off all that have a drop of English blood in them, and their women cry out that the English are only meat for doggs.

55. Neare the Town of Monaghan, they most cruelly murthered one Mr. Foord in his own Garden, most inhumanely tortured his wife, Laying hot Tongs to her hands and feet (to make her tell where his money was) that with the payn thereof she died.

56. They have most villanously ravished Virgins and women, and afterwards have bin so bloody and hard-harted, as to dash their childrens brains out.

Thus have you heard of some part of the miseries and tortures inflicted upon the poor Protestants in Ireland, by the bloody Rebels; many more inhumane murthers they have committed, which I forbear for brevity sake: But such is the care and wisdom of the Parliament to put an end to the bleeding miseries of Ireland, that they have chosen that renowned, faithful, and valiant Commander Major General Skippon to be Field-Marshal over their Forces, and Major General Massey is chosen Lieutenant General of the horse, the Lord crown their endeavours with victory over those inhumane blood-thirsty Rebels, that so dying Ireland may yet live to praise him.

London, Printed for *J. H.* and are to be sold in *Popes head Alley*. 1647.

Plate 7. *Prospect of Bleeding Ireland's Miseries*, 1647.

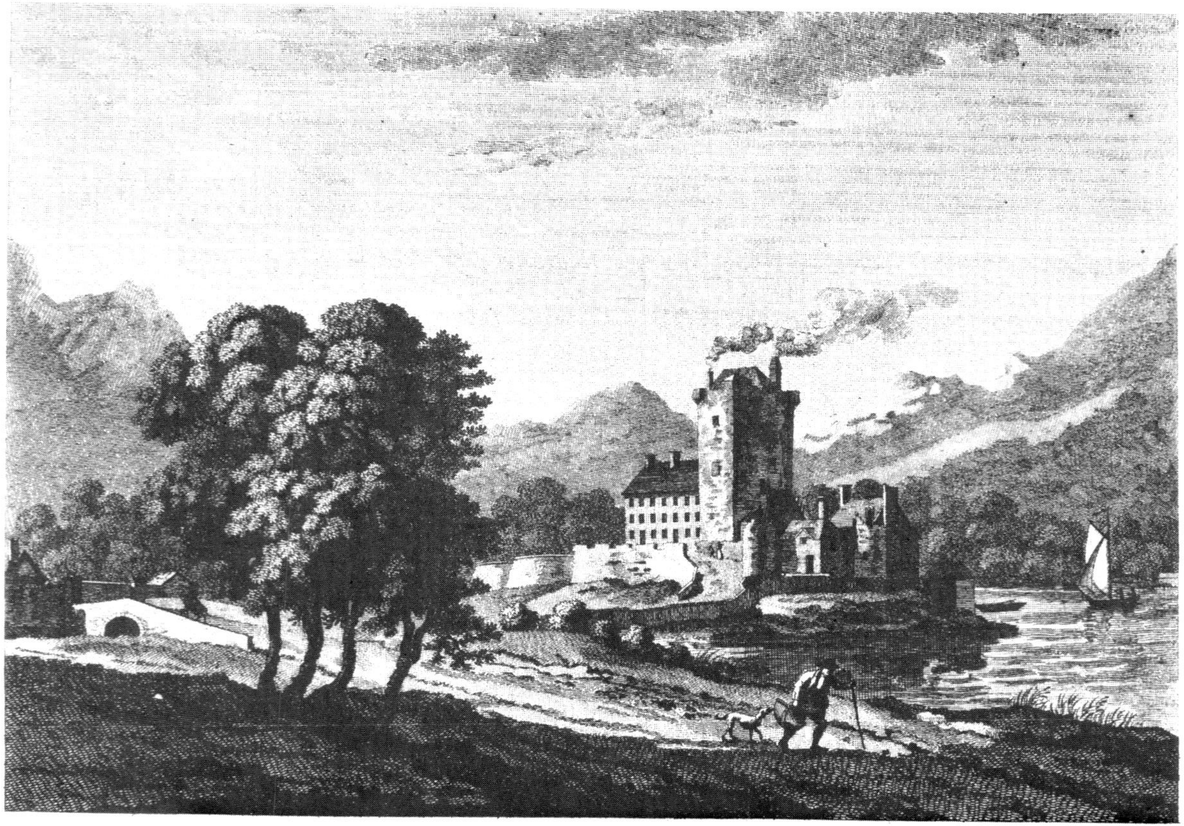

Plate 8. Ross Castle, from P. Sandby's

Plate 9. Dunluce Castle, from P. Sandby's *Tour Through Ireland*, 1746.

Plate 10. Map of Ireland, from R. Twiss' *Tour in Ireland*, 1776.

Plate 11. Mayo mud cabin, from J. Barrow's *Tour Round Ireland*, 1836.

Plate 12. Mayo stone cabin, from J. Barrow's *Tour Round Ireland*, 1836.

Plate 13. Hovel at the Reek, from J. Barrow's *Tour Round Ireland*, 1836.

Plate 14. Better Irish cottage, by Daniel Maclise, from J. Barrow's *Tour Round Ireland*, 1836.

Plate 15. Better Connaught cabin, from J. Barrow's *Tour Round Ireland*, 1836.

Plate 16. Contrasting fashions, 1859.

Plate 17. A village in the west of Ireland, 1859.

Plate 18. Bog village, Roscommon, from *Illustrated London News*, 1881.

Plate 19. Deserted wharves, Westport, from *Illustrated London News*, 1881.

4. THREE TRAVELLERS' OBSERVATIONS OF IRISH LIFE

Quite obviously it is impossible to have a recognisable genre of travel literature without a belief that seeing foreign countries, or, more to the point, reading others' accounts of their travels, does one good. The cliché 'travel broadens the mind' has to be taken seriously. Clearly such literature can be found from the time of classical Greece onwards in the West, in Herodotus, Tacitus, Julius Caesar, Mandeville, Eustache Deschamps, and other writers. Equally one might point to two developments in the Renaissance which increased the importance of travelling as a valuable pursuit in itself: the discovery of the 'New World' and the creation of the science of ethnology to cope with the awareness of mankind's diversity and control (classify) such information, making it 'useful';[1] and the advent of the 'Grand Tour', designed for young gentlemen to acquire and absorb the cultural legacy they had as Europeans by visiting great cities, studying their buildings and art treasures, learning their languages and being introduced at their courts.[2] Ireland, in Brady and Gillespie's words, 'a constitutional anomaly, neither the "kingdom" of England nor a "colony" in North America',[3] did not fit easily into either Eurocentric project, which may help to explain the lack of interest travellers showed until the seventeenth century, when Ireland had supposedly been made 'safe' (a more fundamental reason for not visiting Ireland for cultural experience had, unsurprisingly, been the fear of physical harm). It may have been that Ireland seemed too close to home for Englishmen, devoid of interesting features (complaints about the lack of buildings are almost *de rigeur* and the Romantic attraction of Ireland is of a much later date (see below, p. 238)). It was neither sufficiently European nor exotic enough for travellers, to warrant hazarding its dangers and discomforts. For those who did incorporate their Irish experiences into general travel works, the influence of the genre and its attendant anxieties are apparent. Did one travel to recognise a European heritage, a 'sameness' to be absorbed? Or was the purpose to observe another culture, a 'difference' to learn from and define oneself against?

1) Fynes Moryson (1566–1617)

Moryson was granted a fellowship from Peterhouse College, Cambridge, in 1584, to study civil law, and used it to travel extensively (1591–7), visiting most of Europe, Turkey, North Africa and the Middle East. His brother, Richard, then governor of Dundalk, recommended that he seek employment in Ireland, where he arrived in November, 1600, and acquired, rather fortuitously,[4] the post of chief secretary to the Lord Deputy, Lord Mountjoy. He took part in the campaign to suppress Tyrone and was present at the battle of Kinsale, remaining in Mountjoy's service until the latter's death in 1606. Apart from a brief visit to Ireland in 1613, the rest of Moryson's life was taken up with his attempt to prepare his account of his travels for publication.

It is almost impossible to convey an accurate sense of the rambling copia of Moryson's excursus, but it is probably fair to say that only the Turks receive a worse press than the native Irish in the *Itinerary,* which gives a journal of his travels (part one), a narration of the Nine Years' War and Moryson's part in it (part two), and accounts of the people seen and places visited (parts three and four). The 'meere' Irish serve as an index of barbarism and the passage included here,[5] containing Moryson's description of Irish culinary practices, would provide ample material for an analysis of the significance of the binary opposition, 'culture' and 'nature', along the lines of Lévi-Strauss's *The Raw and the Cooked.*[6]

From the *Itinerary* (1617):[7]

Touching the Irish dyet, Some Lords and Knights, and Gentlemen of the English-Irish, and all the English there abiding, having competent meanes, use the English dyet, but some more, some lesse cleanly, few or none curiously, and no doubt they have as great and for their part greater plenty than the English, of flesh, fowle, fish, and all things for food, if they will use like Art of Cookery. Alwaies I except the Fruits, Venison, and some dainties proper to England, and rare in Ireland. And we must conceive, that Venison and Fowle seem to be more plentiful in Ireland, because they neither so generally affect dainty foode nor so diligently search it as the English do. Many of the English-Irish, have by little and little been infected with the Irish filthiness, and that in the very cities, excepting Dublyn, and some of the better sort in Waterford, where, the English continually lodging in their houses, they more retain the English diet. The English-Irish, after our manner serve to the table joynts of flesh cut after our fashion, with Geese, Pullets, Pigges, and like rosted meats, but their ordinary food for the common sort is of Whitmeates, and they eate cakes of oates for bread, and drinke not English Beere made of Mault and Hops, but Ale. At Corck I have seen with these eyes, young maides starke naked grinding of Corne with certaine stones to make cakes thereof, and striking of into the tub of meale, such reliques thereof as stuck upon their belly, thighes, and more unseemely parts.

And for the cheese and butter commonly made by the English-Irish, an English man would not touch it with his lippes though he were halfe starved; yet many English inhabitants make very good of both kindes. In Cities they have such bread as ours, but of sharpe savour, and some mingled with Anniseeds and baked like cakes, and that onely in the houses of the better sort.

The Irish Aquavitae, vulgarly called Usquebagh, is held the best in the world of that kind; which is made also in England, but nothing so good as that which is brought out of Ireland. And the Usquebagh is preferred before our Aquavitae, because the mingling of Raysons, Fennell seede, and other things, mitigating the heate, and making the taste pleasant, makes it lesse inflame, and yet refresh the weake stomacke with moderate heate, and a good relish. These Drinks the English-Irish drink largely, and in many families (especially at feasts) both men and women use excesse therein. And since I have in part seene, and often heard from others experience, that some Gentlewomen were so free in this excess as they would kneeling upon the knee and otherwise, carausse health after health with men; not to speake of the wives of the Irish Lords or to referre it to the due place, who often drinke till they be drunken, or at least till they voide urine in full assemblies of men, I cannot (though unwilling) but note the Irish women more specially with this fault, which I have observed in no other part to be a woman's vice, but onely in Bohemia. Yet, so accusing them, I meane not to excuse the men, and will also confesse that I have seen Virgins, as well Gentlewomen as Citizens, commanded by their mothers to retyre after they had in curtesie pledged one or two healths. . . .

[. . .]

The wild and (as I may say) meere Irish, inhabiting many and large Provinces, are barbarous and most filthy in their diet. They skum the seething pot with an handfull of straw, and straine their milk taken from the Cow through a like handfull of straw, none of the cleanest, and so cleanse, or rather more defile the pot and milke. They devoure great morsels of beefe unsalted, and they eat commonly Swines flesh, seldom mutton, and all these pieces of flesh, as also the intralles of beasts unwashed, they seeth in a hollow tree, lapped in a raw Cowes hide, and so set over the fier, and therewith swallow whole lumps of filthy butter. Yea (which is more contrary to nature) they will feede on Horses dying of themsleves, not only upon small want of flesh, but even for pleasure: For I remember an accident in the Army, when the Lord Mountjoy, the Lord Deputy, riding to take the ayre out of the Campe, found the buttocks of dead Horses cut off, and suspecting that some soldiers had eaten that flesh out of necessity, being defrauded of the victuals allowed them,[8] commanded the men to bee searched out, among whom a common soldier, and that of the English-Irish, not of the meere Irish, being brought to the Lord Deputy, and asked why hee had eaten the flesh of dead Horses, thus freely answered, Your Lordship may please to eate Pheasant and Partridge, and much good doe it you that best likes your taste; and I hope it is lawfull for me without offence to eat this flesh, that likes me better then beef. Whereupon the Lord Deputy perceiving himself to be deceived, & further understanding that he had received his ordinary victuals (the detaining whereof he suspected, and purposed to punish for example), gave the soldier a piece of gold to drinke in Usquebagh for better digestion, and so dismissed him.

The foresaid wilde Irish doe not thresh their Oates, but burne them from the straw, and so make cakes thereof, yet they seldome eate this bread, much less any better kind, especially in the time of warre. Whereof a Bohemian Baron complained, who having seen the Courts of England and Scotland, would needes, out of his curiosity returne through Ireland in the heate of the Rebellion; and having letters from the King of Scots to the Irish lords then in Rebellion, first landed among them, in the furthest North, where for eight dayes space he had found no bread, not so much as a cake of Oates, till he came to eate with the Earl of Tyrone, and after obtaining the Lord Deputies Passe to come into our Army, related this their want of bread to us for a miracle, who nothing wondred thereat. Yea, the wilde Irish in time of greatest peace impute covetousness and base birth to him that hath any Corne after Christmas, as if it were a point of Nobility to consume all within those Festivall dayes. They willingly eate the herb Schamrock, being of a sharpe taste, which as they runne and are chased to and fro, they snatch like beasts out of the ditches. . .

Many of these wilde Irish eat no flesh, but that which dyes of disease or otherwise of it self, neither can it scape them for stinking.

They desire no broath, nor have any use of a spoone. They can neither seethe Artichokes, nor eate them when they are sodden. It is strange and ridiculous, but most true, that some of our carriage Horses falling into their hands, when they found Sope and Starch, carried for the use of our Laundresses, they thinking them to be some dainty meates, did eate them greedily, and when they stuck in their teeth, cursed bitterly the gluttony of us English churles, for so they terme us. They feede most on Whitmeates, and esteem for a great daintie sower curds, vulgarly called by them Bonaclabbe. And for this cause they watchfully keep their Cowes, and fight for them as for religion and life; and when they are almost starved, yet they will not kill a Cow except it bee old, and yield no Milke. Yet will they upon hunger in time of warre, open a vaine of the cow and drinke the bloud, but in no case kill or much weaken it. A man would thinke these men to be Scythians,[9] who let their Horses bloud under their eares and for nourishment drinke their bloud; and indeed (as I have formerly said), some of the Irish are of the race of Scythians, comming into Spaine, and from thence into Ireland. The wild Irish (as I said) seldome kill a Cow to eate, and if perhaps they kill one for that purpose, they distribute it all to be devoured at one time; for they approve not the orderly eating at meales, but so they may eate enough when they are hungry, they care not to fast long. And I have knowne some of these Irish footemen serving in England, (where they are nothing lesse than sparing in the food of their families), to lay meate aside for many meales, to devoure it all at one time. . .

These wild Irish never set any candles upon tables; What do I speak of Tables? since indeede they have no tables, but set their meate upon a bundle of grasse, and use the same Grasse for napkins to wipe their hands. But I meane that they do not set candles upon any high place to give light to the house, but place a great candle made of reedes and butter upon the floure in the midst of a great roome. And in like sort the chiefe men in their houses make fiers in the middest of the roome, the smoake whereof goeth out at a hole in the top thereof. An Italian Frier comming of old into Ireland and seeing at Armagh this their diet and the nakedness of the women. . . , is said to have cried out,

'Civitas Armachana, civitas vana,
Carnes crudae, mulieres nudae.'

'Vaine Armagh City, I did thee pity,
Thy meates rawness and womens nakedness.'

I trust no man expects among these gallants any beds, much less featherbeds and sheetes, who, like the Nomades removing their dwellings according to the commodity of pastures for their Cowes, sleepe under the Canopy of heaven, or in a poore house of clay, or in a cabbin made of the boughes of trees and covered with turffe, for such are the dwellings of the very Lords among them. And in such places they make a fier in the middest of the roome, and round about it they sleep upon the ground, without straw or other thing under them, lying all in a circle about the fier, with their feete towards it. And their bodies being naked, they cover their heads and upper parts with their mantels, which they first make very wet, steeping them in water of purpose, for they finde that when their bodies have once warmed the wet mantels, the smoake of them keepes their bodies in temperate heate all the night following. And this manner of lodging, not only the meere Irish Lords and their followers use, but even some of the English-Irish Lords and their followers, when after the old but tyrannicall and prohibited manner vulgarly called Coshering, they goe (as it were) on progresse, to live upon their tenants, till they have consumed al the victuals that the poore men have or can get. To conclude, not only in lodging passengers, not at all or most rudely, but even in their inhospitality towards them, these wild Irish are not much unlike to wild beasts, in whose caves a beast passing that way, might perhaps finde meate, but not without danger to be ill intertained, perhaps devoured, of his insatiable host.

2) William Lithgow (1582–1645?)

Lithgow, a native of Lanark, Scotland, but forced to leave in early adolescence after an unfortunate incident,[10] had travelled extensively even before he set off in 1609 on the three voyages that were to make up his *Total Discourse*. In all he claimed to have walked over 36,000 miles (twice the circumference of the earth) and his itinerary is even more extensive than Moryson's,[11] although the description of it considerably shorter. He endured much physical hardship on his travels, most notably when he was imprisoned and tortured by the Spanish Inquisition in Malaga, an incident which led to further imprisonment in the Marshalsea after he had attacked the Spanish ambassador, Gondomar, in 1662, for the failure of the latter's government to compensate him for his sufferings.[12] There were early accounts of his travels published in 1614 and 1616, but the *Total Discourse*, the first collected edition, came out in 1632, which resulted in yet more trouble as the robust narrative of his treatment in Malaga seems to have elicited a response from the Spanish influence at court. Lithgow later witnessed the sieges of Breda (1637) and Newcastle (1645), writing accounts of these, as well as a description of London (1643), probably dying sometime in the mid 1640s.

Lithgow was in Ireland from August 22, 1619, until February 23, 1620. His style is generally more florid than Moryson's (or Brereton's spare and sober diary entries), but his judgements are often similar and his comparison of the Irish to the Turks may well echo Moryson's. Lithgow also detested Irish filth, superstition, inefficiency and women.[13]

From *The Total Discourse of His Rare Adventures* (1632):

And this I dare avow, there are moe Rivers, Lakes, Brookes, Strands, Quagmires, Bogs, and Marishes, in this Countrey, then in all Christendome besides; for Travelling there in the Winter, all my dayly solace, was sincke down comfort; whiles Boggy-plunging deepes kissing my horse belly; whiles over-mired Saddle, Body, and all; and often or ever set a swimming, in great danger, both I, and my Guides of our Lives: That for cloudy and fountayne-bred perils, I was never before reducted to such a floting Laborinth. Considering that in five moneths space, I quite spoyled sixe horses, and my selfe as tyred as the worst of them.

[. . .]

I remember I saw in Irelands North-parts, two remarkable sights: The one was their manner of Tillage, Ploughes drawne by Horse-tayles, wanting garnishing, they are only fastned, with straw, or wooden Ropes to their bare Rumps, marching all side for side, three or foure in a Ranke, and as many men hanging by the ends of that untoward Labour. It is as bad a Husbandry I say, as ever I found among the wildest Savages alive; for the Caramins, who understand not the civill forme of Agriculture; yet they delve, hollow, and turne over the ground, with manuall and Wooden instruments: but they the Irish have thousands of both Kingdomes daily labouring beside them; yet they can not learne, because they wil not learn, to use garnishing, so obstinate they are in their barbarous consuetude, unlesse punishment and penalties were inflicted; and yet most of them are content to pay twenty shillings a yeare, before they wil change their Custome.

The other as goodly sight I saw, was women travayling the way, or toyling at home, carry their Infants about their neckes, and laying the dugges over their shoulders, would give sucke to the Babes behinde their backes, without taking them in their armes: Such kind of breasts, me thinketh were very fit, to be made money bags for East or West-Indian Merchants, being more then halfe a yard long, and as wel wrought as any Tanner, in the like charge, could ever mollifie such Leather.

3) Sir William Brereton (1604–61)

Brereton is most famous for his role as a parliamentary commander in the Civil War, when he enjoyed considerable success against Royalist forces in his native Cheshire. In 1634–5 he travelled through Britain and Ireland, then Holland and the United Provinces, keeping a diary from which the following passage is taken.[14] Why he took these journeys is not stated. A staunch Protestant, Brereton shares the same values as Moryson and Lithgow and is repelled by the inadequacy of Irish towns, the lack of cultivation, superstition instead of 'true' religion, and so on. He seems to have admired Dublin chiefly because it resembled England more than anywhere else.[15]

From *Travels* (1634–5):

Jul. 7. — We left Dromemoore and went to the NEWRIE, which is sixteen miles. This is a most difficult way for a stranger to find out. Herein we wandered, and being lost, fell amongst the Irish towns. The Irish houses are the poorest cabins I have seen, erected in the middle of fields and grounds, which they farm and rent. This is a wild country, not inhabited, planted, nor enclosed, yet it would be good corn if it were husbanded. I gave an Irishmen to bring us into the way a groat, who led us like a villain directly out of the way and so left us, so as by this deviation it was three hour before we came to the Newrie. Much land there is about this town belonging to Mr. Bagnall,[16] nothing well planted. He hath a castle in this town, but it is for most part resident at Green Castle; a great part of this town is his, and it is reported that he hath a £1000 or £1500 per annum in this country. This is but a poor town, and is much Irish, and is navigable for boats to come up unto with the tide. Here we baited at a good inn, the sign of the Prince's Arms. Hence to Dundalke is eight mile; stony, craggy, hilly, and uneven, but a way it is nothing difficult to find. Before you come to Dundalke you may discern four or five towers or castles seated upon the sea side.

This town of DUNDALKE hath been a town of strength, and is still a walled town, and a company of fifty soldiers are here in garrison under the command of Sir Faithful Fortesque. This town is governed by two bailiffs, sheriffs, and aldermen; the greatest part of the inhabitants of the town are popishly affected, and although my Lord Deputy, at the last election of burgesses for the Parliament, commended unto them Sir Faithfull Fortesque and Sir Arthur Teringham,[17] yet they rejected both, and elected a couple of recusants. One of the present baliffs is popish. Abundance of Irish, both gentlemen and others, dwell in this town, wherein they dare to take the boldness to go to mass openly. This town seated upon the sea so as barks may come within a convenient distance with the flood; much low, level, flat land hereabouts, which is often overflowed in the winter, and here is abundance of fowl, and a convenient seat. Here we lodged at one Mris. Veasie's house, a most mighty fat woman; she saith she is a Cheshire woman, near related in blood to the Breretons; desired much to see me; so fat she is, as she is so unweildy, she can scarce stand or go without crutches. This reported one of the best inns in north of Ireland; ordinary 8d. and 6d., only the knave tapster over-reckoned us in drink.

Jul. 8 — We left Dundalke and came to TREDAUGH [Drogheda], which is accounted sixteen mile, but they are as long as twenty-two mile.[18] About five mile hence we saw Sir Faithfull Fortesque's house or castle, wherein for most part he is resident, which he holds by a long lease upon a small rent under my Lord Primate of Armath. This is a dainty, pleasant, healthful, and commodious seat, and it is worth unto him about [gap in MS]. During ten miles riding from this town, much rich corn land, and the country well planted; the other six miles towards Tredaugh, until you come near unto it, not so rich land, nor so well husbanded.

This town, as it is the largest and best built town I have yet seen in Ireland, so it is most commodiously seated upon a good navigable river, called Boyne, whereinto flows the sea in so deep a channel (though it be very narrow) as their ships may come to their doors. This river is built on both sides, and there is on either side a convenient quay; a stone wall built all along the river, so as a ship may lie close unto this quay, and may unload upon her. It is like the quay of Newcastle, and those channels I have seen in Holland in their streets. This town commodiously also situated for fish and fowl. It is governed by a mayor, sheriffs, and twenty-four aldermen; most of these, as also the other inhabitants of the town, popishly affected, insomuch as those that have been chosen mayors, who for the most part have been recusants, have hired others to discharge that office. One man (it is said) hath been hired by deputation to execute that place thirteen times; the present mayor also is but a deputy, and the reason why they make coy to execute that office is because they will avoid being necessitated to go to church.

I observed in this city divers fair, neat, well-built houses, and houses and shops well furnished, so as I did conceive this to be a rich town; the inhabitants civilized and better apparelled.

[. . .]

We came to the city of DUBLIN, July 9, about 10 hour. This is the metropolis of the kingdom of Ireland, and is beyond all exception the fairest, richest, best built city I have met with in this journey (except York and Newcastle).

[. . .]

This city of Dublin is extending his bounds and limits very far; much additions of buildings lately, and some of those very fair, stately and complete buildings; every commodity is grown very dear. You must pay also for an horse hire 1s. 6d. a day: here I met with an excellent, judicious and painful smith. Here are divers commodities cried in Dublin as in London, which it doth more resemble than any town I have seen in the king of England's dominions.

Jul. 14 — Upon Tuesday, Jul. 14, I left Dublin and came to HACQUETTS TOWN, about eleven hour at night. It is accounted twenty-seven miles, but it is as long as thirty-seven. After you pass four miles from Dublin, you travel through the mountains, which are dry land, and some of them good pasture for cattle that are young, and sheep, but these are not sufficiently stocked. Towards evening we passed through troublesome and dangerous ways and woods, and had wandered all night, had we not hired an Irish guide, by whose directions we arrived at eleven hour at Hacquett's Town, where we lodged in a little, low, poor, thatched castle. Here Mr. Wattson, a Lanarkshire man, hath a plantation. As we passed this way, I observed the head of the river Liffe, which comes under the bridge at Dublin, whence it is made navigable by the flood, which goeth a mile above the bridge, and little further; I passed also, about eighteen miles from Dublin, by the head of the Slane, which runs to Waxford, and is there navigable, and twenty miles above Waxford.

5. LAND AND LANDSCAPE

Early modern Ireland appeared to English observers in a variety of guises, but types (or genres) of description can be established. Many colonial pamphlets, like the anonymous 'Discourse' (c. 1599), describe it as the land of opportunity; fertile, relatively empty, full of rich pickings for adventurous 'undertakers', with its people either helpful or quiescent. Parallels with tracts persuading settlers to colonize the Americas are legion and have often been made.[1] One might even call this mode of writing 'Fortunate Islands Literature' as Ireland seems to become transformed into a wandering discursive entity between Britain and the Americas.[2]

Alternatively, there is the Ireland of bogs, fog, impenetrable forests and guerilla warfare, barring the march of civilization. This is the country seen by soldiers like Thomas Gainsford or Henry Bagenal, who could divide Ireland into these two hostile states, affirming the continuity of the lands of peace and war. Often it was the south-west of Munster which was singled out for praise as the best land beyond the Pale. In contrast, Ulster, the least Anglicized province of Ireland, was the centre of Irish resistance and the focus of English fears.

The importance of woodland in Ireland should not be underestimated. Woods were valued as raw material, particularly for the Pipe-staving industry which helped to make the fortune of Richard Boyle (see below, p. 120), and timber was so over-used that a severe shortage occurred in the early 1600s. However, woods also served to hide Irish 'rebels' and were removed for this reason.[3] Ulster, once a vast forest, is still virtually treeless today after the destruction performed to establish the plantation and the re-establishment of woodland is by no means a dead political issue.[4]

1) John Dymmok

Nothing is known of Dymmok, but from the evidence of his 'Treatise' it appears that he went to Ireland with Robert Devereux, the second Earl of Essex, either as part of his personal retinue or as a soldier. The work praises Essex's actions in suppressing rebellion (probably most controversially, his agreement with Tyrone[5]) and as it refers to Essex as the Lord Lieutenant it was probably written between September, 1599, where the narrative of events ends and June 5th, 1600, when Essex was dismissed from holding all offices of state.

The 'Treatise' divides neatly into two parts; the first giving a survey of Ireland's geographical outline and society; the second, a narration of recent events. The description of Ireland emphasises both the negative and positive features noted above.[6]

From 'A Treatise of Ireland' (c. 1599–1600):

The realme of Irelande containeth, from the south forelande to the northe pointe called Thoragh, about 300 myles, and in breadthe, from Dublin to Saint Patriks mounte and the sea beating alongst Connaught, 140 miles Irish, which are somwhat larger then our Engleshe myles.

The cuntry lyeth very low, and therefore watrish, and full of marishes, boggs, and standing pooles, even in the highest mowntaynes, which causeth the inhabitants, but specially the sojoners there, to be subject to rhewmes, catarrs, and flixes, for remedy whereof they drinke great quantity of hott wynes, especially sackes, and a kinde of aqua vitae, more dryinge, and lesse inflamynge, then that which is made in Englande.

The ayre is thicke, and nothinge soe piercynge as here in Englande.

The soile is generally fertill, but litle and badly manured, by reason of the great exactions of the lordes upon their tenants. For the tenant dothe not holde his lands by any assurance for tearmes of yeares, or lyfe, but onely ad voluntatem domini,[7] so that he never buildeth, repareth or enclosethe the grownde; but whensoever the lorde listeth, is turned out, or departeth at his most advantage, which, besides the great want of graine to suffice that cuntrye, breadeth also a generall weakenes, for want of inhabiting and plantynge the people in places certain, beinge of themselves geven to a wanderinge and idle life.

The cuntry yeeldeth great store of beeffes and porkes, excellent horses of a fine feature and wonderfull swyftnes, and are thought to be a kinde of the race of the Spanish Genetts.[8]

There ar many and those very good hawkes, but yt aboundeth cheefly in fysh and fowle, some store of sheepe, but small, and those bearinge a longe course fleze, whereof the rugges are made. Great plenty of woode, except in Leinster, where for the great inconveniences finding them to be ready harboures for the Irish rebell, they have beene cutt downe.

There are also many mynes, especially iron and lead, and some copper, but of what richnes and goodnes I finde not.

The cheefe thinge wantinge in that cuntry is cyvillitie, and dutyfull obedience of the people to their sovereigne, which groweth partly throughe a desyre in the principall kindreds and septes to shake of all foreine obedience, and to governe accordinge to their owne lawes, which is their owne willes, partly throughe the inclination of the common sorte to wildenes, being ledd by the superiours upon whose willes they must of force depend; but generally for lacke of execution of such good lawes as tende to the preservation of the Englishrye, in resreyninge them from marryinge, fosteringe, and allyinge with the Irish, and takinge of coyne and lyvery, which hath beene, and yet is, the only cause of weakeninge the English pale, and of so many degenerate English at this present.

2) Luke Gernon

Gernon was made second justice of Munster in 1619 and remained in Ireland probably until the Restoration. Nothing is known of his early life, but he may have been from Hertfordshire. Gernon's 'Discourse' mentions that he is resident in Limerick and he lived there until the Rebellion of 1641, when, like many English in Ireland, he lost most of his possessions, according to a petition his wife made to Cromwell.[9] He was well connected and he was on friendly terms with Richard Boyle, the Great Earl of Cork;[10] his wife seems to have known Archbishop Ussher.[11] A reference to the administration of his property notes that he died sometime before 1673.

Gernon's 'Discourse' probably dates from the winter of 1620. It is a long letter written to an unnamed friend, describing his impressions of the country to which he has just moved. The bawdy, pornographic blazon[12] of a female Ireland belongs to many iconographic traditions: Ireland as Cathleen Ni Houlihan;[13] Ireland as mother;[14] Ireland as younger sister of England appealing for protection;[15] Ireland as a fragile virgin in contrast to the resilient virgin of England;[16] Ireland as a wench (or whore?) ready to be fertilized by the potent colonial settlers,[17] and so on. The style of the letter is familiar and jokey (whatever the implications of the statements made), hence the comparison of the effects of rebellion to the aftermath of a feast.

From 'A Discourse of Ireland' (c. 1620):[18]

This Nymph of Ireland, is at all poynts like a yong wenche that hath the greene sicknes for want of occupying. She is very fayre of visage, and hath a smooth skinn of tender grasse. Indeed she is somewhat freckled (as the Irish are) some partes darker than other. Her flesh is of a softe and delicat mould of earthe, and her blew vaynes trayling through every part of her like ryvoletts. She hath one master vayne called the Shannon, which passeth quite through her, and if it were not for one knot (one mayne rocke) it were navigable from head to foot. She hath three other vaynes called the sisters, the Seuer, the Noyer & the Barrow, which rysing at one spring, trayle through her middle partes, and joine together in theyr going out. Her bones are of polished marble, the grey marble, the blacke, the redd, and the speckled, so fayre for building that their houses shew like colledges, and being polished, is most rarely embelished. Her breasts are round hillocks of milk-yeelding grasse, and that so fertile, that they contend with the vallyes. And betwixt her leggs (for Ireland is full of havens), she hath an open harbour, but not much frequented. She hath had goodly tresses of hayre arboribusqu' comae,[19] but the iron mills, like a sharpe toothed combe, have notted & poled her much, and in her champion partes she hath not so much as will cover her nakedness. Of complexion she is very temperate, never too hott, nor too could, and hath a sweet breath of favonian winde. She is of a gentle nature. If the anger of heaven be agaynst her, she will not bluster and storme, but she will weepe many dayes together, and (alas) this last summer she did so water her plants, that the grasse and blade was so bedewed, that it became unprofitable and threatens a scarcity. Neyther is she frosenharted, the last frost was not so extreame here as it was reported to be in England. It is nowe since she was drawne out of the wombe of rebellion about sixteen yeares, by'r lady nineteen, and yet she wants a husband, she is not embraced, she is not hedged and diched, there is noo quicksett putt into her.

[. . .]

In every village there is a castle, and a church, but bothe in ruyne. The baser cottages are built of underwood, called wattle, and covered some with thatch and some with green sedge, of a round forme and without chimneys, and to my imaginacion resemble so many hives of bees, about a country farme. In the end of harvest the villages seem as bigg agayne as in the spring, theyre corne being brought into theyr haggards, and layed up in round cockes, in forme of theyr houses. And by the way, there is no meate so daynte as a haggard pigg, a pigg that hath been fedd at the reeke, take him at a quarter old, and use him like a rosting pigg; because his biggness should not be offensive, they serve him up by quarters. Here I would conclude with our buildings, but when I look about I cannot but bewayle the desolation which cyvill rebellion hath procured. It lookes like the later end of a feast. Here lyeth an old ruyned castle like the remaynder of a venyson pasty, there a broken forte like a minced py half subjected, and in another place an old abbey with some turrets standing like the carcase of a goose broken up. It makes me remember the old proverb — It is better to come to the end of a feast, then at the beginning of a fray.

3) Robert Payne

Probably from Nottinghamshire, and a noted agricultural writer, Payne became an undertaker on the Munster plantation in the late 1580s with twenty-five of his neighbours. As they were wary of risking all in Ireland, Payne went over first to report on the situation and wrote his 'Brief Description' to urge them to join him. The tract praises opportunities in Ireland and aims to dispel some prejudices (i.e., the imminence of a Spanish invasion, the evil of the natives), but Payne's name does not appear on the 1622 survey so he may not have settled in Munster. The 'Brief Description' is interesting for the rosy picture it paints of Ireland in its role as colonial propaganda, and also for the assurance it grants the would-be planters that the Irish know and fear the Spanish because of their atrocities in the New World, making it a significant contribution to 'The Black Legend'.[20]

From *A Brief description of Ireland* (c. 1589):[21]

These men will say there is great danger in travelling the countrie, and much more to dwell or inhabite there: yet are they freed from three of the greatest dangers: first, they cannot meete in all that lande any worsse then themselves: secondly, they neede not feare robbing for that they have not anye thing to loose: lastly, they are not like to runne in debte, for that there is none will trust them. The greatest matter which troubleth them is, they cannot get any thinge there but by honest travell, which they are altogether ignorant of. These men cannot tell what good fruits England have, the which Ireland wanteth, neyther can they justly saye, but that it lieth better for the vent of all commodities then England doeth.

What these men have reported or what the simple have credited, that would rather beleeve a runnegate then travell to see, I care not.[22] But what I have discovered or learned in that countrie, I will herein recite unto you.

First, the people are of three sortes, the better sorte are ciuill and honestly given: the most of them greatly inclined to husbandrie, although as yet unskilful, notwithstanding through their great travell many of them are rich in cattell: some one man there milketh one hundred kine, and two or three hundred yeawes and goates, and reareth yeerely most of their breed.

Their entertainment for your diet shalbe more welcome and plentifull, then cleanly and handsome: for although they did never see you before, they will make you the best cheare their countrie yeeldeth for two or three dayes, and take not any thing therefore. Most of them speake good English and bring up their children to learning. I saw in a Grammar schoole in Limbrick, one hundred, & threescore schollers, most of them speaking good and perfit English, for that they have used to conster the Latin into English. They keepe their promise faithfully, and are more desirous of peace than our English men, for that in time of warres they are more charged, And also they are fatter praies for the enemie, who respecteth no person. They are quicke witted and of good constitution of bodie: they reforme them selves dayly more and more after the English manners: nothing is more pleasing unto them, then to heare of good Justices placed amongst them. They have a common saying which I am perswaded they speak unfeinedly, which is Defend me and Spend me: meaning from the oppression of the worser sorte of our countrimen:[23] They are obedient to the laws, so that you may travel through all the land without any danger or injurie offered of the verye worst Irish, and be greatly releeved of the best.

The second sorte being least in number are called Kernes, they are warlike men: most of that sorte were slayne in the late warres.

The third sorte, are a very idle people, not unlike our English beggars, yet for the most parte, of pure complexion and good constitution of bodie: one of the greatest oversights in the better sorte is, for that they make not that idle sort give accompt of their life.

[. . .]

[T]he commodities of the countrie are many moe then eyther

the people can well use or I recite. Their soile for the most parte is very fertil, and apte for Wheate, Rye, Barly, Peason, Beanes, Oates, Woade, Mather, Rape, Hoppes, Hempe, Flaxe and all other graines and fruites that England any wise doth yeelde. There is much good timber in manye places, and that of that streightnesse and so good to reave, that a simple workeman with a Brake axe will cleave a greate Oke to boardes of lesse then one ynche thicke, xiii. ynches broad and xv. footes in length. such a board there is usually sold for ii. d. ob. There is verie riche and greate plentie of Iron stone, and one sort more then we have in England, which they call Bogge myne, of the which a Smith there wil make at his forge Iron presently. Also there is great store of Lead Ore, & Wood sufficiente to mayntayne divers Iron and lead workes (with good husbandrie) for ever. A barrell of Wheate or a barrel of bay Salt contayning three bushels and a halfe of Winchester measure, is sold there for iiii. s. Malt, Peason, Beanes, for ii. s. viii. d. Barly for ii. s. iiii. d. Oates for xx. d. a fresh Sammon worth in London x. s. for vi. d. xxiiii. Herrings or vi. Makerels vi. sea breames, a fat hen, xxx. Egges, a fat Pigge, one pound of Butter, or ii. gallones of new milke for a penny. A reede Deare without the skinne, for ii. s. vi. d. A fat Beefe for xiii. s. iiii. d. A fat Mutton for xviii. d.

There be great store of wild Swannes, Cranes, Pheasantes, Partriges, Heathcocks, Plovers, greene and grey, Curlewes, Woodcockes, Rayles, Quailes, & all other fowles much more plentifull then in England. . . . You may keep a better house in Ireland for L. li. a yeere, then in England for CC. li. a yeere.

4) Thomas Gainsford

Gainsford, like Churchyard and Rich, was another prolific soldier-author, although his work is rather more geographical and historical than literary. Born in Surrey, he served in Mountjoy's army against Tyrone, was present at Kinsale, and then purchased land on the Ulster Plantation in 1610. He probably died in 1624.

The following extract comes from an account of his Irish experience appended to Book One of *The Glory of England*, a patriotic geographical survey in the genre dominated by Camden and Speed,[24] comparing all the eminent kingdoms of the earth unfavourably to England. Gainsford describes Ireland as seen by the soldier.[25]

From 'The Description of Ireland' in *The Glory of England* (1618):[26]

The country and kingdome of Ireland is generally for naturall aire, and commoditie of blessings, sufficient to satisfie a covetous, or curious appetite: but withall divided into such fastnes of mountaine, bogg, and wood, that it hath emboldened the inhabitants to presume an hereditary securitie, as if disobedience had a protection. For the mountaines denie any cariages, but by great industry and strength of men (so have we drawne the Cannon over the deepest boggs, & stoniest hils) and the passages are every way dangerous both for unfirmnes of ground, & the lurking rebell, who will plashe downe whole trees over the paces and so intricately winde them, or laye them, that they shall be a strong barracado, and then lurke in ambush amongst the standing wood, playing upon all commers, as they intend to goe along. On the bogg they likewise presume with a naked celeritie to come as neere our foote and horse, as is possible, and then flie off againe, knowing we cannot, or indeed dare not follow them: and thus they serve us in the narrow entrances into their glins, and stony paths, or if you will dangerous quagmires of their mountaines, where a 100 shot shall rebate the hasty approch of 500; and a few muskets (if they durst carry any) well placed, will stagger a pretty Armie, not acquainted with the terror, or unpreventing mischeefe.

5) 'A Treatise of Ireland' (Sept. 1644):[27]

The title page of this anonymous tract is missing, which limits the chance of finding out anything about the circumstances of its composition. The author explicitly criticises the Irish policy of the present king, Charles I, and his two predecessors, Elizabeth and James, claiming that the monarch's duty is to the English people who should not have had to face the rebellion of Catholics within the ruler's realms. The writer argues that Ireland is a good place for the religiously disaffected who would be able to convert the Irish through their zeal and thus be free from the restraints of England and more popular with the ecclesiastical powers that be,[28] as well as having the opportunity to test the strength of their faith. Ireland is seen as a solution to the dilemma, as there is a clear, identifiable enemy in the Catholic majority, freedom from inter-party squabbles, and plenty for all. In Ireland, English wounds will be healed and rifts joined.

And now a few arguments to perswade these people to go to Ireland.

First, Ireland hath room enough, and the land is cheap enough; room enough its easie to prove: that there may dwell tenne times as many, as now are there, and live better then they ever lived in

Ireland: land is cheap, it might be had for sixpence, twelve pence, eighteen pence the acre when Ireland was in its greatest glory, and there are many houses undemolished, so that a man may possess himself of as good an estate there for an hundred pound: as he can do in new England for a thousand pound, considering the length of the voyage: the charge of clearing, and building.

Secondly, Ireland stands bravely for trade, near to all parts of Christendom, especially Spaine, France, and England; hath good commodities for export, and may have far better: settle there once artists, and men of ingenuity, and it may equall moste partes of Christendome: the contrary, as the remotenesse, and want of artists in New England hath undone them, and had they arts, yet they want materialls, and besides, the voyage is so long, that ordinary commodities invite not, and if, yet the expence of the voyage makes them not able to sell: but every one that hath the commoditie nearer, will under sell them, which was fully manifest, when passengers stopt, trade ended there; and this may be said of any part of America that we can plant in.

Thirdly, the like sole content may there be had, nay better, for want, is an impediment; give me not poverty: when in an handsome easie way of using the things of this life we may increase, its a most singular way to drive on the designes of Heaven, whether generall or particular, want brings cares, cares eat out grace, as well as abundance: nay far more in a gracious soul.

Fourthly, God will have more Glory, in reason: for why may not a wise, a pious, and loving terrour, not only subdue those people, but convert them? It was the great argument that carried people to America, the conversion of those people to beleeve in Jesus Christ: shew one man that ever was converted, or civilized to this day: the Irish acknowledge the Creator of Heaven and Earth, Jesus Christ, the Holy Ghost, they are reasonable Creatures in the practice, may be wonne by teaching, and example; consider what by two or three godly Ministers was done in a few years in Wales, many hundreds brought home to Christ, and at this day shew forth the vertue of him that hath called them, above any its beleeved in the world.[29] yet now by reason of the War, wandring up and down in sheep skins, & goats skins, a sufficient triall of their integrity in leaving large possessions, & why should any think the Irish should not do the same? are they Popish? so were the Welsh, are they heathenish? so were the other: Theres no question but such cords of Love as these, holy examples, unblamable life, forgiving, exhortings, instructing in the way of Heaven, with meeknesse, may bring in many thousands: its confest there is great reason that capital offenders should be destroyed, or rooted out, whether of one kind or other, which done, the people are wax, which it may be at first may be a little brittle, but after a little of the warmth of love mixt with the wisdom of the Serpent, you may impresse civility, industry, and if God please, grace.

7) Two comments on Irish woodland

a) From 'Address to the Lord Deputy of Ireland and Council on Redress of Grievances' (1621):[30]

The making of pipe staves and yron worke, wil in short tyme destroy the woode of this kingdom, yf speedy course be not taken for planting and preservation of the woode.

b) From 'A Discourse of Ireland' (c. 1599), p. 160:

The woodes be over greate and thicke serving for a covert unto Rebells and Theeves Which nevertheless (amongst civil people) will be found no inconvenience, the use of woodes beeing so great for building of shippes and houses and other necessaries also for fewell, Irone-workes, and other mettalls whereof Ireland hath both diversity and planty if the same might be sought for and safety wrought upon.

6. IRISH SOCIETY

To compare societies requires the ability to distinguish salient structural features which are similar to or different from a norm. For English observers of Ireland in the early modern period the norm was not some abstract sociological or ethnographic construct, but their own society or, rather, a rationalized, idealised, form of it.[1] Irish deviation from this standard often resulted in their being placed as barbarian or savage in contrast to the civilized English,[2] and they were seen as comparable to the Amerindians of the New World, or the ancient Britons of England's past who had been forcibly 'civilized' by the Romans, as the English were about to metamorphosise the Irish.[3] Frequently singled out for criticism was the Irish family unit, which appeared to the English as loose and self-destructive, based on the non-committal form of marriage, with inadequate parental affection shown to the children and a disastrously haphazard system of inheritance.[4] The English family structure, in contrast, was perceived as cohesive, patriarchal and secure through primogeniture.[5] Similarly, Irish agricultural methods were represented as simply pastoral and thus also unstable (though, as modern historians have pointed out, this does not tell the whole story),[6] in contrast to the sophisticated method of English cultivation; Irish legal systems were believed to undermine order rather than establish it;[7] Irish poets (bards) to incite rebellion instead of encouraging civility and courtesy; clothes, such a vital subject in the Renaissance,[8] were designed to foster disobedience, and so on. The pattern observed before again applies: when Irish practices differ they are to be stopped, when they are recognisably the same, they can be permitted to continue.

1) Fynes Moryson: 'On childbirth' (1617):[9]

Touching child-bearing, women within two hours after they are delivered, many times leave their beds to go fop and drink with women coming to visit them; and in our experience a soldier's wife delivered in the camp did the same day, and within few hours after her delivery, march six miles on foot with the army to the next camping place. Some say that commonly the women have little or no pain in child-bearing, and attribute the same to a bone broken when they are tender children; but whatever the cause be, no doubt they have such easy deliverance, and commonly such strange ability of body presently after it, as I never heard any woman in the world to have the like; and not only the mere Irish, but most of the English-Irish dwelling in the cities. Mid-wives and neighbours come to help women to be delivered commonly more for fashion than any great need of them; and here is no talk of a month's lying-in, or solemn churching at the end of the month, as with us in England. They seldom nurse their own children, especially the wives of lords and gentlemen (as well mere Irish as English-Irish). For women of good wealth seek with great ambition to nurse them, not for any profit, rather spending much upon them while they live, and giving them when they die sometimes more than to their own children. But they do it only to have the protection and love of the parents whose children they nurse. And old custom is so turned into a second nature with them as they esteem the children they nurse more than their own, holding it a reproach to nurse their own children. Yea, men will forbear their wives' bed for the good of the children they nurse or foster, but not nursing their own. Yea, the foster-brothers — I mean the children of the nurse and strangers that have sucked her milk — love one another better than natural brothers, and hate them in respect of the other. And by frequent examples we have seen many mourn for their foster-brothers much more than they would have done for their natural brothers; and some to oppose their own brothers to death that they might save their foster-brothers from danger thereof. The worst is that these nurses with their extreme indulgence corrupt the children they foster, nourishing and heartening the boys in all villainy, and the girls in obscenity.

2) Edmund Spenser (1552?–1599)

Spenser's connection with Ireland dates from at least 1580 when he went over as secretary to Lord Grey de Wilton, the Lord Deputy, and possibly as early as 1577.[10] He held a series of official posts in Dublin and Munster and in 1586 acquired Kilcolman Castle on the escheated lands of Lord Desmond which formed the Munster Plantation, settling there in 1588. He returned to England only twice in the last nineteen years of his life; in 1589, apparently on Walter Raleigh's insistence,[11] and in 1596, both times to promote his poetry and seek preferment at court, which he failed to achieve.[12] He was involved in a protracted legal dispute with his neighbour, Lord Roche, in the early 1590s, and was married for the second time in 1593 to Elizabeth Boyle, a 'kinswoman' of the Great Earl of Cork.[13] Soon after Tyrone's victory at the Yellow Ford (August 14, 1598), Spenser was appointed sheriff of Cork (September 30), but in October Munster was overrun, Kilcolman was sacked and burnt, and, after writing the desperate 'A brief note of Ireland',[14] he was sent to London by the President of Munster, Sir Thomas Norris, where he died in January, 1599.

Spenser's *A View of the Present State of Ireland*, probably written in 1596, entered into the Stationer's Register on April 14, 1598, but not published until 1633,[15] has been the most discussed early modern English tract on Ireland.[16] The first two of the three extracts included here come from Irenius's attempt to prove to his fellow disputant, Eudoxus, that the Irish are descended from the barbarous race of the Scythians[17] by way of a comparison of the social practises of the two peoples. The discussion of the bards is perhaps more ambivalent: is Spenser using the Irish respect for poets as a stick with which to beat his intended English audience, for whom, in Sidney's words, poetry had fallen 'from the highest estimation of learning. . . to be the laughing-stock of children'?[18] After all it is an English poet (feeling, perhaps, that he has failed to gain the recognition he deserves) who is exposing the seditious nature of the bards' writing and thus performing a useful action worthy of respect and honour in neutralizing their claims to speak the truth.

From *A View of the Present State of Ireland* (c. 1596):[19]

Irenius [T]here is one use amongst them [the Irish] to keep their cattle and to live themselves the most part of the year in Bollies,[20] pasturing upon the mountain and waste wild places, and removing still to fresh land as they have depastured the former days; the which appeareth plain to be the manner of the Scythians as ye may read in Olaus Magnus et Johannes Boemus,[21] and yet is used amongst all the Tartarians and the people about the Caspian Sea which are naturally Scythians, to live in herds as they call them, being the very same that the Irish Bollies are, driving their cattle continually with them and feeding only on their milk and white meats.

Eudoxus: What fault can ye find with this custom, for though it be an old Scythian use, yet it is very behoveful in this country of Ireland where there are great mountains and waste deserts full of grass, that the same should be eaten down and nourish many thousand of cattle, for the good of the whole realm, which cannot, methinks, well be any other way than by keeping those Bollies as there ye have showed?

Iren: But by this custom of Bollying there grow in the meantime many great enormities unto that commonwealth. For, first, if there be any outlaws or loose people, as they are never without some which live upon stealths and spoils, they are ever more succored and find relief only in those Bollies being upon the waste places; where else they should be driven shortly to starve, or to come down to the towns to seek relief, where by one means or another they would soon be caught. Besides, such stealths of cattle as they make they bring commonly to those Bollies where they are received readily, and the thief harboured from danger of law or such officers as might light upon him. Moreover, the people that live thus in these Bollies grow thereby the more barbarous and live more licentiously than they could in towns, using what means they list, and practising what mischiefs and villainies they will, either against the government there generally by their combinations, or against private men, whom they malign by stealing their goods or murdering themselves; for there they think themselves half exempted from law and obedience, and having once tasted freedom do, like a steer that hath been long out of his yoke, grudge and repine ever after to come under rule again.

Eud: By your speech, Irenius, I perceive more evil come by these Bollies than good by their grazing, and therefore it may well be reformed, but that must be in his due course.

3) Sir John Davies (1569–1626)

Davies was a lawyer who wrote poetry which has served to make him famous. He was called to the bar in 1595, was briefly disbarred after a fight, became an M.P. at the same time as he was readmitted (1601), and was important enough to be part of Lord Hunsdon's entourage when the latter travelled to the Scottish court on behalf of Elizabeth (March, 1603). Winning James's favour, Davies was appointed Solicitor-General for Ireland, arriving in Dublin in November, 1603. He presented a report on the state of Ireland at court in April, 1605, encouraging the vigilant suppression of Catholic priests, and was appointed Attorney General in May, 1606. In this role Davies frequently toured the country inspecting the courts, helped to establish the Ulster plantation and became so confident of Ireland's reformed nature that he often begged to be recalled, feeling his job was over. In 1613 he was made speaker of the Irish House of Commons and took his chair only after an attempt by Catholic members to install their man, Sir John Everard, had been violently suppressed.[22]

Davies's major work on Ireland is *A Discovery of the True Causes Why Ireland Was Never Entirely Subdued* (1612), which argues that the failure to sweep away the laws and habits of the native Irish resulted in the division of the country. He claimed that only in James's reign had full control been asserted and the chance to build anew established. The extract from the work given here illustrates Davies's assessment of Irish customs, institutions and social conventions.[23]

From *A Discovery of the True Causes Why Irleand was Never Entirely Subdued* (1612):[24]

For, if we consider the Nature of the Irish customes, wee shall finde that the people which doth use them must of necessitie be rebels to all good Government, destroy the commonwealth wherein they live, and bring Barbarisme and desolation upon the richest and most fruitful Land of the world. For, whereas by the just and Honourable Law of England, & by the Lawes of all other well-governed Kingdomes and Commonweals, Murder, Manslaughter, Rape, Robbery, and Theft are punnished with death; By the Irish Custome, or Brehon Law, the highest of these offences was punished only by Fine, which they call an Ericke. Therefore, when Sir William Fitzwilliams, being Lord Deputy,[25] told Maguyre that he was to send a sheriffe into Fermanaugh, being lately before made a County, Your sheriffe (sayde Maguyre) shall be welcome to me; but let me knowe his Ericke, or the price of his head, aforehand; that if my people cut it off I may cut the Ericke upon the Countrey. As for Oppression, Extortion, and other trespasses, the weaker had never anie remedy against the stronger: whereby it came to passe that no man coulde enjoy his Life, his Wife, his Lands or Goodes in safety if a mightier man than himselfe had an appetite to take the same from him. Wherein they were little better than Canniballes, who doe hunt one another, and hee that hath most strength and swiftnes doth eate and devoure all his fellowes.

Againe, in England and all well ordered Common-weales men have certaine estates in their Lands & Possessions, and their inheritances discend from Father to Son, which doth give them encouragement to builde and to plant and to improove their Landes, and to make them better for their posterities. But by the Irish Custom of Tanistry the cheefetanes of every Countrey and the chiefe of every Sept had no longer estate then for life in their Cheeferies, the inheritance whereof did rest in no man. And these Cheeferies, though they had some portions of land alloted unto them, did consist chiefly in cuttings and Cosheries, and other Irish exactions, whereby they did spoyle and impoverish the people at their pleasure: And when their chieftanes were dead their sonnes or next heires did not succeede them, but their Tanistes, who were Elective and purchased their elections by stronge hand; And by the Irish Custome of gavellkinde, the inferior Tennantries were partible amongst all Males on the Sept, both Bastards and Legittimate; and after partition made, if any one of the Sept had died, his portion was not divided among his Sonnes, but the cheefe of the Sept made a new partition of all the Lands belonging to that Sept, and gave evere one his part according to his antiquity.

These two Irish Customes made all their possessions uncertain, being shuffled, and changed, and removed so often from one to another, by new elections and partitions, which uncertainty of estates hath bin the true cause of such Desolation & Barbarism in this land, as the like was never seen in any Countrey that professed the name of Christ. For though the Irishry be a Nation of great Antiquity, and wanted neither wit nor valour, and though they had received the Christian Faith, above 1200 yeares since; and were Lovers of Musicke, Poetry, and all kind of learning, and possessed a land abounding with all thinges necessary for the Civill life of man; yet (which is strange to be related) they did never build any houses of Brick or stone (some few poor Religious Houses excepted) before the reign of King Henrie the second, though they were Lords of this Island for many hundred yeares before, and since the Conquest attempted by the English: Albeit, when they sawe us builde Castles uppon their borders, they have only in imitation of us, erected some few piles for their Captaines of the Country: yet I dare boldly say, that never any particular person, eyther before or since, did build any stone or bricke house for his private Habitation; but such as have latelie obtained estates, according to the course of the Law of England. Neither did any of them in all this time, plant any Gardens or Orchards, Inclose or improve their Lands, live together in setled villages or Townes, nor made any provision for posterity, which, being against all common sense and reason, must needes be imputed to those unreasonable Customes which made their estates so uncertaine and transitory in their possessions.

For who would plant or improove, or build upon that Land, which a stranger whom he knew not, should possesse after his death? For that (as Solomon noteth) is one of the strangest Vanities under the Sunne. And this is the true reason Ulster and all the Irish Countries are found so wast and desolate at this day, and so would they continue till the worlds end if these Customes were not abolished by the Law of England.

Again, that Irish custom of Gavell-kinde did breed another michiefe, for thereby every man being borne to Land, as well Bastard as Legitimate, they al held themselves to be Gentlemen. And though their portions were never so small, and them-selves never so poor (for Gavelkind must needs in the end make a poor Gentility) yet did they scorne to discend to Husbandry or Merchandize, or to learn any Mechanicall Art or Science. And this is the true cause why there were never any Corporate Towns erected in the Irish Countries. As for the Maritine Citties and Townes, most certaine it is that they were peopled and built by Ostmen or Easterlings:[26] for the natives of Ireland never perfourmed so good a worke as to build a City. Besides, these poor Gentlemen were so affected unto their small portions of Land, as they rather chose to live at home by Theft, Extortion, and Coshering, than to seek any better fortunes abroad, which increased their Septs or Syrnames into such numbers, as there are not to bee found in any Kingdome of Europe, so many gentlemen of one Blood, Familie, and Surname as there are of the O'Nealles in Ulster; of the Bourkes in Conaght, of the Geraldines, and Butlers, in Munster & Leinster. And the like may be saide of the Inferiour Bloodes and Families; whereby it came to passe in times of trouble & Dissention, that they made great parties and factions adhering one to another, with much constancie because they were tyed together Vinculo Sanguinis;[27] whereas Rebels and Malefactors which are tyed to their Leaders by no band, either of Dutie or Blood, do more easily breake and fall off one from another: And besides, their Coe-habitation in one Countrey or Territory, gave them opportunity suddenly to assemble, and Conspire, and rise in multitudes against the Crowne. And even now, in the time of peace, we finde this inconvenience, that ther can hardly be an indifferent triall had between the King & the Subject, or between partie and partie, by reason of this generall Kindred and Consanguinity.

But the most wicked and mischeevous Custome of all others was that of Coigne and livery, often before mentioned; which consisted in taking of Man's meat, Horse meat & Money of all the inhabitants of the Country, at the will and pleasure of the soldier, who as the phrase of Scripture is, 'Did eat up the people as it were bread', for that he had no other entertainment. This Extortion was originally Irish, for they used to lay Bonoght[28] uppon their people, and never gave their Soldier any other pay. But when the English had Learned it, they used it with more insolency, and made it more intollerable; for this oppression was not temporary, or limited either to place or time; but because there was everywhere a continuall warre, either Offensive or Defensive; and every lord of a Countrey and every Marcher made war and peace at his pleasure, it became Universall and Perpetuall; and was indeed the most heavy oppression that ever was used in any Christian of Heathen Kingdom. And therfore, Vox Oppressorum,[29] this crying sinne did draw down as great, or greater plagues uppon Ireland, then the oppression of the Isrelites, did draw upon the land of Egypt. For the plagues of Egypt, though they were griveous, were but of a short continuance. But the plagues of Ireland, lasted 400 years together. This extortion of Coigne and Livery, did produce two notorious effects. First, it made the Land waste; Next, it made the people, ydle. For, when the Husbandman had laboured all the yeare, the soldier in one night, did consume the fruites of all his labour, Longique perit labor irritus anni.[30] Had hee reason then to manure the Land for the next year? Or rather might he not complaine as the Shepherd in 'Virgil': —

> 'Impuris haec tam culta novalia miles habebit?
> Barbarus has segetes? En quo discordia Cives
> Perduxit miseros! En queis conservimus agros!'[31]

And hereupon of necessity came depopulation, banishment, & extirpation of the better sort of subjects, and such as remained became ydle and lookers on, expecting the event of those miseries and evill times: So as this extreame extortion and Oppression, hath been the true cause of the Idleness of this Irish Nation; and that rather the vulgar sort have chosen to be beggars in forraigne Countries, than to manure their own fruitfull Land at home.

5) Fynes Moryson (c. 1617)[32]

Our Captaines, and by their example (for it was otherwise painefull) the common souldiers, did cut downe with their swords all the Rebels corne, to the value of ten thousand pound and upward, the onely meanes by which they were to live, and to keepe their Bonaghts (or hired soldiers). It seemed incredible, that by so barbarous inhabitants, the ground should be so manured, the fields so orderly fenced, the Townes so frequently inhabited, and the high waies and paths so well beaten, as the Lord Deputy here found them. The reason whereof was, that the Queenes forces, during these warres, never till then came among them.[33]

6) Luke Gernon (1620)[34]

Lett us converse with the people. Lord, what makes you so squeamish — be not affrayed. The Irishman is no Canniball to eate you up nor no lowsy Jack to offend you.

The man of Ireland is of a strong constitution, tall and bigg limbed, but seldom fatt, patient of heate and colde, but impatient of labour. Of nature he is prompt and ingenious, but servile crafty and inquisitive after newes, the simptomes of a conquered nation. Theyr speach hath been accused to be a whyning language, but that is among the beggars. I take it to be a smooth language, well commixt of vouells and of consonants, and hath a pleasing cadence.

The better sorte are apparelled at all poynts like the English onely they retayne theyr mantle which is a garment not indecent. It differs nothing from a long cloke, but in the fringe at the upper end, which in could weather they weare over their heades for warmth. Because they are commanded at publicke assemblies to come in English habit, they have a tricke agaynst those times, to take off the fringe, and to putt on a cape, and after the assembly past, to resume it agayne. If you aske an Irishman for his cloke, he will tell you it is in his pockett and show you his cape. The churle is apparrelled in this maner. His doublett is a packe saddle of canvase, or coarse cloth without skirtes, but in winter he weares a frise cote. The trowse is a long stocke of frise, close to his thighes, and drawne on almost to his waste, but very scant, and the pryde of it is, to weare it so in suspense, that the beholder may still suspecte it to be falling from his arse. It is cutt with a pouche before, whiche is drawne together with a string. He that will be counted a spruce ladd, tyes it up with a twisted band of two colours like the string of a clokebagge. An Irishman walking in London a cutpurse took it for a cheate, and gave him a slash. His broges are single soled, more rudely sewed then a shoo but more strong, sharp at the toe, and a flapp of leather left at the heele to pull them on. His hatt is a frise capp close to his head with two lappetts, to button under his chinne. And for his weapon he weares a skeyne which is a knife of three fingers broad of the length of a dagger and sharpening towards the poynt with a rude wodden handle. He weares it poynt blanke at his codpiece. The ordinary kerne seldome weares a sword. They are also wedded to theyr mantle, they plow, they ditch, they thressh with theyr mantles on. But you look after the wenches.

The weomen of Ireland are very comely creatures, tall, slender and upright. Of complexion very fayre & cleare-skinned (but frecled), with tresses of bright yellow hayre, which they chayne up in curious knotts, and devises. They are not strait laced nor plated in theyr youth, but suffred to grow at liberty so that you shall hardly see one crooked or deformed, but yet as the proverb is, soone ripe soone rotten. Theyr propensity to generation causeth that they cannot endure. They are wemen at thirteene, and olde wives at thirty. I never saw fayrer wenches nor fowler calliots, so we call the old wemen. Of nature they are very kind and tractable. At meetings they offer themselves to be kiste with the hande extended to embrace you. The yong wenches salute you, conferre with you, drinke with you without controll. They are not so reserved as the English, yett very honest. Cuckoldry is a thing almost unknowne among the Irish. At solemne invitements, the Benytee, so we call the goodwife of the house meets at the hall dore with as many of her femall kindred as are about her all on a row; to leave any of them unkist, were an indignity though it were done by the lord president.

I come to theyr apparrell. About Dublin they weare the English habit, mantles onely added thereunto, and they that goe in silkes, will weare a mantle of country making. In the country even among theyr Irish habitts they have sundry fashions. I will beginne with the ornament of theyr heads. At Kilkenny they weare broad beaver hatts coloured, edged with a gold lace and faced with velvett, with a broad gould hatt band. At Waterford they weare capps, turned up with furre and laced with gold lace. At Lymerick they weare rolles of lynnen, each roll contayning twenty bandles of fyne lynnen clothe (A Bandle is half an ell), and made up in forme of a myter. To this if it be could weather, there is added a muffler over theyr neck and chinne of like quantity of linnen; being so muffled, over all they will pinne on an English maske of blacke taffety, which is most rarely ridiculous to behold. In Connaught they weare rolles in forme of a cheese. In Thomond they weare kerchiefs, hanging downe to the middle of theyr backe. The maydes weare on the forepart of theyr head about foure yards of coloured ribbon smoothly layd, and theyr owne hayre playted behind. In other places they weare theyre hayre loose and cast behind. They weare no bands, but the ornament of theyr neckes is a carkanett of goldsmyths worke besett with precious stones, some of them very ritch, but most of them gawdy and made of paynted glasse and at the end of them a crucifixe. They weare also braceletts, and many rings. I proceed to theyr gowns. Lend me your imaginacion, and I will cutt it out as well as the tayler. They have straight bodyes, and longe wasts, but theyr bodyes come no closer, but to the middle of the ribbe, the rest is supplyed with lacing, from the topp of their breasts, to the bottome of theyr plackett, the ordinary sort have only theyr smockes between, but the better sort have a silk scarfe about theyr neck, which they spread and pinne over theyre breasts. On the forepart of those bodyes thay have a sett of broad silver buttons of goldsmiths worke sett round about. A sett of those buttons will be worth 40s, some are worth £5. They have hanging sleeves, very narrow, but no arming sleeves, other then theyre smocke sleeves, or a wastcoate of stripped stuffe, onely they have a wrestband of the same cloth, and a lyst of the same to joyne it to theyr winge, but no thing on the hinter part of the arme least they should weare out theyr elbowes. The better sort have sleeves of satten. The skyrt is a piece of rare artifice. At every bredth of three fingers they sew it quite through with a welte, so that it seemeth so many lystes putt together. That they do for strength, they girde theyr gowne with a silke girdle, the tassell whereof must hang downe poynt blanke before to the fringe of theyr peticotes, but I will not descend to theyr petycotes, least you should thinke that I have bene under them. They beginne to weare knitt stockins coloured, but they have not disdayned to weare stockins of raw whyte frise, and broges. They weare theyr mantles also as well with in doors as with out. Theyr mantles are commonly of a browne blew colour with the fringe alike, but those that love to be gallant were them of greene, redd, yellow, and other light colours, with fringes diversified. An ordinary mantle is worth £4, those in the country which cannot go to the price weare whyte sheets mantlewise. I would not have you suppose that all the Irish are thus strangely attyred as I have described. The old women are loath to be shifted out of theyr auncient habitts, but the younger sort, especially in gentlemens houses are brought up to resemble the English, so that it is to be hoped, that the next age will weare out these disguises. Of theyr cleanlynes I will not speak.

7) Edmund Spenser (c. 1596)[35]

Irenius: [The Irish] have another custom from the Scythians, that is the wearing of mantles and long glibs, which is a thick curled bush of hair hanging down over their eyes, and monstrously disguising them, which are both very bad and hurtful. . . For the inconveniences which thereby do arise are much more many, for it is a fit house for an outlaw, a meet bed for a rebel, and an apt cloak for a thief. First the outlaw being for his many crimes and villanies banished from the towns and houses of honest men, and wandering in waste places far from danger of law, maketh his mantle his house, and under it covereth himself from the wrath of heaven, from the offence of the earth, and from the sight of men: when it raineth it is his pentice, when it bloweth it is his tent, when it freezeth it is his tabernacle; in summer he can wear it loose, in winter he can wrap it close; at all times he can use it, never heavy, never cumbersome. Likewise for a rebel it is as serviceable: for in his war that he maketh (if at least it deserves the name of war) when he still flyeth from his foe and lurketh in the thick woods and straight passages waiting for advantages, it is his bed, yea and almost his household stuff. For the wood is his house against all weathers, and his mantle is his cave to sleep in. There he wrappeth his self round ensconseth himself strongly against the gnats, which in the country do more annoy the naked rebels whilst they keep the woods, and do more sharply wound them than all their enemies' swords or spears which can seldom come nigh them; yea and oftentimes their mantles serveth them when they are near driven, being wrapped about their left arm instead of a target, for it is hard to cut through it with a sword; besides, it is light to bear, light to throw away, and being as they then commonly are naked, it is to them all in all. Lastly, for a thief it is so handsome, as it may seem it was first invented for him, for under it he can cleanly convey any fit pillage that commeth handsomely in his way, and when he goeth abroad in the night on freebooting it is his best and surest friend, for lying as they often do, two or three nights together abroad to watch for their booty, with that they can prettily shroud themselves under a bush or a bankside till they may conveniently do their errand. And when all is done he can, in his mantle, pass through any town or company, being close hooded over his head as he useth from knowledge of any to whom he is endangered. Besides all this he or any man else that is disposed to mischief or villainy may, under his mantle, go privily, armed without suspicion of any, carry his headpiece, his skene or pistol, if he please to be always in a readiness. Thus necessary and fitting is a mantle for a bad man. And surely for a bad housewife it is no less convenient. For some of them that be these wandering women, called of them Monashutt,[36] it is half a wardrobe, for in summer ye shall find her arrayed commonly but in her smock and mantle to be more ready for her light services; in winter; and in her travel it is her cloak and safeguard, and also a coverlet for her lewd exercise, and when she hath filled her vessel, under it she can hide both her burden and her blame; yea, and when her bastard is born it serves instead of all her swaddling clothes, her mantles, her cradles with which others are vainly cumbered, and as for all other good women love to do but little work, how handsome it is to lie in and sleep, or to louse themselves in the sunshine, they that have been but a while in Ireland can well witness. Sure I am that ye will think it very unfit for good housewives to stir in or to busy herself about the housewifery in sort as they should. These be some of the abuses for which I would think it meet to forbid all mantles.

Eudoxus: O evil minded man, that having reckoned up so many uses of mantles, will yet wish it to be abandoned.

9) Barnaby Rich, *The Irish Hubbub or the English Hue and Cry* (1617):[37]

[T]o weepe Irish[38] is to weepe at pleasure, without either cause or greefe, when it is an usuall matter amongst them, upon the buriall of their dead, to hire a company of women, that for some small recompence given them, they will follow the corps, and furnish out the cry (as Master Stanihurst hath said) with such howling and barbarous outcries that hee that should but heare them, and did not know the ceremony, would rather thinke they did sing then weep. Such a brutish kinde of lamentation, as in the judgement of any man that should but heare, and did not know their custome, would thinke it to be some prodigious presagement, prognosticating some unluckie or ill successe, as they use to attribute to the howling of doggs, to the croaking of Ravens, and the shrieking of Owles, fitter for Infidels and Barbarians, then to bee in use and custome among Christians.

And yet in Dublin it selfe, there is not a corps carried to the buriall, which is not followed with this kinde of mourners, which you shall heare by their howling and their hollowing, but never see them to shed any teares. And from hence I thinke indeed ariseth the proverb, to weep Irish. So that it appeares, how the Irish have wit and discretion, both to weep when they list, and to laugh at their pleasure. And I am glad of it: for I will make a little bold to borrow some of their agilitie; yet not to weepe without a cause, for that were right to weepe Irish; but to laugh, and to give the Hubbub; when I see a cause, and neither to forbeare Irish nor English. For we daily see the pride, the drunkennesse, the swearing, the bawdery, the bribery, the popery, all the most lewd and idle vices: the beastly and diuellish fashions the one doth use, the other doth imitate; wherefore then should I not let them see themselves, and their abominations, that so they may amend. If not, yet to let the honest plaine men view their follies, that so he may laugh at their fooleries. Doth not this deserve the Hubbub to see ugly vice doth beare the name of seemly vertue, and drunkennesse reputed good fellowship, murther called manhood, lechery named honest love, impudency good audacitie, pride they call decency, and wretched misery they call good husbandry, hypocrisie they call sinceritie, and flattery doth beare the name of eloquence, truth and veritie, and that which in former ages was called flat knavery, passeth by the name of wit and policie. If I should weepe for any thing, it should bee for some madde conceited griefe: Like the woman, that when her Husband was hanged on the fore-noone, shee fell a-weeping in the after-noone, and did lament with such vehement shewes of sorrow, that her neighbours comming about her, began to exhort her to patience, telling her that she was not the first woman that had had a Husband hanged, and although the manner of his death was somewhat disgraceful to the world, yet they wisht her to play a wise womans part, and not to take such greefe whereby to hurt her selfe for that which could not be holpen: True, true indeed, answered this sorrowful woman, it cannot now be holpen, and I would be loath to hurt my selfe by playing too much the foole; neither doe I take this greefe[39] for that my Husband was hanged, but for that he was not hanged in a cleane shirt: if his linnen had bin cleanly about him, his hanging would never have greeved me.

11) Edmund Spenser (c. 1596)[40]

Irenius: There is amongst the Irish a certain kind of people called the bards, which are to them instead of poets, whose profession is to set forth the praises and dispraises of men, in their poems or rhymes, the which are had in so high regard and estimation amongst them that none dare displease them for fear to run into reproach through their offence and to be made infamous in the mouths of all men;[41] for their verses are taken up with a general applause, and usually sung at all feasts and meetings by certain other persons whose proper function that is, which also receive for the same great rewards, and reputation besides. . . [P]oets as in their writing do labour to better the manners, and through the sweet bait of their numbers to steal into the young spirits a desire of honour and virtue, are worthy to be had in great respect, but these Irish bards are for the most part of another mind, and so far from instructing young men in moral discipline, that they themselves do more deserve to be sharply disciplined, for they seldom use to choose unto themselves the doing of good men for the ornaments of their poems, but whomsoever they find to be most licentious of life most bold and lawless in his doings, most dangerous and desperate in all parts of disobedience and rebellious disposition, him they set up and glorify in their rhymes, him they praise to the people, and to young men make an example to follow. . . such licentious parts as these, tending for the most part to the hurt of the English, or maintainance of their own lewd liberty, they themselves being most desirous thereof, do most allow, besides these evil things being decked and suborned with the gay attire of goodly words, may easily deceive and carry away the affection of a young mind that is not well stayed, but desirous by some bold adventure to make proof of himself. For being (as they all be) brought up idly without awe of parents, without precepts of masters, without fear of offence, not being directed nor employed in any course of life which may carry them to virtue, will easily be drawn to follow such as any shall set before them, for a young mind cannot rest if he be not still busied in some goodness. He will find himself such business as shall soon busy all about him, in which, if he shall find any to praise him and to give him encouragement, as those bards and rhymers do for little reward or a share of a stolen cow, then waxeth he most insolent and half mad, with the love of himself and his own lewd deeds. And as for words to set forth such lewdness it is not hard for them to give a goodly gloss and painted show thereunto, borrowed even from the praises which are proper unto virtue itself[.] . .

Eud: [T]ell me, I pray you, have they any art in their composition or be they anything witty or well savoured, as poems should be?

Iren: Yea, truly, I have caused diverse of them to be translated unto me, that I might understand them, and surely they savoured of sweet wit and good invention, but skilled not of the goodly ornaments of poetry. Yet were they sprinkled with some pretty flowers of their own natural devise, which gave good grace and comeliness unto them, the which it is great pity to see so abused to the gracing of wickedness and vice, which would with good usage serve to beautify and adorn virtue. This evil custom, therefore, needeth reformation.

7. HUGH O'NEILL, SECOND EARL OF TYRONE (1540–1616)

O'Neill was taken into the care of the Sidneys after the murder of his elder brother. He was possibly educated at Penshurst, then went to court (nothing is known about this period of his life), before returning to Ireland in 1568 when his uncle, Shane, was killed, the English government hoping to use him as a counter-weight to the influence of Turlough Liuineach. He fought against Turlough; later helped Walter Devereux in Ulster; fought against the Earl of Desmond in Munster and was present at the massacre at Smerwick (see Chapter 6), being commended for his overall service to the crown. By the 1580s he was firmly established in Tyrone (he was made earl in 1585) and involved in conflict with other rival chieftains. Many now began to suspect his ambition and motives, despite his continuing cooperation with the government in taking his seat in the Irish parliament (1585), agreeing to have his land shired, allowing the Blackwater fort to be built in his territory, and professing his desire to have his followers adopt English dress, systems of land tenure and customs. In 1593 he married Mabel Bagenal, daughter of the English-born Irish Knight-Marshal and achieved recognition from Turlough as the master of Tyrone. The invasion of Louth in May, 1595 signalled the start of the Nine Years' War; Tyrone's attack pre-empting one by crown troops. There is dispute as to the exact form and purpose of the war: was it just another rebellion of a disaffected chieftain who saw the writing on the wall as the English closed in? Or do O'Neill's appeals to Catholic Spain make it a religious conflict and, very possibly, a truly national one?[1] There is no disputing the danger the war signalled to English dominance and government in Ireland as Irish forces secured previously unheard of victories (most famously at the Blackwater) and swept into Munster in 1598. But after the debacle of Essex's campaign, Mountjoy's ruthless tactics forced Tyrone back into Ulster, so that when the Spanish finally arrived at Kinsale in September, 1601, his troops had to traverse the length of the country only to be disastrously defeated. O'Neill eventually surrendered in

March, 1603, on generous terms (he was allowed to keep most of his lands), but fled to Italy via France in September, 1607,[2] where he died, his appeals for permission to return to a portion of former estates having been refused, and the Ulster plantation established.

O'Neill troubled and enraged English writers not just because of the danger and disruption he caused, nor simply for the audacity of his nearly successful war, but because he was a transgressive and hybrid figure who in many ways resembled them, having acquired courtly values (see Harington), an English wife (see Gainsford), diplomatic skills (see Lee). Perhaps there is a sense of betrayal that the culture of Castiglione, Machiavelli and Ariosto had been turned against them, possibly better understood.

1) Sir Thomas Lee (d. 1601)

Lee probably came to Ireland with Walter Devereux in 1574. He acquired property through marriage and was used by numerous Lord Deputies as a soldier against rebels throughout the 1580s and 1590s. He obtained land in Ulster and helped in negotiations with Tyrone whom he appears to have been familiar with and whom he defended against Lord Deputy Fitzwilliam. The latter, in turn, hated Lee and mistrusted Tyrone. Lee continued to serve against rebels, but he remained a believer in Tyrone's good-will, and in August, 1598, after the Battle of the Yellow Ford he was imprisoned on suspicion of holding treasonable communication with him. Released owing to the necessity of war, he visited Tyrone again and, unable to secure a submission, turned against him, having found him 'quite changed from his former disposition'. Lee returned to England with Essex (the second Earl) in 1599. He was arrested in February, 1601, charged with attempting to spring Essex and Southampton from gaol and executed.

Lee's 'Brief Declaration' was probably written in 1595 to defend Tyrone against the accusations of Fitzwilliam.[3]

From 'A Brief Declaration of the state of Ireland' (c. 1595):

Let those devices of theirs take effect, or otherwise to have him cut off, your majesty's whole kingdom there would moan it most pitifully; for there was never man bred in those parts, who hath done your majesty greater service than he, with often loss of his blood upon notable enemies of your majesty's; yea, more often than all other nobles of Ireland. And what quietness your majesty had these many years past in the northern parts of that kingdom, it's neither your forces there placed, (which have been but small) nor their great service who commanded them, but only the honest disposition of and carriage of the earl, hath made them obedient in those parts to your majesty. And what pity it is that a man of his worth and worthiness shall be thus dealt withal by his adversaries (who are men who have had great places of commandment) and neither they, nor their friends for them, are able to set down they ever did your majesty one good day's service, I humbly leave to your majesty.

If he were so bad as they would fain enforce (as many as know him and the strength of his country, will witness thus much with me) he might very easily cut off many of your majesty's forces which are laid in garrison in small troops, in divers parts bordering upon his country; yea, and overrun all your English pale, to the utter ruin thereof; yea, and camp as long as should please him even under the walls of Dublin, for any strength your majesty yet hath in that kingdom to remove him.

These things being considered, and how unwilling he is (upon my knowledge), to be otherwise towards your majesty than he ought, let him (if it please your highness) be somewhat hearkened unto and recovered (if it may be) to come in unto your majesty to impart his own griefs, which no doubt he will do, if he will like his security. And then, I am persuaded, he will simply acknowledge to your majesty how far he hath offended you; and besides (notwithstanding his protection) he will, if it so stand with your majesty's pleasure, offer himself to the marshall (who hath been the chiefest instrument against him) to prove with his sword, that he hath most wrongfully accused him. And because it is no conquest for him to overthrow a man ever held in the world, to be of most cowardly behaviour, he will, in defence of his innocency, allow his adversary to come armed against him naked, to encourage him the rather to accept of his challenge.

2) Thomas Gainsford

From *The True, Exemplarie and Remarkable History of the Earl of Tirone* (1619):[4]

[H]e moved awhile in the highest orbe of prosperity, and from our English supportation commanded his country, as a Prince of the North, and except an open displaying of his colours of Rebellion, performed, what he durst, and durst does any thing, which tended not to manifest treason, and dangerous innovation. For not long after, under colour of corroborating the peace of his country and insinuation with some English affinity, hee made Sir Samuel Bagenols sister beleeve, that the great Oneale of Ireland was captiuated to her love, and in which, if the time could have served, hee would have shewed himselfe as brave and complete an Amorist, as the formallest Courtier in England: To this the Lady seemed no great opposite, onely with some shew of modesty depending on her brother, she refered the successe to his approbation, who somwhat too stubborne, interposed as it were a negative, not without exprobation of the barbarous customs of the North of Ireland, which Tirone interpreted disgracious to his exaltation, and finding no other remedy to appease his wilfulnesse, in a manner by force of armes took her to his wife; whereupon hee was denied her dowry, and that exasperated his displeasure to which when the Deputy added the suppressing of MacMahond his neighbour, I am afraid it exculcerated his loyalty.

3) Sir John Harington (1561–1612)

Harington was the godson of Elizabeth. He was a lawyer who turned to the court for advancement, where his epigrams, translation of Ariosto's *Orlando Furioso*, and *The Metamorphosis of Ajax* (a satirical tract on the water-closet[5]) made him well known. He went to Ireland with Essex in 1599 and was one of the many knights created by the Lord Lieutenant.[6] He fell into disgrace after Essex's rebellion and was forced to retire to his family home when he returned from Ireland in November (1599). Restored to the court in 1602, he tried to find favour with James, but his attempt to gain the Chancellorship of Ireland after the death of Adam Loftus was unsuccessful[7] and his petitioning was doomed to failure until the king, recognising Harington's erudition, made him a tutor to prince Henry shortly before he died.

Harington's visit to Tyrone took place during the fateful truce organised by Essex, and after the Earl's departure for London.[8]

To Justice Carey, October, 1599:[9]

Having expected shipping till the 8th of this month [October], and meeting with none convenient, (in respect that all were taken up with sick souldiers, or with my Lord Lieutenant's horses,) I was desirous to make some use of the time that I should stay here, and therefore was easily persuaded to go with Sir William Warren,[10] my kind friend, with whom I had been formerly acquainted in England, and to see some part of the realme northward, and the arch-rebel himself, with whom Sir William was to entreat.

But staying at Dundalk till the 15th of this month, and no news certain of the earl's coming, I went to see the Newry, and from thence to Darlingford by the narrow water, and was hindered by waters that I could not come back to Sir William Warren before his first meeting with the Earl Tyrone, which was on the 17th day; what time how far they proceeded I know not, but it appeared that the earl was left in good dysposition, because he kept his hour so well, the next morning: and, as I found after, Sir William had told him of me, and given such a report of me above my desert, that the next day, when I came, the earl used far greater respect to me than I expected; and began debasing his own manner of hard life, comparing himself to wolves, that fill their bellies sometime, and fast as long for it; then excusing himself to me that he could no better call to mind myself, and some of my friends that had done him some courtesy in England; and been oft in his company at my Lord of Ormond's; saying, these troubles had made him forget almost all his friends.

After this he fell to private communication with Sir William, to the effecting of the matters begun the day before; to which I thought it not fit to intrude myself, but took occasion the while to entertain his two sons, by posing them in their learning, and their tutors, which were one Fryar Nangle, a Franciscan; and a younger scholer, whose name I know not; and finding the two children of good towardly spirit, their age between thirteen and fifteen, in English cloths like a nobleman's sons; with velvet gerkins and gold lace; of a good chearful aspect, freckle-faced, not tall of stature, but strong, and well set; both of them [learning] the English tongue; I gave them (not without the advice of Sir William Warren) my English translation of 'Ariosto', which I got at Dublin; which their teachers took very thankfully, and soon after shewed it to the earl, who call'd to see it openly, and would needs hear some part of it read. I turn'd (as it had been by chance) to the beginning of the 45th canto, and some other passages of the book, which he seemed to like so well, that he solemnly swore his boys should read all the book over to him.

Then they fell to communication again, and (calling me to him) the earl said, that I should witness, and tell my Lord Lieutenant, how, against all his confederates wills, Sir William had drawn him to longer cessation, which he would never have agreed to, but in confidence of my lord's honourable dealing with him; for, saith he, 'now is my harvest time, now have my men their six-weeks pay afore-hand, that they have nothing to do but fight; and if I omit this opportunity, and you shall prepare to invade me the mean time, I may be condemned for a fool.'

Also one pretty thing I noted, that the paper being drawn for him to sign, and his signing it with O'Neill, Sir William (though with very great difficulty) made him to new write it, and subscribe, Hugh Tyrone. Then we broke our fasts with him, and at his meat he was very merry, and it was my hap to thwart one of his priests in an argument, to which he gave reasonable good ear, and some approbation. He drank to my lord's health, and bade me tell him he loved him, and acknowledged this cessation had been very honourably kept. He made likewise a solemn protestation that he was not ambitious, but sought only safety of his life, and freedom of his conscience, without which he would not live, though the Queen would give him Ireland.

Then he asked of Sir Henry Harington,[11] and said he heard he had much wrong, to have imputation of want of courage, for the last defeat at Arkloo;[12] protesting, that himself had known Sir Henry serve as valiently as ever any man did, naming the time, place, and persons, all known to Sir William Warren.

Other pleasant and idle tales were needless and impertinent, or to describe his fern table and fern forms, spread under the stately canopy of heaven. His guard, for the most part, were beardless boys without shirts; who, in the frost, wade as familiarly through rivers as water-spaniels. With what charm such a master makes them love him I know not, but if he bid come, they come; if go, they do go; if he say do this, they do it. He makes apparent show to be inclinable to peace; and some of his nearest followers have it buzzed amongst them, that some league of England, with Spain or Scotland, or I know not where, may endanger them. But himself, no doubt, waits only to hear what my Lord Lieutenant intends, and according to that will bend his course.

Fryar Nangle swears all oaths, that he will do all the good he can, and that he is guiltless of the heinous crimes he is indicted of; for, if he had his pardon, perhaps there might be made good use of him.

This is all I remember any way worthy the writing to you, not doubting but Sir William Warren, that had the sole charge of this business, will give you much better account of the weightier affairs than I, that only went to see their manner of parting.

I remain, in much duty,
John Harington.

4) 'The Supplication of the Blood of English most lamentably murdered in Ireland, crying out of the yearth for revenge' (1599):[13]

The 'Supplication', directly addressed to Elizabeth, is the work of an anonymous Munster planter eager to press forward the colonial perspective of the New English in its trenchant criticisms of official English policy in Ireland allegedly lenient towards the Irish rebels. The tract, datable to November-December, 1598,[14] prefigures later 'atrocity literature',[15] testifies to the fear caused by Tyrone's actions, and shows how different interest groups interpreted the situation in Ireland and their own status there.

Never shall you reade in the stories of the Gothes and Vandelles, in the recordes of the Turkes and Infidells, in the most barbarous and cruell warres that ever were, suche brutishe crueltie, such mounsterous outrage. O that yore highnes might without hazard to yore royall person have seen the demeanour of those savage beasts, for men we can not call them, whose doinges shewe such Contrarietie to manhoode.

There should you have seen, some smothered out of theire houses, others hewen to peeces most unmercifully, others driven for feare of fier and sword into the waters, where they were drowned. There should you have seen younge infants scarce yett seasoned with the ayre of the world, most lamentably brained: some dashed against the walles: others tombled from highe towers. There should you have seene the widowe lamentinge over the dead bodie of her husband: the Child bewaylinge the death of his father: the mother runinge into the thikest of the swordes to save her sonne, miserablie rentinge and tearing herselfe for the abusinge of her daughter before her face.

The lamentable and woofull cryes of those desolate widdowes, wretched orphanes, comfortlesse mothers, defloured virgins, and foule abused women, which then peirced the Cloudes, and ascended to the very throne of majestie had ben sufficient to have drawen revenge from heaven, had theire wickednes been come to her full measure: or had not god reserved that revenge for you to worke, O Queene, as his faithfull minister, whom next him selfe they have most dishonored. . .

They sleep not in their busines: They have possessed every parte of the Contry: their forces are everywhere: Ulster is their owne: They have made a riddance of the English pale: Connaught is at their owne Comaund, redie to cutt the governors throte when they please: Mounster is generally revoulted, In the Contry they possesse all: the townes only which god knowes are but fewe, Ill manned, worse minded, are yet yours, but god knowes what they are like to be: and the smale remnaunt of yore poore subjectes, that live there yett pend up by the rebelles shall feele, and yore selfe finde, If you sent not force, and that a royall force to suppresse the rage of these monsters very shortly.

5) Thomas Gainsford

From *The True, Exemplaire and Remarkable History of the Earl of Tirone* (1619):[16]

At the first entrance into the roome, euen at the threshold of the doore, hee prostrated himselfe groueling to the earth, with such a deiected countenance, that the standers by were amazed, and my Lord Depauty himselfe had much a doe to remember the worke in hand. For whether the sight of so many Captaines and Gentlemen, whether ashamed of himselfe, when he saw such a number of his owne nation spectators of his wretchednesse, whether the consideration of his fortunes, that had thus embased him contrary to expectation: whether the view of my Lord to be his Iudge, whom once he reputed to be at his mercy: whether hee repented this course of submission, and degenerating begging of life, when a noble death had beene both honourable, and the determiner of misery: or whether mans naturall imperfection, to bee confounded and altred with affliction, depressed his spirits, I know not, but it was one of the deplorablest sights that euer I saw: and to looke vpon such a person, the author of so much trouble, and so formerly glorious, so deiected, would haue wrought many changes in the stoutest heart, and did no doubt at this instant raise a certain commiseration in his greatest aduersary.

After a while the Deputy beckned him to come neere: beleeue it, hee arose: but with such degrees of humility, as if misfortune had taught him cunning to grace his aduersity. For he passed not two steps, before hee yeelded to a new prostitution, which might well bee called a groueling to the ground, and so, by diuided ceremonies, fell on his knees, beginning an apology for some of his actions, but at euery word confessing, in how many treasons hee had plunged himselfe, offending God and Her Maiesty, how hee had abused her fauours, disturbed her Kingdome, disobeyed her lawes, wronged her subiects, abandoned all ciuility, and wrapped himselfe in the very tarriers of destruction; so that nothing remained, but to flie to the refuge of her Princely clemency, which had so often restored both his life and honour.

8. WAR AND REBELLION

The nature of conflict in early modern Ireland was a complex phenomenon. Whilst Sir Henry Sidney was outraged that the court refused to grant his struggle with Shane O'Neill the status of a 'war',[1] a later Lord Deputy, Lord Grey de Wilton, and his secretary, Edmund Spenser, although disagreeing over crucial details,[2] both justified the slaughter of combatants at the Fort d'Oro, Smerwick (1580), after they had surrendered, on the grounds that they were 'rebels and traitors' and therefore not worthy of the 'custom of war and law'. Given the supposed constitutional status of Ireland as a kingdom ruled by the English monarch, the latter is the more frequently made interpretation of the status of the Irish bearing arms against the English government. A comparison of the treatment of Irish and English rebels illustrates not only the similarity of their gruesome fates, but also the link between those enforcing the status quo in both nations.[3] Hooker and Churchyards' neat, moralistic descriptions of the fate of the Irish rebels perhaps owe much to *The Mirror for Magistrates* and the tradition of complaint,[4] as well as the writings of Henrican propagandists such as Richard Moryson, Thomas Starkey, and others,[5] and the Elizabethan homilies.[6] Spenser's harrowing and famous account of the Munster famine, where the rebels become what they eat, 'anatomies of death', can be read in the same way, but the cannibalistic self-consumption perhaps implies a New World context, where the anthropophagi had recently been 'rediscovered'.[7] Here the Irish seem to become the 'other' of both a domestic and an exotic discourse. The narrative of Sir Henry Sidney shows how routine such slaughter and destruction were in the suppression of rebellion and how they often required no justification at all.

1) John Hooker: The sons of Clanricard (1586):[8]

And then his lordship [FitzWilliam] prepareth to take a journie towards Waterford . . . . But when he was passed a daies journey, word was brought unto him from the bishop of Meth, who laie then upon the confines of Meth and Connagh for ordering of matters in these parties; and the like from the maior of Gallewaie, and from diverse others, who affected well the state, crieng out with trembling termes and dolefull reports, that the earle of Clanricard his sonnes that basterlie brood, which not scarse two moneths past had humbled themselves to the lord deputie, confessed their faults, and craved pardon, and had most firmelie protested and sworne most dutifull and continuall obedience.

These (I saie) not without the counsell and consent of their father, were on a night stollen over the river of Shennon, and there cast awaie their English apparell, and clothed themselves in their old woonted Irish rags, and sent to all their old friends to come awaie to them, and to bring the Scots whom they had solicited, and their Gallowglasses, and all other their forces with them. Who when they met togither, they forthwith went to the towne of Athenrie, and those few houses which were newlie builded, they sacked, set the new gates on fire, beat awaie the masons and labourers which were there in working, brake and spoiled the queenes armes, and others, there made and cut to be set up. Bad and wicked they were before, but now ten times worse than ever they were; being come, even as it is said in the scriptures, that the wicked spirit was gone out of the man, and wanting his woonted diet, returneth unto the house from whense he came, and finding the same swept cleane, he goeth and seeketh out other seven wicked spirits, and entreth and dwelleth where he did before, and the last state of that man is woorse than the first. And if a man should aske of these bastardlie boies, and of their sier, what should be the cause that they should thus rage, and so wickedlie and suddenlie revolve, as dogs to their vomits, so they to their treasons and treacheries, having beene so courteouslie used, so gentlie interteined, so friendlie countenanced, so fatherly exhorted, so pithilie persuaded, & so mercifullie pardoned in hope of amendment: surelie nothing can they answer, but that they would not be honest, nor in anie part satisfie a little of infinite the robberies, thefts, and spoiles which they had made. For bastardlie slips cannot bring forth better fruits, neither can thornes bring foorth grapes.

2) Thomas Churchyard (1520?–1604).

Churchyard's literary career stretched from the reign of Edward VI to that of James I and his output is immense, albeit neglected and ridiculed.[9] As a soldier he served in Scotland and the Low

Countries as well as Ireland, under such commanders as Sir William Drury and Lord Grey de Wilton. He spent a great deal of his life searching for patrons, apparently almost always unsuccessfully. A literary joke he may seem to be, but his career tells us much about the changing conditions of patronage and taste in the sixteenth century,[10] as well as the opinions of the gentry, not least, in his numerous tracts on Ireland.[11]

From Churchyard's *Choise* (1579):[12]

And by a good occasion maister John Malbie, with three score and fowre horsemen, and a fewe footemen, he made suche a slaughter, that five and thirtie of his beste men, that followed Neall Bryan Artte were licked up and slaine, and a greate preye and bootie taken from hym, and brought awaie, he beeyng twoo hundreth footemen, and fourtie horsemen in the feelde. Among those menne that was slaine, was one Con Mackmeloeg, who before caused maistre Smithe to be eaten up with Dogges, after he had been boiled,[13] and this same Con Mackmeloeg beying slaine, was lefte among wolves 5 dayes, and was had into a house, where his freendes howled, and cried over his dedde bodie so long, that by mischaunce a greate deale of pouder caught fire, and sett the house in a flamme: the Doggs in the toune smellymg this ded bodie ranne in, and tooke it out of the house, and so tore it in peeces, and fedde uppon his carraine fleshe openly. Whiche was a thyng to bee muche marvueiled at, and thought to bee sent from God, for a terrour to all tyrauntes hereafter.

3) Edmund Spenser (c. 1598)[14]

Eudoxus: Surely of such desperate persons as wilfully follow the course of their own folly, there is no compassion to be had, and for the others ye have proposed a merciful means, much more than they have deserved. But what then shall be the conclusion of this war, for you have prefixed a short time of his continuance?

Irenius: The end I assure me will be very short and much sooner than can be in so great a trouble (as it seemeth) hoped for. Although there should none of them fall by the sword, nor be slain by the soldier, yet thus being kept from manurance, and their cattle from running abroad by this hard restraint, they would quickly consume themselves and devour one another. The proof whereof I saw sufficiently ensampled in those late wars in Munster, for notwithstanding that the same was a most rich and plentiful country, full of corn and cattle, that you would have thought they would have been able to stand long, yet ere one year and a half they were brought to such wretchedness, as that any stony heart would have rued the same. Out of every corner of the woods and glens they came creeping forth upon their hands, for their legs could not bear them. They looked anatomies of death, they spake like ghosts crying out of their graves, they did eat of the dead carrions, happy were they could find them, yea and one another soon after in so much as the very carcasses they spared not to scrape out their graves, and if they found a plot of water cress or shamrocks, there they flocked as to a feast for the time, yet not able long to continue therewithal, that in short space there were none almost left and a most populous and plentiful country suddenly left void of man or beast. Yet sure in all that war there perished not many by the sword, but all by extremity of famine, which they themselves had wrought.

4) Sir Henry Sidney (1529–86)

Sidney served under Mary and Elizabeth in Wales as Lord President and Ireland as Lord Deputy. His terms of office in Ireland are notable for the advocation of extensive colonisation as a means of ordering the country,[15] the killing of Shane O'Neill[16] and his attempt to raise a permanent revenue in the Pale by replacing 'cess' with an annual land tax ('Composition'), which was fiercely resisted.[17] Sidney's intermittent career in Ireland came to an end when he was finally recalled in September, 1578 for failing to govern as economically as was desired. He is often regarded as one of the ablest of Tudor politicians in Ireland.[18]

From Sidney's 'Memoir addressed to Sir Francis Walsingham' (1581):[19]

So (wasting and spoyling all that country) with as convenient speed as I could, I came to the city of Corke, where I found the abovewritten captains and soldiers [Collier and Chestynde]. I in manner received the poore afflicted ladie, and comforted the citizens of the same city. I there heard of the arrival of the Earl of Ormond, whom I addressed to meete me at Lymericke; and after I had refreshed me and my men a few days, I departed from thence and encamped in a country of the Earl of Desmond's, called Kiriewherie, and destroyed the same, wynning the principall castle thereof, called Carreg-Ilyn, and left in it a ward. From thence I marched into Mack-Donoghe's country, which confyneth with Desmond, the Earl of Clancare's country; and there I won and pulled down castles, burned and spoiled villages and fields; which, while I was in doing, the lord of the country, O'Kueefe, Mac Aulley, the eldest son of O'Swillivan Moore (the father for aige and corpulency not being able to travel) and O'Swillivan-Bere, without protection came to me and submitted themselfs, lyves and lands; and taking of them othe and hostage for their fidelitie, without pardon, I dismissed them to expect the queen's mercie. I then turned into a great territorie of lande of the Viscount Barry's, the name of the country I have forgotten, but the principall castle thereof beareth a French name called Bowte de vawne,[20] which I took, and repossessed the right owner in it; so I did divers landlords and freeholders whose lands and castles had been taken and withheld from them, some of long tyme by the Earl of Desmond, and some of late tyme by James Fitzmaurice.

5) William Farmer (fl. 1612–15)

Almost nothing is known of Farmer, except that he was an intimate friend of Sir Arthur Chichester, Lord Deputy, 1604–14, and referred to himself as a surgeon. Two treatises on Ireland remain extant.[21] The piece included here serves as a parallel to Spenser's description.

From 'Chronicles of Ireland' (1615?):

Here it is to be noated that in this yeare happened a great famine and scarcitie of victualles in the northe as well among the English, as the Irish, that all things weare growne to verie high rates and excessive prices amonge the Englishe, not withstandinge that they wear some times relieved and their wants supplyed by shipping out of England, and other places, but the Irishe that had no suche supplies were brought to extreme miserie, in such sorte that they wear driven to eate the flesh of horses garrans[22] and other kinds of beasts, unfit and unnatural for any Christian to eat, and as I have heard it credibly reported that some of the Irish have lyene secretly with pieces to kill people, either friends or enemies, that passed by, to the intent to eat them.

But this is most true, and as lamentable as true, that Sir Arthur Chichester, the governor, travelling on a journey with soldiers to do some service, as he travelled through a wood there was felt a great savour, as it were roasting or broiling of flesh; the governor sent out soldiers to search the wood, and they found a cabin where a woman was dead, and five children by her made fire to her thighs and arms and sides, roasting her flesh and eating it. The governor wet to the place to see it, and demanded of them why they did so; they answered they could not get any other meat. It was demanded where their cows were, and they said the English men had taken them away. Also it was demanded when the wod kerne were there, and they answered not in three days before. It was asked of them whether they would have meat or money to relieve them; they answered both meat and money; so the governor commanded to collect a proportion of victuals from among the soldiers' knapsacks, and left it with them, and so departed and went on his journey.

6) Lord Arthur Grey de Wilton (1536–1593)

A soldier virtually all his life, Grey had served in the Netherlands[23] and Scotland, and acquired a reputation as a staunchly Protestant magistrate in his native Buckinghamshire before becoming Lord Deputy of Ireland in July, 1580. Warned by Elizabeth to temper his religious zeal, he became a by-word for treacherous butchery in Ireland (and in some quarters in England) from which he has never recovered,[24] after his action at Smerwick (1580) during the Desmond rebellion. At the same time an uprising in the Pale threatened to get out of hand; there was a renewed threat from Turlough O'Neill in Ulster. Grey was forced to march back to Dublin, then north, where he achieved spectacular, if temporary, military success. At odds with Elizabeth's more cautious approach in matters of religion, he petitioned frequently for his recall and his wish was eventually granted in August, 1582.[25]

The passages below detail both Grey's and Spenser's accounts of the events at Smerwick and their respective defences of the Lord Deputy's actions.

From Grey to Elizabeth, 12 November, 1580:[26]

There was presently sent unto me one Alexandro, their campmaster; he told me that certain Spaniards and Italians were there arrived upon fair . . . speeches and great promises, which altogether vain and false they found, and t[hat] it was no part of their intent to molest or take any government from your Majesty, for proof that they were ready to depart as they came, and deliver in [to] my hands the fort. Mine answer was, that for that I perceived their people to stand of two nations, Italian and Spanish, I would give no a [nswer] unless a Spaniard were likewise by. He presently went and returned [with] a Spanish captain. I then told the Spaniard that I knew their nation [to] have an absolute Prince, one that was in good league and amity with your Majesty, which made me marvel that any of his people should be found associate . . . them that went about to maintain rebels against you and to disturb . . . any your Highness' governments, and taking it that it could not be his Kings' will, I was to know by whom and for what cause they were sent. His reply was, that the King had not sent them, but that one John Martinez de Ricaldi, Governor for the King, at Bilboa, had willed him to levy a band and to repair with it to St. Andrews, and there to be directed by this their colonel here, whom he followed as a blind man, not knowing whither. The other avouched that they were all sent by the Pope for the defence of the Catholica fede. My answer was, that I would not greatly have marvelled if men being commanded by natural and absolute princes did sometimes take in hand wrong actions, but that men, and that of account as some of them made show of, should be carried into unjust, desperate, and wicked actions by one that neither from God nor man could claim any princely power or empire, but indeed a detestable shaveling, the right Antichrist and general ambitious tyrant over all right principalities, and patron of the diabolica fede, I could not but greatly rest in wonder, their fault therefore, far to be aggravated by the vileness of the commander, and that at my hands no condition of composition they were to expect, other than that simply they should render me the fort, and yield their selves to my will for life or death.

With this answer he departed, after which there was one or two courses to and fro more, to have gotten a certainty for some of their lives, but finding that it would not be, the colonel himself about sunsetting came forth and requested respite with surcease of arms till the next morning, and then he would give a resolute answer.

Finding that to be but a gain of time for them and loss of the same for myself, I definitely answered, I would not grant it, and therefore presently either that he took my offer or else return, and I would fall to my business. He then embraced my knees simply putting himself to my mercy, only he prayed that for that night he might abide in the fort, and that in the morning all should be put into my hands. I asked hostages for the performance; they were given. Morning come; I presented my companies in battle before the fort, the colonel comes forth with 10 or 12 of his chief gentlemen, trailing their ensigns rolled up, and presented them unto me with their lives and the fort. I sent straight, certain gentlemen in, to see their weapons and armours laid down, and to guard the munition and victual there left for spoil. Then put I in certain bands, who straight fell to execution. There were 600 slain.

7) Edmund Spenser (c. 1598):[27]

Eudoxus: I remember that in the late government of that good Lord Gray, when after long travail and many perilous assays, he had brought things almost to this pass that ye speak of, that it was even made ready for reformation, and might have been brought to what Her Majesty would. . . complaint was made against him, that he was a bloody man, and regarded not the life of her subjects, no more than dogs, but had wasted and consumed all, so as now she had almost nothing left but to reign in their ashes. . . . [H]e was always known to be a most just, sincere, godly and right noble man, far from such sternness, far from such unrighteousness. But in that sharp execution of the Spaniards at the fort of Smerwick, I heard it specially noted, and if it were true, as some reported, surely it was a great touch to him in honour. For some say that he promised them life, others that at least he did put them in hope therof.

Iren: Both the one and the other is most untrue, for this I can assure you, myself being as near then as any, that he was so far from either promising or putting in hope, that when first their secretary, called, as I remember, Signor Jeffrey, an Italian, being sent to treat with the Lord Deputy for grace, was flatly refused, and afterwards their Colonel named Don Sebastian came forth to entreat that they might part with their armours like soldiers, at least with their lives, according to the custom of war and law of nations, it was strongly denied him, and told him by the Lord Deputy himself, that they could not justly plead either custom of war or law of nations, for that they were not any lawful enemies, and if they were, willed them to show by what commission they came thither into another princes dominions, to war, whether from the Pope or the King of Spain, or any other. The which when they said they had not, but were only adventurers, that came to seek fortune abroad and serve in wars, amongst the Irish who desired to entertain them, it was then told them that the Irish themselves, as the Earl and John of Desmond with the rest were no lawful enemies, but rebels and traitors, and therefore they that came to succour them no better than rogues and runagates, specially coming with no licence nor commission from their own King, so as it should be dishonourable for him in the name of his Queeen to condition or make any terms with such rascals; but left them to their choice to yield and submit themselves or no, whereupon the said colonel did absolutely yield himself and the fort with all therein, and craved only mercy; which it being thought good not to show them, both for danger of themselves, if, being saved, they should afterwards join with the Irish, and also for terror of the Irish, who were much emboldened by those foreign succours and also put in hope of more ere long. There was no other way but to make that short end of them which was made. Therefore most untruly and maliciously do these evil tongues backbite and slander the sacred ashes of that most just and honourable personage, whose least virtue of many most excellent which aboundeth in his heroic spirit, they were never able to aspire unto.

Eudox: Truly, Irenius, I am right glad to be thus satisfied by you in that I have often heard questioned, and yet was never able till now to choke the mouth of such detractors with the certain knowledge of their slanderous untruths.

8) Edmund Ludlow

Edmund Ludlow (?1617–1692), regicide, was the son of a Wiltshire MP. He became closely involved with Cromwell then alienated from him on the latter's kingly aspirations. Ludlow was among those who signed Charles I's death warrant, and he was promoted second in command to Ireton when Cromwell departed from Ireland in 1650. After Ireton's death in November Ludlow assumed military responsibility in Ireland until Ooctober 1752, when Fleetwood arrived to take charge. His Irish campaigns included the taking of Galway in April 1652 and the acceptance of the surrenders of Lord Muskerry and Clanricarde (June 1652). In August 1660, as the revolution settlement collapsed, Ludlow fled to Dieppe. He spent most of his later life abroad. In the following extract he summarises in a succinct fashion the partition policy for Ireland set in train by the victorious English and Scottish forces.

From *The Memoirs of Edmund Ludlow*:[28]

The Irish being reduced to extremity, and most of the country in the hands of the English, the Parliament resolved to give the adventurers possession of lands proportionable to the several sums they had advanced, and also to satisfy the arrears of the army out of the same, as they had formerly promised: which that they might be enabled to perform, they passed an Act, confiscating so much of the estates of those who had acted against the English, as they judged the quality of their crimes to require, and extending their clemency to those who had carried themselves peaceably. In the mean time that I might bring such as remained yet in arms against us to a necessity of submitting, I marched with a party of about four thousand horse and foot; and having scoured the counties of Wexford and Wicklo, placing garisons where I thought convenient, I went to Tredagh, where I met the rest of the Parliament's Commissioners; and having staid eight days in that place to settle affairs, I continued my march into the country of Meath, and coming to Carrick Mac Ross, a house belonging to the Earl of Essex, where the rebels had barbarously murdered one Mr. Blany a justice of peace in that country, I caused it to be fortified, and put a garison in it, being advantageoulsy situated to restrain the enemy's excursions. From hence I went to visit the garison of Dundalk, and being upon my return, I found a party of the enemy retired within a hollow rock, which was discovered by one of ours, who saw five or six of them standing before a narrow passage at the mouth of the cave. The rock was so thick, that we thought it impossible to dig it down upon them, and therefore resolved to try to reduce them by smoak. After some of our men had spent most part of the day in endeavouring to smother those within by fire placed at the mouth of the cave, they withdrew the fire, and the next morning supposing the Irish to be made uncapable of resistance by the smoak, some of them with a candle before them crawled into the rock. One of the enemy who lay in the middle of the entance fired his pistol, and shot the first of our men into the head, by whose loss we found that the smoak had not taken the designed effect. But seeing no other way to reduce them, I caused the trial to be repeated, and upon examination found that tho a great smoak went into the cavity of the rock, yet it came out again at other crevices; upon which I ordered those places to be closely stopped, and another smother made. About an hour and half after this, one of them was heard to groan very strongly, and afterwards more weakly, whereby we presumed that the work was done; yet the fire was continued till about midnight, and then taken away, that the place might be cool enough for ours to enter the next morning. At which time some went in armed with back, breast, and head-piece, to prevent such another accident as fell out at their first attempt; but they had not gone above six yards before they found the man that had been heard to groan, who was the same that had killed one of our men with his pistol, and who resolving not to quit his post, had been, upon stopping the holes of the rock, choaked by the smoak. Our souldiers put a rope about his neck, and drew him out. The passage being cleared, they entred [sic], and having put about fifteen to the sword, brought four or five out alive, with the priest's robes, a crucifix, chalice and other furniture of that kind. Those within preserved themselves by laying their heads close to a water that ran through the rock. We found two rooms in the place, one of which was large enough to turn a pike; and having filled the mouth of it with large stones, we quitted it, and marched to Castle-Blany, where I left a party of foot, and some horse, as I had done before at Carrick and Newry, whereby that part of the county of Monaghan was pretty well secured.

9. COLONISATION

Why colonise? The answer given by K. R. Andrews that commercial profit was the sole motive may well provide a satisfying explanation for the establishment of many of the colonies which formed the basis of the British Empire.[1] The same might be said of George Peckham's 'Report of the discovery of Newfoundland by Sir Humphrey Gilbert' (1583),[2] where he argues that civilized peoples have a right to establish outposts in the lands of savages because it is the moral duty of all nations to trade. They are further able to defend those settlements from attack, conquering the host country if needs be.[3] However this must be set against the tortuous early history of the Ulster Plantation which was forced upon the London companies, who were obliged to back what they saw as a potentially unprofitable venture (rightly as it turned out).[4] Clearly the motives for creating such a colony go beyond the problem of what to do with younger sons in a system of primogeniture when there was 'no room at the top',[5] the access to cheap raw materials, need for new trade routes and centres, pressure of economic problems at home, and other staples of promotional literature for colonies.[6] The same can be said of the theoretical explorations of classical models of colonisation preceding Sir Thomas Smith's Ards' project, unearthed by Lisa Jardine's examination of Gabriel Harvey's annotations and marginalia.[7] What is at issue is social control, making the ungovernable governable. This is the focus of Beacon's treatise, but it is also evident in Blenerhasset's overtly propagandist tract, designed to encourage settlers through the promise of a better life in Ireland.

Richard Beacon (fl. 1594)

Beacon was a crown official in Munster from December, 1586, and possessed land there which he sublet to other Englishmen. Although his post was conferred on another in 1591, Beacon is mentioned as an Irish landowner as late as 1611.

Beacon's *Solon his Follie* (1594), one of the few works on Ireland printed in the 1590s,[8] is an easily decipherable allegory, being a 'dream vision'[9] dialogue between the Athenians, Solon and Epimenides (a character called Pisistratus makes a fleeting appearance concerning the policy their state should pursue towards the newly conquered Salamina, recently conquered by Solon, the lawgiver[10] (thus, 'his follie'). Salamina is clearly Ireland, and Athens, England, as recent events described and names make clear.[11] The work has not excited much comment until recently,[12] but it demonstrates a thorough familiarity with Machiavelli's *Discourses* and *The Prince*,[13] as well as a general interest in contemporary theories of politics, statecraft and war, through Solon and Epimenides' discussion of the means of subduing, manipulating and becoming popular with a subject people. Included here is the last part of Epimenides' argument for 'the reformation of commonwealths', which concludes the substance of the dialogue with the recommendation that establishing colonies is the best way of achieving Athens' aims. Solon leaves to fight the Maganian navy, praising Epimenides' wisdom, and the narrator wakes up, remembering that Solon instructed him to write the dialogue down 'in pelting prose and not in heroicall verse'.[14]

From *Solon his Follie* (1594):[15]

Epimenides: There remaineth now that we deduct colonies, which is the last, but not the least meanes to suppresse this distemperature, which of all others is the most beneficiall for the containing of a nation conquered in their duty and obedience; wherein foure matters are worthily considered: first the necessitie of deducting colonies; secondarily the benefite that redoundeth thereby unto common-weales; thirdly what order and manner in deducting colonies is to bee used and observed; lastly, the impedimentes which are usuallie given unto the deducting of colonies.

Solon: Shew us the necessitie of collonies.

Epi: A nation conquered may not be contained in their obedience without the strength of colonies or garrisons: for may we be induced to beleeve, that that people or nation, who daily bewaileth & accuseth his present state and condition, may persist therein longer then they be pressed therunto by necessitie? and more then this in the act of Absentes, the meere native borne people of Salamina, are tearmed to be mortall and naturall enemies unto their conquerer and all his dominions[16] . . . for how many waies did this people incite the French King, how oft have they provoked the Pope to invade this lande of Salamina? Againe the Emperour and all other Princes and Potentates, what fortes and holdes have they not taken, and how many of our garrisons have they most cruelly slaine and murdered, the same, in the several actes of Attainder of Shane Oneile, Garralde Fitz Garralde, James of Desmond, and by severall other recordes, may appeare at large.[17] Neither doth this forme of government drawe with it a perpetuall discontentment onelie, but also an infinite and continuall charge in maintaining these severall garrisons, as well to the Prince, as to the subject; for so in the act of subsidie and other recordes it may appeare. Neither be these all the discommodities that perpetual garrisons drawe with them, for these notwithstanding, we have beene forced to send at sundry times armies roiall to suppresse disorders and rebellions, as the same more at large may appeare in the act of restraining of tributes; so as wee may conclude, that where colonies are not strongly and faithfully deducted, there the ende of the first warres, is but a beginning of the second more dangerous than the first; the which maie appeare by the recordes of Salamina: for no sooner were the people or sects, called Omores, Odempsies, Oconores, and others, expelled by great forces and strengthes, to our great charges, out of the severall countries of Liece, Slewmarge, Irry, Glimnarliry, and Offalie, but eftsones for that we deducted not colonies, they traiterouslie entered the said countries by force, and long detained the same, untill they were with greater forces expelled, all which more at large may appeare in the act made for the deviding of countries, into shire groundes, so as we may conclude, that it is not for wise Princes to persevere in that course of government, which doth nourish as it were a perpetuall interest in troubles, charges, and expenses: for the which causes chiefely did the Venetians willingly abandon the government of Bybienna and Pisa, and wee of Athens, Salamina, the which did chiefly arise unto us, for that in steede of planting colonies, we placed garrisons. . . . [L]et us loose no opportunity of deducting of colonies, for they be deducted and maintained with small or no charges, & with no great offence, but onely to such whose landes and houses they possesse, the which remaine for the most part pacified, in that they enjoy their life which stoode in the hands of the Prince, as well as their landes to dispose, for their offences: and if they should remaine discontented, for that having respect to the whole kingdome they be but a handfull, and also dispersed and poore, they may never be able to hurt or disturbe the state, & all others which finde themselves free from their losses, shall rest pacified, partely fearing, least they commit any thing rashly or foolishly, and partly doubting, least the like befalleth them as to those which remaine spoyled for their offences.

[. . .]

Sol: Nowe sith the necessity of colonies doeth manifestly appeare by unfallible proofs and examples, let us proceede unto the profite and benefite that groweth thereby.

Epi: The benefites that hereby arise to the common-weale, are sundry and diverse: first the people poore and seditious which were a burden to the common-weale, are drawen forth, whereby the matter of sedition is remooved out of the Cittie; and for this cause it is said, that Pericles sent into the country of Cherronesus, a thousand free men of his Cittie there to dwell, and to devide the landes amongst them; five hundreth also into the Ile of Naxus, into the Ile of Andros others, some he sent to inhabite Thracia, and others to dwell with the Bisaltes;[18] as well thereby to ridde the Cittie of a number of idle persons, who through idlenes began to be curious and to desire a change of thinges, as also to provide for the necessity of the poore towns-men that had nothing, which being naturall Citizens of Athens served as garrisons, to keepe under those which had a desire to rebell, or to attempt any alteration or change: secondly by translating of colonies, the people conquered are drawen and intised by little and little, to embrace the manners, lawes, and governement of the conquerour: lastly the colonies being placed and dispersed abroade amongest the people, like Beacons[19] doe foretell and disclose all conspiracies. . . . lastly, they yeelde a yearely rent, profite, or service unto the crowne for ever.

2) Thomas Blenerhasset (1550?–1625?)

Blenerhasset was another soldier-writer, who spent much of his time stationed on Guernsey where he wrote his contributions to the expansion of *The Mirror for Magistrates* (1577),[20] dealing with the Matter of Britain. In the early seventeenth century he was stationed in Ireland where he wrote his important pamphlet, *A Direction for the Planting of Ulster* (1610) when he became an undertaker for the plantation. Blenerhasset received 2000 acres in Fermanagh in 1611 and in 1612 petitioned, with others, for more land in Sligo, planning to settle colonists there. In 1624 he was noted as the owner of yet more estates in Fermanagh.

The pamphlet was dedicated to Prince Henry, a keen promoter

of colonies,[21] and describes the plantation as a 'New Troy', which links the Irish project to the British legends.[22] Blenerhasset envisages the new colony as a self-sufficient enterprise surviving without Irish help and he frequently stresses the need to root out the 'wood-kern' systematically, making him a colonial propagandist in the 'purest', etymological sense (see Introduction, p. 12). As with so much material of this type, it is almost impossible to gauge its influence and effect.

From *A direction for the Plantation of Ulster* (1610):[23]

For these undertakers to plant themselves so in this time of quiet, I doe verilie beleeve it would be to small availe, and not the best way to secure themselves with their goods, and that wilde country to the Crowne of England; for although there be no apparent enemy, nor any visible maine force, yet the wood-kerne and many other (who now have put on the smiling countenance of contentment) doe threaten every houre, if opportunitie of time and place doth serve, to burne and steale whatsoever: and besides them there be two, the chief supporters of al their insolencie, the inaccessable woods, & the not passible bogs: which to subject to our desires is not easie, and that not performed, it is not possible to make a profitable improvement, no not by any meanes in any place.

Moreover the frowning countenance of chance and change, (for nothing so certaine as that all thinges are moste uncertaine[24] doth also incite a provident undertaker to lay such a foundation, as it should be rather a violent storme than a fret of foule weather that should annoy him. A scattered plantation will never effect his desire: what can the countenance of a Castle or Bawne with a fewe followers doe? even as they at this present doe: which is nothing to any purpose.

What shall we then say? or to what course shall we betake ourselves? surely by building of a wel fortified Towne, to be able at any time at an houres warning with five hundred men well armed, to encounter all occasions: neither will that be sufficient, except that be seconded with such another, and that also (if it may be, as easily it may) with a third: so there will be helpe on every side, to defend, & offend: for as in England, if a privy watch be set, many malefactors are apprehended, even amongst their cuppes: so there when the spaces in the Woods be cut out, and the bogges be made somewhat passible, then these new erected townes intending a reformation, must ten times at the first set a universall great hunt, that a suddaine search may be made in all suspitious places, for the

Woolfe and the Wood-Kerne, which being secretly and wisely appointed by the governors, they with the helpe of some Irish, well acquainted with the holes and holdes of those offenders, the generalitie shall search every particular place.

[. . .]

Throughout all Ireland where there be Fortes and garrisons in paye, if all those places were planted with this kinde of undertaking, & the old worthy Soldiers, who in those places have garrisons in pay, with every one of their Soldiers, if they were rewarded with the fee simple thereof, to them & to their heires, paying after one life yearely unto his Majestie a fee farme, as the other undertakers doe:[25] but these Captaines and Soldiers would have their pay continued, otherwise they shall not be able to procede with the charge of planting, and then other lands there next adjoining laide also to such places, that many might joine with them to erect corporations: which may be performed now ten times better cheape then it will be hereafter: their security would be much better and the societye farre excell, & so the charge of the garrisons might be withdrawne, the olde worthy warriour who hath gone already through with the brunt of that busines, shall with a good satisfaction be rewarded, and all Ulster a whole hundred times better secured unto the Crowne of England: for the generation of the Irish, (who doe at this time encrease ten to one more then the English, nay I might say twenty) will never otherwise be sufficiently brideled.

[. . .]

The Conclusion, contayning an exhortation to England.

Fayre England, thy flourishing sister, brave Hibernia, (with most respective terms) commendeth unto thy due consideration her youngest daughter, depopulated Ulster: not doubting (for it cannot but come into thy understanding) how the long continuance of lamentable warres, have raced & utterly defaced, whatsoever was beautiful in her to behold, and hath so bereaved all her royalties, goodly ornaments, & well beseeming tyers, as there remaineth but onely the Majesty of her naked personage, which even in that plite is such, as whosoever shall seeke and search all Europe's best Bowers, shal not finde many that may make with her comparison. Behold the admirable worth of her worthiness! even now shee gives to the world to understand by testimoniall knowne sufficiently to all that knowe her, that if thou wilt now but assist her with meanes to erect her ruynes, she will nourish thee with much dainty provision, and so furnish thee, as thou shalt not neede to send to thy neighbour-kingdomes for corne, nor to the Netherlands for fine Holland:[26] shee will in requitall of thy kindnesse provide those thinges, with some other, such as thy heart most desireth. Art thou overcharged with much people? Ulster her excellency will imbrace that thy overplus in her amourous sweete armes: she will place them as it were Euphrates, and feed them with better Ambrosia then ever Jupiter himselfe knew.

10. THE REBELLION OF 1641

The facts surrounding the rebellion have been a matter of dispute from the event until to the present day.[1] The main question concerns the authenticity of the 'Depositions', the testimonies of the Protestant survivors of the 'massacre'.[2] Some, like A.T.Q. Stewart, argue that there can be no smoke without fire,[3] whereas other historians are less sanguine.[4] The rebellion started on 22 October in Ulster, led by the Catholic gentry with the plan to put pressure on the Dublin administration to scotch the threat to their land titles,[5] but had soon developed into a religious war fought by an unstable alliance of Old English and Old Irish which spread throughout Ireland, with Kilkenny becoming a centre of military organisation.[6] What cannot be doubted is the traumatic effect of the writings that came to represent the rebellion; in the words of one historian, 'they resemble a pornography of violence'.[7] Probably the two most influential works were Bishop Henry Jones's *Remonstrance* (March, 1642) and Sir John Temple's *History of the Irish Rebellion* (1646),[8] which provided a catalogue of the horrors supposedly perpetrated by the Catholics. However, 'atrocity literature' was by no means in short supply as the first two texts reproduced here indicate. An implication as to how influential the uprising was in forming attitudes is found in the post hoc rationalisations of the course of events: 'It had been no hard matter to have been a prophet and, standing upon the top of Holyhead, to have foreseen those black clouds, engendering in the Irish air, which broke out after wards into such fearful tempests of blood', asserted one author in 1643.[9] The voices of those like Sir James Ware, who saw an end to strife in the 1630s (see Introduction, p. 12) were silenced[10] and, as Patricia Coughlan has noted, 'Throughout the 1640s, any mention of the Irish seems to require an epithet such as "bloody", "cruel" or "inhuman" to be communicatively effective'.[11]

1) Thomas Morley

From *A Remonstrance . . . Being the Examinations of many who were eye-witnesses of the same, and justified upon oath by many thousands* (London, 1643):[12]

In the County of Monaghan M. Blany a Justice of the peace and Knight of the shire, and Committee for the Subsidies, hanged up, stript and buried in a ditch by the rebels (in The County of Monaghan), because he would not turne and goe to masse; and the next night one Luke Ward hang'd and throwne into a ditch; and they and divers others were robbed, and the rest kept in prison, without reliefe from them that robd them.

[. . .]

A man who had severall young children borne and alive, and his wife neere her time of delivery of another, was most cruelly murthered by the rebels, his wife, flying into the mountaines, the rebels, hastily pursued her and her little children, and found her newly delivered of her child there; they pittying no such, nor any distresse, presently murthered her and her other children which runne with her thither, and in most inhumane and barbarous manner suffered their dogs to eate up and devoure the new borne child.

[. . .]

The rebels would send their children abroad in great troopes, especially neere kindred, armed with long wattles and whips, who would therewith beate mens privy members until they beat or rather threshed them off, and then they would returne in great joy to their parents, who received them for such service, as it were in triumph.

If any women were found dead, lying with their faces downward, they would turne them upon their backes, and in great flockes resort unto them, censuring all the parts of their bodies, but especially such as are not to be named; which afterwards they abused so many waies and so filthily, as chaste cares would not endure the very naming thereof.

[. . .]

The rebels themselves confessed and told it to Dr. Maxwell while he was prisoner among them, that they killed 954 in one morning in the County of Antrim; and that besides them they supposed they had kild 1100 or 1200 more in that County.

[. . .]

Reference being had to the number in grosse which the Rebels themselves have upon enquiry found out and acknowledged, which notwithstanding will come farre short of all those that have been murthered in Ireland, there being above one hundred fifty four thousand wanting of British within the very precincts of Ulster in March 1641 as by their monethly bills brought in and made by their Priests by speciall direction appeareth.

It is proved by divers witnesses that after the drowning of many Protestants at Portadowne, strange visions and apparitions have been seen and heard there upon the water; sometimes a spirit assuming the shape of a man hath been seen there with his hands held up and closed together; and sometimes in the likenesse of a woman, appearing waste high above the water, with haire disheveled, eyes twinkled, elevated and clasped hands, crying out, revenge, revenge, &c. and appearing, and crying so many nights together. Other visions and strange voices, and fearful scritchings have been heard where they have drowned the English at other places, as at Beltubat river in the County of Cavan; a lough near Loghgall in the County of Armagh, which have also deterred and affrighted the Irish soldiers and others, that they durst not stay neere the place, but fled away.

In the Countie of Armagh, it was ordinary and common for the rebels to expose the murthered bodies of the British so long unto publique view and censure, that they began to stinke and infect the ayre, (which being a thing very strange) would not sometimes happen untill foure or five weekes after the murther committed. Then at length they would permit some of their bodies to be recovered and cast into ditches, but so as they must be laid with their faces downward. The reason they gave for the same was, that they so placed them to the intent they might have a prospect and sight of Hell onely. And therefore when they kild any of the Protestants they used alwaies these words, Aurius Dewll, which is, thy sole to the divell.

[. . .]

They tooke [a] Scotchman[13] and ripped up his belly, that they might come to his small guts. The one end whereof they tied to a Tree and made him go round untill he had drawne them all out of his body. Then they saying, they would try whether a dog, or a Scotchman's guts were longer.

[. . .]

In the County of Cavan, James O'Rely, Hugh Brady, and other rebels often tooke the Protestant Bibles and wetting them in puddle water, did five or six severell times dash the same in the faces of the Protestants, saying, come I know you love a good lesson, here is a most excellent one for you, and come tomorrow and you shall have as good a Sermon. And as the Protestants were going to the Church the rebels tooke and dragged them into the Church by the haire of the head; where they whipt, rob'd, stript, and most cruelly used them, saying, that tomorrow you shall heare the like sermon.

That Rory MacGuire, Sir Phelim O'Neale, and the Northern Rebells in the Counties of Monaghan, Armagh, Lowth, Cavan, Meath and other places where they came, burnt, tore, or otherwise trampled under their feete, and spoyled all the Protestants Bibles, and other good Bookes of the Protestants.

[. . .]

The Generall cruelty to Ministers against Protestants and that religion duly exercised by the Papist-rebells scornfull malicious and contemptuous words and blasphemies, are so many and frequently used, and by too wofull experience found and proved by a multitude of witnesses.

2) Anon., *A True and Credible Relation* (London, 1642):[14]

Their Cruell and Damnable Design was first to have surprised the Castle of Dublin upon the 23. day of October Anno predicto, upon a Saturday; the same night all the Popish houses were to be marked with a Crosse to be knowne from the Protestant houses, their intent being upon the Sunday following to have surprised all the protestants and to have stript them naked, as they did many thousands of men, women and children in other parts of the kingdome of Irelande upon the same day, and also to have surprised all the English shipping, riding at Anchor at a Harbour commonly called the Rings End, about a mile distant from the City of Dublin. But God that saw that bloudy intent discovered their practice by one of their owne faction suffering them to run in their owne wicked hope and cruell imagination, untill the night before their practise should have been put in execution, for the same night the Lord Mack-Gueere an Irish man, and Captaine Mack-Mahowne also an Irish man (who confessed the whole plot) were apprehended, the one in Cookstreet within the City of Dublin, the other neere Dublin in Saint Mary Abbey in the suburbes of the same City, both which have been ever since imprisoned in the Castle of Dublin, and doe still remaine there.

[. . .]

It is too manifest thet the Jesuits those firebrands of hell, and Popish priests were the plotters of this and other Treasons, which can at their pleasure absolve subjects of their obedience to their princes and give power to murther and depose kings, neither could they worke upon a more rebellious and forward nation to doe mischiefe.

[. . .]

It is too well knowne (the more is the pittie and to be lamented) that they have murthered, and starved to death of the English in the province of Ulster and other provinces where they are risen up in (re)bellion of men, women and children alone 20,000.

Their manner is and hath beene, cowardly and treacherously to surprise them upon great advantages, and without respect of persons, to rob them of all they have, but being not content therewith (but as insatiable of bloud) hunting after their pretious lives, stript ladies and gentlewomen, Virgins and Babies, old and young, naked as ever they were borne, from their clothes, turning them into open fields, (where having first destroyed the husbands and the Parents, before their wives and childrens faces) many hundreds have beene founde dead in ditches with cold for want of food and rayment, the Irish having no more compassion of their age or youth, then of Doggs.

As for the protestant Ministers, those they take (which have been many) they use them with such cruelty, as it would make any heart so melt into teares that doth but heare this relation; Their manner is first to hang them up, and then they cut off their heads, after they quarter them, then they dismember their secret parts, stopping their mouths therewith, a thing indeed for modestie sake, more fit to bee omitted then related.

Many of their wives, they have ravished in their sights before the multitude, stripping them naked to the view of their wicked Companions, taunting and mocking them with reproachful words, sending them away in such a shamefull or rather shamelesse manner that they have (most of them) either dyed for griefe, or starved with want and cold, such cruelty was never knowne before.

[. . .]

As for the murder of Rebels, it is not certainly knowne; but without question there is a great many of them, but not the third part of them armed, and those armes they have, they have taken from the English, in surprising and murthering them cowardly and treacherously, and some of them under pretence of being rob'd by the Rebells, have deceiptfully gotten Armes to goe fight against them, and then have run away from their Captaines to the Rebells, and indeed there is no trust nor confidence to be put in them, they are so treacherously perfidious.

It is supposed that the chiefe Rebells doe intend to steale away by Sea (having gotten a great estate from the English Plantators whom they have robbed and murthered) and so leave the ignorant rabble of Irish in the lurch.

[. . .]

It is to be beleeved that the Rebells will never give a Battell, and that in short time they will be starved for want of food, for they have gotten in most parts from the English all they can get, and they wast and devoure that plenty they have, and there is neither plowing nor sowing in those parts, so that it will be impossible for them to subsist long.

[. . .]

They report and allege that Religion is the cause of their war, but that is false for they have had too much liberty and freedome of conscience in Ireland, and that hath made them Rebell. I hope that God that hath discovered their bloudy practice, will confound their devices, and bring them to confusion. To the which God be all honour, praise and Glory for ever.

3) Richard Boyle, first Earl of Cork (1566–1643)

Feeling unable to gain an adequate income in England, Boyle landed almost penniless in Ireland in June, 1588, and soon amassed a huge fortune through his first marriage and dealing in lands after he had found an entrance into high places. This initial prosperity was swept away when the Nine Years War reached Munster in the late 1590s and he returned to England. He settled in Ireland once more, having been offered a post in the patent office by Essex. Although his activities were often under suspicion and attracted official hostility, culminating in his notorious feud with Wentworth,[15] Boyle built up another massive fortune in Munster, through the establishment of iron-works and (more importantly), the systematic acquisition of lands, many of which came from the Catholics he persecuted so zealously that the government publicly commended him. He became Lord High Treasurer in 1631. The sudden outbreak of rebellion in 1641 saw the Earl better prepared than many and he helped organise defences with much success; as a respected elder statesman he submitted a report to the Irish parliament on the crisis. Interestingly enough Cork still found time and energy, at his advanced age and in a time of such dire emergency, to worry about the unifying theme of his life; money.[16]

Richard Boyle to the Speaker of the House of Commons, 1642:[17]

Sir, I pray ['let' erased] give me leave to present unto your selfe and that honourable house, that this great and generall rebellion brake forth in October last, at the very instant when I landed here out of England; and though it appeared first in Ulster, yet I who am 76 yeares of age, and have eate most parte of my bread in Ireland these 54 yeares, and by reason of my severall employments and commands in the government of this province and kingdome could not [but suspect] that the infection and contagion was generall and would by degrees quickly creep into this province, as forthwith it did. And soe that I found to my great griefe that by the course the late Earle of Strafford had taken, all or the greatest part of the English and Protestants in this province, were deprived ['debarred' erased] of their Armes, and debarred from having any powder in their houses, and the King's Magazines in ['this province' erased] heer, being soe ['very' erased] weakely furnished as in a manner they were empty. I without delay furnished all my Castles in these two Counties with such Ammunition as my owne poore Armory did afford, and sent 300li. ster. into England to bee bestowed in Ammunition for my selfe and [my] tenants, and putt in sufficient guards, and 9 monethes victualls into every of my ['victuall' erased] Castles; all which I thanke God, I have hitherto preserved and made good, not without giving great annoyance out of those Castles to the rebels. And for that the late Lord President did judiciously observe that the preservation of this importart Towne and harbour of Yoghall, was of principall consequence to bee maintayned and kept for the service of the Crowne, and presuming that noe man did exceed me in power and abilitie to make it good, hee prevayled [with mee] soe farre, for the advancement of his Majestie service and securing of this considerable towne and harbour, as to leave my owne strong and defensible house of Lismore (which was well provided of Ordnance and all things fitting for defence) to the guard of my sonn Broghill with 100 horse and 100 foot, and to retyre hither; whither I brought two foot Companies of 100 a peece, all compounded of English Protestants and well disciplined, and these at my chardges armed, being men experienced and formerly seasoned with the ayre of this Countrey, wherein they are good guides. And hitherto I doe thanke my God, this Towne and harbour, are made good and is a receptacle not onely for all shipping but also for multitudes of distressed English, which have been ['stript' erased] dispossessed and stript by the rebells, and found succour and saftie heere.

11. THE TRANSPLANTATION TO CONNAUGHT: 1655–9

Recent historians have argued that the advent of Cromwellian Ireland did not signal a break with the past as was once thought, but a continuity dictated by forces of circumstance and lack of real interest.[1] Although some zealots like John Cook might have used the traditional image of Ireland as a blank 'white paper' on which to write new legislation and draw up a new society,[2] policies were often employed for more pragmatic reasons. Transplantation itself was not a radical theoretical departure, but a commonplace of colonial theory,[3] although nothing on this scale had been attempted before. As Karl Bottigheimer has pointed out, it was probably the result of fiscal considerations as much as anything else, with the English government needing to pay off and settle the army, having fought in Ireland using the promise of land as security for loans to prosecute the war.[4] - hence the acts of 1652–3 alleging Irish responsibility for the war and the deliberate circulation of the gory details of Bishop Jones's depositions to stifle moderate opinion and justify confiscation.[5] These guilty Irish[6] were then deprived of their lands and apportioned new ones in Clare and Connacht, enclosed between the Shannon and the Atlantic. The area was chosen for its remoteness from the English settlers to ensure their safety (Ulster was still considered to be the poorest province in the 1650s). Exactly who went and who came from England to replace them is still a matter for conjecture and enquiry is hampered by the incomplete state of the extant data.[7] Wholesale transplantation did not occur. It would have been impossible to organise and English yeomen were notably unwilling to take over from Irish peasants. It can be conjectured that the Irish who did go West were mainly 'uninfluential landowners'.[8] The nature of the settlers who replaced them is also hard to gauge, as so many adventurers and soldiers sold their land; but, again, what changes did take place seem to have involved mainly the upper classes, as it was the large-scale entrepreneurs who were the principal beneficiaries of the policy, buying up vast blocks of land and becoming a significant social phenomenon as Restoration landlords.[9]

The debate between Gookin and Lawrence, the most well-known concerning transplantation, is rich and complex, and, in many ways, illustrates the vague form the plan took and the confusing mode of its authorisation. But the fundamental matter which divides the two disputants is the question of the nature of the Irish, which takes us back to the very heart of the problem the Tudors faced. Who were the Irish? Could they be 'reformed'? It might not be too far-fetched to see Gookin and Lawrence playing out a dialogue like Spenser's *View*, with Gookin as Eudoxus (good-doctrine?) and Lawrence as Irenius (the man who knows Ireland? the angry one? he whose council leads to peace?)

1) Vincent Gookin (1616?–1659).

Gookin's father had been a tenant of Richard Boyle's and had risen, like his landlord, to be one of the wealthiest men in Ireland, before fleeing to England after a vicious outburst against the native Irish had threatened him with imprisonment. Gookin soon sold his father's English property and returned, to remain in Ireland until his death. He was a firm believer in the benefits of English colonisation for Ireland and saw the projected transplantation as a betrayal of its [colonisation's] virtue of spreading civility. He was also a staunch republican and supporter of Henry Cromwell, often defending the latter against criticism.[10] He was M.P for Kinsale and Bandon and worked with Sir William Petty in establishing the details of land distribution as payment for the adventurers and soldiers, but is remembered mainly for his dispute with Lawrence and the resulting tracts.[11]

From *The Great Case of Transplantation Discussed* (1655):[12]

For future Inhabitants, Adventurers, Souldiers, and such others as shall engage in the planting of Ireland. The first and chiefest Necessaries to the settlement and advancement of a Plantation, are those natural riches of Food, Apparel, and Habitations. If the first be regarded, there are few of the Irish Commonality but are skilfull in Husbandry, and more exact than any English in the Husbandry proper to that Country. If the second, there are few of the Women but are skilfull in dressing Hemp and Flax, and making of Linnen and Woollen Cloth. If the third, it is believed, to every hundred Men there are five or six Masons and Carpenters at least of that Nation, and these more handy and ready in building ordinary Houses, and much more prudent in supplying the defects of

Instruments and Materials, than English Artificers. Since then 1000 Acres of Land (Plantation measure) being but of indifferent goodnes, with the rest of the Lands in Ireland, shall require as much Stock as whose original price and charge of transporting will amount to 1500 or 2000l. Since likewise Husbandmen and Tradesmen that are laborious, can subsist by their Labours and Trades comfortably in England, and most will not probably leave their native soyl on any terms; and those who will, on extraordinary terms. It is necessarily consequent, that the transplantation of the Irish doth not onely deprive the Planter of those aforementioned advantages, but also so exceedingly aggravates his charge and difficulty in planting (by his irredeemable want of whatever he brings not with him out of England) that his charge will manifestly appear to be more than his profit; and it is not easily conceivable how or when five or six Millions of Acres are like to be planted or inhabited upon so clear an account of expence and loss.

Objection. Against all these advantages it is onely objected, that the English may degenerate, and turn Irish, unless a separation by transplanting the one from the other be observed; and to this purpose experience of former ages is urged.

Answer. Of future contingents no man can pass a determinate judgement; but if we speak morally, and as probably may be, it may much rather be expected that the Irish will turn English. Those Topicks before instanced concerning Religion do infer it as very probable, that with the Religion professed by the English, it is likely they may receive their Manners also. And this is confirmed by experience of all that Nation who embraced the Protestant Religion. And as to the former experience, even that likewise seems to add weight to this expectation, because whatever inducements perswaded the English formerly to turn Irish, the same more strongly invite the Irish now to turn English.

1. When England was reformed from Popery, no care was took, nor endeavours used to spread the reformation in Ireland; by which means the English Colonies there continued still Papists, and so in Religion were alienated from the English, and fastened to the Irish: But now it being most probable that most of the Irish will embrace the Protestant Profession, it is upon the same grounds most probable that they will embrace the English Manners.

2. Former Conquests of Ireland were either the undertakings of some private persons, or so managed by publick persons, that the power and profitable advantages of the Land remained in the hands of the Irish: But as in the present Conquest the Nation of England is engaged, so is the power and advantage of the Land in the hands of the English. For instance.

1. The Irish were the Body of the People, and too potent for the English (especially at such times as the troubles of England caused the Armies to be called thence, which Historians observe to have been the times of degeneration,[13] as a means to self-preservation.

2. The Irish were the general Proprietors of Land, and an English Planter must be their Tenant; and the temptation of this relation and dependence is very prevelant (at least) to bring the Posterity to a complyance, and that to a likeness, and that to a sameness.

3. The Irish were the chiefly estated, and the intermarriages with them were accompanied with greater Friends and Fortunes than with the English, who were not onely Strangers, but for the most part (till of late years) comparatively poor.

4. The Lawyers were Irish, the Jurors Irish, most of the Judges Irish, and the major part of their Parliament Irish; and in all Disputes between Irish and English, the Irish were sure of the favour.

But now the condition of Ireland is (through Gods goodness) so altered, that all these Arguments are much more forcibly perswasive, that the Irish will turn English.

3. The frequent use of the Irish Language in all commerce, and the English habituating themselves to that Language, was one great means of Irishying the English Colonies: But now the Language will be generally English; and if the Irish be mingled with the English, they will probably learn and be habituated to the English Tongue, which is found by experience to be suddenly learn'd by the Irish; whereas if they be transplanted into Connaught, the distinction of the English and Irish tongue will not onely be continued, but also the Irish left without means of learning English.

3. Concerning the Security of the English, and their Interests.

1. For the present, This Plantation will necessarily make many Tories.[14] For,

1. Many inhabitants, who are able to subsist on their Gardens in their present Habitations, are unable to subsist in travelling to Connaught, and for the present to derive subsistence from the wast Lands of Connaught, when they come thither; and therefore will rather choose the hazard of Torying, than the apparent danger of starving.

2. Many Irish Masters will disburthen themselves of their attendants and servants on this occasion, in regard the charge of retaining them will be greater, and their imployment of them less, both in the journey, and journeys end; and these servants, however

disposed to honest labour and industry, yet being thus secluded from means of subsistence, necessity will enforce to be Tories.

3. The range of the Tories will be so great, and advantages thereby of securing themselves and Cattel so much, that untill the whole Land be otherwise planted, it will not be probable that our Armies should either have intelligence of their places of abode in their fastnesse, or be enabled to find them, those who are acquainted with the service of Tory hunting, know much of this difficulty. And impossible it is, that those parts of the Land which adjoin to those Fastnesses, should be planted in many ages, if Tories (secured in them) make incursions on such as shall plant.

4. The Irish numbers (now abated by Famin, Pestilence, the Sword, and Forein Transportations) are not like to overgrow the English as formerly, and so no fear of their being obnoxious to them hereafter: but being mixed with, they are likelyer to be swallowed up by the English, and incorporated into them; so that a few Centuries will know no difference present, fear none to come, and scarce believe what were pas'd. The chiefest and eminentest of the Nobility, and many of the Gentry, have taken Conditions from the King of Spain, and have transported at several times 40000 of the most active spirited men, most acquainted with danger and discipline of War, and inured to hardness; the Priests are all banished; the remaining part of the whole Nation are scarce the sixth part of what were at the beginning of the War, so great a devastation has God and Man brought upon that Land, and so far are they from those formidable numbers they are (by those that are strangers to Ireland) conceived to be; and that handfull of Natives left, are poor laborious usefull simple Creatures, whose design is onely to live, and their Families, the manner of which is so low, that it is a design rather to be pitied, than by any body feared, envyed, or hindered.

2) Richard Lawrence (fl. 1643–82)

Lawrence was a successful soldier who accompanied Cromwell to Ireland in 1649. In 1650–1 he became a governor of Waterford and a plan to settle 1200 men in Waterford was approved by Ireton.[15] He was also one of the commissioners who dealt with the Irish at Kilkenny (1652). His first pamphlet, an exposure of the subtlety of the forms the Popish antichrist takes, had been published in 1647 and he felt moved to respond to Gookin's attack on transplantation in 1655. Like his adversary, Lawrence became involved with Petty when he publicly quarrelled with the latter over who had the right to survey forfeited lands and he later had the satisfaction of helping to eject Petty from public employment (1659). He acquired some lands in Dublin, Cork and Kildare and somehow survived the Restoration with them intact despite a proposal to deprive him of them all as one of thirty fanatics opposing the king and defending regicide. After retiring from the army, he became involved in schemes for the improvement of commerce, being a member of the council of trade along with (ironically enough) William Petty. He also wrote an important tract on the subject.[16]

From *The Interest of England in the Irish transplantation Stated* (1655):[17]

Therefore consider what punishment it was they did incur by their offence, which will be the better done, First, by considering the offence it self, which was the most horrid causless Rebellion, and bloudy Massacre that hath been heard of in these last Ages of the world,[18] and the Offenders not particular persons or parties of the Irish Nation (for that had been another case) but the whole Irish Nation it self consisting of Nobility, Gentry, Clergy, and Commonality, are all engaged as one Nation in this Quarell, to root out and wholly extirpate all English Protestants from amongst them, who had (for the most of them) as legal and just right to their Estates and interest in Ireland, as themselves, many of them possessing nothing, but what they had lawfully purchased, and dearly paid for, from the Irish, and others of them possessing by right of grant from the Crown of England, time out of minde what they did enjoy, and the Irish Nation enjoying equal privileges with the English, if not much more . . . so that they were under no provocation, nor oppression, under the English Government at that time when the bloudy Rebells in 1641 committed that inhumane Massacre upon a company of poor, unarmed, peaceable, harmless people living quietly amongst them, wherein neither Age nor Sex were spared. . . in which rebellious practices and cruel War they persisted to the ruining of that flourishing Nation, and making of it near a waste Wilderness, thereby necessitating England (in the time of its own Trouble) to maintain an Army in Ireland, to preserve a footing there, and at last forced them to send over and maintain a potent Army, greatly exhausting their Treasure and People to recover their Interest out of the hands of this bloudy Generation, and bring the Offenders to condign punishment . . . Ireland having cost England more money and men to recover it, than it is or ever is like to be worth to them many a time over, and for England now at the close of all to heal up this wound slightly, and to leave the Interest and People of England in Ireland at as eminent uncertainties as ever, (whereby the posterity of this present Generation (if not themselves) shall after a few years to come to be at the mercy and disposition of this bloudy people again (except a few inwalled Towns and Garisons) if it may be any lawfull and prudent means prevented) I judg those who are wise and ingenious of the Irish themselves would acknowledg it a weakness, and great neglect in those in whose hand God hath placed the power, much more all true hearted Englishmen who are so much concerned therein.

And therefore it remains now to prove that the work of Transplantation (at least so far as it is at present declared and intended) is the most probable means to secure the present English Interest in Ireland, and obtain one there able to secure it self without such immediate dependence upon England (as hitherto hath been) for men and money to effect the same.

And for the better making out of this:

First, confident wherein the advantage of the Irish above the English consisted at the first breaking out of the late horrid Rebellion, whereby the many thousands of English People then inhabiting in that Countrey became so inconsiderable either as to the preservation of their own Lives and Estates, or the publick Interest of England there; which chiefly proceeded from their not being imbodied, or from their not cohabiting together, whereby they might have been in a capacity to imbody, they being scattered up and down the whole Nation, here and there, a few families, being thereby wholly subjected to the mercy of the Rabble Irish, to the general destruction and ruine of them, before the Enemy had either Army, Arms, or Ammunition, more than Skeanes and Stayes, whereas had those English that were then in Ireland been cohabiting together in one entire Plantation, or in several Plantations, so they had been but entire Colonies of themselves, and Masters of the Countrey in which they lived, the Irish would hardly have had confidence to have attempted a War, much less a Massacre upon them . . . Whereas by their promiscuous and scattered inhabiting among the Irish, who were in all places far the greatest number and in most a hundred to one, they were even as sheep prepared for the slaughter, that the very Cripples and Beggars of several of the Countreys where they lived (if they toke against them) were able to destroy them.[19]

[. . .]

And therefore I would propose (as essential to the security of the English interest and People in Ireland) that the England inhabitating in that Nation should live together in distinct Plantations or Colonies, separated from the Irish, and (so far as the natural advantage of the Countrey, or their own ability will afford it) to maintain frontier Garrisons, upon Lines or Passes, for the security of every Plantation, and to admit no more Irish Papists (that they had not eminent grounds to believe were or would be faithful to the English interest) to live within them . . . it is my judgement it would not be safe to admit in any English Plantation, above the fifth part to be Irish Papists, either in the capacity of Tenants or Servants, unless in such cases where two Justices of the Peace, with two godly Ministers of that English Plantation should receive satisfaction of their being converted to the Protestant Religion, and English Civil Manners and Customs.

For though the Lord hath been pleased so far to own the English Cause and Interest in the late War, that they have been able to engage them with far less numbers, that one hath put ten, and ten one hundred to flight, yet in the work of surprisings and unexpected assaults and inroads upon the English, the Irish have been usually more expert and vigilant, for the Irish are naturally a timorous, suspicious, watchfull People; and on the other hand, the English are a confident, credulous, careless People, as our daily experience in Ireland teacheth us. And therefore if their numbers should be near equal, that advantage which they would have of their Irish Neighbours to correspond with them, and fall into their assistance, would much add to their encouragement to attempt mischief upon the English, with or among whom they lived, though they were far less numbers. And if this be not admitted, that it is essential in order to the safety of the English interest and people, that their Plantation should consist of many more English than Irish (as above,) then there is a necessity (in order thereto) that some of the Irish should be removed out of some parts of Ireland, to make way for the English Plantations, and if so, then a Plantation must be admitted to be essential in order to the security of the English interest and People there.

[. . .]

[A]s to that concerning Religion, where he [Gookin] endeavoureth to hold forth that the not transplanting of the Irish, would no ways hazard the perverting of the English, and would be much in order to the converting of the Irish, which the Transplantation (saith he) will wholly prevent . . . I do not judge the Discussor can suppose that the continuing of the popish, superstitious Souldier and Proprietor among and over the common people will be a means to make way for their conversion to the Protestant Religion, more than to continue their Priests, but it is so evident it will much rather tend to the contrary, even shutting that door of hope, that may otherwise be opened to that work, that to spend time about arguing of it would not be to profit, and besides require more Lines than I am willing to swell this paper into, it being much larger already than I intended it.

3) Edmund Ludlow

Ludlow's complex of feelings in the following extract is not without interest, or national significance. He is quite unaware of any latent irony in his words. He laments the plight of the geographical entity of Ireland. This he describes as a 'poor wasted country' brought low by the Irish people's insistence upon living there. He reveals how the new English and Scottish possessors of Ireland, without delay, fell to squabbling over their respective shares, and how they settled the problem: a committee would be instituted to adjudge the legality of claims.

From *The Memoirs of Edmund Ludlow*:[20]

The Commissioners also by order of the Parliament published a declaration to inform the publick, and particularly the adventurers, who had advanced money upon the Irish lands, that the war in Ireland was concluded. This they did as well that the said adventurers might have what was justly due to them, as that the poor wasted country of Ireland might have the assistance of their own purses and labour, to recover the stock and growth of the land; the Irish having all along eaten out the heart and vigour of the ground, and of late much more than ever, being in daily apprehension of being removed.

All arrears due to the English army in Ireland were satisfied by the Parliament out of the estates forfeited by the rebels, which were delivered to them at the same rates with the first adventurers. In this transaction those of the army shewed great partiality, by confining the satisfaction of arrears only to such as were in arms in August 1649, which was the time when the English army commanded by Lieutenant-General Cromwel arrived in Ireland; and tho the hardships endured by those who were in arms before had been much greater, yet nothing could be obtained but such a proportion of lands in the county of Wicklo, and elsewhere, as was not sufficient to clear the fourth part of what was due to them. Those who solicited the affairs of the army in Ireland with the Parliament, having perswaded the adventurers that there were forfeited lands enough in one moiety of nine principle counties, they accepted of them for their satisfaction, and the other moiety was assigned by the Act for the satisfaction of the souldiers; the rest of Ireland was also disposed of, only the province of Connaught was reserved for the Irish under the qualifications agreed upon by the Parliament; according to which they were to be put into possession of the several proportions of land which had been promised them in the said province; that so the adventurers, souldiers, and others to whom the Parliament should assign their lands, might plant without disturbance, or danger of being corrupted by intermixing with the natives in marriages or otherwise, which by the experience of former times the English had been found to be, rather than to have bettered the Irish either in religion or good manners: and that the natives being divided by the River Shannon from the other provinces, and having garisons placed round and amongst them in the most proper and convenient stations, they might not have those opportunities to prejudice the English as formerly they had. An Act being drawn up to this purpose, the parliament passed it, reserving the counties of Dublin, Kildare, Carlo and Cork, (together with the remaining part of the lands formerly belonging to the Bishops, Deans and Chapters of Ireland, whereof some had been already applied, to augment the revenues of the College of Dublin) to be disposed of as the Parliament should think fit.

The forfeited lands were divided between the adventurers and souldiers by lot, according to an estimate taken of the number of acres in the respective counties, in conformity to an order from the Commissioners of Parliament; by whom were appointed sub-commissioners to judg of the qualifications of each person, and others, who upon certificate from the sub-commissioners for determining qualifications, were required to set out so much land in the province of Connaught as belonged to every one by virtue of the said Act. They also established a committee to sit at Dublin to receive and adjudg all claims of English and others to any lands, limiting a time within which they were obliged to bring in and make appear their respective claims to be legal; to the end that the adventurers, souldiers, and others, might be at a certainty, and after such a time free from any molestation in the possession of their lands; and that none through ignorance or absence might be surprized, they prorogued the said time twice or thrice to a longer day.

12. PASSAGE AND TRAVEL

Travelling between mainland Britain and Ireland could be easy, but more often was long drawn out and worrying. At times it proved highly dangerous. Sir William Brereton gives a lively description of his all-night-long journey in 1635, depressing and terrifying by turns, from Scotland to Islandmagee on Ireland's north-east-coast.[1] A parallel experience on the other side of the country was John Stevens's approach to Bantry Bay and then Cork, just before travelling north to fight at the Boyne.[2] In 1748 two English travellers record being caught by a Spanish privateer near Kinsale.[3] Arthur Young's first journey in 1776 lasted 22 'tedious' hours from Holyhead to 'Dunlary'.[4] De Quincey in 1800 describes a woman bringing her carriage on deck and shielding herself from the discomfort of the elements and the notice of the other passengers by making the journey tucked inside it.[5] Before steam transport helped to regularise contact between the two countries this unpredictable, uncomfortable journeying must have been the norm.

There is a literary significance in the fact. If English travellers, venturing into Scotland or Wales, found the new landscape they were travelling through varied from the one they had left at home, it was also a natural extension of it; the same travellers, venturing into Ireland, found no such affinity. Ireland consistently impressed visitors by its foreign quality. Their mode of arrival had an effect on this new apprehension; since, to see Ireland, travellers first had to lose sight of their starting place, their first anxiety was drawn from their loss of contact with the solid land of their own country. Add to this unease a bad or an uncertain journey, and the mess of disembarkation, and one sees how the anxiety might deepen into resentment at Ireland. As some of the following extracts show, visitors' nerves were not always in the best condition when they set foot on Irish soil. The anonymous author of an 1836 tour formed a distinctly unfriendly first impression of Ireland, arriving at shabby Cork after an uncomfortable crossing, and his sense of let-down must have been often shared.[6] Thackeray's first note is a jaundiced one.[7] Of the various routes, Holyhead to Dublin became the chief one. Ways of writing about it became conventionalised. A typical description of the impact Dublin made on the incoming traveller is Sir John Carr's remark in 1806 that Dublin bay wants only a volcanic mountain at one side to equal the Bay of Naples.[8] Carr was behind the times. His analogy was such a tired one by 1800 that travellers were making a point of challenging it.

Travel around Ireland's perimeter could also mean trusting to the sea. Arthur Young saw the Giant's Causeway in this fashion, and Richard Pococke before him had also approached the Causeway and inspected its details in a rowing boat, writing these up for insertion in the *Philosophical Transactions.*[9] Pococke also visited a number of Ireland's western and south-western islands by embarking on sizeable expeditions from the mainland. Anne Plumptre describes a frightening experience sailing to Rathlin Island. Inland, horse transport and, less commonly, horse-drawn carriages provided the only means of getting around. Travellers have some praise for Ireland's roads, but they were put to their shifts in places. Pococke describes the elaborate techniques used to enable horses to proceed through boggy ground.[10] Inns were few and poor, so that most travellers sought to stage themselves from mansion to mansion among the network of the Anglo-Irish ruling class establishment.

1) Richard Pococke

Richard Pococke (1704–65) combined an Irish clerical career with obsessive travel. He was born in Southampton and after graduating from Oxford became successively precentor of Lismore cathedral (1720) and of Waterford (1744), archdeacon of Dublin (1745), bishop of Ossory (1756), bishop of Elphin (1765) and bishop of Meath (1765). Meanwhile he had toured extensively through Europe and the Middle East as well as England, Scotland and Ireland. Pococke showed little respect for 'accepted' routes. His Egyptian travel was more an exploratory expedition than anything else. In Europe too he made a point of striking out into unattempted regions, as when he led a party into the Vale of Chamounix; a renowned tourist's area for Shelley and Byron, this was virtually unknown in Pococke's time.[11] In Ireland Pococke showed a similar desire to get off the beaten track. The following extract describes one of his rowing-boat ventures in the south west to observe life on the offshore islands.

From a tour of 1758:[12]

Dear Madam Cape Clear July 24th 1758

On the 24th I set out in a row boat, went down the river & passing by the Island of Inibeg & Donegal, we came in a league opposite to Baltimore, where are remains of an Old Castle, & only a few Cabins the Fort having been burnt by the Algerines in 1631. It is a corporation & sends Members to Parliament & there is a church a little to the north of the Castle. We went a mile further to the Island of Iniskertain which is in the parish of Baltimore, & defends the harbour against the Southwest winds. There was formerly a Barrack with 19 guns & a Fort with 17 guns. The Island is about two miles long & ½ a mile broad containing 9½ ploughlands & about 100 families eight of which are Protestants with Captn Becher the proprietor of the Island at the head of them, who lives here. We went ashore to see what they called the Abbey, which was a Friory of Minorites of observance, founded by Florence O'Driscol in 1460. The Church is a good building, with a Tower rais'd on an Arch & there are large pillars in a south Isle. There is a greenish freestone in this Island & Cape Clear as well as about Crookhaven: They are all fishermen both in this Island & Cape Clear; & they have on the coast places for curing fish, commonly call'd fish palaces, & come to these parts from Cork & Kingsale, & especially about Crookhaven, which abounds in fish, & make up little huts in which they live during the summer; & in time of peace the French came over here to fish: When the Pilchards came great fortunes were made by them: now they get chiefly mackrel during the month of July & August Herrings also come in at that time, they catch likewise Hake, Ling & Cod, all which they salt, & barrel up the Mackrels & Herrings. The mackrels sell well, as they give only half a mackrel to the Negroes, which they call a fish with one eye. In Crookhaven they are out in the evening, & as soon as they see the scholes by the motion in the water they draw their Sein nets across & enclose 'em, they take also, Breme, Turbot, Plaice, & John Dory: & in the season the people live on fish. they have great plenty of Salmon, but it does not sell under a peny a pd., Lobsters, Crayfish & Crabs sell for pence apiece & are very good. Wild fowl are sold by the couple, — Plover 2d. Partridge 3d. Teal 4d. Duck 8d. They have small black cattle, which at 3 years old sell for 10s., & when fat weigh about 300. We went to Cape Clear, the most Southern Island & the Old Head of Kingsale is reckon'd the most Southern land; it is about half a league to the South of Iniskerham, is 3 miles long & a mile & half broad. We went into the North Cove, — on this bay is a stone on which two crosses are cut, as its s[d]. by S[t]. Kiaran & in another part of the Island are two Stones near one another about 8 feet high, & half way up a hole cut in the middle of each of them, probably for fixing a stone cross in order it may be to form a Greek Cross. they keep S[t]. Kiaran's & S[t]. Clara's days as their Patrons the original of the name being the Isle of S[t]. Clara. The great vice here is drinking Spirits, which they do excessively even some of them, they say, to a gallon a day. over which is a ruin'd Church dedicated to S[t]. Kiaran, Founder of the Sea of Ossory; who according to Archbp Usher was born in this Island, & a little beyond it is an old Castle on a rock, which is a Peninsula with a narrow passage to it. The Island consists of twelve plough lands, & there are about 200 families in it, all Romans. It is a parish which commonly goes with Affadown. They were alarm'd at seing our boats, thinking it was the Kings, as they had laid in great Store of Rum from the West India fleet which had lately pass'd. They were glad to be undeceiv'd, tho when the officers not long ago made a seizure, the women rescued it. They brought in a bottle of rum by way of civility & dealt it round, & we return'd this civility by a piece of mony. They have here very fine flags. There is a lake in this Island, with a particular kind of soft worm in it which 'tis supposed cleanses all vessels put into it of whatever filth they have contracted. The water is very soft, occasioned probably by the softness of the soil from the sea spray. I am &c.

2) Arthur Young

Arthur Young (1741–1820) was the son of the rector of Bradfield in Suffolk. He left school at seventeen and went into apprenticeship but plans for a mercantile career came to nothing. In 1763 he began farming, married Martha Allan of Lynn in 1765, and published *The Farmer's Letters to the People of England* in 1767. This was followed by his numerous tours through the agricultural regions of England — the southern counties in 1768, the north in 1770, the eastern counties in 1771. Young also toured France in 1769. He visited Ireland in 1776 and spent two years as Lord Kingsborough's agent in County Cork. His *Tour in Ireland* appeared in 1780. Young returned to France in 1787, and in later years, and spent the remainder of his life publishing on politics, economics and agriculture. The Irish tour lacks some of the gossipy detail of Young's other tours, much of his notes having been lost at sea.

Young praises Irish roads, considering them superior to those in England, and, a follower of Adam Smith,[13] offers the typical explanation that enlightened self-interest has been the governing principle behind their construction.

From *A Tour in Ireland* (1780):[14]

The following is the system on which the cross ones are made. Any person wishing to make or mend a road, has it measured by two persons, who swear to the measurement before a justice of the peace. It is described as leading from one market town to another (it matters not in what direction)[,] that it will be a public good, and that it will require such a sum, per perch, of twenty-one feet, to make or repair the same; a certificate to this purpose (of which printed forms are sold) with the blanks filled up, is signed by the measurers, and also by two persons called overseers, one of whom is usually the person applying for the road, the other the labourer he intends to employ as an overseer of the work, who swears also before the justice the truth of the valuation. The certificate, thus prepared, is given by any person to some one of the grand jury, at either of the assizes, but usually in the spring. When all the common business of trials is over, the jury meets on that of roads; the chairman reads the certificates, and they are all put to the vote, whether to be granted or not. If rejected they are torn in pieces and no farther notice taken, if granted they are put on the file.

This vote of approbation, without any farther form, enables the person, who applied for the presentment, immediately to construct or repair the road in question, which he must do at his own expence, he must finish it by the following assizes, when he is to send a certificate of his having expended the money pursuant to the application; this certificate is signed by the foreman, who also signs an order on the treasurer of the county to pay him, which is done immediately. In like manner are bridges, houses of correction, gaols, &c. built and repaired. If a bridge over a river, which parts two counties, half is done by one, and the other half by the other county.

[. . .]

Any persons are eligible for asking presentments; but it is usually done only by resident gentlemen, agents, clergy, or respectable tenantry. It follows necessarily, that every person is desirous of making the roads leading to his own house, and that private interest alone is considered in it, which I have heard objected to the measure; but this I must own appears to me the great merit of it.

Whenever individuals act for the public alone, the public is very badly served; but when the pursuit of their own interest is the way to benefit the public, then is the public good sure to be promoted; such is the case of presentment roads; for a few years the good roads were all found leading from houses like rays from a center, with a surrounding space, without any communication; but every year brought the remedy, until in a short time, those rays, pointing from so many centers, met, and then the communication was complete. The original act passed but seventeen years ago, and the effect of it in all parts of the kingdom is so great, that I found it perfectly practicable to travel upon wheels by a map; I will go here, I will go there; I could trace a route upon paper as wild as fancy could dictate, and every where I found beautiful roads without break or hindrance, to enable me to realize my design. What a figure would a person make in England, who should attempt to move in that manner, where the roads, as Dr. Burn has very well observed, are almost in as bad a state as in the time of Philip and Mary. In a few years there will not be a bad road, except turnpikes, in all Ireland. The money raised for this first and most important of all national purposes, is expended among the people who pay it, employs themselves and their teams, encourages their agriculture, and facilitates so greatly the improvement of waste lands, that it ought always to be considered as the first step to any undertaking of that sort.

3) Anne Plumptre

Anne Plumptre (1760–1818), the daughter of Anne Newcome and Dr Robert Plumptre, the president of Queen's College, Cambridge, is best known as a writer for her English translations of the plays of the German dramatist Kotzebue. Her *Pizarro* attained some notice in 1799, rivalling Sheridan's play of the same name. But she was also a confirmed traveller and travel writer. She lived in France between 1802 and 1805 and published a narrative of her residence there in 1810. Her Irish journey of 1814–15 had an inauspicious start. It took her 24 hours to get from Liverpool to Holyhead. Although by dawn the day after her departure she saw the Hill of Howth, it was not till six in the evening that she could step ashore: a total of 57 hours of travel. Her description of Ireland is loquacious and full, but informative.

From *Narrative of a Residence in Ireland* (1817):[15]

The next day, as I was told by the fishermen (the only mariners of the place) that the weather was remarkably favourable for sailing round the Head and to the island of Rathlin, I engaged a boat and set out on my voyage. Though very desirous of visiting this island, and very glad when I was safe back again that I had been there, yet I believe if I had previously had any idea of the sea I was to navigate, I should entirely have relinquished the idea of venturing upon it. Round the Head the swell of the sea was very powerful, sufficient to give me a sensation of fear, to which I am not subject upon the water; but once round, all was calm again, and the rocks form a most sublime spectacle indeed; a boat can go almost close to their foot. We landed on the other side of the promontory, and walked about for near an hour till the tide would serve for going to the island. If I thought the swell round the Head extraordinary and awful, how much more tremendous appeared the monstrous waves by which we were now surrounded for the greater part of the voyage. I was disposed to be very angry with the boatmen for having, as indeed I thought they had, deceived me in the state of the weather, and enticed me out when the sea was so violently agitated. They assured me that what I saw was nothing, that they considered the sea as very quiet, and begged me to notice that there really was no wind, scarcely sufficient to fill the sails. So far was certainly true, the breeze was as light as possible, but the sea notwithstanding rolled in mountains: — of such a swell without wind I could not have formed an idea if I had not seen it. To add to the misery of the thing, we were obliged to tack repeatedly in order to make the island, so that we were thus tossed about for a most tedious length of time. Indeed, I began to think that instead of being off the coast of Ireland I was off that of Sicily, and had fallen into the vortex of Charybdis. To the fishermen who are accustomed to this sea its present state was mere play, and they seemed astonished that any body could be alarmed; but I, who now saw it for the first time, could almost say that what was play to them was death to me. I do not know that I ever felt so alarmed upon the water, inadequate as our frail bark appeared to stemming such a mighty force: but we did stem it, and I am alive to recount my fears. It should seem that the true cause of this extraordinary effect is yet among the hidden secrets of the deep, for no attempt hitherto made to explain it is by any means satisfactory. To ascribe it to the narrowness of the channel is far from being so, since that is eight miles over, and no such effect is seen in many a channel not approaching to that breadth. A great conformity is said to exist between this sea and the straits of Reggio which divide Sicily from Italy.

4) Thomas Carlyle

Carlyle's connections with Ireland were complex. On his 1846 and 1849 visits he found the country's miserable condition disgusting. He was also shocked by the people, and despised their supersitious adherence (as he judged it) to the Catholic religion. As with the slave population of the West Indies, Ireland's beaten state turned Carlyle hostile rather than sympathetic.[16] But he insisted on England's responsibility for Ireland's reduced condition, which he termed the breaking point of the suppuration of Europe.[17] Carlyle was always critical of mere charity, emphasising the need to tackle the sources of poverty and the importance of psychological as well as material improvement. At the beginning of his Irish journal Carlyle remarks that he was sleepless and ill throughout the tour. This certainly influenced his critical tone, as did his impatience with the sentimentality of much current writing on Ireland.[18] Carlyle's tour was first published in 1882.

From *Reminiscences of my Irish Journey in 1849*:[19]

It turned out now there had a man been *lost* last night. The good old Captain so reported it. On Saturday evening, most of the poor Irish wretches of 'invalids' got more or less completely drunk; some of them even on entering, had needed no completing. One of them a lean, angry, misguided, entirely worthless looking creature, age perhaps 40, came staggering upon the quarter-deck, and made a turn there: turn nearly completed, he came right upon the captain who of course ordered him off, — which order, tho' given mildly enough the poor drunk wretch felt to be insulting to his honour, and swore fiercely not to comply with. A scuffle had ensured (Captain's hand got 'twisted'): all of us started up to conjure the poor wretch &c.; he did then turn off, abashed, perhaps repentant, had taken more drink for consolation was 'last seen about midnight': it was now he that was never to be seen more! The Irish physiognomies I studied often from the upper platform: besides my yellow friend with the cap, I had made out some five or six type-physiognomies, which I could recognize as specimens of Irish *classes* of faces: there was the angry-bewildered, for instance the poor wretch that went overboard, or a still better yet left on beard, a lean withered show of a creature with hanging brows, droop nose, mouth corners drooping, chin narrow, narrow, eyes full of sorrow and rage: 'I have a right to be here, sir, I want my ration!'

said he once. There was there a blonde big tiger-face (to whom I lent a light for his pipe); this is of mixed breed, I think a north country face; noble possibility quite marred. Irish sailor at the helm in wig and storm hat; bulky, with aquiline face and closed mouth, wild cunning little eye: like Jock McDonald of my early years. Ah me! These faces are still very clear to me; and were I a painter, I could draw them; others, one or two, not thought of again till now, have got erased; I was struck in general with the air of faculty *misbred*, and gone to waste, or more or less 'excellent possibility much marred,' in almost all these faces. The man had found himself so enveloped in conditions which he deemed unfair, which he had revolted against, but had not been able to conquer, that he had so to speak, *lost his way*; a sorry sight, the *tragedy* of each of these poor men; but here too surely is a 'possibility'; if the Irish faculty be good, you *can* breed it, put it among conditions which *are* fair or at least fairer.

5) Lord John Manners

In his tour of Ireland in 1849 Manners visited Dublin, then headed west and south to Limerick, Kilkeel, Killarney and Valentia. He was impressed by the wild region, describing the Kenmare to Glengariff road as the grandest in Europe, barring the Alpine passes. He returned to Dublin, then went north; he found the Giant's Causeway unexciting, but Dunluce Castle, by contrast, deeply romantic.

From *Notes of an Irish Tour* (1849):[20]

Our communicative skipper told us that gannets breed on the Skelligs: he described them as being large as swans: when plucked they sell for eightpence a-piece. Puffins and curlews are also eaten, and are said to be good when properly prepared, as follows. The breasts of a good number are cut open, they are then put between two boards, and squeezed; an oil exudes from the breast, and the bird is then sweet and good: the oil is also made use of. Even in this ultima Thule, I found Teetotalism triumphant; only one of our crew would touch a drop of the cratur, wherewith we had provided ourselves, and he seemed to lead but a sorry life, being constantly girded at by his pledged companions. With wind and tide in our favour we spun back at a great rate, and passing the town of Valentia, essayed to enter the open sea on the other side of the island; but in vain; the waves and surf exceeded anything I had ever seen. On one side of our little boat, in which it was no easy matter to remain, over some rocks almost within arm's reach dashed the huge waves, sending up clouds of spray; on the other the iron-bound coast rose high above us, while our craft now glided down a steep inclined place of some twenty or thirty yards into the yawning heart of a billow, or rose to meet a swelling monster which seemed about to swallow up boat and us in one gulp. Most terrific and glorious it was. I own I was heartily glad when our skipper proposed putting about, for I saw by the face of the sailor nearest me, that it was not in his opinion either pleasant or safe to continue our fight with the Atlantic. Near the lighthouse we witnessed the hawling [sic] in of a successful fish-take. The scene was very animated: as the two boats containing the seine came nearer and nearer together, and the fish at the bottom began to feel and protest against, by various energetic movements, their hitherto unperceived imprisonment, the cries, shouts, prayers, and ejaculations of all on board, as well as of a large concourse of their friends on shore, became more and more frantic, till at last they resembled wild Indians howling with insane energy at the moon, rather than Christian Irishmen pursuing a peaceful and profitable avocation. It was a great haul, 2,000 fish, or so; and twenty beautiful mackerel were sold that hour to our worthy hostess of the Valentia hotel for eighteen pence. The epithet worthy is in this instance no mere expletive for be it known to all tourists that the neatest, cleanest, and most comfortable little hotel in all Ireland is at Valentia, kept by Mrs. Roper. The whole island, six miles long and two or three miles broad, with the exception of one farm, belongs to the Knight of Kerry, and contains 4,000 inhabitants, of whom 300 are employed in the slate quarries, and all the gross rental is estimated at £2,400 a year, and the county rate is assessed at £400! The show-room of the slate works contained all manner of works elaborated out of that rather common material. Inkstands, tables, drawers, basinss, table ornaments, garden seats, even fonts; but the taste of the last-mentioned item was detestable, and with a gentle admonition to that effect I left the yard, agreeably surprised at the beauty of the Valentia slate, and the forms in which it may be worked up.

The Knight of Kerry lives on this little island-kingdom, and is busily engaged in improving the cultivation of flax. At the recent show of the Royal Irish Agricultural Society, at Limerick, he carried off the first prize with flax grown on the island. By the way, though nothing can be prettier to look at than a field of flax in bloom, with its delicate pale flower, nothing can be more abhorrent to one's sense of smelling than the said flax spread out to dry after having been steeped in some pool, or used-up peat cutting. The stench poisons the air for miles.

On quitting the clean little inn early this morning for a bathe in the Atlantic, I was startled by the quick though measured, plash of oars in a hundred directions; it was the fishing power of the island hurrying after a great shoal of fish that had been descried in the channel: each boat was rowed by six oars, and strenuous indeed were the exertions made to arrive first at the scene of action. This day we devoted to seeing the island by land: with the exception of its rocks, coast, and slate quarries, there is nothing to admire in the way of scenery. About two-thirds of the island are bog or sheep-walks; the rest grows barley, flax, oats, potatoes.

6) Harriet Martineau

Harriet Martineau (1802–1876) was born in Norwich to Unitarian parents whose stern influence turned her into a gloomy and sensitive child. She was a compulsive reader, having most of *Paradise Lost* by heart at seven years of age. When the family fell into bankruptcy in 1829 she turned to writing. She first visited Dublin in 1831, staying with her brother, then toured America, Egypt and Palestine. Her Irish writings appeared as separate essays in the *Daily News* in 1851, and were republished in book form in 1852. Rather unusually, Martineau landed in Ireland at Portrush, County Antrim. She travelled from there to Dublin, then to Galway and Connemara and Clare, Killarney, Valentia.

From *Letters from Ireland* (1852):[21]

August 29, 1852

The railway from Dublin to Galway carries the traveller completely across Ireland — from the Irish Channel to the Atlantic — in six hours. The speed is not great — a little short of twenty-one miles an hour; but the punctuality is remarkable. The Dublin and Galway Railroad is not a very easy one to travel on in regard to steadiness. For the third of the line nearest to Dublin there are many curves, and pretty severe ones, so that the shaking of the carriages is disagreeable. For the rest of the way the road cuts straight through bog, with very narrow intervals of more solid ground; and a little jumping is not therefore to be wondered at, or found fault with. The marvel would have been, a quarter of a century ago, that the weight of a railway train should ever be carried across the bog at all.

The road traverses the great limestone basin which occupies the centre of Ireland; and there is scarcely any variation of level all the way. The engineer's difficulties were wholly with the consistency of the soil, and not at all with any hills and dales. One pleasant consequence of this is that the traveller sees for miles on either hand, and is not blinded and stunned by being whirled through cuttings. To us it appears as if there was scarcely a mile of cutting the whole way. Some who know the road may ask what is the good of this, considering what it is that is to be seen. But when one's object is to study the face of a country, nothing comes amiss, — neither Salisbury Plain nor the Bog of Allen. We (two of us) determined to use our opportunity of passing through a dead level of nearly 125 miles, to see everything on both sides the road, — and a diligent look-out we kept.

First, about the potatoes. We can safely say that we did not see one healthy ridge of them between Dublin and Galway; and we believe there is not one. It appeared indeed as if, in despair, the people had left the potatoes to their fate without a struggle. In the greater number of cases the field was so gay with poppies and other weeds as to leave only a black shadow of the potato-plant in the midst; and, quite universally, the ridges were so choked with grass and weeds that no care could possibly have been taken of the crop at any time this season. The oats were as weedy as many that we have before described; and some of the pastures as overgrown with thistles and ragwort; but they did not present the same evidences of reckless despair as the numerous potato-fields. Some of the pastures were so fine, of so pure a grass and so brilliant a verdure, that there would have been unmingled pleasure in looking on them but for the drawback that the hay is not yet carried. There it stands in cocks, in these last days of August, to catch the rains which are coming up with this west wind from the Atlantic: and a sad pity it seems. We do not expect to see much more such grass; and we can scarcely see finer anywhere. The limestone bottoms favour pasturage so much, that we hope the day may come when, in all the intervals of the great central bog, there may be a most advantageous stock farming carried on. In those days the hay will, we suspect, be saved six weeks earlier; though it should in fairness be said that we are told that English critics have no idea what allowance it is necessary to make for the caprices of the Irish climate.

As we proceeded, we looked with a regretful interest on the trees, where we saw them grouped in any beauty — as they were, if we are rightly informed, nearly the last we shall see for some time to come. Among the wild scenery of the west coast we shall see quite another kind of beauty. The College at Maynooth appears to be surrounded by gardens and thriving plantations; and some old trees hang about the neighbouring ruins of the ancient castle of the Fitzgeralds of Leinster, and clothe the entrance to the estate of the Duke of Leinster. There are large plantations again on the estates of Lord Clancarty, at Ballinasloe, though there we have entered on the bog country, which extends all the way to Galway. A more desolate tract of country than that which stretches forward from the boundary of Lord Clancarty's liberal improvements, we are hardly likely ever to see. It makes the imagination ache, like the eye. What it must be may be in some measure conceived, if we remember that Ireland contains very nearly 3,000,000 of acres of bog: that six-sevenths of this amount lie between lines drawn from Wicklow Head to Galway, and from Howth Hill to Sligo; and that, within that space, the greater proportion of bog lies west of the Shannon. When Cromwell transplanted all disaffected families from other parts to Connaught, and when Connaught became the proverbial alternative of hell,[22] the great bog was no doubt the uppermost image in men's minds. The disgraces of Connaught certainly recur with strong force to the traveller's mind when he traverses that bog for the first time.

The depth is at the deepest part forty-two feet: at the shallowest, where it is worked, about six feet. The deep and wide drains are satisfactory to look upon; and so are the blue smokes where heaps of peat are burning with an intermixture of clay, — working the process of reclamation; and so, perhaps, are the dismal patches of thin and feeble oats, where, wholly surrounded by black bog, the reaper and his children, bare-legged and half clad, suspend their work to see the train go by. The vast 'clamps' (stacks) of peat, the acres upon acres covered with little heaps of the drying 'bricks' of turf, the brown and black terraces, just sprinkled with new heather and weeds, may be dreary; but they are not dismal; for they tell of industry, and some harvest of comfort, however small. But there are other sights, — groups of ruins, as at Athenry — staring fragments of old castles, and churches, and monasteries; and worse than these, a very large number of unroofed cottages. For miles together, in some places, there is scarcely a token of human presence but the useless gables and the empty doorways and window-spaces of pairs or rows of deserted cottages. There is something so painful — so even exasperating in this sight, that one wishes that a little more time and labour could be spared to level the walls, as well as take off the roof, when tenants are either ejected, or go away of their own accord. Yet, while substantial stone walls are thus staring in the traveller's face, what cabins — actual dwellings of families — are here and there distinguishable in the midst of the bog! styes of mud, bulging and tottering, grass-grown, half-swamped with bog-water, and the soil around all poached with the tread of bare feet. In comparison with such places, the stony lands near Galway (a vivid green ground, strewn with grey stones) look wholesome, and almost cheerful, but for the wrecks of habitations. From the time that we enter upon the district of the red petticoats — the red flannel and frieze, which form a part of the dress of most of the Galway people — things look better than in the brown and black region of the bog.

13. THE SENSE OF DIFFERENCE

British visitors to Ireland registered a country different in landscape, in atmosphere, in material and social existence. The intensity of the realisation varied, as historical pressures changed consciousness, but was always a factor; and it applied to Irish people no less than to Ireland itself.

When planters and soldiers up to the time of Cromwell and beyond were fighting the Irish people in Ireland for the control of religion, land and power it was inevitable, perhaps, that their attitude to the Irish should have tended towards simplistic hostility. Despite persistent questioning voices, the Irish, as military foes, were always likely to be cast as sub-civilised, therefore justly destroyed or removed. After 1700 such functional hostility, though still in evidence, was less overwhelming, if only because by that time the country had been militarily and politically conquered, shared out among the victors and then subordinated, economically, to the interests of London and Britain. But it never disappeared, and in fact was to reappear with some ferocity, as A. P. Curtis has demonstrated, among popular journalists in the British press during the Repeal agitation of the nineteenth century.[1] Ignorance of Ireland of course remained high; John Gough's English servant in 1813 had expected to find there only bogland, whiskey and potatoes and not a single stone-built house.[2] A change of emphasis during the eighteenth and early nineteenth centuries saw (among other attitudes) the notion of beautiful, suffering Ireland begin to replace that of devilish Ireland, accompanied by a more distinct consciousness of the country's down at heel aristocracy and incapable peasantry: that is, a perception developed of Irish ills interlinked with Irish mismanagement. Later, the picture became still more sharply drawn: the degraded people of a starving land could not organise their own survival. But alongside and against these variations on a common theme — Irish incompetence — questions were raised too about the justice of such stereotyping. Bell and Plumptre challenge the notion of the feckless Irishman, and other travellers stress how little is really known about Ireland among the ordinary people of Great Britain. Cobbett lists the conventional reasons adduced for Ireland's backward condition (lazy people, Catholicism, emancipation denied, tithes, the Union, absenteeism, political agitation) and denies them all as false.[3] As the Famine years approached, functional pity replaced functional hostility in the English traveller. This may represent a moral improvement. Both attitudes though cast the Irish as human inferiors. Victorian commentaries on Ireland, ostensibly as well as really sympathetic to the suffering country, are studded with analogies between the Irish people and remote savages or (in the modern terminology) the inhabitants of 'under-developed' cultures in the far parts of the earth.[4]

As suggested, attitudes to the Anglo-Irish also changed. Mid-eighteenth century travellers like Richard Pococke often describe them approvingly, but a little later other travellers such as Wesley and Richard Cumberland, and nineteenth century visitors like De Quincey and Engels note their disproportionate houses and eccentric personalities. The two last writers are particularly alive to the ambiguous, even unbalanced existence forced upon the Anglo-Irish gentry by history.[5] Alienated as they were from their neighbours and their immediate surroundings, and removed too from real contact with London, the true basis of their power, they appeared anomalous — slightly mad.

1) Arthur Young, *Tour in Ireland* (1780):[6]

In the variety of theories which have been started to account for the formation of bogs, difficulties occur which are not easily solved: yet are there many circumstances which assist in tracing the cause. Various sorts of trees, some of them of a great size, are very generally found in them, and usually at the bottom, oak, fir, and yew the most common; the roots of these trees are fast in the earth; some of the trees seem broken off, others appear to be cut, but more with the marks of fire on them. Under some bogs of a considerable depth there are yet to be seen the furrows of land once ploughed. The black bog is a solid weighty mass, which cuts almost like butter, and upon examination appears to resemble rotten wood. Under the red bogs there is always a stratum, if not equally solid with the black bog, nearly so, and makes as good fuel. There is upon the black as well as the red ones a surface of that spungy vegetable mass which is cleared away to get at the bog for fuel, but it is shallow on these. Sound trees are found equally in both sorts.

Both differ extremely from the bogs I have seen in England in the inequality of the surface; the Irish ones are rarely level, but rise into hills. I have seen one in Donnegal which is a perfect scenery of hill and dale. The spontaneous growth most common is heath; with some bog myrtle, rushes, and a little sedgy grass. As far as I can judge by roads, laying gravel of any sort, clay, earth, &c. improves the bog, and brings good grass. The depth of them is various, they have been fathomed to that of fifty feet, and some are said to be still deeper.

From these circumstances it appears, that a forest cut, burnt, or broken down, is probably the origin of a bog. In all countries where wood is so common as to be a weed, it is destroyed by burning; it is so around the Baltick, and in America at present. The native Irish might cut and burn their woods enough for the tree to fall, and in the interim between such an operation and successive culture, wars and other intestine divisions might prevent it in those spots, which so neglected afterwards became bogs. Trees lying very thick on the ground would become an impediment to all streams and currents, and gathering in their branches, whatever rubbish such waters brought with them, form a mass of a substance which time might putrefy, and give that acid quality to, which would preserve some of the trunks though not the branches of the trees. The circumstance of red bogs being black and solid at the bottom, would seem to indicate that a black bog has received less accession from the growth and putrefaction of vegetables after the formation than the red ones, which from some circumstances of soil or water might yield a more luxuriant surface vegetation, till it produced that mass of spunge which is now found on the surface. That this supposition is quite satisfactory I cannot assert, but the effect appears to be at least possible, and accounts for the distinction between the two kinds. That they receive their form and increase from a constant vegetation appears from their rising into hills, if they did not vegetate the quantity of water they contain would keep them on a level. The places where the traces of ploughing are found, I should suppose were once fields adjoining to the woods, and when the bog rose to a certain height it flowed gradually over the surrounding land.

2) Robert Bell (1804)

Most of Robert Bell's *Description* of the Irish (more a survey than a tour) appeared in the *Weekly Dispatch* before being published in book form in 1804. Bell argues that legislation for Ireland requires a truer knowledge of the people's condition than either the Irish gentry possess, or English writers have sought; given this, he is sure Ireland will stay loyal to Britain. As this suggests, although Bell points out that all British accounts of Ireland have been hostile, as usual when conquerors have written of the conquered, he seeks a reinforced tie between the countries. Seeking to render something characteristic of Irish life, Bell describes a wedding among the better-off peasants, then an Irish wake, and finally an Irish pattern, or patron-feast.

From *A Description of the . . . Peasantry of Ireland* (1804):[7]

It must be recollected that the writers who speak of the Irish in terms of reproach, were natives of Britain, and that the hostility of mind which always existed between a conquered people and the conquerors, (and which to this hour has never been effaced in Ireland), must have thrown no weak tint of prejudice on the picture which they drew. The accounts which men give of a people whom they either fear or despise, are not to be received as authentic: and still less are they to be relied on, if it be considered that the authors, from the very nature of their situation, are unable to acquire a knowledge of those whose manners they attempt to describe. Can it be supposed that English governors or English officers going to Ireland in the character of enemies, unacquainted with the language of the country, and having no intercourse with the people except the ceremonial visits of perfidious Chieftains who pretended to enter into their views, were capable of giving a true description of Irish manners? Among the fragments of Irish literature which still remain, there is sufficient evidence to prove that many of the accounts of Giraldus Cambrensis are false or exaggerated. Yet this author is quoted by modern historians as an unquestionable authority.

It was not until the present enlightened era that men of liberal and philosophic minds came forward to assert the antiquity of Ireland, to examine the few records that had escaped the ravages of her invaders, and to vindicate her character from unmerited obloquy.

But whatever grounds the English historians might have had for representing the native Irish as savage and ferocious, it has been clearly ascertained that they were not so previously to the invasion of Henry II. The cause of their degeneracy must therefore be obvious to every person who has read the history of conquered countries where the dominion of the victor was only to be retained by force: and still more to those who will take the trouble of reading Dr. Leland's History of Ireland. It is a fact as well authenticated as most parts of antient history, that there were many seminaries of learning in this island for four or five centuries before it was conquered by England; that numbers of persons from other countries resorted thither for instruction; (the greater part of Europe being at that time in a state of deplorable ignorance): that there were Princes in the country who displayed the talents of great statesmen and generals; that the Irish were often as successful as their English neighbours in repelling Danish invasions; and that in the reign of William the Conqueror they had made a generous though unsuccessful, struggle to restore the exiled family of Harold to the throne of England.

3) Richard Colt Hoare

Richard Colt Hoare (1758–1838), a member of the famous banking family and grandson of a Lord Mayor of London, began travelling in 1785 as a distraction after his wife's death. He made a first European journey from 1785 to 1787, visiting France, Switzerland and Italy, and a second to Germany and the Adriatic from 1788 to 1791. When France closed Continental Europe to British travellers he toured Wales, then in 1806 visited Ireland, publishing his journal of Irish travel in 1807. As the passage below shows, Hoare's reason for recommending Irish travel was, so to speak, a secondary one: Ireland was worth visiting while Europe was unavailable. He emphasises the paucity of information currently available about Ireland compared with continental countries.

From *Journal of a Tour* (1807):[8]

To the traveller, who fond of novelty and information, seeks out those regions, which may either afford reflection for his mind, or employment for his pencil, and especially to him, who may be induced to visit the neglected shores of HIBERNIA, the following pages are dedicated.

While the opposite coasts of WALES and SCOTLAND, have for many successive years attracted the notice and admiration of the man of taste, and of the artist; whilst the press has so teemed with publications, pointing out their natural beauties, and works of military and monastick art, that little more is left to be described; whilst WALES and SCOTLAND, I say, have had the assistance of the Historian's pen to record their annals, and of the artist's pen to pourtray their natural and artificial curiosities; the Island of HIBERNIA still remains unvisited and unknown. And why? Because from the want of books, and living information, we have been led to suppose its country rude, its inhabitants savage, its paths dangerous. 'Were we to take a view [says an Irish Historian] of the wretched condition in which the History of IRELAND stands, it would not be a matter for astonishment, that we should be considered as a people, in a manner unknown to the world, except what little knowledge of us is communicated by merchants, sea-faring men, and a few travellers; while all other nations of Europe have their historians, to inform their own people as well as foreigners, what they were, and what they are.'[9]

[. . .]

The traveller who makes IRELAND the object of his excursions, will experience a double mortification, in finding the books relating to that country so few, when compared to those descriptive of every other part of our kingdom; and in finding so few amongst the natives who are able to give him such general information as he could wish, concerning the objects most worthy of his attention; but he will every where find a *hand* ready to assist, and a *heart* open to receive, him in all his difficulties.

The love of liberty and independence is by nature implanted in the breast of every Englishman; it is not only his birth-right, but his guide and upholder through life. On no occasion, and in no place, will *independence* be more requisite, or more useful, than during the progress of an *Irish Tour.* The traveller must not expect to find those comforts and conveniences which he will meet with on the Bath road, or even in many of the remotest provinces of England; he must not expect to find post chaises and post horses, ready at a moment's notice, to waft him from the LAKE OF KILLARNEY to the GIANT'S CAUSEWAY; for these accommodations are to be found only on the great roads of communication from one city to another. On the *cross* roads, he must bear with patience the delays of postboys, and the indifference of postmasters; his purse will be taxed, and his time lost. To remedy these inconveniences, the tourist must make himself *independent*, by being his own post-master, and his own post boy; in short, he must travel with his own carriage, and with his own horses; all difficulties will then cease; for if he makes a proper choice of resting places, and avoids such a *gite* as BALLYSHANNON (more of which hereafter) all will go on smoothly; for he will find excellent roads, with better inns and fare than he would expect from the descriptions he has heard, and the impressions he may have formed of the general state of the country.

4) Anne Plumptre

From *Narrative of a Residence in Ireland* (1817):[10]

I shall be thought, perhaps, by my own countrymen to cast the severest reflection that can be cast upon the Irish, when I say that they perpetually reminded me of the French. There is a much stronger resemblance in them to the French national character than to the English; and this resemblance is equally forcible in the lower as in the higher classes of society. Nothing is more comic than to observe the difference between an English mechanic and a French or Irish one. I once, when travelling in France, wanted something done to the lid of a trunk, which I thought in some danger of splitting in two. I did not wish, however, to be long delayed by the job; and recollecting how an English carpenter or trunk-maker would have chiselled and planed a piece of wood, and fitted and fitted it over again before he could have been satisfied to nail it upon the trunk, and how much time all this would take, I was rather afraid of submitting my wounded servant to such a process; I thought I should be *impatienté* at the *longueur*, and I tried to persuade myself that the case was not of a very pressing nature. Yet the more I examined, the more imminent the danger appeared; and at length I desired that a carpenter might be sent for, stating what I wanted. *Veni, vidi, vici*, says Caesar; and so it was with the carpenter: I need not have been so much afraid of delay. He brought with him a hammer, a few nails, and a rough spline: the latter was knocked on in two minutes, and all was accomplished. It did not look quite so neat as if it had come from the hands of an English workman: it held the lid together, however, and all was well: but the rapidity with which the whole was performed was amusing and highly characteristic. The same is very much the case with the Irish: — ardent in their pursuits, rapid in their movements, they blaze brilliantly for a while, but the ardour is too apt easily to subside; while with the Englishman, who is less alive at catching fire, when the flame within him is once lighted, it burns on even and steady, nor is readily exhausted. It is perhaps extraordinary, considering the state of depression in which the Irish have been kept for such a lengthened series of years, that they still retain so much of their native wit, ardour, and vivacity; but even now an Irishman, like a Frenchman, will have his joke if it comes in his way, *coute-qui-coute* .[11]

A very marked difference is, however, to be observed between the inhabitants of the two extremes of Ireland which I visited, the north-east or county of Antrim, and the south-west, including the counties of Cork and Kerry, strongly supporting the belief that their origin is to be traced to different sources. In the south of Ireland the people are much darker than in the north; and here was the country where the Milesians from Spain, according to all the traditions, both written and oral, were first established. Now the dark complexion, eyes and hair, have been ever, and still are, the distinguishing characteristics of all the Southern nations of Europe; as the fair complexion, blue eyes, and light hair, sometimes deviating into red, were, and are still, of the Northern. The one are bleached by colds and snows, the others darkened by the warmth of the sun. Now, every possible presumptive evidence leads to the belief that the north of Ireland, or perhaps all Ireland and Scotland, were originally peopled from the Northern nations of Europe, the parts which formed the ancient Scandinavia; while the south, if originally peopled by the same, afterwards became the settlement of an Iberian colony, whose descendants remain there to this day. A close and constant intercourse has always subsisted between the inhabitants of the north of Ireland and Scotland, so that they ever have been, as it were, one and the same people.[12] In more than one part the coasts come so near as within eighteen miles of each other: the distance is no more between Port Patrick in Scotland and Donaghadee in Ireland, and between the Mull of Cantire in Scotland and the county of Antrim in Ireland. Indeed there can scarcely be a doubt, from the name, that Port Patrick was originally an establishment of the Irish. It is well known that the Irish are in ancient records called *Scots*; but at the Milesian conquest, these people coming from the land of Iberia, one of the leaders also bearing the name *Heber*, thence the name of *Hibernia*, afterwards given to the island, was derived; whilst the natives driven constantly northwards, many of them probably at that time migrating to Scotland, transferred thither with themselves the name they bore. There is besides more of the true Irish quickness and vivacity in the south of Ireland than in the north; the people of the north partake somewhat of the solemnity of their neighbours the Scots.

6) William Bennett

William Bennett travelled to Ireland in 1847 with seed provision for the victims of famine. He visited Dublin, then toured Belmullet, Sligo, Ballyshannon, Donegal, the Rosses and Gweedore and returned to Dublin by way of Letterkenny, Omagh, Armagh and Portadown. He next went by train to Carlow and Kilkenny, Killarney, Cahirciveen; then by boat to Valentia. Bennett's assessment of Ireland is mixed. He traces the sufferings of nineteenth century Ireland to a string of natural calamities rather than to the combination of natural causes with political and economic circumstances built up over time. Behind his wish for Irish economic growth lies a perception of the advantage to England of a flourishing market near at hand. To the English visitor the Irish seem to inhabit a different world; they are an object of study. Nevertheless, in the following passage Bennett challenges the analogy common among some writers of the time between Irish life and remote savage culture — an attitude which tends to obscure the extent of English involvement in Irish history.

From *Narrative of a recent journey* (1847):[13]

Take the line of the main course of the Shannon, continued north to Lough Swilly, and south to Cork. It divides the island into two great portions, east and west. In the eastern there is distress and poverty enough, as part of the same body, suffering from the same causes; but there is much to redeem. In the west it exhibits a people, not in the centre of Africa, the steppes of Asia, the backwoods of America, — not some newly-discovered tribes of South Australia, or among the Polynesian Islands, — not Hottentots, Bushmen, or Esquimeaux, — neither Mahomedans nor Pagans, — but some millions of our own Christian nation at home, living in a state and condition low and degraded to a degree unheard of before in any civilized community; driven periodically to the borders of starvation; and now reduced, by a national calamity, to an exigency which all the efforts of benevolence can only mitigate, not control; and under which *absolute thousands* are not merely pining away in misery and wretchedness, but are dying like cattle off the face of the earth, from want and its kindred horrors! Is this to be regarded in the light of a Divine dispensation and punishment? Before we can safely arrive at such a conclusion, we must be satisfied that human agency and legislation, individual oppressions, and social relationships, have had no hand in it.

[. . .]

Is there anything inherent in the national character fatal to improvement? The Irish are accused of being lazy, improvident, reckless of human life. I doubt their being much more so than the

English, the Americans, or any other nation would be under the like circumstances. The distances to which an Irish labourer will go for work, and the hardships he will submit to, are notorious; and the private correspondence of all who have entered into the subject teems with evidence of the alacrity of the poor women and peasant girls for employment of any kind, and of the teachableness and skill they exhibit. The appeal to a wider range of facts is irresistible. Who come over in such numbers to reap our harvests, dig our canals, construct our railroads, in fact wherever hard work is to be obtained? Who save up what money they can, during harvest-time, and such-like seasons of extra employment, to take back to their families at home? Who, in a country where labour is better remunerated, send over sums exceeding all that the wealthy have raised in charity, to comfort those they have left behind, or help over their poor friends and relatives to what they think that happier land? The generosity of the Irish was never questioned. Their peaceableness has been put to the severest test. In no other country, probably, could such a state of things have endured so long, and to such an extremity, without ten-fold more outrages than have been committed. They are naturally a contented and a happy race. The charge of recklessness of human life — apart from those deplorably aggravated deeds arising invariably out of natural jealousies — is answered by the perfect safety of a stranger amongst them; and it has further been placed on the right shoulders in another quarter, more fearlessly than I durst have penned it here.

7) Queen Victoria

Queen Victoria's liking for Ireland does not appear strong. She visited the country on a few occasions for official reasons such as the Dublin Great Exhibition of 1851, but not for pleasure. 'Holidays, to her, meant the Continent.'[14] When Albert went on shore to look at Irish cabins, she remained on board ship, writing and sketching. However, Victoria registers the feeling of difference — a sense that they were abroad — which Ireland produced in English visitors. Driving around Cork city, she can specify nothing definite about the town, just a feeling of confusion; yet the characteristic looks of Cork women had caught her attention.

From *Victoria Travels* (1970):[15]

Friday, August 3. — The day was grey and excessively 'muggy', which is the character of the Irish climate. The ships saluted at eight o'clock, and the 'Ganges' (the flag-ship and a three-decker) and the 'Hogue' (a three-decker cut down, with very heavy guns, and with a screw put into her), which are both very near us, made a great noise. The harbour is very extensive, and there are several islands in it, one of which is very large. Spike Island is immediately opposite us, and has a convict prison; near it another island with the depot, &c. In a line with that is the town of Cove, picturesquely built up a hill. The two war-steamers have only just come in. The Admiral (Dixon) and the Captains of the vessels came on board. Later, Lord Bandon (Lord-Lieutenant of the county), Lord Thomond, General Turner, Commander of the Forces at Cork, presented their respects, and Albert went on shore, and I occupied myself in writing and sketching. Albert returned before our luncheon, and had been walking about and visiting some of the cabins.

We left the yacht at two with the ladies and gentlemen, and went on board the 'Fairy', which was surrounded with rowing and sailing boats. We first went round the harbour, all the ships saluting, as well as numbers of steamers and yachts. We then went into Cove and lay alongside the landing-place, which was very prettily decorated; and covered with people; and yachts, ships and boats crowding all round. The two Members, Messrs. Roche and Power, as well as other gentlemen, including the Roman Catholic and Protestant clergymen, and then the members of the Yacht Club, presented addresses. After which, to give the people the satisfaction of calling the place Queenstown, in honour of its being the first spot which I set foot upon Irish ground, I stepped on shore amidst the roar of cannon (for the artillery were placed so close as quite to shake the temporary room which we entered): and the enthusiastic shouts of the people. We immediately re-embarked and proceeded up the river Lee towards Cork. It is extremely pretty and richly wooded, and reminded me of the Tamar. The first feature of interest we passed was a little bathing-place, called Monsktown, and later Blackrock Castle, at which point we stopped to receive a salmon, and a very pretty address from the poor fishermen of Blackrock.

As we approached the city we saw people streaming in, on foot, on horseback, and many in jaunting-cars. When we reached Cork the 'Fairy' again lay alongside, and we received all the addresses: first, from the mayor and Corporation (I knighted the Mayor immediately afterwards), then from the Protestant Bishop and clergy; from the Roman Catholic Bishop and clergy; from the Lord Lieutenant of the county, the Sheriffs, and others. The two Judges, who were holding their courts, also came on board in their robes. After all this was over we landed, and walked some few paces on to where Lord Bandon's carriage was ready to receive us. The ladies went with us, and Lord Bandon and the General rode on each side of the carriage. The mayor preceded us, and many (Lord Listowel among the number), followed on horseback or in carriages. The 12th Lancers escorted us, and the Pensioners and Infantry lined the streets.

I cannot describe our route, but it will suffice to say that it took two hours; that we drove through the principle streets; twice through some of them; that they were densely crowded, decorated with flowers and triumphal arches; that the heat and dust were great; that we passed by the new College which is building — one of the four which are ordered by Act of Parliament; that our reception was most enthusiastic; and that everything went off to perfection, and was very well arranged.

Cork is not at all like an English town, and looks rather foreign. The crowd is a noisy, excitable, but very good-humoured one, running and pushing about, and laughing, talking, and shrieking. The beauty of the women is very remarkable, and struck us much; such beautiful dark eyes and hair, and such fine teeth; almost every third woman was pretty, and some remarkably so. They wear no bonnets, and generally long blue cloaks; the men are very poorly, often raggedly dressed; and many wear blue coats and short breeches with blue stockings.

We re-embarked at the same place and returned just as we came.

14. FROM WAR TO UNION

The seventeenth century in Ireland had been characterised by military conflict — not only the set piece wars, but simmering confrontations like that between English troops and Irish tories described by Arthur Capel in 1675.[1] These small incidents may not have changed history but they kept alive the antagonisms which did — 1689, 1798, 1916. In another tiny example Samuel Mullenaux gives us a brief sharp glimpse into the jittery condition of Dublin Protestants as they sat at home in 1690, wondering who had won at the Boyne,[2] and of the latter historic event a well known, vivid eyewitness account (not included here) will be found in John Stevens's *Journal*.[3] Yet between the 1690s and 1790s there was no battle fought on Irish soil. To match this experience of a whole century free from war on their soil the Irish had to go back a long way. Civil tumult came to predominate over, though not replace, military tumult in Irish life, as it has done ever since: agrarian disturbances, sectarian and religious conflict, hooliganism, pattern fights and tenant-landlordism recur or yield place to each other after 1700. Thus the deep antagonisms planted in Irish life over history were modified but not cured.

As the seventeenth century receded, the Ireland of battlefields also yielded place, temporarily, to one less disrupted. To the traveller's eye Ireland after 1700 seemed to be a country heavily unequal, certainly, in its social organisation, but at peace, dotted with grand houses generously thrown open to the genteel visitor and boasting impressively romantic scenery. Much travel writing from the period emphasises this aspect: beauty, wealth and power in the lives of the Ascendancy rulers, by whom the travellers' journeys were often made easy. There is occasionally a touch of criticism. The attractive prospect was set off by the evidence of material and cultural degradation in the surrounding population. And even in some of the members of the ruling minority of Anglo-Irish landowners, episcopal as well as secular, a Wesley or a Pococke could note evidence of a doubtful temperament, failure of judgement or character imbalance.

Some of the turning points in Irish history are included here, as English observers saw and described them, or sought to influence them. The passages selected offer to the reader not vital historical information but revealing attitudes. They uncover some of the assumptions (whether of the writers, or of the persons described) about what was judged to be significant in Irish affairs. They were, in other words, instrumental attitudes; they shaped English policy towards the country and its inhabitants over the centuries. Sir William Petty's paper redisposition of Irish land, for example — a rewriting of Ireland if ever there was one — might strike a modern reader as no less chilling in its unemotional pragmatism than Ludlow's account (quoted above, chapter 11) of the victorious English soldiers re-distributing vast confiscated territories, or, even, than Cromwell's cruel transplantations. Even where, as in De Quincey on the Union, a document may strike us as the highly impressionistic account of an event as it happened rather than a blueprint for future action, it is never without a political edge. De Quincey analyses corruption among the politically degenerate — the Anglo-Irish rulers of Ireland, ready to sell their power. (It is a fifteen-year-old who passes the stern judgement.) In all this discussion Ireland in its own right comes lower in the scale of importance. Even the sympathising English visitors of the Famine years, like Cobbett and Martineau, see in Ireland, primarily, a pattern for English life, a political lesson. Thus a version of Ireland is inscribed, whether sympathetic or hostile, heavily loaded towards English priorities and English expectations. The process anticipates near at home that fabrication of remote cultures which, as Lévi-Strauss remarked, a modern anthropologist can produce instantaneously by means of modern equipment, a set of organising preconceptions, and a willingness not to probe deeply into the actuality of the lives and histories being described.[4]

1) William Petty

Sir William Petty (1623–1687), the son of a Hampshire clothier, lived and studied on the Continent until 1646, when he returned to England, began writing on textiles and other subjects, and helped to found the Royal Society. In 1652 he became physician-general to the English army in Ireland, and, having criticised Benjamin Worsley's survey of Ireland as inaccurate, offered to do a better job himself. The result was the 'Down Survey' of Irish estates which were judged to have been forfeited, so named because, for the first time, it was a survey not limited to verbal description but also measured down on maps. (Hence 'Lansdowne', the name Petty assumed when rewarded for his work.[5]) Petty's survey, which assimilated Strafford's earlier survey of Tipperary but was otherwise new, has been praised then and since for its accuracy. Petty wrote *The Political Anatomy of Ireland* in 1672, recommending the union of the two countries of England and Ireland. In the first of the following extracts he summarises the political relationships between Ireland and England after the Cromwellian period. His 'anatomy' of Ireland may echo Spenser, the advocate of firm government, but Petty admits that English meddling in Irish affairs has been a historical blunder and concedes that it might advantage the English to 'abandon their whole Interest in that Countrey'. However, Petty's remedy is not abandonment, but real union implemented by means of the cross-transplantation, or wholesale shipments, of English and Irish people into one another's country, with carefully regulated intermarriage between the two nations. This, he designs, will produce a homogeneous nation — homogeneous, but not equal: Petty's stipulations are to ensure that the English character predominates.

From *The Political Anatomy of Ireland* (1691):[6]

The English invaded *Ireland* about 500 years since; at which time, if the *Irish* were in number about 1,200,000. *Anno* 1641. they were but 600 M. in number, 200 years ago, and not above 300,000 M. at the said time of their Invasion; for 300,000 people will, by the ordinary Course of Generation, become 1200 M. in 500 years; allowance being made for the Extraordinary Effects of Epidemical Diseases, Famines, Wars, *&c.*

There is at this Day no Monument or real Argument that, when the *Irish* were first invaded, they had any Stone-Housing at all, any Money, any Foreign Trade, nor any Learning but the Legend of the Saints, Psalters, Missals, Rituals, *&c. viz.* nor Geometry, Astronomy, Anatomy, Architecture, Enginery, Painting, Carving, nor any kind of Manufacture, nor the least use of Navigation, or the Art Military.

Sir *John Davys* hath expressed much Wit and Learning, in giving the Causes why *Ireland* was in no measure reduced to *English* Government, till in Queen *Elizabeths* Reign, and since; and withal offers several means, whereby what yet remains to be done, may be still effected.

The Conquest made by the *English*, and desribed in the Preamble of the Act of Parliament past *Ann.* 1662. for the Settlement of

Ireland, gave means for any thing that had been reasonable of that kind; but their Forfeiters being abroad, and suffering with His Majesty from the same usurping hands, made some diversion.

Wherefore (*Rebus sic stantibus*) what is now to be done is the Question, *viz.* What may be done by natural possibility, if Authority saw it fit?

Some furious Spirits have wished, that the *Irish* would rebel again, that they might be put to the Sword. But I declare, that motion to be not only impious and inhumane, but withal frivolous and pernicious even to them who have rashly wish'd for those occasions.

That the *Irish* will not easily rebel again, I believe from the memory of their former Successes, especially of the last, had not many Providences interpos'd; and withal from the consideration of these following Particulars, *viz.*

1. That the *British Protestants* and *Church* have 3/4 of all the Lands; 5/6 of all the Housing; 9/10 of all the Housing in wall'd Towns, and Places of strength 2/3 of the Foreign Trade. That 6 of 8 of all the *Irish* live in a brutish nasty Condition, as in Cabins, with neither Chimney, Door, Stairs nor Window; feed chiefly upon Milk and Potatoes, whereby their Spirits are not dispos'd for War. And that although there be in *Ireland* 8 *Papists* for 3 others; yet there are far more Soldiers, and Soldierlike-Men of this latter and lesser Number, than of the former.

That His Majesty, who formerly could do nothing for, and upon *Ireland*, but by the help of *England*, hath now a Revenue upon the Place, to maintain, if he pleases, 7000 Men in Arms, besides a Protestant Militia of 25000 more, the most whereof are expert in War.

That the *Protestants* have Housing enough within Places of strength within 5 Miles of the Sea-side, to receive and protect, and harbour every Man, Woman and Child belonging to them, and have also places of strength of their own properly, so situate in all parts of *Ireland*, to which they can easily travel the shortest day of the year.

That being able to secure their Persons, even upon all sudden Emergencies, they can be easily supplied out of *England* with Food sufficient to maintain them, till they have burnt 160 M. of their afore-described Cabins, not worth 50 M.l. destroy'd their Stacks and Haggards of Corn, and disturbed their Tillage, which the embody'd *British* can soon and easily atchieve.

That a few Ships of War, whereof the *Irish* have none, nor no Skill or Practice of Navigation, can hinder their relief from all Foreign help.

That few Foreigners can help them if they would. But that none, not the King of *France*, can gain advantage by so doing, even tho he succeeded. For *England* hath constantly lost these 500 years by their meddling with *Ireland*. And at this day, than when *Ireland* was never so rich and splendid, it were the advantage of the *English* to abandon their whole Interest in that Countrey; and fatal to any other Nation to take it, as hath been elsewhere (as I think) demonstrated; and the advantage of the Landlords of *England*, to give them the Equivalent of what they should so quit out of their own Estates in *England*.

Lastly, Let the *Irish* know, That there are, ever were, and will be men discontented with their present Conditions in *England*, and ready for any Exploit and Change, more than are sufficient to quell any Insurrection they can make and abide by.

Wherefore, declining all Military means of setling and securing *Ireland* in peace and plenty, what we offer shall tend to the transmuting one People into the other, and the thorough union of Interests upon natural and lasting Principles; of which I shall enumerate several, tho seemingly never so uncouth and extravagant.

1. If *Henry* the II. had or could have brought over all the people of *Ireland* into *England*, declining the Benefit of their Land; he had fortified, beautified and enrich'd *England*, and done real Kindness to the *Irish*. But the same Work is near four times as hard now to be done as then; but it might be done, even now, with advantage to all Parties.

Whereas there are now 300 M. *British*, and 800 M. *Papists*, whereof 600 M. live in the wretched way above mentioned: If an Exchange was made of but about 200 M. *Irish*, and the like number of *British* brought over in their rooms, then the natural strength of the *British* would be equal to that of the *Irish*; but their Political and Artificial strength three times as great; and so visible, that the *Irish* would never stir upon a National or Religious Account.

3. There are among the 600 M. above-mentioned of the poor *Irish*, not above 20 M. of unmarried marriageable Women; nor would above two thousand *per Ann.* grow and become such. Wherefore if 1/2 the said Women were in one year, and 1/2 the next transported into *England*, and disposed of one to each Parish, and as many *English* brought back and married to the *Irish*, as would improve their Dwelling but to an House and Garden of 3l. value, the whole Work of natural Transmutation and Union would in 4 or 5 years be accomplished.

The charge of making the exchange would not be 20,000 l. *per Ann.* which is about 6 Weeks Pay of the present or late Armies in *Ireland*.

If the *Irish* must have Priests, let the number of them, which is now between 2 and 3 thousand Secular and Regulars, be reduced to the competent number of 1000, which is 800 Souls to the pastorage of each Priest; which let be known persons, and *Englishmen*, if it may be. so as that when the Priests, who govern the Conscience, and the Women, who influence other powerful Appetites, shall be *English*, both of whom being in the Bosom of the Men, it must be, that no massacring of *English*, as heretofore, can happen again. Moreover, when the Language of the Children shall be *English*, and the whole Oeconomy of the Family *English*, *viz.* Diet, Apparel, *&c.* the Transmutation will be very easy and quick.

Add hereunto, That if both Kingdoms, now two, were put into one, and under one Legislative Power and Parliament, the Members whereof should be in the same proportion that the Power and Wealth of each Nation are, there would be no danger such a Parliament should do any thing to the prejudice of the *English* Interest in *Ireland*; nor could the Irish even complain of Partiality, when they shall be freely and proportionably represented in all Legislatures.

2) John Stevens

Little is known of John Stevens. According to his biographer Robert H. Murray he had served in Portugal as an army officer, then worked as an excise officer in Wales before visiting Drogheda and Limerick in 1685–6.[7] For a time he lived well in Dublin. After the Williamite war he was to devote himself to literature, translating a number of Spanish works into English and writing ecclesiastical history. While in Ireland he fought at the Boyne with the losing Jacobite army, of which he writes contemptuously as a mountainy rabble ill led by unsoldierly officers. But in the following passage, though also critical, in places, of Jacobite policy or firmness, Stevens acknowledges the stubborn defence of Limerick put up by Catholic troops against Protestant attack.

From *The Journal of John Stevens* (1689–91):[8]

Saturday the 9th: the Prince of Orange invested the town, enclosing with his army all that is not surrounded by the Shannon. Detachments of our foot, supported by the dragoons, disputed every field with the enemy, lining the hedges and retiring orderly from one to another after several volleys and some execution till they came within shelter of our cannon or outworks, and there they continued in small bodies in the ditches and kept their ground all night. In this skirmishing we lost but very few men, nor indeed could we spare them so that it was done only for form and to amuse the enemy. Giving way still as they pressed upon us, there was never an officer killed but Sir Maurice Eustace had his horse shot under him in the midst of us, and Fitzpatrick's major his in a field below us, but neither they nor any of us hurt. I will not be too exact in affirming what garrison we had, I know both to encourage us and terrify the enemy we were given out to be 15,000 strong, but I can be positive that to my knowledge we were not in all 10,000, including the unarmed men which were a considerable number. This day the Grand Prior with the regiments joined, which I shall no more repeat, mounted the hornwork, Hamilton the east side trenches, Maxwell's Dragoons from the south-east to the south-west tower, on the west side Bellew and Gormanstown. Detachments mounted the redoubts, the walls and English town being posts of less consequence, and never falling to these that were the best regiments, except the walls when the siege grew hot; I shall make no mention of them, not being able to give a general account of all places, being constantly tied to the duties of my post, which being in a regiment of such repute was commonly where there was most probability of service. I shall be brief in my relation of the siege, affirming only what I saw or received from eyewitnesses of credit, for considering my post at that time very much cannot be expected, and I had rather be brief with truth and omit small passages than by pretending to more particulars than I can affirm deliver falsehoods or at least uncertainties. There was within the bornwork a small stone half-moon that covered Mungret Gate, now quite made up. This place was appointed for a party of horse and here constantly stood about thirty of Luttrell's regiment ready upon all occasions.

[. . .]

Wednesday the 27th: the enemy's batteries played furiously, the farthest off being the least at Ball's Bridge, the great one at the breach till they had laid it open above thirty paces and made the ascent plainer on their side than it was from the town. About noon the trenches were to be relieved which in part was done, only the Grand Prior's to which, as was said before, because of the weakness of regiments were joined Slane's and Boisseleau's, stood at arms in the street in order to have relieved the hornwork. It had been before ordered that as they relieved one regiment should still stand at arms till another came in. It was our good fortune to attend then when on a sudden we were commanded to light our matches and that scarce done to march towards St. John's Gate and man the walls, but before we could reach it our governor, Major-General Boisseleau, came running and, ordering us to the left, led to the breach. Before we could come up the running we perceived the breach possessed by the enemy, a great number came down into the retrenchment made within it and above twenty of them were got into the street. Having heard no firing of small shot before, we at the first sight thought they had been our guards retiring out of the counterscarp, they being all in red coats, till we discovered the green boughs in their hats which was the mark of distinction worn by the rebels, whereas ours was white paper. Besides an officer on the breach brandishing his sword called upon his men to follow, crying the town was their own. Our guards, who were in the counterscarp, on the first appearance of the enemy abandoned their post without firing a shot, flying with such precipitation that many of them forced their way through our dragoons, who were posted on the right of them towards St. John's Gate. These dragoons behaved themselves with much bravery presenting their pieces upon such of the guards as had not pierced through them, which obliged many to stand as did some of their officers ashamed of the infamous flight of their men. With these few that stood by them the dragoons made good their post during the whole time of the action. Meanwhile the Grand Prior's Regiment had well lined the retrenchment within the breach and, being undeceived that the enemy and not our own men were those that rushed in so impetuous, the word was given to fire, which was performed so effectively that a considerable number of the rebels dropped, and our men renewed their charges with such vigour that in a very short space they had not left one enemy within the breach, though still nothing daunted they pressed over, fresh men succeeding those that were killed or wounded. This sort of fight was continued near an hour, our battalion alone making good their ground against that multitude of enemies which being still backed with new supplies was all that while insensible of its losses. During this dispute most of the inhabitants of the Irish town giving it for lost fled into the English town, as did also the regiment of Colonel Butler of Ballyraggett to which three others were joined, and all ordered to support us that bore the brunt at the breach. The guards that were upon the gate of the English town at Ball's Bridge shut it against these regiments, which by that means were again formed and marched to the breach, but not till the heat of the action was over the enemy having been beaten, from it, which was in this manner. Our continual fire having made a great slaughter among the rebels and they beginning to abate of their first fury, M. de Beaupré, a Frenchman, and Lieutenant-Colonel to Boisseleau our Governor, leaped over the retrenchment making to the breach. Most men strove to be foremost in imitating so good an example, so that being followed by a resolute party he soon recovered the top of the breach. Here the fight was for some time renewed and continued with sword in hand and the butt end of the musket. Our other men upon the walls were not idle this while, some firing and others casting stones upon the enemy beneath, which did no small execution, but the greatest havoc was made by two pieces of cannon playing from the citadel and two others from the King's Island, as also two others from the Augustine chapel near Ball's Bridge, which last scoured all along our counterscarp then filled with rebels, and the other four swept them in their approach on the south and east sides. The enemy thus cut off on all sides came on faintly, and a barrel of powder which lay near the south-east tower accidentally taking fire and blowing up some that were near it, the rest conceived it had been a mine and fled, neither fair words nor threats of officers prevailing to bring them back. The action continued hot and dubious for at least three hours, and, above half an hour after, went in diminution till the enemy wholly drew off. A great slaughter was made of them: deserters and prisoners who spoke the least, affirming above 3,000 were killed and wounded but others spoke of much greater numbers, and I am apt to believe by what we afterwards found unburied there could not be much less than 3,000 killed. On our side the dead and wounded amounted not to 500, among the first were Lieutenant Beaupré before mentioned and Colonel Barnewell who had no post there but being under some imputation of cowardice came to clear his honour at the expense of his life; among the latter a French major of the regiment of Boisseleau and others of less note, as also Lieutenant-Colonel Smith, captain of a company of foot guards killed, and Sir James Mockler, Lieutenant-Colonel of Dragoons wounded. It was God's providence that the enemy attacked not the hornwork at the same time as the breach, for those regiments that were in it, though never assaulted apprehending the town was lost quitted it, and fled down to the river wihout reflecting there was no way for them there to escape and that their only security was in their arms; but God had not ordained the town should be lost at this time. After the enemy was wholly withdrawn from the attack the guards repossessed themselves of the counterscarp. Those who had made good the breach continued in arms about it all the night without receiving any molestations from the enemy, unless the firing now and then of a cannon, as it had been to keep us waking, and the casting a few bombs and carcasses which had little or no effect.

Thursday the 28th: the enemy played their cannon very hot at the breach to enlarge it towards the south angle, and to beat down a small part of that tower which sheltered our men on the south wall from their host, and had been prejudicial to them mounting the breach. The first they performed as to laying the breach wider open, but their design on the remaining part of the tower took no effect. From their lower battery next to the bog they plied the bridge so warmly it was very dangerous to pass. This, as was remarked before, is not the great bridge over the main body of the Shannon, but a small one over a branch of it, and joins the English and Irish towns; the communication between which they laboured to cut off, which if effected must have proved fatal to us, but the damage they did was inconsiderable. In the morning only the Grand Prior's regiment was relieved with orders to refresh only for four hours and then to be at arms again, which being done, 250 men were drawn in five detachments of 50 each and posted in several places. That which I commanded was ordered to the middle tower on the east wall which was much shaken and still battered, where we continued all the rest of the day and night following. Several were this day killed in the counterscarp by the stones that flew from the wall.

Friday the 29th: the enemy's cannon played as before and enlarged the breach to above forty paces. At the bridge one shot cut both the chains of the drawbridge and did some other damage but not of much moment, because the enemy's battery had not a full view of it, and their shot came slanting towards one end, yet the passage was very dangerous. The Grand Prior's detachments were all relieved this afternoon except that where I commanded, which continued in the same place till night, when being relieved we only marched into the street, and having joined the rest of the regiment to the trenches on the south-west side of the town, where we continued all night expecting an attack. The night was extreme cold, dark and rainy and we almost spent for want of rest. For my own particular as appears by this relation I had had none at all for three nights before this and but very little during the whole siege, nor indeed was it possible to have much being upon duty every other day and continually alarmed when we expected to rest. Our cannon and small shot fired the whole night round the walls, and much railing was betwixt our men and the enemies, for we were so closed up on all sides that though the night was stormy we could easily hear one another.

Saturday the 30th: in the morning we observed there was great silence in the enemy's works and day appearing we could not perceive anybody in them, which at first was looked upon as a stratagem to draw us out of our works, but some few being sent out to discover returned and brought the news that all abroad was clear. Immediately the word was carried about all our works that the rebels had raised the siege and stole away in the dead of night, which at first seemed incredible to many. In a short space our men could not be contained within the works but running out found the enemy's trenches and batteries abandoned, and their dead lying everywhere in great numbers unburied, being those that were killed at the assault. All that had anything they stripped but the plunder was very poor, the clothes being old and coarse and having lain two days and upwards in the dirt and rain upon those carcasses.

3) George Story

George Story wrote his account of the Williamite Irish war from personal observation; he was chaplain to one of the English regiments.[9] In the following passage he describes an encounter between Irish rapparees (guerilla fighters, in modern terminology) and English forces.

From *An Impartial History (1693)*:[10]

At this time Colonel *Byerley* being at *Mountmelick* with part of his own Regiment, and some of Colonel *Earl*'s Foot, he was frequently Allarmed; as well by Parties of the *Irish* Army, as by Considerable Numbers of Rapparees, who had a design to burn the Town, as they had done several others thereabouts; but the Colonel was very watchful, and kept good Intelligence (a main Matter in this Affair.) He was told of a Party that designed to burn the Town; and he took care to have all his Men, both Horse and Foot, in readiness to welcome them; but they heard of his Posture and durst not Venture; however on the third of *December* he had notice of a Body of Rapparees, that were not far from the Town, and designed him a Mischief; he sends out Lieutenant *Dent* with Twenty Horse, and ordered each Horseman to take a Musqueteer behind him; when the Horse came almost within sight of the Rapparees, they dropt their Foot, who marched closely behind the Hedges unperceived by the Enemy. When the Enemy espied so small a Party of Horse, they Advanced from the side of the Bog towards them; the Horse seem'd to Retreat a little, till the Rapparees were

Advanced within Musquet-shot of our Foot, who firing amongst them, kill'd several, and then Lieutenant *Dent* fell in with his Horse; as also the Foot charged them a second time, that after some resistance they kill'd Thirty nine, and took Four, whom they hanged without any further Ceremony. The rest escaped to the Bogs, and in a manner all disappeared; which may seem strange to those that have not seen it, but something of this kind I have seen my self; and those of this Party assured me, that after the Action was over, some of them looking about amongst the Dead, found one *Dun* a Serjeant of the Enemies, who was lying like an Otter, all under Water in a running Brook, (except the top of his Nose and Mouth;) they brought him out, and although he proffer'd Forty Shillings in *English* Money to save his Life (a great Ransom as he believed) yet he was one of the Four that was hanged. When the Rapparees have no mind to show themselves upon the Bogs, they commonly sink down between two or three little Hills, grown over with long Grass, so that you may a soon find a Hair [sic] as one of them: they conceal their Arms thus, they take off the Lock and put it in their Pocket, or hide it in some dry Place; they stop the Mussle close with a Cork, and the Tutch-hole with a small Quil, and then throw the Piece it self into a running Water or a Pond; you may see an hundred of them without Arms, who look like the poorest humblest Slaves in the World, and you may search till you are weary before you can find one Gun; but yet when they have a mind to do mischief, they can all be ready in an Hours warning, for every one knows where to go and fetch his own Arms, though you do not.

4) John Wesley

John Wesley (1703–91), the fifteenth child and second son of Samuel Wesley, rector at Epworth in Lincolnshire, was educated at Charterhouse and Oxford and followed his father into the ministry. In the 1720s he formed at Oxford the holy club known as methodists, and in 1735 undertook a mission to Georgia which lasted two years and was described as 'troubled' on account of resistance in the colony to his too precise notions. He returned to England in 1737–8, travelled through Holland and Germany, and began open-air preaching. Wesley first visited Ireland in 1747 and made a total of twenty one visits between that year and 1789. These were missionary visits first and foremost. Wesley had little interest in Ireland or the Irish for their own sake, but unlike most English travellers of his period he mixed with the poor as well as the rich, and his journal contains a good deal on ordinary life in the Irish countryside, towns and roads. The following passage describes a hostile reception given to him in Enniskillen in 1773.[11]

From *The Journal of . . . John Wesley* (1909–16):

One of my horses having a shoe loose, I borrowed Mr. Watson's horse, and left him with the chaise. When we came near Enniskillen, I desired two only to ride with me, and the rest of our friends to keep at a distance. Some masons were at work on the first bridge, who gave us some coarse words. We had abundance more as we rode through the town; but many soldiers being in the street, and taking knowledge of me in a respectful manner, the mob shrunk back. An hour after Mr. Watson came in the chaise. Before he came to the bridge many ran together and began to throw whatever came next to hand. The bridge itself they had blocked up with large stones, so that a carriage could not pass; but an old man cried out, 'It this the way you use strangers?' and rolled away the stones. The mob quickly rewarded him by plastering him over with dirt and mortar from head to foot. They then fell upon the carriage, which they cut with stones in several places, and wellnigh covered with dirt and mortar. From one end of the town to the other the stones flew thick about the coachman's head. Some of them were two or three pounds' weight, which they threw with all their might. If but one of them had struck him it would have effectually prevented him from driving any farther; and then, doubtless, they would have given an account of the chaise and horses.

I preached at Sidaire in the evening and morning, and then set out for Roosky. The road lay not far from Enniskillen. When we came pretty near the town both men and women saluted us, first with bad words, and then with dirt and stones. My horses soon left them behind; but not till they had broke one of the windows, the glass of which came pouring in upon me, but did me no further hurt.

About an hour after John Smith came to Enniskillen. The masons on the bridge preparing for battle, he was afraid his horse would leap with him into the river, and therefore chose to alight. Immediately they poured in upon him a whole shower of dirt and stones. However, he made his way through the town, though pretty much daubed and bruised.

At Roosky Mr. Macburney, one of our preachers, gave me the following account: On Thursday, March 4, he went to Mr. Perry's a quarter of a mile from Aghalun, a village six or seven miles from

Enniskillen. In the evening he was singing a hymn, when a large mob beset the house. Six of these rushed in, armed with clubs, and immediately fell upon the people; but, many of them joining together, thrust them out, and shut and fastened the door. On this they broke every pane of glass in the windows, and threw in a large quantity of stones. They then broke into the house, through a weak part of the wall, and, hauling out both men and women, beat them without mercy. Soon after they dragged out Mr. Macburney, whom M--- N--- instantly knocked down. They continued beating him on the head and breast, while he lay senseless on the ground. Yet, after a while, coming a little to himself, he got up; but not being quite sensible, staggered, and fell again. Then one of them set his foot upon his face, swearing he would tread the Holy Ghost out of him. Another ran his stick into his mouth. As soon as he could speak he said, 'May God forgive you! I do.' They then set him on his horse, and M--- N--- got up behind and forced him to gallop down the rocky mountain to the town. There they kept him, till a gentleman took him out of their hands, and entertained and lodged him in the most hospitable manner. But his bruises, on his head and breast in particular, would not suffer him to sleep; and ever since he has felt such inward pain and weakness that it is a wonder that he is still alive.

One of those that was much abused was Mr. Mitchell, who lives about a mile from the town. On Saturday the mob came to his house, about eight in the evening, swearing they would have his father's heart's blood. They threw many large stones at the windows, and broke a great hole in the door. Through this hole Mr. Mitchell, seeing no other remedy, fired twice with small shot. At the second shot they ran away with all speed, no man looking behind him.

Mr. Perry and Mitchell applying to Mr. Irwin, of Green Hill, he granted warrants for six of the rioters; and the next week, for fifteen more; but the constable would not take them; and the next week, at the Assizes held in Enniskillen, the Grand Jury threw out all the bills! Therefore, it is to these honourable gentlemen I am obliged for all the insults and outrage I met with. But, meantime, where is liberty, civil or religious? Does it exist in Aghalun or Enniskillen?

5) Thomas De Quincey

Thomas De Quincey (1785–1859) was born at Greenheys, Manchester, the son of a merchant who died when the boy was seven; thereafter he was brought up by his evangelistic mother. He went to Eton, where he met Lord Westport (son of Lord Altamont the Irish peer) and with this school friend he travelled to Dublin and the west of Ireland in his fifteenth year. The last sitting of the Irish House of Lords took place while De Quincey was in Dublin, and in the following passage he describes this formal event. De Quincey recalled as formative the interesting experiences he met on his Irish journey from Dublin to Westport, but gives few details. He made a second journey to Ireland in 1857 to visit his daughter, who had married in 1853 and settled in Ireland.[12]

From *Autobiography from 1785 to 1803* (1889):[13]

Lord Westport and I were determined to lose no part of the scene, and we went down with Lord Altamont to the House. It was about the middle of the day, and a great mob filled the whole space about the two Houses. As Lord Altamont's coach drew up to the steps of that splendid edifice, we heard a prodigious hissing and hooting; and I was really agitated to think that Lord Altamont, whom I loved and respected, would probably have to make his way through a tempest of public wrath — a situation more terrific to him than to others, from his embarrassed walking. I found, however, that I might have spared my anxiety; the subject of the commotion was, simply, that Major Sirr, or Major Swan, I forget which (both being so celebrated in those days for their energy as leaders of the police), had detected a person in the act of mistaking some other man's pocket-handkerchief for his own — a most natural mistake, I should fancy, where people stood crowded together so thickly. No storm of any kind awaited us, and yet at that moment there was no other arrival to divide the public attention; for, in order that we might see everything from first to last, we were amongst the very earliest parties. Neither did our party escape under any mistake of the crowd: silence had succeeded to the uproar caused by the tender meeting between the thief and the major; and a man, who stood in a conspicuous situation, proclaimed aloud to those below him the name or title of members as they drove up. 'That,' said he, 'is the Earl of Altamont; the lame gentleman, I mean.' Perhaps, however, his knowledge did not extend so far as to the politics of a nobleman who had taken no violent or factious part in public affairs. At least the dreaded insults did not follow, or only in the very feeblest manifestations. We entered; and, by way of seeing everything, we went even to the robing-room. The man who presented his robes to Lord Altamont seemed to me, of all whom I saw on that day, the one who wore the face of deepest depression. But, whether this indicated the loss of a lucrative situation, or was really disinterested sorrow, growing out of a patriotic trouble at the knowledge that he was now officiating for the last time, I could not guess. The House of Lords, decorated (if I remember) with hangings representing the battle of the Boyne, was nearly empty when we entered — an accident which furnished to Lord Altamont the opportunity required for explaining to us the whole course and ceremonial of public business on ordinary occasions.

Gradually the House filled: beautiful women sat intermingled amongst the peers; and, in one party of these, surrounded by a bevy of admirers, we saw our fair but frail enchantress of the packet. She, on her part, saw and recognised us by an affable nod; no stain upon her cheek, indicating that she suspected to what extent she was indebted to our discretion; for it is a proof of the unaffected sorrow and the solemn awe which oppressed us both, that we had not mentioned, even to Lord Altamont, nor ever *did* mention, the scene which chance had revealed to us. Next came a stir within the house, and an uproar resounding from without, which announced the arrival of his Excellency. Entering the house, he also, like the other peers, wheeled round to the throne, and made to that mysterious seat a profound homage. Then commenced the public business, in which, if I recollect, the Chancellor played the most conspicuous part — that Chancellor (Lord Clare) of whom it was affirmed in those days, by a political opponent, that he might swim in the innocent blood which he had caused to be shed. But nautical men, I suspect, would have demurred to that estimate. Then were summoned to the bar — summoned for the last time — the gentlemen of the House of Commons; in the van of whom, and drawing all eyes upon himself, stood Lord Castlereagh. Then came the recitation of many acts passed during the session, and the sounding ratification, the jovian contained in the *Soit fait comme il est desiré*, or the more peremptory *Le Roi le veut*.[14] At which point in the order of succession came the royal assent to the Union Bill, I cannot distinctly recollect. But one thing I *do* recollect — that no audible expression, no buzz, nor murmur, nor *susurrus* even, testified the feelings which, doubtless, lay rankling in many bosoms. Setting apart all public or patriotic considerations, even then I said to myself, as I surveyed the whole assemblage of ermined peers, 'How is it, and by what unaccountable magic, that William Pitt can have prevailed on all these hereditary legislators and heads of patrician houses to renounce so easily, with nothing worth the name of a struggle, and no reward worth the name of an indemnification, the very brightest jewel in their coronets? This morning they all rose from their couches Peers of Parliament, individual pillars of the realm, indispensable parties to every law that could pass. To-morrow they will be nobody — men of straw — *terrae filii.*[15] What madness has persuaded them to part with their birthright, and to cashier themselves and their children for ever into mere titular Lords?' As to the Commoners at the bar, *their* case was different: they had no life estate at all events in their honours; and they might have the same chance for entering the Imperial Parliament amongst the hundred Irish members, as for re-entering a native Parliament. Neither, again, amongst the peers was the case always equal. Several of the higher had English titles, which would, at any rate, open the central Parliament to their ambition. That privilege, in particular, attached to Lord Altamont. And he, in any case, from his large property, was tolerably sure of finding his way thither (as in fact for the rest of his life he *did*) amongst the twenty-eight Representative Peers. The wonder was in the case of petty and obscure lords, who had no weight personally, and none in right of their estates. Of these men, as they were notoriously not enriched by Mr. Pitt, as the distribution of honours was not very large, and as no honour could countervail the one they lost — I could not, and cannot, fathom the policy. Thus much I am sure of — that, had such a measure been proposed by a political speculator previously to Queen Anne's reign, he would have been scouted as a dreamer and a visionary, who calculated upon men being generally somewhat worse than Esau — viz., giving up their birthrights, and *without* the mess of pottage. However, on this memorable day, thus it was the Union was ratified; the bill received the royal assent without a muttering, or a whispering, or the protesting echo of a sigh. Perhaps there might be a little pause — a silence like that with follows an earthquake; but there was no plain-spoken Lord Belhaven as on the corresponding occasion in Edinburgh, to fill up the silence with, 'So, there's an end of an auld sang!' All was or looked courtly, and free from vulgar emotion. One person only I remarked whose features were suddenly illuminated by a smile, a sarcastic smile, as I read it; which, however, might be all a fancy. It was Lord Castlereagh; who, at the moment when the irrevocable words were pronounced, looked with a penetrating glance amongst a party of ladies. His own wife was one of that party; but I did not discover the particular object on whom his smile had settled. After this I had no leisure to be interested in anything which followed. 'You are all,' thought I to myself, 'a pack of vagabonds henceforward, and interlopers, with actually no more right to be here than myself. I am an intruder; so are you.' Apparently they thought so themselves; for, soon after this solemn *fiat* of Jove had gone forth, their lordships, having no farther title to their robes (for which I could not help wishing that a party of Jewish old-clothesmen would at this moment have appeared and made a loud bidding), made what haste they could to lay them aside for ever. The House dispersed much more rapidly than it had assembled. Major Sirr was found outside, just where we left him, laying down the law (as before) about pocket-hankerchiefs to old and young practitioners; and all parties adjourned to find what consolation they might in the great evening event of dinner.

6) Thomas Reid

Thomas Reid toured Ireland in 1822 to explore the country's social and economic evils, including prison conditions. He sailed from Liverpool to Dublin, then toured the southern half of Ulster before travelling south, west and north in a large sweep which took in Kilkenny, Waterford and Cork, Killarney, Valencia, Limerick, Galway, Westport and Sligo. From here, via Edgeworthstown, Enniskillen and Belfast, he made his way back to Dublin. Reid's account of his journey shows him to be a clear observer with an eye for telling detail (such as the children he found in an empty cabin in Monaghan, tied to the bed to keep them from the fire).[16] For Reid Ireland appears an 'anomaly among nations',[17] and political factors, unsurprisingly, are named as the cause.

From *Travels in Ireland* (1823):[18]

This being the anniversary of the ever-memorable battle of the Boyne, a day hallowed in the calendar of certain persons in this part of the country, self-denominated *Orangemen*, and by them always devoted to unbounded festivity. I was desirous to observe what might happen at a place where it was understood several bodies of them had determined to assemble. A small town called Middleton, about seven miles from Armagh, was the place of rendez-vous appointed: the cause of this place being selected was openly declared by some of those brave, highminded gentry, and was simply this; — some three or four years back, a number of them had met as usual to celebrate the *'glorious memory'*, and insult their fellow-subjects, the Catholics, who, at length, driven to resentment, repelled the aggressors, and the affray terminated in the glorious-memory-men getting 'gloriously' thrashed. This stain on their chivalry they were determined to wipe off, and for this purpose their forces were this day to be concentrated on the ground which had before been the theatre of defeat.

At an early hour the road between Dungannon and Caledon was crowded with men, boys, women, and children: most of them wore shoes, many had stockings, and all were provided with flags, scarfs, or ribands of an orange colour; some of these indeed were discoloured by smoke and soot-rain, but their owners (or more properly their wearers, for it was said that many of them were borrowed), did not appear to prize them the less on that account. The importance of the occasion was heightened by drums, fifes, and bugles, which produced exhilarating discord. Some of the Orangemen and *Orangewomen* were mounted on horses that appeared certainly to stand more in need of a feed of oats than the airing intended for them in this procession.

Having passed the preceding night at the house of a relation close to the road, I was enabled to observe minutely every particular of this irregular and grotesque assemblage. There lived in the neighbourhood a poor man, named John Beaviers, almost worn out by disease, — hoemoptysis[19] had brought him to the verge of the grave. I had myself prescribed for him, and most rigidly enjoined abstinence and quiet: but so irresistible was the desire to swell the ultra-loyal ranks, that this infatuated creature was staggering along in the crowd, nobly supported by his wife. On my expressing astonishment and regret at the fatal folly of this man, an acquaintance who was standing by, and who was an Orangeman, said, 'The boys must all show themselves; else how could we tell whether they are of the right or wrong sort?' I asked, would any of those 'right or wrong' fellows support the poor man's widow and children if he were called from them. This seemed treading on tender ground; — I got no reply, and my 'right or wrong' friend walked off, not at all pleased at my curiosity.

It would appear that part of the infantry, I mean the Orangewomen, got tired on the march, as many of them were seen returning during the forenoon, not preserving the best possible order. Their native thriftiness, which had been awhile smothered by orange ardour, seemed to revive with increased keenness; for most of those who in the morning wore stockings and shoes, had now divested themselves of those unusual, and to them unnecessary, incumbrances. About three in the afternoon I rode to Caledon, a distance of four miles; the way was strewed with orange-lilies, and at particular places were thrown over it triumphal arches, decorated with orange-festoons, and garlands innumerable. The scene was quite delightful, and reminded me of the fabled stories of fairy-land I had read at school.

From Caledon I had three miles further to travel to Middleton; and this road would have been more enchanting, if possible, than the former, had it not been rendered less so by meeting straggling parties of the Orangemen, who had taken a premature departure from the aggregate body; not, however, before they had laid in a large store of whiskey and irresistible loyalty. So desirous were they of an opportunity to display this exalted sentiment, that the cry 'Five pounds for the face of a black-*moutht Papish*', (meaning, I suppose, Papist,) was shouted incessantly. Many of them were mounted on horses, which, I knew, were not their own; almost every horse had two riders; and the violence with which those half-starved animals were driven, fully verified the old saying, 'Borrowed horses have hard hoofs.' It was really disgusting to hear the shout from boys whose ages could not have exceeded sixteen or seventeen years; but some of whom, it would seem, were officers, as they bore standards, and were invested with other insignia indicative of authority.

About half-way between Caledon and Middleton, I met a large body of them; they had fourteen flags, each of which, I was told, belonged to a distinct lodge. In this crowd, I should think, there were between eleven and twelve hundred persons; and I can safely and solemly [sic] assert, that in the whole number there was not one decent-looking individual. This did not disappoint me; for I was assured that men who had any pretensions to respectability could not be found in brotherhood, or in any way associating with such *canaille.* I do not mean to say that decent-looking men are not to be found in the Orange ranks at all: I am acquainted with some gentlemen of respectability belonging to that association, who would reflect credit on any institution; but I cannot believe they would so entirely forget what they owe to society as gentlemen, and to themselves as men, to herd with such persons as have just been noticed.

The latter part of the road to Middleton exhibited a more complete picture of drunkenness and violence than the former. Extirpation of the unoffending Catholics was a cherished object. In the arms of apparent death, the faint cry of 'Five pound — for the face of a — black-*moutht* Papish,' was the last articulate sound that could be collected from those heroes, when they fell overwhelmed by the effects of extreme intoxication.

Having heard some of the Orangemen, several weeks before this, avow their determination to avenge some indignity that had been offered to their party on a former occasion, and knowing that a considerable portion of the population of that part of the country were Catholics, who, it was reasonable to suppose, would oppose force to violence, I apprehended serious consequences from the agitation that was likely to prevail; but was much pleased to find less riot and confusion in the town than I expected. Most of the Orangemen had left it; and as those who remained could find no Catholics to fight with, a quarrel there could not easily be excited. It is barely doing justice to say, that the conduct of the Catholics this day was orderly, decent, and peaceable in a most creditable degree.

After sauntering through the town about an hour, and witnessing many acts of extravagance, I proceeded to Blackwater Town, and that short journey presented a striking contrast to the parade of the morning. the condition of one of the 'ultras' was both ludicrous and disgusting. A great many falls had extensively rent the hinder part of his nankeen trowsers, which was not observable as he lay on the ground; but some kind friends, desirous of getting him home, placed him across the back of a horse, as they would *spoleen* or horse-beef, his arms and head hanging down on one side, and his legs on the other, which exposed the accident. Dangling in this position, sickness speedily came on; and, in all probability, apoplexy would have terminated his 'glorious' career, had I not interposed, and requested them to set him down. While suspended across the back of the horse, his loyalty must have experienced considerable diminution, as it was escaping at both extremities.

Others of these worthies, having exhausted their loyal abuse on the yielding air, had supplied the vacuum with copious libations to the demon of ebriety, and were getting home with various proofs of constitutional ability; but many were incapable of proceeding unless supported by their wives or sisters, who, expecting this result, had come to their assistance. The scene resembled groups of *calibans* intermingled with angelic forms, who were smiling with sober compassion on the unwieldy and senseless burdens they endeavoured to help along. What pity that men should deprive themselves of the blessings of reason, and be rendered incapable of appreciating the enjoyment of civil liberty amidst the delights and charms of female society!

7) William Cobbett

William Cobbett (1762–1835) was born at Farnham, Surrey. After some time spent working as a field labourer he became an attorney's clerk in London, then enlisted, and travelled as a soldier to Nova Scotia. In 1791 he returned to England and left the military service, having been a soldier for eight years. He visited France, then in 1792 emigrated to America, where he taught French refugees to speak English and became a political and literary journalist. He returned to England in 1800, started a bookshop in 1801 and in the next year began publishing his weekly *Political Register*; this continued to appear for over thirty years. In 1803 Cobbett began reporting Parliamentary debates; Hansard grew out of his venture. About 1804 Cobbett went over to the popular side in politics, and he was imprisoned in 1810 for two years for publishing an attack on military flogging. In 1816 he vastly increased the *Political Register*'s circulation by lowering its price to two pence. In 1817 he went to America for two years, farming and writing; he returned with the bones of Thomas Paine. From 1821 Cobbett undertook political tours of England on horseback; the eventual 'Rural Rides'. He took a leading part in the journalistic movement for reform. He was prosecuted for sedition in 1831 but defended himself, and was acquitted. He became MP for Oldham in the reformed Parliament. Cobbett's writings on Ireland show him against absenteeism, against potatoes, against Scotch economic philosophy. He sees Ireland as a political testing ground for England, and writes on Ireland with England principally in mind, but, at the same time, urges on his working class readers solidarity with the needy people of Ireland. Cobbett cultivates a style which, as the following extract shows, is direct, repetitive, personal and racy.

From *Cobbett in Ireland* (1984):[20]

Dublin, 27 September 1834.
MARSHALL,

After I wrote to you, the other day, about the MENDICITY, I went again at the dinner time. You know, I saw the breakfast! that is the *ground oats* and *butter-milk* or *water*, or *skim-milk*, (sometimes one and sometimes the other), boiling in great coppers for the breakfast; and now I went to see the *dinner*; and the gentlemen, who have the management of the place, showed me all about it. There are about *three thousand* persons fed here, and, if they were not thus fed, they must either *die*, or *thieve* or *rob*; or more properly *take by force*; for, in such a case, the words *theft* or *robbery* do not, according to the just laws of England, apply to the act; though they do apply, and I hope, always will apply, in England.

I saw this 'dinner'. In one long room, there were about 500 women, each with some potatoes in a bowl, mashed, as you mash them to mix with meal, for your hogs. These people go to one end of the room, and, one at a time, get their mess. There are persons to put the potatoes into the bowl, which they do by taking the potatoes out of a tub, with a tin measure, holding about a quart, and putting the thing full into the bowl, which is then carried away by the person who is to eat it; and all these persons are, as they eat, *standing up* in the room, as thick as they can stand. Each, as soon as the mess is eaten, goes away; and, as there is room made, others come in; and there were about three hundred then waiting in the yard to take their turn.

There were about a hundred little girls in a *school*, and about as many boys in another; neither had shoes or stockings, and the boys had *no shirts*. Their faces were pale, the whole hundred not having so much red as your little round-faced chap that was set to keep the birds away from the cabbage seed in Dodman's field. Yes, Marshall, that little chap, with his satchel full of bread and cheese or bacon; he was at the *proper school*! He and Tom Deadman and little Barratt will make strong and able men like their fathers; will live well, and be well clothed; and will be respected like their fathers; and be happy in that state of life in which it has pleased God to place them; and will not, I hope, listen to any fanatical man, who would persuade them, that to starve in rags, in this world, has a tendency to give them a crown of glory in the next.

In another place I saw a great crowd of women sitting and doing nothing, each with a baby in her arms. They were sitting in rows, waiting, I believe, for the messes. Some of them were young and naturally handsome; but made ugly by starvation, rags, and dirt. It was one mass of rags; not rags such as you see on the beggars or gipsies that go to hopping at Farnham; but far worse than any that you ever saw tied round a stake to frighten the birds from our wheat and our peas; far worse than the Kentish people and South Hampshire people put on a scare-crow to keep the birds from their cherries. And this is the condition, Marshall, in which the Scotch *feelosofer*[21] vagabonds wish to persuade the Parliament to reduce the wives and the daughters of the working people of England! while they talk of *educating* you all, at the same time! Ah! Marshall, these vagabonds want to give you *books*, and to take away the *bread* and *meat* for themselves.

In another place I saw the most painful sight of all: *women*, with heavy hammers, *cracking stones* into very small pieces, to *make walks in gentlemen's gardens*! These women were as ragged as the rest; and the sight of them and their work, and the thoughts accompanying these, would have sunk the heart in your body, as they did mine. and [sic] are the women and girls of England to be brought to this state? Would not every man in Normandy suffer every drop of blood to be let out of his body rather than see your sisters and daughters and mothers and wives brought to this state? If I were not *sure* that Tom Farr would perish himself rather than see his sister brought to this, he should not live under my roof a moment longer. And what, then, of his good and industrious and kind and tender mother! The bare thought would drive him mad! Yet, Marshall, it is my duty to tell you, that the half-drunk and half-mad and greedy and crawling Scotch vagabonds, whose counsel have beggared the Scotch working people, are endeavouring to persuade the Parliament to bring your wives, mothers, sisters, and daughters into this very state! Be on your guard, therefore; be ready to perform *your* duty to prevent the success of these crawling villains, who hope to get rewarded for their schemes for making you work for 6d. a day, and for putting your wages into the pockets of the landlords. When I get back we will have a meeting at Guildford to petition the king and Parliament on the subject; to this meeting you must all come; for, though the law does not give you the right of *voting*, it always gives you the right of *petitioning*; and as I shall hereafter show you, it gives you a *right* to *parish relief* in case you are *unable* to *earn* a sufficiency to keep you in a proper manner. This is as much as your *birth-right* as is the lord of the manor's right to his estate; and of this we will convince the crawling and greedy vagabonds before we have done. It is our duty, too, to exert this right to endeavour to better the lot of our suffering fellow-subjects in Ireland. Mr Dean will tell you, that I have always set my face against the ill-treatment of Irish people who go to get work in England. Their own food is sent away from them to England, for the benefit of their landlords; we receive the food, and it is monstrous injustice in us to frown upon them, if they come and offer their labour in exchange for a part of that very food which they themselves have raised.

8) John Forbes

John Forbes journeyed through Ireland in 1852, first touring the south-western parts, then the west and finally the north. He throws into his topographical descriptions a miscellany of essays on Catholic Ireland, Irish history and education, round towers, teetotalism and Union workhouses. Emigration, which Forbes here describes, was a long-standing Irish problem. In the following extract emigrants leaving Killaloe say goodbye to their families and friends.

From *Memorandums made in Ireland* (1853):[22]

We found the steamer waiting for us, and the little pier thickly crowded with people waiting to go on board or to see their friends on board. The deck was, indeed, so crowded, that it was not an easy matter to get from one part of it to another: and the crowding and confusion were still further increased by the whole of the fore part of the vessel being occupied by cattle.

It was soon seen that a party of emigrants had come or were coming on board, and were now taking leave of their friends with every token of the most passionate distress. With that utter unconsciousness and disregard of being the observed of all observers, which characterises authentic sorrow, these warm-hearted and simple-minded people demeaned themselves entirely as if they had been shrouded in all the privacy of home, clinging to and kissing and embracing each other with the utmost ardour, calling out aloud, in broken tones, the endeared names of brother, sister, mother, sobbing and crying as if the very heart would burst, while the unheeded tears ran down from the red swollen eyes literally in streams. It was a sight that no human being could see unmoved; and when the final orders were given to clear the ship and withdraw the gangway, the howl of agony that rose at once from the parting deck and the abandoned pier, was perfectly overpowering. 'O Mary! O Kitty! O mother dear! O brother! O sister! God bless you! God preserve you! The Lord in Heaven protect you!' and a thousand other wild and pious ejaculations, broken and intermixed by agonising cries and choking sobs, literally filled the air, and almost drowned the roar of the engine and the wheels that tore the loving hearts that uttered them asunder.

Amid the crowds of people on the pier, swaying to and fro as they shouted aloud and waved their hats and handkerchiefs, several women were seen kneeling on the stones, kneeling and weeping, with their hands raised fixedly above them, and so continuing as long as they could be distinguished from the receding vessel.

The scene was altogether a most painful one to witness, and not soon to be forgotten by those who witnessed it. If it told, in language not to be misunderstood, of the warm and strong affections of a most cordial people, it brought home the truth to the fancies of all, and to the memories and hearts of many — that there is no greater pang in the store of life's ills than Separation. And, indeed, such a separation as this, is often a greater pang, to one of the sufferers at least, than death itself is; for here, on both sides, nature still retains her full consciousness of loss and her full strength to suffer; while Providence has most kindly so ordered it, in the great separation of all, that the woe, on one side at least, is more than half lost in the weakness.

There were about twenty of these emigrants, all destined, in the first place, to Liverpool by way of Dublin. The majority of them were going to the United States, but several, particularly the young women, were bound for Australia. Everyone was going out on funds supplied by their friends who had preceded them to the land of their exile.

One woman, with two children, was going to Philadelphia to join her husband, having already received 15*l.* from him, although he had left Ireland less than a year. He had borrowed a good part of the money, the wife said, from his brother, who had been longer settled than himself.

Several young unmarried women were going to Australia, expecting to be taken as domestic servants immediately on their arrival. They too had been invited, on the same irresistible terms, by their absent friends and relations, to share their exile. There were one or two complete families, father and mother and children; but most of them were but links of a broken chain which had its ends in the opposite quarters of the earth.

Among the most deeply affected of these poor exiles were two young girls, who, at the invitation of some friends in Australia, were leaving nearly all the links of their chain of affection behind them. I believe one of the kneelers on the pier was their mother, as when dragged forcibly from them, she had sunk on her knees as she had reached the shore. They had a brother also, a strong, rough, long-coated young fellow, who, notwithstanding all remonstrances and entreaties that he would leave his sisters and go on shore, had so many last words and fresh leave-takings, that when he at last broke loose from them, he found the gangway hauled up, and the ship's side some distance from the pier. I don't think he intended this, but his stay was an evident respite both to himself and his sisters. In his various subsequent attempts to cheer his sisters, he at length adopted one expedient, which I presume must be regarded as completely national: he set-to, with right good will and with all his might, to dance jigs before them! Poor fellow, it was at once laughable and melancholy to see the mingled grotesque and sorrowful expression of his countenance, more especially when, amid his formal mirth, he now and then caught a glance of his sisters rubbing their swollen eyes. He, however, held up wonderfully well until our arrival at the next stopping-place (Williamstown), when the final leave-taking was made, and he took his departure from the ship, setting up, as soon as he descended into the boat, such another portentous howl, as had signalised the parting at Killaloe.

15. IRISH LIFE AND CUSTOMS

After the Cromwellian and Williamite wars, the Ascendancy rulers of Ireland found themselves as powerful as monarchs within their immediate territories, but uncertain in their wider tenure. Over their heads on a single thread — the support of English governments — hung an unsheathed sword. How long could their enviable dominion hold out? Goldsmith comments on the strange transformation which, he observed, took place in English men and women transferring themselves to Ireland.[1] And travellers both before and after Edgeworth's *Castle Rackrent*, where the type is first memorably fictionalised, notice the mixture of generosity and eccentricity,[2] or instability, which characterises this class, condemned to a historical dead end in which they might go mildly insane.

Perhaps because the war had been won and the Irish defeated, English travellers to Ireland after the Williamite period could spare time to observe the latter in their ordinary lives. This could mean some unexpected rethinking. As John Dunton admitted in 1699, he went to Ireland prepossessed with a 'mean opinion' of the country but was surprised and impressed with what he found.[3] The stereotyping habit returns, however, with the spread of poverty and the approach of famine conditions; every traveller felt obliged to record the solicitous beggar, the neglected fields, the wretched cabin. English travellers noted with interest the food and eating habits of Irish people. Richard Pococke details the amazingly prodigality of mealtime provision, or 'Milesian feasts' as he calls them, among the Anglo-Irish who entertained him on his journey through Kerry in 1758, and the deep drinking habits of the inhabitants of some of the offshore islands.[4] At the other extreme Henry Inglis notes the Derry style of mashing potatoes in the nineteenth century, and carefully reproduces the recipe as a novelty.[5]

English visitors focus on the anthropology and sociology of Irish life with a variety of shades of the same negative (or at best detached) attitude: contemptuous, amused, indignant, compassionate, curious. They are rarely admiring. Though John Gough in 1813 found a 'soothing pleasingness' in the Irish howl,[6] most English travellers ran from the experience. The blinkered attitude induced by the centuries-old superiority complex leads to a representation interesting for its racialist character; few English observers can describe the Irish scene, so to speak, straight. Hence in the following extract the Irishness of the customs described seems to call for them to be rendered comic or extravagant or uncivilised. At the same time a representation like that of Farewell, written in the burlesque mode, is governed by the conventions of the genre perhaps more then by national feeling as such, and it would be a mistaken reading which took everything it says as literally intended. Nonetheless, it seems to Farewell that, by definition, describing the Irish scene in heroic terms is a good joke. One should not forget that travel writing is a self-referential mode. If much of the literature reiterates the anti-Irish material found in preceding accounts, another recurrent theme in eighteenth-and nineteenth-century writing and later is its condemnation of these inaccurate slurs.

1) William Petty

From *The Political Anatomy of Ireland* (1691):[7]

The Priests are chosen for the most part out of old *Irish* Gentry; and thereby influence the People, as well by their Interest as their Office.

Their Preaching seems rather Bugbearing of their flocks with dreadful Stories, than persuading them by Reason, or the Scriptures. They have an incredible Opinion of the Pope and his Sanctity, of the happiness of those who can obtain his Blessing at the third or fourth hand. only some few, who have lately been abroad, have gotten so far, as to talk of a difference between the Interest of the Court of *Rome*, and the Doctrine of the Church. The Common Priests have few of them been out of *Ireland*; and those who have, were bred in Covents [sic], or made Friars for the most part, and have humble Opinions of the *English* and Protestants, and of the mischiefs of setting up Manufactures, and introducing of Trade. They also comfort their Flocks, partly by Prophecies of their Restoration to their Ancient Estates and Liberties, which the abler sort of them fetch from what the Prophets of the Old-Testament have delivered by way of God's Promise to restore the *Jews*, and the Kingdom to *Israel*. They make little esteem of an

Oath upon a Protestant Bible, but will more devoutly take up a Stone, and swear upon it, calling it a Book, than by the said Book of Books, the Bible. But of all Oaths, they think themselves at much liberty to take a Land-Oath, as they call it: Which is an oath to prove a forg'd Deed, a Possession, Livery or Seisin, payment of Rents, *&c.* in order to recover for their Countrey-men the Lands which they had forfeited. They have a great Opinion of Holy-Wells, Rocks, and Caves, which have been the reputed Cells and Receptacles of men reputed Saints, They do not much fear Death, if it be upon a Tree, unto which, or the Gallows, they will go upon their Knees toward it, from the place they can first see it. They confess nothing at their Executions, though never so guilty. In brief, there is much Superstition among them, but formerly much more than is now; for as much as by the Conversion of Protestants, they become asham'd of their ridiculous Practices, which are not *de fide.* As for the Richer and better-educated sort of them, they are such Catholicks as are in other places. The Poor, in adhering to their Religion, which is rather a Custom than a Dogma amongst them, They seem rather to obey their Grandees, old Landlords, and the Heads of their Septes and Clans, than God. For when these were under Clouds, transported into *Spain,* and transplanted into *Connaught,* and disabled to serve them as formerly, about the year 1656. when the Adventurers and Soldiers appeared to be their Landlords and Patrons, they were observ'd to have been forward enough to relax the stiffness of their pertinacity to the Pope, and his Impositions. *Lastly,* Among the better sort of them, many think less of the Pope's Power in Temporals, as they call it, than formerly; and begin to say, that the Supremacy, even in Spirituals, lies rather in the Church diffusive, and in qualified General-Councils, than in the Pope alone, or than in the Pope and his Cardinals, or other *Juncto.*

The Religion of the Protestants in *Ireland,* is the same with the Church of *England* in Doctrine, only they differ in Discipline thus, *viz.*

The Legal Protestants hold the Power of the Church to be in the King, and that Bishops and Arch-Bishops, with their Clerks, are the best way of adjusting that Power under him. The Presbyterians would have the same thing done, and perhaps more, by Classes of Presbyters National and Provincial. The Independents would have all Christian Congregations independent from each other. The *Anabaptists* are Independent in Discipline, and differ from all those aforemention'd in the Baptism of Infants, and in the inward and spiritual Signification of that Ordinance. The Quakers salute not by uncovering the Head, speak to one another in the second Person, and singular Number; as for Magistracy and Arms, they seem to hold with the *anabaptists* of *Germany* and *Holland*; they pretend to a possibility of perfection, like the Papists; as for other Tenents, 'tis hard to fix them or to understand what things they mean by their Words.

The Diet of the poorer *Irish*, is what was before discoursed in the [blank in text] Chapter.

The Cloathing is a narrow sort of Frieze, of about twenty Inches broad, whereof two foot, call'd a Bandle, is worth from 3½ to 18*d*. Of this, Seventeen Bandles make a Man's Suit, and twelve make a Cloak. According to which Measures and Proportions, and the number of People who wear this Stuff, it seems, that near thrice as much Wooll is spent in *Ireland*, as exported; whereas others have thought quite contrary, that is, that the exported Wooll is triple in quantity to what is spent at home.

As for the Manners of the *Irish*, I deduce them from their Original Constitutions of Body, and from the Air; next from their ordinary Food; next from their Condition of Estate and Liberty, and from the Influence of their Governours and Teachers; and lastly, from their Ancient Customs, which affect as well their Consciences as their Nature. For their Shape, Stature, Colour, and Complexion, I see nothing in them inferior to any other People, nor any enormous predominancy of any humour.

Their Lazing seems to me to proceed rather from want of Imployment and Encouragement to Work, than from the natural abundance of Flegm in their Bowels and Blood; for what need they to Work, who can content themselves with *Potato*'s, whereof the Labour of one Man can feed forty; and with Milk, whereof one Cow will, in Summer time, give meat and drink enough for three Men, when they can every where gather Cockles, Oysters, Muscles, Crabs, *&c.* with Boats, Nets, Angles, or the Art of Fishing; can build an House in three days? And why should they desire to fare better, tho with more Labour, when they are taught, that this way of living is more like the Patriarchs of old, and the Saints of later times, by whose Prayers and Merits they are to be reliev'd, and whose Examples they are therefore to follow? And why should they breed more Cattel, since 'tis Penal to import them into *England*? Why should they raise more Commodities, since there are not Merchants sufficiently Stock'd to take them of them, nor provided with other more pleasing foreign Commodities, to give in Exchange for them? And how should Merchants have Stock, since Trade is prohibited and fetter'd by the Statutes of

England? And why should Men endeavour to get Estates, where the Legislative Power is not agreed upon and where Tricks and Words destroy natural Right and Property?

They are accused also of much Treachery, Falseness, and Thievery; none of which, I conceive, is natural to them; for as to Treachery, they are made believe, that they all shall flourish again, after some time; wherefore they will not really submit to those whom they hope to have their Servants; nor will they declare so much, but say the contrary, for their present ease, which is all the Treachery I have observed; for they have in their hearts, not only a grudging to see their old Proprieties enjoyed by Foreigners, but a persuasion they shall be shortly restor'd. As for Thievery, it is affixt to all thin-peopled Countries, such as *Ireland* is, where there cannot be many Eyes to prevent such Crimes; and where what is stolen, is easily hidden and eaten, and where 'tis easy to turn the House, or violate the Persons of those who persecute these Crimes, and where thin-peopled Countries are govern'd by the Laws that were made and first fitted to thick-peopled Countries; and where matter of small moment and value must be try'd, with all the formalities which belong to the highest Causes. In this case there must be thieving, where is withal, neither encouragement, nor method, nor means for Labouring, nor Provision for Impotents.

As for the Interest of these poorer *Irish*, it is manifestly to be transmuted into *English*, so to reform and qualify their housing, as that *English* Women may be content to be their Wives, to decline their Language, which continues a sensible distinction, being not now necessary; which makes those who do not understand it, suspect, that what is spoken in it, is to their prejudice. It is their Interest to deal with the *English*, for Leases, for Time, and upon clear Conditions, which being perform'd they are absolute Freemen, rather than to stand always liable to the humour and caprice of their Landlords, and to have every thing taken from them, which he pleases to fancy. It is their Interest, that he is well-pleased with their Obedience to them, when they see and know upon whose Care and Conduct their well-being depends, who have Power over their Lands and Estates. Then, to believe a Man at *Rome* has Power in all these last mentioned Particulars in this World, and can make them eternally happy or miserable hereafter, 'tis their Interest to joyn with them, and follow their Example, who have brought Arts, Civility, and Freedom into their Country.

On the contrary, What did they ever get by accompanying their Lords into Rebellion against the *English*? What should they have gotten if the late Rebellion had absolutely succeeded, but a more absolute Servitude? And when it fail'd, these poor People have lost all their Estates, and their Leaders encreas'd theirs, and enjoy'd the very Land which their Leaders caus'd them to lose. The poorest now in *Ireland* ride on Horse-back, when heretofore the best ran on foot like Animals. They wear better Cloaths than ever; the Gentry have better Breeding, and the generality of the *Plebeians* more Money and Freedom.

2) James Farewell

Of James Farewell nothing certain is known. His poem's interest lies in its guying of Virgil's description in book six of the *Aeneid* of the descent into the underworld — a favourite subject in English satires from Ben Jonson's *Famous Voyage* to Pope's *The Rape of the Lock*. Farewell undermines both subject and literary model by adopting the octosyllabics and silly rhymes of Butler's *Hudibras*. English readers would have found the epic style and Ireland a ludicrous mixture, but would have also recognised that the satirical convention was dictating the nature of what was being said. A reading of the poem as a seriously intended description of Irish life would misinterpret it. Farewell's introduction disavows national prejudice and national reflections. The poem is probably more a satire directed against poetic form and epic convention than against Ireland, but note the national reflection implied in this manoeuvre: Irish life is an absurd candidate for epic treatment.

From *The Irish Hudibras or Fingallian Prince* (1689):[8]

Meanwhile the Rout to work do fall,
To Celebrate the Funeral.
And first with Turff from Bog, and Blocks,
They made a Fire wou'd roast an Oxe.
Some lay the Pipkins on, and some
With Holy-water bathe his Bum.
There was the Priest forgiving Sins,
Busie as Hen with two Chick-eens,
'Nointing his Forehead, and his Nose,
And downwards to his Pettitoes;
After the Method of his Function,
With Holy Oyl of Extreme Unction,
Which Office decently perform'd,
The Guests, with Usquebagh well warm'd,
They raise the Cry. And so they fout [sic] him
Unto a Crate, to howl about him;

Built without either Brick or Stone,
Or Couples to lay Roof upon:
With Wattles unto Wattles ty'd,
(Fixt in the ground on either side)
Did like a shaded Arbour show,
With Seats of Sods, and Roof of Straw.
The Floor beneath with Rushes laid, stead
Of Tapestry; no Bed nor Bedstead;
No Posts, nor Bolts, nor Hinges in door,
No Chimney, Kitchin, Hall, or Windor;
But narrow Dormants stopt with hay
All night, and open in the day.
On either side there was a door
Extent from roof unto the floor,
Which they, like Hedg-hogs, stop with straw,
Or open, as the Wind does blow:
And tho they reach from top to floor,
His Grace crept in upon all-four.
Betwixt the door there was a spot
I' th' middle, to hang o're the pot;
And had an Engine in the nick,
For pair of Tongues, a broken stick.
I' th' presence was no stool, but one
Old Creel, for *Nees* to sit upon:
For all the rest, as they did come,
Made Stools and Cushions of their Bum.
In this so rich and stately Cabbin,
To lie in state came this Sea-Crab in,
Dy'd for the nonce in liquid Sable,
And laid him underneath the Table;
Where in one end the parted Brother
Was laid to rest, the Cows in t' other,
With all his Followers and Kin
Who far and near came crowding in
With *Hub-bub-boos*, besides what Cryers
For greater state his Highness hires;
Who all come crowding in; and in comes
Monk Coron too, with all his Trinkums;
Who when he had his Office paid,
And for the Dead a while had pray'd,
To their own Sports, (the *Masses* ended,)
The Mourners now are recommended.
  Some for their Pastime count their Beads,
Some scratch their Breech, some louse their Heads;
Some sit and chat, some laugh, some weep
Some sing *Cronans*,[9] and some do sleep;
Some pray, and with their prayers mix curses;

Some Vermin pick, and some pick Purses;
Some court, some scold, some blow, some puff,
Some take Tobacco, some take Snuff;
Some play the Trump, some trot the Hay,
Some at *Macham,*[10] some *Noddy* play;
With all the Games they can devise;
And (when occasion serves him) cries.
  Thus did they mix their grief and sorrow,
Yesterday bury'd kill'd to morrow;
And mounted him upon a Beer;
Through which the Wattles did appear;
Like Ribbs on either side made fast,
With a White Velvet over-cast:
So poor *McShane,* Good rost his Shoul,
Was after put him in a hole;
In which, with many sighs and scrietches,
They throw his Trouses and his Breeches;
And tattar'd Brogue was after throw,
With a new heel-piece on the toe;
And Stockins Fine as *Friez* to feel,
Worn out with praying at the heel;
And in his mouth, 'gainst he took Wherry,
Dropt a white Groat to pay the Ferry.
Thus did they make this last hard shift,
To furnish him for a dead lift.

3) John Dunton

John Dunton (1659–1733) was born in Graffham, Huntingdonshire, the son of a clergyman who retired to Ireland after his wife's death in 1660 and became chaplain to Sir Henry Ingoldsby; in 1668 he returned to England and became rector of Aston Clinton, Buckinghamshire. The younger Dunton, who had been left in England in the meantime, became a bookseller's apprentice in London, but in 1665–6 visited New England, where he studied Indian customs, then visited Holland and Rhineland Germany until settling down in 1688 as a London bookseller for a number of years. Dunton travelled to Ireland in 1698 and described his visit in a poem entitled 'The Dublin Scuffle' and six prose letters *Teague Land.* Although Dunton incorporates some Irish anecdotes from earlier writers he stresses his own observations and corrects Echard on Ireland in a number of places.[11] In later life Dunton became increasingly eccentric and perhaps deranged. He published his *Life and Errors* in 1705.

From *Teague Land* (1699):[12]

And now I think I may say something to you of the sports used among the Irish on their holidays. One exercise they use much is their hurling, which has something in it not unlike the play called Mall. When their cows are casting their hair, they pull it off their backs and with their hands work it into large balls which will grow very hard. This ball they use at the hurlings, which they strike with a stick called commaan about three foot and a half long in the handle. At the lower end it is crooked and about three inches broad, and on this broad part you may sometimes see one of the gamesters carry the ball tossing it for 40 or 50 yards in spite of all the adverse players; and when he is like to lose it, he generally gives it a great stroke to drive it towards the goal. Sometimes if he miss his blow at the ball, he knocks one of the opposers down: at which no resentment is to be shown. They seldom come off without broken heads or shins in which they glory very much. At this sport one parish sometimes or barony challenges another; they pick out ten, twelve, or twenty players of a side, and the prize is generally a barrel or two of ale, which is brought into the field and drunk off by the victors on the spot, though the vanquished are not without a share of it too. This commonly is upon some very large plain, the barer of grass the better, and the goals are 200 or 300 yards one from the other; and whichever party drives the ball beyond the other's goal wins the day. Their champions are of the younger and most active among them, and their kindred and mistresses are frequently spectators of their address. Two or three bag pipes attend the conquerors at the barrel's head, and then play them out of the field. At some of these meetings two thousand have been present together. They do not play often at football, only in a small territory called Fingal near Dublin the people use it much, and trip, and shoulder very handsomely. These people are reckoned the best wrestlers of the Irish, though I think the best would come off badly in Moorfields. They have a sort of jargon speech peculiar to themselves, and understand not one word of Irish, and are as little understood by the English. I'll give a sample of it in a lamentation which a mother made over her son's grave, who had been a great fisher and huntsman Ribbeen a Roon, Ribbeen Mourneen, thoo ware good for loand stroand and mounteen, for rig a tool and roast a whiteen, reddy tha taakle gather tha baarnacks drink a grote at nauny hapennys.[13]

The Irish have another custom, to plant an ash or some other tree which will grow big in the middle of the village, though I never observed them to be planters of them anywhere else. In some towns these trees are old and very great, and hither all the people resort with a piper on Sundays or Holydays in the afternoon, where the young folks dance till the cows come home (which by the by they'll do without anyone to drive them). I have seen a short truss young woman tire five lusty fellows, who hereby gets a husband: I am sure I should hardly venture myself with one who had been so able for so many. The elder people sit spectators telling stories of their own like feats in days of yore, and now and then divert themselves with a quill full of sneezing or a [wh]if[f] of tobacco; for one short foul pipe of an inch long, the shorter and fouler the better, will serve a dozen of them men and women together, the first holding the smoke in his mouth until everyone has whiffed once or twice, and when the pipe returns to him he blows it out of his nose. If in the dance the woman be tired, the man throws her to the piper, whose fee is half a penny, and the man if tired is served after the same manner.

4) Richard Pococke

From *Tour in Ireland in 1752*:[14]

Going from church in the morning I observed a circumstance, which added to the Romantic view of the mountains to the south: In the side of one of them a sort of Amphitheatre is formed in the rock; here I saw several hundred people spread all over that plain spot and the priest celebrating Mass under the rock, on an altar made of loose stones, and tho' it was half a mile distant, I observed his Pontifical vestment with a black cross on it; for in all this country for sixty miles west and south as far as Connaught, they celebrate in the open air, in the fields or on the mountain; the Papists being so few and poor, that they will not be at the expence of a public building.

5) Arthur Young

From *Tour in Ireland* (1776–8):[15]

i) Dancing is very general among the poor people, almost universal in every cabbin. Dancing-masters of their own rank travel through the country from cabbin to cabbin, with a piper or blind fiddler; and the pay is six pence a quarter. It is an absolute system of education. Weddings are always celebrated with much dancing; and a Sunday rarely passes without a dance; there are very few among them will not, after a hard day's work, gladly walk seven miles to have a dance. *John* is not so lively, but then a hard day's work with him is certainly a different affair from what it is with *Paddy.* Other branches of education are likewise much attended to, every child of the poorest family learning to read, write, and cast accounts. There is a very antient custom here, for a number of country neighbours among the poor people, to fix upon some young woman that ought, as they think, to be married; they also agree upon a young fellow as a proper husband for her; this determined, they send to the fair one's cabbin to inform her, that on the sunday [sic] following *she is to be horsed,* that is, carried on men's backs. She must then provide whisky and cyder for a treat, as all will pay her a visit after mass for a hurling match. As soon as she is *horsed,* the hurling begins, in which the young fellow appointed for her husband has the eyes of all the company fixed on him; if he comes off conqueror, he is certainly married to the girl, but if another is victorious, he as certainly loses her, for she is the prize of the victor. These trials are not always finished in one sunday, they take sometimes two or three, and the common expression when they are over is, that *such a girl was goal'd.* Sometimes one barony hurls against another, but a marriageable girl is always the prize.

From *Tour in Ireland* (1776–8):[16]

b) The food of the common Irish, potatoes and milk, have been produced more than once as an instance of the extreme poverty of the country, but this I believe is an opinion embraced with more alacrity than reflection. I have heard it stigmatized as being unhealthy, and not sufficiently nourishing for the support of hard labour; but this opinion is very amazing in a country, many of whose poor people are as athletic in their form, as robust, and as capable of enduring labour as any upon earth. The idleness seen among many when working for those who oppress them is a very contrast to the vigour and activity with which the same people work, when themselves alone reap the benefit of their labour. To what country must we have recourse for a stronger instance than lime carried by little miserable mountaineers thirty miles on horses back to the foot of their hills, and up the steeps on their own. When I see the people of a country, in spite of political oppression, with well formed vigorous bodies, and their cottages swarming with children; when I see their men athletic, and their women beautiful, I know not how to believe them subsisting on an unwholesome food.

At the same time, however, that both reason and observation convince me of the justice of these remarks, I will candidly allow that I have seen such an excess in the laziness of great numbers, even when working for themselves, and such an apparent weakness in their exertions when encouraged to work, that I have had my doubts of the heartiness of their food. But here arise fresh difficulties; were their food ever so nourishing, I can easily conceive an habitual inactivity of exertion would give them an air of debility compared with a more industrious people. Though my residence in Ireland was not long enough to become a perfect master of the question, yet I have employed from twenty to fifty men for several months, and found their habitual laziness or weakness so great, whether working by measure or by day, that I am absolutely convinced 1s. 6d. and even 2s. a day, in Suffolk or Hertfordshire, much cheaper than six-pence halfpenny at Mitchelstown: it would not be fair to consider this as a representation of the kingdom, that place being remarkably backward in every species of industry and improvement; but I am afraid this observation would hold true in a less degree for the whole. But is this owing to habit or food? Granting their food to be the cause, it decides very little against potatoes, unless they were tried with good nourishing beer instead of their vile potations of whisky. When they are encouraged, or animate themselves to work hard, it is all by whisky, which though it has a notable effect in giving a perpetual motion to their tongues, can have but little of that invigorating substance which is found in strong beer or porter, probably it has an effect as pernicious, as the other is beneficial.[17] One circumstance I should mention, which seems to confirm this, I have known the Irish reapers in Hertfordshire work as labouriously as any of our own men, and living upon potatoes which they procured from London, but drinking nothing but ale. If their bodies are weak, I attribute it to whisky, not potatoes; but it is still a question with me whether their miserable working arises from any such weakness, or from an habitual laziness. A friend of mine always refused Irishmen work in Surrey, saying his bailiff could do nothing but settle their quarrels.

But of this food there is one circumstance which must ever recommend it, they have a bellyfull, and that let me add is more than the superfluities of an Englishman leaves to his family: let any person examine minutely into the receipt and expenditure of an English cottage, and he will find that tea, sugar, and strong liquors, can come only from pinched bellies. I will not assert that potatoes are a better food than bread and cheese; but I have no doubt of a bellyfull of the one being much better than half a bellyfull of the other; still less have I that the milk of the Irishman is incomparably better than the small beer, gin, or tea of the Englishman; and this even for the father, how much better must it be for the poor infants; milk to them is nourishment, is health, is life.

If any one doubts the comparative plenty, which attends the board of a poor native of England and Ireland, let him attend to their meals: the sparingness with which our labourer eats his bread and cheese is well known; mark the Irishman's potatoe bowl placed on the floor, the whole family upon their hams around it, devouring a quantity almost incredible, the beggar seating himself to it with a hearty welcome, the pig taking his share as readily as the wife, the cocks, hens, turkies, geese, the cur, the cat, and perhaps the cow — and all partaking of the same dish. No man can often have been a witness of it without being convinced of the plenty, and I will add the chearfulness that attends it.

6) Philip Luckombe

Philip Luckombe praises Dublin, which he described at some length before travelling to Wexford and Waterford with an eye out for public buildings and private seats and so returning to Dublin. His second journey took him to Kilkenny, Cork, Killarney and the south west, and his third to the further south western parts, including Bantry, Baltimore, Cape Clear and the Reeks. Journey number four was to the north: Drogheda, Newry, Armagh and Lough Neagh, Belfast, Antrim, the Giant's Causeway, Derry, and back to Dublin via Lough Erne, Enniskillen and Athlone.

From *A Tour through Ireland* (1780):[18]

Upon this stream, about a mile below Callan, is a very famous iron mill, that brings great profit to the proprietors. The town is built in the form of a cross; and in the centre a cross is erected, with a square glass lanthorn that gives light in the night to travellers that come from the four cardinal points of the compass. One would imagine this town should be in a more thriving condition, since the two great roads of Cork and Limerick go thro' it. There is one handsome seat, just out of the town, in the Limerick road, belonging to a gentleman of the Ormond family; but we had not an opportunity of seeing the inside. It was market-day when we stopped there, where we observed great numbers of what they call the ancient Irish race. Men and women mostly wore large frize cloaks, though a warm day. The women's heads were wrapped up in thick handkerchiefs besides their ordinary linen head dress. We observed a man mounted upon a little horse, that most of the others seemed to pay an extraordinary respect to, tho' I thought neither his figure, nor dress, seemed to draw it upon him. I had the curiosity to ask a gentleman in our company the meaning of paying him so much civility, who informed us that person was of an ancient race, and derived his birth from some of the noted clans in the county; and though the patrimony might have been in the hands of others for more than seven centuries, yet from father to son, since that time the survivor still calls the estate his, though not a penny of the profits ever come into his pocket; but he enjoys it in imagination, and when he talks concerning it, says, 'My house, my land, my mountains, meadows and rivers, &c.' They are often allowed a cabin, and a small parcel of ground rent free, or on a trifling acknowledgement from the proprietor, and expect to be treated with the utmost respect by every one. The old Irish give him the title of his ancestors, make him and his lady (if he has one) little presents, cultivating his spot of ground, not suffering him or his to do the least work to degrade his airy title. I own this account, (if true, and I have no reason to contradict it) gave me a secret pleasure: it called to my memory an idea of many ages past; and when I observed this man, I looked upon him as one of the ancient Milesian race,[19] so much renowned for their wisdom and victories, even before christianity had a being in the world. Alas! let us think what Egyptian, Grecian, and Roman greatness were, and the state they now are in.

7) John Edwin

John Edwin (1749–1790), the son of a London watchmaker and a Yorkshire mother, joined a Cheapside spouting club at fifteen years of age, then turned actor. In 1765 he acted in Manchester for a summer season before removing to Dublin. Here he lived a vagabond's life, left his engagement, and returned to England. In 1768 he appeared at Bath and later at the Haymarket. From 1777 onwards he acted regularly at the latter theatre, transferring to Covent Garden in 1779, where he stayed until 1790. Edwin had a charming presence on the stage and earned a reputation as a singer.

Like the Farewell passage above, this extract shows the literary mode to some extent governing what is written: the biographer describing a comic actor at the intrinsically comic scene of an Irish funeral (comic to English thinking, that is), produces an 'act' on the page which corresponds to Edwin's stage performance. The result is excruciatingly arch writing.

From *The Eccentricities of John Edwin* (1791):[20]

A few days previous to EDWIN's quitting WATERFORD, a misfortune occured [sic]; it was simply this — A poor fellow of the name of PATRICK O'KEAGHEGAN, in the honest endeavour to find his way home from a *shebeen* house after dark, made a small mistake, took the helm of a Norway brig in the harbour for his own house, and in labouring to enter, stumbled over an eighteen-inch cable, fell plump into the river, and was drowned. The body was taken up the next day, and agreeably to the customs of Ireland was to be *waked* the ensuing night — to this ceremony EDWIN as a stranger was invited, and the more especially as he had often given the deceased a glass full of beverage, vulgarly called WHISKEY. The Comedian went and found the *mourners* assembled in a cellar under an usquebaugh shop on the quay — after a formal introduction to the relative of the deceased, he took his seat among the rest of the visitors, and had his allotment of a pipe of tobacco, some grilled cake, snuff, and half a pint of spirits — the body was deposited in a heavy elm coffin, which was placed upon two stools in the middle of the apartment with the lid half removed. — Over this hung the gentle relict of the departed, bathing the cold forehead of her dead lord with tears. — After many ghostly admonitions from PETER BALLYBOUGH, the parish priest, the wretched lady permitted herself to be dragged from the corpse — took *a sup of the Crater* — sat down — hid her countenance in her hands — and profusely wept like another *Alcyone*! — The seat of lamentation however was not long unoccupied — JUGGY PONSONBY, who was cousin-german to O'KEAGHEGAN'S foster-mother, uprose from the corner of the room — flew to the wooden case of benumbed mortality, and vented her grief in accents that were probably heard at a league's distance. — When she had repeatedly ejaculated with great earnestness, wringing her hands, 'Arrah now PADDY why did you die?' the whole company united in a general *pullulleloo*, the noise of which almost breaking the drum of poor EDWIN's ears, he was in the act of stopping them with his thumbs, which being perceived by his immediate neighbour, BRIAN O'ROW, who dealt in *fruit* and *timber*, at Dungarvan, he griped the left wrist of the tremulous comedian, and vociferated, 'why bl — d-a nouns man what are you about?' This salutation brought EDWIN to his senses, and he zealously joined in the pious orgies with all the devotion of a mad bacchanal. —

When this ceremony was concluded, SHELAH MULLOWNEY was called upon for a chaunt — after three loud hems, and two coarse apologies, the fair digger of turf sung, or rather bellowed as follows —

As my true love and I went truffing togedder,
We called at the sign of the grisken and meddar:
Och there we danced launstram poney togedder,
And often cried whack for the other brown medder:
Sing furillulloo, turiddleliddlelull, burillulloo,
turiddleliddlelull, furiddle, turiddle, furiddle,
and now boys go merrily WHACK!

When the lovely offspring of beauty came to the concluding monosyllable *Whack*, all the assembly clapped their hands loudly in unison, as if by instinct, and repeated the word with a sonorous emphasis — every thing went on as well as decency could expect, until four in the morning, when an inconsiderable affray took place — FATHER BALLYBOUGH, who had been drowning his grief in vast potations of the Lethean juice, got up with much difficulty and reeled in a zig-zag direction towards his clay-cold friend, whom he seized by the hand, and crossing his breast thus ejaculated, 'bad luck to you, Paddy now, why was you after going to that same *shebeen* house without first asking my *lave* my jewel? get out of that with your laughing, you comical bastard,' said he tapping the forehead of the deceased, 'to be sure you don't remember when I *cotched* you tickling KATTY MACFOOSTER'S under petticoat in the chapel itself you *Spalpeen*, last Lammas; but I forgive you with all the veins in my heart so I do — here you *taaf* of the world, take this and put it under your wig;' continued the disciple of Christ, sticking a short pipe between the teeth of the corpse, 'it will *kape* you comfortable in the winter months my honey.' At this instant an old crony of PADDY'S started up, and thundering out a tremendous oath, 'by this book and I swear it,' uttered he, kissing the skirt of his coat, 'but he shall have some suction as well as all tobacco d'ye see;' and in an endeavour to fix a bottle of spirits at his right ear, in which attempt he was violently opposed by the Priest, a scuffle ensued, which brought the contending parties, dead body and all to the ground — the head of the coffin pitched unluckily upon the temple of THADY FOGARTY, who lay stretched upon the floor in a sound sleep, and had not his head been as thick and as impenetrable as the great wall of Tartary, or the Cones of Cherburgh, the abrupt visitation must have shivered his skull to atoms — however the Fates interfered, and THADY gave an unerring testimony of his being in the land of the living, by entertaining his friends for about ten minutes with a hideous roar, not entirely dissimilar to the tones of a dying hog in the victualling office — the lifeless trunk was rolled by the concussion some yards on the floor, and stopped by EDWIN'S feet, who was so much alarmed at the accident, that to use an Irish phrase, he *gathered up his duds* — made but three strides from the cellar to the street, and did not even think himself secure when he got nestled, and trembling between the dowlass sheets at his own dormitary.

8) Thomas De Quincey

From *Autobiography from 1785 to 1803:*[21]

Making but short journeys on each day, and resting always at the house of some private friend, I thus obtained an opportunity of seeing the old Irish nobility and gentry more extensively, and on a more intimate footing, than I had hoped for. No experience of this kind, throughout my whole life, so much interested me. In a little work, not much known, of Suetonius,[22] the most interesting record which survives of the early Roman literature, it comes out incidentally that many books, many idioms, and verbal peculiarities belonging to the primitive ages of Roman culture, were to be found still lingering in the old Roman settlements, both Gaulish and Spanish, long after they had become obsolete (and sometimes unintelligible) in Rome. From the tardiness and the difficulty of communication, the want of newspapers, &c., it followed, naturally enough, that the distant provincial towns, though not without their own separate literature and their own literary professors, were always two or three generations in the rear of the metropolis; and thus it happened that, about the time of Augustus, there were some grammatici in Rome, answering to our black-letter critics, who sought the material of their researches in Boulogne (*Gessoriacum*), in Arles (*Arelata*), or in Marseilles (*Massilia*). Now, the old Irish nobility — that part, I mean, which might be called thr rural nobility — stood in the same relation to English manners and customs. Here might be found old rambling houses, in the style of antique English manorial chateaux, ill planned, perhaps, as regarded convenience and economy, with long rambling galleries, and windows innumerable, that evidently had never looked for that severe audit to which they were afterwards summoned by William Pitt; but displaying, in the dwelling-rooms, a comfort and 'cosiness', combined with magnificence, not always so effectually attained in modern times. Here were old libraries, old butlers, and old customs, that seemed all alike to belong to the era of Cromwell, or even an earlier era than his; whilst the ancient names, to one who had some acquaintance with the great events of Irish history, often strengthened the illusion. Not that I could pretend to be familiar with Irish history *as* Irish; but, as a conspicuous chapter in the difficult policy of Queen Elizabeth, of Charles I., and of Cromwell, nobody who had read the English history could be a stranger to the O'Neils, the O'Donnells, the Ormonds (*i.e.*, the Butlers), the Inchiquins, or the De Burghs, and many scores besides.[23] I soon found, in fact, that the aristocracy of Ireland might be divided into two great sections: the native Irish — territorial fixtures, so powerfully described by Maturin; and those, on the other hand, who spent so much of their time and revenues at Bath, Cheltenham, Weymouth, London, &c., as to have become almost entirely English. It was the former whom we chiefly visited; and I remarked that, in the midst of hospitality the most unbounded, and the amplest comfort, some of these were conspicuously in the rear of the English commercial gentry, as to modern refinements of luxury. There was at the same time an apparent strength of character, as if formed amidst turbulent scenes, and a raciness of manner, which were fitted to interest a stranger profoundly, and to impress themselves on his recollection.

9) Sir John Carr

Sir John Carr (1772–1832) was born in Devonshire and trained as a lawyer. For health reasons he travelled round many European countries and published regular accounts of his journeys which, his biographer writes in the *D.N.B.*, circulated widely without possessing much intrinsic interest. They included *The Stranger in France* (1805), *A Northern Summer, or Travels round the Baltic* (1803), *The Stranger in Ireland* (1806), *Caledonian Sketches* (1808) and *Descriptive Travels* (1811) in Spain and the Balearic Isles. Other countries visited by Carr included Denmark, Sweden, Russia, Poland and Prussia. *The Stranger in Ireland* was mocked for its conceit in 1807 by one Edward Dubois and an inconclusive lawsuit followed. Byron satirised Carr as Erin's Green Knight in some suppressed cantos in *Childe Harold.*[24] Carr is frequently quite interesting on Ireland, but his English superciliousness and pomposity may be seen in his account of an incident in Glendalough. His action of chipping away (for a souvenir) some of the hardened cement holding up the round tower in this place had shocked, he observed, the 'superstitious veneration' which an Irish observer had for the place, until the 'whimsical fellow' was 'tranquillized' with money.[25]

From *The Stranger in Ireland* (1806):[26]

(i) Upon Thomond's bridge, for the first time since I had been in Ireland, I heard beggars imploring alms, and peasants conversing in the Irish language. Some words sounded very sweet, and I think my reader will not object to pause a little, previous to our setting off for the lakes of Killarney, to take a brief review of the language.

It is remarkable for the varieties of its powers: it is affecting, sweet, dignified, energetic, and sublime; and so forcibly expressive, that the translation of one compound epithet would fill two lines of English verse. The number of synonima with which it abounds, prevents the ear from being satiated by a repetition of the same word. It has upwards of forty names to express a ship, and nearly an equal number for a house.

In the county of Meath, which borders upon the metropolis, it has been said that a justice of the peace must understand Irish, or keep an interpreter. In the north-west and south-west counties, the English language is scarcely known: the low Irish who understand English and Irish, have a proverbial saying, 'When you plead for your life, plead in Irish.' In the county of Wexford English customs and habits prevail universally, and the Irish language is quite forgotten.

At Limerick I heard one peasant address another, by saying. 'Commas ta tu,' how are you? I am told that the same salutation in Italian is 'Come stai?' The following words will give a little specimen of the Irish language.

Heaven, ceal	A fever, fiabras
An angel, aingeal	A rose, rosa
The devil, diabal	A cottage, caban
The sun, sol	A cow, bo
The moon, luan	A nightingale, rosin-ceol
A pint, pinta	

(ii) At Ten Mile-house I was fortunate enough to meet with a female companion, an inteligent, sprightly Irish girl, who had been educated at one of the convents at Cork, whither she was going, and who relieved the dreariness of the road, by talking the Irish language, and singing some ancient Irish airs; the former sounded very mellifluous, and the latter were very delightful.

10) Richard Cumberland

Richard Cumberland (1732–1811) was the son of Denison Cumberland, clergyman at Stanwick near Northampton. He was educated at Bury St Edmund's, Westminster, and Cambridge, where he graduated in 1750–51. Cumberland was a committed Whig. He became private secretary to Lord Halifax, and when George II died and Halifax became Lord Lieutenant of Ireland Cumberland was made Ulster secretary; his father became one of Halifax's chaplains, later Bishop of Clonfert, and in 1772 was translated to Kilmore. Cumberland turned to playwriting when, in 1762, Halifax became secretary of state and a rival claimant gained the under-secretaryship in Cumberland's place. Dramatic and critical writing became his main business, though he never entirely forsook politics. For instance, in 1780 he went on a secret mission to Spain which cost him an estimated £4,500 — never repaid. Cumberland's characterisation of the Irish, which follows, overlays its repetition of the stereotype — warm-hearted, risible and wayward — with a humane moralism typical of the dramatist of the age of sentiment. Compare Cumberland's characterisation of the Anglo-Irish, which follows this entry.

From *Memoirs* (1807):[27]

a) Amongst the labourers in my father's garden there were three brothers of the name of O'Rourke, regularly descended from the kings of Connaught, if they were exactly to be credited for the correctness of their genealogy. There was also an elder brother of these, Thomas O'Rourke, who filled the superior station of hind, or headman; it was his wife that burnt the bewitched turkies, whilst Tom burnt his wig for joy of my victory at the cock-match, and threw a proper parcel of oatmeal into the air as a votive offering for my glorious success. One of the younger brothers was upon crutches in consequence of a contusion on his hip, which he literally acquired as follows — When my father came down to Clonfert from Dublin, it was announced to him that the bishop was arrived:

the poor fellow was then in the act of lopping a tree in the garden; transported at the tidings, he exclaimed — 'Is my lord come? Then I'll throw myself out of this same tree for joy —.' He exactly fulfilled his word, and laid himself up for some months.

When I accompanied my mother from Clonfert to Dublin, my father having gone before, we passed the night at Killbeggan, where Sir Thomas Cuffe, (knighted in a frolic by Lord Townshend) kept the inn. A certain Mr. Geoghegan was extremely drunk, noisy and brutally troublesome to Lady Cuffe the hostess: Thomas O'Rourke was with us, and being much scandalized with the behaviour of Geoghegan, took me aside, and in a whisper said — 'Squire, will I quiet this same Mr. Geoghegan?' When I replied by all means, but how was it to be done? — Tom produced a knife of formidable length, and demanded — 'Haven't I got this? And won't this do the job, and hasn't he wounded the woman of the inn with a chopping knife, and what is this but a knife, and wou'dn't it be a good deed to put him to death like a mad dog? Therefore, Squire, do you see, if it will pleasure you and my lady there above stairs, who is ill enough, God he knows, I'll put this knife into that same Mr. Geoghegan's ribs, and be off the next moment on the grey mare; and isn't she in the stable? Therefore only say the word, and I'll do it.' This was the true and exact proposal of Thomas O'Rourke, and as nearly as I can remember, I have stated it in his very words.

We arrived safe in Dublin, leaving Mr. Geoghegan to get sober at his leisure, and dismissing O'Rourke to his quarters at Clonfert. When we passed a few days in Kildare-Street, I well remember the surprise it occasioned us one afternoon, when without any notice we saw a great gigantic dirty fellow walk into the room, and march straight up to my father for what purpose we could not devise. My mother uttered a scream, whilst my father with perfect composure addressed him by the name of Stephen, demanding what he wanted with him, and what brought him to Dublin — 'Nay, my good lord,' replied the man, 'I have no other business in Dublin itself but to take a bit of a walk up from Clonfert to see your sweet face, long life to it, and to get a blessing upon me from your lordship; that is all.' So saying he flounced down on his knees, and in a most piteous kind of howl, closing his hands at the same time cried out — 'Pray, my lord, pray to God to bless Stephen Costello —.' The scene was sufficently ludicrous to have spoiled the solemnity, yet my father kept his countenance, and gravely gave his blessing, saying as he laid his hands on his head — 'God bless you, Stephen Costello, and make you a good boy!' The giant sung out a loud amen, and arose, declaring he should immediately set out and return to his home. He would accept no refreshment, but with many thanks and a thousand blessings in recompence for the one he had received, walked out of the house, and I can well believe resumed his pilgrimage to the westward without stop or stay. I should not have considered this and the preceding anecdotes as worth recording, but they are in some degree characteristic of a very curious and peculiar people, who are not often understood by those who profess to mimic them, and who are too apt to set them forth as objects for ridicule only, when oftentimes even their oddities, if candidly examined, would entitle them to our respect.

b) On this visit to Mr. Talbot I was accompanied by Lord Eyre of Eyre Court, a near neighbour and friend of my father. This noble Lord, though pretty far advanced in years, was so correctly indigenous, as never to have been out of Ireland in his life, and not often so far from Eyre Court as in this tour to Mr. Talbot's. Proprietor of a vast extent of soil, not very productive, and inhabiting a spacious mansion, not in the best repair, he lived according to the style of the country with more hospitality than elegance: whilst his table groaned with abundance, the order and good taste of its arrangement were little thought of: the slaughtered ox was hung up whole, and the hungry servitor supplied himself with his dole of flesh, sliced from off the carcase. His lordship's day was so apportioned as to give the afternoon by much the largest share of it, during which, from an early dinner to the hour of rest, he never left his chair, nor did the claret ever quit the table. This did not produce inebriety, for it was sipping rather than drinking, that filled up the time, and this mechanical process of gradually moistening the human clay was carried on with very little aid from conversation, for his lordship's companions were not very communicative, and fortunately he was not very curious. He lived in an enviable independance [sic] as to reading and of course he had no books. Not one of the windows of his castle was made to open, but luckily he had no liking for fresh air, and the consequence may be better conceived than described.

He had a large and handsome pleasure boat on the Shannon, and men to row it; I was of two or three parties with him on that noble water as far as to Portumna, the then deserted castle of Lord Clanrickarde.[28] Upon one of these excursions we were hailed by a person from the bank, who somewhat rudely called to us to take him over to the other side. The company in the boat making no reply, I inadvertently called out — 'Aye, aye, Sir! stay there till we come.' Immediately I heard a murmur in the company, and Lord

Eyre said to me — 'You'll hear from that gentleman again, or I am mistaken. You don't know perhaps that you have been answering one of the most irritable men alive, and the likeliest to interpret what you have said as an affront.' He predicted truly, for the very next morning the gentleman rode over to Lord Eyre, and demanded of him to give up my name. This his lordship did, but informed him withal that I was a stranger in the country, the son of Bishop Cumberland at Clonfert, where I might be found if he had any commands for me. He instantly replied, that he should have received it as an affront from any other man, but Bishop Cumberland's was a character he respected, and no son of his could be guilty of an intention to insult him. Thus this valiant gentleman permitted me to live, and only helped me to another feature in my sketch of Major O'Flaherty.

A short time after this, Lord Eyre, who had a great passion for cock-fighting, and whose cocks were the crack of all Ireland, engaged me in a main at Eyre Court. I was a perfect novice in that elegant sport, but the gentlemen from all parts sent me in their contributions, and having a good feeder I won every battle in the main but one. At this meeting I fell in with my hero from the Shannon bank. Both parties dined together, but when I found that mine, which was the more numerous and infinitely the most obstreperous and disposed to quarrel, could no longer be left in peace with our antagonists, I quitted my seat by Lord Eyre, and went to the gentleman above-alluded to, who was presiding at the second table, and seating myself familiarly on the arm of his chair, proposed to him to adjourn our party, and assemble them in another house, for the sake of harmony and good fellowship. With the best grace in life he instantly assented, and when I added that I should put them under his care, and expect from him as a man of honour and my friend, that every mother's son of them should be found forthcoming and alive the next morning — 'Then by the soul of me, he replied, and they shall; provided only that no man in company shall dare to give *the glorious and immortal memory* for his toast, which no gentleman, who feels as I do, will put up with.' To this I pledged myself, and we removed to a whiskey house, attended by half a score pipers, playing different tunes. Here we went on very joyously and lovingly for a time, till a well-dressed gentleman entered the room, and civilly accosting me, requested to partake of our festivity, and join the company, if no body had an objection — 'Ah now, don't be too sure of that,' a voice was instantly heard to reply, 'I believe you will find plenty of objection in this company to your being one amongst us.' — What had he done the gentleman demanded — 'What have you done,' rejoined the first speaker, 'Don't I know you for the miscreant, that ravished the poor wench against her will, in presence of her mother? And didn't your Pagans, that held her down, ravish the mother afterwards, in presence of her daughter? And do you think we will admit you into our company? Make yourself sure that we shall not; therefore *get out of this* as speedily as you can, and away wid you!' upon this the whole company rose, and in their rising the civil gentleman made his exit and was off. I relate this incident exactly as it happened, suppressing the name of this gentleman, who was a man of property and some consequence. When my surprise had subsided, and the punch began to circulate with a rapidity the greater for the gentleman's having troubled the waters, I took my departure, having first cautioned a friend, who sate by me, (and the only protestant in the company) to keep his head cool and beware of the *glorious memory*; this gallant young officer, son to a man, who held lands of my father, promised faithfully to be sober and discreet, as well knowing the company he was in; but my friend having forgot the first part of his promise, and getting very tipsy, let the second part slip out of his memory, and became very mad; for stepping aside for his pistols, he re-entered the room, and laying them on the table, took the cockade from his hat, and dashed it into the punch-bowl, demanding of the company to drink *the glorious and immortal memory of King William* in a bumper, or abide the consequences. I was not there, and if I had been present I could neither have stayed the tumult, nor described it. I only know he turned out the next morning merely for honour's sake, but as it was one against a host, the magnanimity of his opponents let him off with a shot or two, that did no execution. I returned to the peaceful family at Clonfert, and fought no more cocks.

11) Robert Bell

From *Description of the . . . Peasantry of Ireland* (1804):[29]

Those peasants who could afford the expence, used to give a feast to all their relations and neighbours when any female belonging to their family was married. The dinner, which was the only meal on this occasion, generally consisted of mutton, salt pork, bacon and poultry; with an abundance of potatoes and common garden vegetables. All these articles were supplied from the stock of the person who furnished the entertainment: but sometimes the relations of the parties would each contribute a share towards the wedding dinner. No part of the fare was purchased by money except the whiskey or beer: the latter was not always to be procured. The chief personage at this entertainment was the parish Priest, or his deputy. The next in pre-eminence was the Squire: but it was not every country gentleman who could attain the honour of being present at a wedding feast: for if he had not resided long in the neighbourhood; if he had not by a gentle and familiar deportment, but above all, by conversing with the peasants in the Irish language; commanded their esteem, and conciliated their affections, he would not have been invited. The Squire, however, could have been easily dispensed with: but, next to the Priest, the Musician was the most necessary person to render the entertainment complete. He was generally a performer on the bagpipes; and the host was often obliged to send for one to the distance of near 20 or 30 miles. Doors taken off the hinges and laid on benches, constituted a dinner table, of which no part was covered with a cloth except the head: here the Priest sat as president or lord over all the guests, and had the most delicate of the viands placed before him. The others sat in order according to their rank; which was estimated by the consideration of their property, their age, and their reputation. The meat was usually cut into pieces about the size of brickbats, and placed along the table in large wooden platters, out of which the guests helped themselves often without the aid of knives or forks: for the few instruments of this kind which could be procured, were appropriated to the service of the Priest and the select party whom he chose to honour with his conversation. The host and hostess, instead of sitting down to dinner, waited upon the company, and pressed them to eat with an earnestness and familiarity that would have been highly disgusting to persons of more refined manners. The marriage ceremony was generally perfomed before dinner; and on this occasion it was sometimes necessary to force the timorous bride from the place where she had concealed herself on the first approach of the company. The company afterwards amused themselves in dancing, singing and drinking. The Priest retired about eight or nine o'clock: and if great care was not taken after that hour, to prevent the distribution of liquor, the night would have ended in intoxication, riot, quarrelling and bloodshed. In the course of a week or fortnight, the bridegroom took his wife home to his own habitation; the portion he received with her, consisted chiefly in cattle. In places where English law and English manners were unknown, the married women were always called by their maiden names.

[. . .]

The amusements of the native Irish chiefly took place on Sundays and holidays. On Sunday morning they regularly went to their popish chapel, which was sometimes not sufficient to contain one half of the people: those therefore who could not gain admittance prayed in the open air, near the doors of the chapel. As soon as the service was over, the greater part of the congregation went home and dined: after which during the summer season, they assembled in large bodies in some adjacent field; where the old sat in circles and entertained each other with stories, and the young danced to whatever music they could procure, and some of the young men exercised themselves in feats of bodily strength. Good humour and contentment always prevailed at those meetings as long as they drank no whiskey: but whenever that fiery spirit was introduced, intoxication and quarrels were the inevitable consequences.

In the winter season, they assembled on Sunday evenings at some house where whiskey was sold: but more commonly where some one belonging to the family played on an instrument of music. The people belonging to the later description of houses never demanded or expected any recompence for the accommodation thus afforded their neighbours, except the satisfaction arising from the consciousness of having contributed to the happiness of others. The love of society was, in short, so prominent a part of the character of those people that hardly any part of a peasant's family remained at home on a Sunday evening; and in winter they would often go a distance of three or four miles, through swamps and bogs, to any place where a considerable number of people were assembled. Even in their ordinary occupations both in the field and in the house, they shewed an uncommon fondness for social intercourse. Every evening in the week throughout the winter season, a party of young females went successively to the houses of their respective parents, with their spinning wheels, and dedicated a great part of the night to the double purpose of industry and innocent amusement. Hither they were generally followed by their lovers: the song and the tale went round, and labour ceased to be a toil. The happiness enjoyed by those simple rustics in places where oppression had not spread her iron hand, was such as those who live in polished societies might envy.

But of all the amusements of the native Irish, there were none so remarkable for variety, for the multitudes that partook of them, and for the interest they excited, as those which were called *Patrons*: nor were any of their meetings oftener concluded with drunkenness and broils than these. An Irish patron resembled, in some manner, the old English wake: probably they both sprung from the same origin. It was a large assemblage of people from all parts within a distance of ten or twenty miles, collected together round a sacred fountain dedicated to, and called after the name of the Saint, in honour of whom this festival was celebrated. In the morning or forenoon the priest of the parish performed mass on a large stone, which was called an altar. Several old men and women at the same time performed penance round the well. Here were all sorts of hawkers, mountebanks, conjurers and itinerant musicians: and tents and booths were erected chiefly for the sale of liquor. The day was not uncommonly concluded by a general battle. Outrages of this kind sometimes proceeded from family feuds; but more frequently from local animosities. If there were none others than the people of two parishes collected together; these, when elevated and maddened with liquor, would fight against each other, for what reason they knew not. If the assemblage of people had been collected from more distant places, the inhabitants belonging to one barony or county would contend with those of another. The battle was most commonly preceded by a challenge. Some fellow, whose bodily strength — whose boisterous and ferocious temper, gave him such an ascendancy over others as to be chosen their leader; would come forth, and flourishing his cudgel over his head, bid defiance to all who did not belong to his clan, parish, barony, or county. A champion on the adverse side would instantly rush forward to meet him. Their followers soon joined them and the engagement became general.

12) John Gough

John Gough toured Ireland in 1813, 1814 and 1816 and wrote about it in 1817. He writes contemptuously of other erroneous accounts (for example Priscilla Wakefield's *English Travellers in Ireland*, and Richard Twiss) and of the anti-Irish prejudice prevalent among the English. Gough stresses instead his own observation of the country. He arrived at Donaghadee and toured the north of Ireland, then proceeded down the east coast to Dublin and from there, after touring the neighbourhood, south west to Limerick, Cork and Waterford. Despite his honest intentions Gough does not produce an easily readable text.

From *A Tour in Ireland* (1817):[30]

Six mail coaches daily pass through the town, both backwards and forwards, and for posting are kept about a dozen post chaises, as good, and as well attended, as they are on the roads in England, and not such as Miss Edgeworth's caricature of an Irish post-chaise in one of her novels, I forget whether it is in her Ennui or her Absentee.[31] And now that I have been led to mention this deservedly admired female writer, I must beg leave to make a few remarks, as they struck me in my journey. Some may think them foreign from the purport of my writing; but the Reader may easily perceive that the whole is a heterogeneous medley, where no regular order is observed; yet I hope these remarks will not appear quite irrelevant to my subject. In some parts of Miss Edgeworth's writings, it appears to me hard to guess, whether she means to defend her countrymen, or turn them into ridicule. Certainly their accent and manner of speech, particularly in Munster, is very disagreeable to an English ear; but the improprieties of their expressions, do not exceed those of the inhabitants of some counties in England; and in all my journies in Ireland, I never heard any one say *shister*, for *sister*, nor upon my *showl*; though they pronounce the word *soul*, as *sowle*, instead of *sole*, and which is the most proper might admit of some dispute; neither did I ever hear *Jauntleman*, instead of *Gentleman*. I never heard the name of Teague in Ireland, though I knew many of the name of Paddy. The word *yees* instead of *you*, is confined very much to the city and neighbourhood of Dublin; but neither those who make use of that expression, nor Miss Edgeworth herself, seem to be aware of its origin, which I can very easily comprehend. In the Irish, as well as every other ancient language, the distinction between *thou* and *you* is still observed. Of course, those whose native language was Irish, on becoming imperfectly acquainted with English, perceiving that *you* was used in the singular number, and concluding that it must have a plural, and finding that in general the plural was formed by adding *s* to the singular, they immediately made a plural to *you*, by adding that termination, and made our *yous* or *yees*; and though many who now use these words, know nothing of the Irish language, I am fully persuaded, that from hence they had their origin, as I never knew them used in the singular number; though Miss Edgeworth has sometimes so applied them.

The very lowest of the vulgar in Dublin use the words *folly* for *follow*, *swolly*, for *swollow* [sic], and *windy*, instead of *window*. At a private lodging in Dublin, where I had the service of the woman servant of the house, I once overheard a curious dialogue between this woman and my man, who was a true born Londoner. The woman, while lighting the fire, desired my man to shut the *windy*; he, who knew her meaning very well, but prided himself on his superior knowledge and education, as being from *Lunnon*; asked her whether she meant the *vindore*; you fool, retorted the woman, sure I dont want you to shut the *fender*.

13) Henry Inglis

Henry David Inglis (1795–1835) was born in Edinburgh, the son of a Scottish advocate, and was educated for business but turned away from it for literature and travel. He published tales under the pen name of Derwent Conway. Later he toured Norway, Sweden and Denmark, Switzerland, southern France and the Pyrenees; subsequently, Spain, the Tyrol, Bavaria and other countries. His Irish tour was made in 1834. The published account attained some success. It reached a fifth edition by 1838 and was quoted as an authority in parliamentary debates. Inglis was certainly a favoured traveller. According to one source he visited Ireland equipped with over a hundred and thirty letters of introduction to important people.[32]

From *A Journey throughout Ireland* (1835):[33]

The spirit of faction is brought into court by almost every witness in these prosecutions. I saw a witness, a woman, brought in support of the prosecution for a homicide committed on some cousin, — who on being desired to identify the prisoners, and the court-keeper's long rod being put into her hand, that she might point them out, struck each of them a smart blow on the head. As for finding out the truth, by the mere evidence of the witnesses, it is generally impossible. Almost all worth knowing, is elicited on the cross-examination: and it is always, by the appearance and manner of the witness, more than by his words, that the truth is to be gathered. All the witnesses, examined for the prosecution, were, by their own account, mere lookers on at the battle; nor stick, nor stone had they. *Their* party had no mind to fight that day; but, in making this assertion, they always take care to let it be known, that, if they had had a mind to fight, they could have handled their shillelahs to some purpose. On the other hand, all the witnesses for the prisoner aver just the same of themselves; so that it is more by what winesses wont [sic] tell, than by what they do tell, that truth is discovered. Half the witnesses called, on both sides, have broken heads; and it is not unfrequently by a comparison of the injuries received on both sides, and by the evidence of the doctor, that one is helped to the truth.

It will be easily seen, from what I have said, that I found ample confirmation of what I had often heard, — the small regard for veracity among the Irish peasantry, and their general disregard of an oath. To save a relation from punishment, or to punish any one who has injured a relation, an Irish peasant will swear anything. This would be called, by some, hatred of the law; but, although, in swearing falsely, the Irish peasant wishes to defeat the ends of justice, he does not do so, merely because he hates justice and the law, but because he thinks he is bound to save his relation, or any one of his faction. If the name of the man who was killed be O'Grady, then every witness, who comes up to be sworn for the prosecution, is also an O'Grady; or, if they be women, they were O'Gradys before they were married; and, if the name of the prisoner be O'Neil, then all the witnesses, for the defence, are O'Neils; or, if there be any exceptions in name, still there is a relationship of some kind.

[. . .]

The most numerous class of cases (with one exception), and the most important class, as throwing the greatest light on the character and state of the people, were those homicides of which I have spoken. The exception in point of number of cases, is rape: of these cases, I think nearly forty were entered for trial: but only a very few of that number were heard; and all of them terminated in acquittal. In nine cases out of ten, the crime is sworn to, merely for the purpose of getting a husband; and the plan generally succeeds. The parties are married before the cause is called for trial; and I have myself seen an earnest negotiation carried on under the piazzas of the court-house, a little while before a case was called. There was the 'boy' indicted for a capital crime, but out on bail, as he generally is; and the girl, about to swear away a man's life; and the attorneys, and a large circle of relations, all trying to bring about a marriage, before Pat should be called upon to appear, and answer to the indictment that he, 'not having the fear of God before his eyes, and being instigated by the devil,' did so and so. In the case to which I was a listener, Pat and the fair one could not agree: the trial went on; and Pat was acquitted.

[. . .]

I saw tried, one of those singular cases of abduction which very frequently occur in Ireland; and which also throw considerable light on the state of society among the lower ranks. Sham cases of abduction are frequent. The 'boy' and the girl are agreed;

but the girl's relations being dissentient, owing to her being an heiress, and entitled to a better match, it is made up between the young people, that the girl shall be carried away by apparent force. The youth makes known the case to his friends, and collects a number of associates: they come during the night to the house of the girl, force open the door, seize upon the maid, who, though 'nothing loth,' screams and makes all the opposition in her power, place her on horseback, and, after escorting her a sufficient distance, deliver her over to the 'boy,' on whose account the abduction was got up. The charge of abduction which I saw tried at Ennis, was a real abduction however, and a very shameless one, attended with circumstances of great cruelty; and originating, as indeed they always do, in love of money. These abductions are most detrimental to the peace of the country; because a feud is instantly generated, between the relatives of the girl, and those of the aggressor; and many subsequent fights invariably result from these outrages.

One of the cases tried at the Ennis assizes, was in many respects similar to that celebrated case, which was the foundation for that excellent novel, 'The Collegians.'[34] A man was tried for the murder of a girl whom he had seduced; he killed her, and buried her in a peat-rick; and the similarity is the stronger, inasmuch as he was at the time in treaty to marry another, not so light-born a damsel indeed, as Anne Chute; but high enough and rich enough, to induce him to sacrifice *his* Elie O'Connor. In this case, one of the witnesses, on being desired to identify the prisoner, and being asked the question, 'Is that the man?' turned round and recognizing the prisoner, said, 'That's him,' and added 'How are you Paddy?' nodding familiarly and good-humouredly to the accused. The man was convicted, and hanged.

Another case tried, arose out of one of those disputes, which so frequently originate in the possession of, and competition for, land. It was a case wherein a widow paid an enormous rent for a bit of potato land; and the rent not being paid, and the mischievous power of distraining being resorted to, the possessor endeavoured to save some portion of the potatos. This gave rise to a fight; and the fight occasioned man-slaughter. In this case, there was much false swearing, and much difficulty in arriving at the truth; and the case strongly impressed upon me the conviction, that the power of distraining, in the hands of the lower orders, is a most mischievous power.

I noticed, that great importance is attached to kissing the book; and sometimes, this ceremony is required, for greater security, to be performed two or three times. Without kissing the book, a witness looks upon his oath as very imperfectly taken; and it is necessary that in the act of kissing, the witness be narrowly watched, lest he kiss his own thumb — with which he holds the book — in place of the book itself.

I noticed also, in the examination of one of the witnesses, a proof of the prevailing belief in the 'good people,' or fairies. A witness, being asked upon his oath, whether a certain individual could have made his way out of a room, the door and windows of which had been fastened, said, with the utmost gravity, it was impossible he could have got out, unless by enchantment; meaning by this, without the assistance of the good people.

To attend an Irish assize, is certainly not the means by which a stranger is likely to obtain favourable impressions of Irish character. Few of its favourable traits are exhibited there; while all the darker shades are made but too manifest. Want of veracity, on the most solemn occasion on which veracity is ever called for, is but too plainly established. We find the very reverse of that straightforwardness, which it is so delightful to see exhibited in the examination of a witness. If positive falsehood will serve the end, it is unhesitatingly resorted to; and as for telling the *whole* truth, I saw no one instance of it.

But the most striking defect of character which is brought to light, is a perfect contempt of human suffering, and an utter disregard even of the value of human life. Weapons, of the most deadly description, are brought into court as evidence, — sticks and whips loaded with lead; and stones, that might crush the head of a horse. A ruffian may occasionally be found in England, who would slay a man alive to become possessed of his purse; but I greatly question whether out of Ireland, fifty men could be found in any one parish, in any country in Europe, ready to beat one another's brains out with stick and stones, and all but glorying in the deed. And, as I have already observed, the same ferocity which has been exhibited at the fight, is brought into court: false oaths are the substitutes for weapons: and by these, witnesses seek to avenge the death of a relative who has been more unfortunate, but probably not more criminal, than the accused.

16. IRISH TOWNS

If English travellers before 1700 describe in Ireland a war-torn, savage country with wrecked cities and neglected landscapes, after 1700, for a century, a new note is struck. Dublin draws admiring attention for its spacious architecture, if not for its beggars and uncleanly streets; to a lesser extent, so do Waterford and other towns. After the turn of the nineteenth century Belfast's growing wealth is noted, as in Plumptre below. Otherwise, travellers regularly lament the poverty and planlessness of small Irish towns, often with the most rudimentary provision for prisons and schools; Thomas Reid and James Glassford undertook tours of Ireland with a particular eye on these features in the nineteenth century.[1] Thackeray (quoted here on Cork) gives also an interesting account of Galway, whose character and atmosphere he tries to put on paper.[2] English visitors, arriving in Ireland with expectations drawn from their own wealthier cities, boroughs and towns enriched by long, peaceful commerce, beautified over time and secured and valued by a confident population, perceived a country appearing to belong to some pre-modern age. Of the roughness and danger still a part of provincial Irish life, George Fox, Wesley and other preachers' accounts provide examples.

1) Richard Cumberland

From *Memoirs* (1807):[3]

I found the state of society in Dublin very different from what I had observed in London; the professions more intermixt, and ranks more blended; in the great houses I met a promiscuous assembly of politicians, lawyers, soldiers and divines; the profusion of their tables struck me with surprise; nothing that I had seen in England could rival the Polish magnificence of Primate Stone,[4] or the Parisian luxury of Mr. Clements. The style of Dodington was stately, but there was a watchful and well-regulated economy over all, that here seemed out of sight and out of mind. The professional gravity of character maintained by our English dignitaries was here laid aside, and in several prelatical houses the mitre was so mingled with the cockade, and the glass circulated so freely, that I perceived the spirit of conviviality was by no means excluded from the pale of the church of Ireland.

I had more than once the amusement of dining at the house of that most singular being George Faulkner,[5] where I found myself in a company so miscellaneously and whimsically classed, that it looked more like a fortuitous concourse of oddities, jumbled together from all ranks, orders and descriptions, than the effect of invitation and design. Description must fall short in the attempt to convey any sketch of that eccentric being to those, who have not read him in the notes of Jephson, or seen him in the mimickry of Foote, who in his portraits of Faulkner found the only sitter, whom his extravagant pencil could not caricature; for he had a solemn intrepidity of egotism, and a daring contempt of absurdity, that fairly outfaced imitation, and like Garrick's Ode on Shakespeare, which Johnson said 'defied criticism,'[6] so did George in the original spirit of his own perfect buffoonery defy caricature. He never deigned to join in the laugh he had raised, nor seemed to have a feeling of the ridicule he had provoked: at the same time that he was pre-eminently and by preference the butt and buffoon of the company, he could find openings and opportunities for hits of retaliation, which were such left-handed thrusts as few could parry: nobody could foresee where they would fall, nobody of course was fore-armed, and as there was in his calculation but one supereminent character in the kingdom of Ireland, and he the printer of the Dublin Journal, rank was no shield against George's arrows, which flew where he listed, and fixed or missed as chance directed, he cared not about consequences. He gave good meat and excellent claret in abundance; I sate at his table once from dinner till two in the morning, whilst George swallowed immense potations with one solitary sodden strawberry at the bottom of the glass, which he said was recommended to him by his doctor for its cooling properties. He never lost his recollection or equilibrium the whole time, and was in excellent foolery; it was a singular coincidence, that there was a person in company, who had received his reprieve at the gallows, and the very judge, who had passed sentence of death upon him. This did not in the least disturb the harmony of the society, nor embarrass any human creature present. All went off perfectly smooth, and George, adverting to an original portrait of

Dean Swift, which hung in his room, told us an abundance of excellent and interesting anecdotes of the Dean and himself with minute precision and an importance irresistibly ludicrous. There was also a portrait of his late lady Mrs. Faulkner, which either made the painter or George a liar, for it was frightfully ugly, whilst he swore she was the most divine object in creation. In the mean time he took credit to himself for a few deviations in point of gallantry, and asserted that he broke his leg in flying from the fury of an enraged husband, whilst Foote constantly maintained that he fell down an area with a tray of meat upon his shoulder, when he was journeyman to a butcher: I believe neither of them spoke the truth. George prosecuted Foote for lampooning him on the stage of Dublin; his counsel the prime serjeant compared him to Socrates and his libeller to Aristophanes; this I believe was all that George got by his course of law; but he was told he had the best of the bargain in the comparison, and sate down contented under the shadow of his laurels. In process of time he became an alderman; I paid my court to him in that character, but I thought he was rather marred than mended by his dignity. George grew grave and sentimental, and sentiment and gravity sate as ill upon George, as a gown and square cap would upon a monkey.

Mrs. Dancer, then in her prime and very beautiful, was acting with Barry at the Crow-Street theatre, and Miss Elliot, who had played in Mr. Bentley's *Wishes*,[7] came over with the recommendation of Mr. Arthur Murphy, who interested himself much in her success; this young uneducated girl had great natural talents, and played the part of Maria in her patron's farce of *The Citizen* with admirable spirit and effect. The whimsical mock-opera of *Midas* was first brought upon the Dublin stage in this season, and had all the protection which the castle patronage could bestow, and that could not be more than its pleasantry and originality deserved.

2) Sir John Gough

In the following passage Gough sketches for his reader something of the thronged and bustling market life of the real Dublin city.

From *Tour in Ireland* (1817):[8]

Notwithstanding the perseverance of the butchers of Patrick-street, in refusing to remove to the new erected market, many of the stalls soon became occupied by other butchers, and it is now the principal market for the poor in this part of the city; very few others ever attending it; sixty three of its stalls are actually occupied. Mutton and Lamb are the only flesh meat ever exposed to sale here, except sometimes, in the spring a small quantity of Pork. The market place is kept very dirty, many of the sheep being killed in the very stalls where they are to be sold; and no fountain throughout its whole extent. The average of the sales by retail in this market, amounts to upwards of one thousand sheep (including lambs in summer) per week. Besides which, as most of them are wholesale butchers, the prime of their mutton is sold to other markets to be retailed there. Even in the slaughtering season, when beef is in the greatest plenty, I never saw any beef in this market.

Ormond market was formerly accounted one of the first markets in Europe. It has not decreased, but others in Dublin have increased. The passages in the market are flagged, and kept tolerably clean; but they are all inconveniently narrow, for the very great business done here. Besides the seventy three stalls occupied by butchers, most of which are of great extent, and all well filled every day, with little variation, there are numerous stalls for poulterers, bacon, butter, cheese, fruit, vegetables, and every kind of fresh fish; in short there is not one article of food possible to mention (consonant with our climate and the season of the year) nor any sauce that luxury or intemperance could require, that may not be had in Ormond-market, on any day, or at any hour.

Castle-market, though not so extensive, is as well furnished in proportion to its extent as Ormond-market, with every article of provision. The market-place is neater than Ormond, though the passages are still too narrow.

Clarendon market is situated very near this latter. It consists of handsome stalls, of which only eighteen are occupied by butchers; a few others by poulterers, &c. but several still remain unemployed.

Cole's Lane or Rotunda market from a small beginning, and that but a few years ago, is now become, as to extent, the greatest in Dublin. The passages are too narrow, and though larger and having a greater number of butchers, to take it all together it is inferior, as to variety, to Ormond market.

Leinster market near Carlisle bridge, newly erected, though very small, is by far the neatest market-place in Dublin; we enter it from three different streets by handsome iron gates. The passage is very handsomely flagged, and the flags are kept as clean as those in a gentleman's hall. It contains about twenty eight stalls, of which as yet only five are occupied by butchers, and three or four more by poulterers, retailers of bacon, &c. the rest remain untenanted.

To these 405 butcher's stalls, we must add about sixty shops of poulterers, scattered through those different markets, who each keep three or four journey-men, constantly employed in drawing and skewering the fowl (as they are plucked before they come to market) an employment much more suitable to women than to men. Those shops are profusely furnished, according to the season, with chickens, barn-door and crammed fowl, geese, turkeys, rabbits, hares, and all kinds of game. Neither have we taken an account of the numerous stalls in each market for fish, or any other provisions than fresh butcher's meat. Besides there are several markets for bacon, butter, eggs &c. held early every morning, and a person walking through the streets of Dublin, and taking a view of the numerous shops where bacon is retailed, in large quantities, in every part of the town, might be led almost to conclude, that the quantity exceeded all other kinds of food put together. Eggs are in exceeding great plenty, and to be had in vast numbers in every obscure street in Dublin either in shops, or in baskets in the streets. The egg-market which supplies these shops, is held every morning, and two hundred thousand eggs is not an uncommon sale in one day; besides the great number sold to private families, by country people, who have each but [a] small quantity.

The butcher's meat is of the most excellent quality. And all those markets are supplied with poultry of every kind, in great perfection and the greatest abundance. It is not therefore in Dublin, as it is in London, that poultry is confined principally to the tables of the opulent and luxurious; the very lowest of the working people, when they have employment, come in for their share. Notwithstanding the number of regular poulterers, who keep shops, there are great numbers of fowls, particularly geese and turkeys, exposed to sale daily in other places; and for about two weeks before Christmas every year, there are at least one thousand geese and turkeys together sold daily in Thomas-street only, principally to labouring people; and likewise large quantities at the different entrances into the city. The barn door and crammed fowl are very fine, and the turkeys, which are in very great plenty, in all the markets, are probably the finest exhibited for sale at any market.

The quantity of fish consumed in Dublin is very considerable, and of excellent quality. They have turbot in great plenty. Cod, haddock, ling, ray, flounders, herrings, oysters, cockles and most fish are very reasonable in price, except lobsters. They have no sprats, and it is seldom that any shrimps are brought to Dublin market. They have abundance of Salmon from the Liffey and Boyne, but it is not equal in quality to what comes by the mail coach from Limerick, Ross and Waterford, but the good Munster salmon they could never have in perfection, as it is frequently from 24 to 30 hours out of the water before it reaches Dublin. Now the connoisseurs in the south of Ireland say, that to have salmon in perfection, it must be put on the fire within two hours after it is taken; of course a real epicure in Dublin, if he wishes to get a good meal of salmon, instead of sending to Limerick for the fish, ought to go thither to eat it; which would not be quite so long a journey as to go to the West Indies to eat turtle. But I have seen very good people in London eat salmon, and think it excellent, and yet it was such as a Munster-man would not taste, except he was really hungry, and could not get any thing else.

To go into Smithfield market, on Monday or Thursday mornings, in the seasons of the year, when there is not any slaughtering for export, and of course the cattle must be for the use of Dublin and its extensive neighbourhood solely, a stranger would be amazed at the great number exposed to sale; for besides beef and veal, it is not uncommon to have five thousand sheep and lambs sold in one day, and this market is twice a week. Now we go on the supposition that Belfast, including Ballimacarret, contains one seventh part of the number of inhabitants that Dublin does; and allowing for a greater number of rich gentry still remaining in Dublin, and that the inferior people more generally live on flesh meat, than those of the same class in Belfast, yet we may reasonably suppose, that Belfast market might require one tenth part of the quantity of meat sold in Dublin. Of this, as far as I could percieve [sic], it falls infinitely short. The flesh most generally used in all parts of Ireland (except in Ulster) particularly by the poor, is mutton and bacon. Beef is the most used in the north, and that generally very poor.

In Dublin there are several thousands of sheep killed every week; in Belfast flesh-market I never saw two hundred at once. The quantity of meat of all kinds sold in Dublin is nearly equal every day; in Belfast, though meat is to be had every day, the quantity sold on Friday (their weekly market) far exceeds that on any other day, or perhaps all the other days in the week; and, even independent of mutton, which is very scarce throughout the north, the meat sold weekly in the single market in Belfast, would, both as to quantity and quality, make but a very middling market among the many in Dublin. Lamb is not often to be met with in Belfast; whereas it is to be got in Dublin for nine months in the year; and, during five months, it is by far the most plentiful, and the cheapest of any kind of meat.

3) Anne Plumptre

Anne Plumptre gives an impression of pre-industrial Belfast, with citizens' holiday homes and a general air of opulence making it an attractive prospect. She caught the town at the period of its transformation into the dominating city of the later nineteenth century, and recognises the flurry of new buildings and newly laid out streets which marked the beginning of this process.

From *Narrative of a Residence* (1817):[9]

Here the road enters the county of Antrim, and continues along the valley of the Lagan quite to Belfast, where the river joins the Bay of Belfast, or Belfast Lough. This valley and the lough run in a direction from south-west to north-east, and the valley is skirted from a very little way beyond Lisburn by a continued chain of mountains. The country constantly improves, till in the neighbourhood of Belfast it becomes very beautiful, being scattered over with a number of villas, the summer residences of the citizens of Belfast. The town stands exactly at the junction of the river with the bay, or perhaps it should rather be said that the bay from its mouth is constantly contracting itself till at Belfast it is narrowed to the breadth only of a river; when it assumes the name of the Lagan. The same is the case with Carlingford Bay in the county of Down; it narrows up to the river called Newry-water; and such also is the Kenmare river in the county of Kerry, a bay narrowing gradually till it becomes no wider than a river. The Lagan is crossed at Belfast by a very old bridge of twenty-one arches, which, like most old bridges, is very narrow, with the arches very small. Three of the arches are in the county of Antrim, the remainder of the bridge is in the county of Down.

Belfast is one of the most opulent towns in Ireland: it is the largest town in the county of Antrim, though not the county town, and is a principal deposit of the linen-trade. It has increased in wealth and size very much within a few years; there are many streets entirely new-built, and nearly at the entrance of the town is a spacious and handsome linen-hall almost new. For its present flourishing state it is much indebted to the late Marquis of Donegal: this family has a large property in the town; many of the new streets are upon ground leased from them. The late Marquis built at his own expense a handsome assembly-room over the Exchange.

Large as the town is, it contains only one parish; the church is a neat one, but has nothing in it particularly striking. A very large portion of the inhabitants are not, however, of the church of England. This county and Down, approaching the nearest to Scotland of any part of the island, have been very much colonised by Scotch families, consequently dissenters from the church of England; yet many do not adhere to the religion they brought over with them, but have adopted other persuasions. Unitarianism is more prevalent here than in any part of Ireland; the catholics are not numerous, though they have two chapels. There are eight congregations of protestant dissenters of different descriptions, including a quakers and a methodists meeting.

As the church had become too small for the increased size of the town, a chapel of ease was in considerable forwardness when I was there. It was raised from the spoils of one out of the many houses built by the late Earl of Bristol, and bishop of Derry. Besides that at Ickworth in the county of Suffolk, he built two in the county of Derry; Down Hill, now the property of Sir Hervey Bruce, and that in question, I think, near Derry.[10] The heir to his estates has thought proper to pull down the latter, and selling the materials, sufficient were purchased by the town of Belfast to build a chapel; among these materials were some fluted Ionic columns, which form a very handsome portico.

The principal charitable institutions at Belfast are, a general infirmary [sic] for the sick poor, a fever hospital, a lying-in hospital, an asylum for the blind where, as in similar institutions in other places, they are taught such works as they are capable of executing, particularly basket-making; — an asylum for aged men and women and orphan children; the latter are fed, clothed, and educated, till of age to be bound out as apprentices; — a house of industry intended to abolish mendicity, — and indeed in no part of Ireland are so few beggars to be seen; perhaps this is rather to be ascribed to the country hereabouts being in a more flourishing state than most other parts.

A plan was formed some years ago for establishing an university, principally with a view to the education of protestant dissenters. Not much progress had at this time been made in it, and it seemed probable that the scheme would fall entirely to the ground. There are literary societies for the promotion of philosophy, the medical sciences, and music: — the latter has principally in view the revival of that ancient national instrument, the harp, such as it was in former days, not with any of those modern *improvements* which entirely deprive the instrument of its true national character. This town is considered as a very literary place, it is a sort of metropolis of the north. Besides the great staple article of manufactory — the linen, there are large manufactories of cotton, sail-cloth, sugar, glass, and earthenware. The streets are well paved with *trottoirs*, and well lighted. All round the town there are very large bleaching-grounds.[11]

The Bay at the flow of the tide is truly beautiful, scattered over on each side for a short distance from the water with country-seats finely wooded, and high hills rising behind them; the hills on the northern shore are much the highest. When the tide is down, a very large portion of the Bay is but a continued sand or rather mud, with a small channel winding through it up to the town. This channel is marked by posts for the direction of vessels coming up at high water, and the depth is then sufficient to admit vessels of a considerable size. Oysters, muscles, and cockles, abound in the Bay, and the shores at low water are scattered over with the shells; but there are no other shells, and no weed or pebbles worth notice. Further down the Bay, towards Carrickfergus, the shore becomes more pebbly, and some shells are to be found of the genera *Buccimum, Venus*, and *Arca*.

4) Henry Inglis

Inglis gives a favourable report of Enniskillen ten years before the Famine. He sees a town blessed by natural advantages which could be further improved. Socially, Inglis can see nothing to quarrel with in the set-up in the town and its district. He sees Enniskillen run by comparatively responsible landlords, secure in its Protestant power, benefitting economically from the military troops based in the town, who also helped to shore up the whole structure, and with the labouring poor kept quiet by a cycle of full employment during two thirds of the year followed by economic hardship during the remainder.

From *A Journey throughout Ireland* (1835):[12]

The situation of Enniskillen is in every way delightful. Loch Erne, the noblest in point of extent, of any of the Irish lakes, and which has been called the Winandermere of Ireland, — an appellation, which I shall by an by endeavour to shew, it is well entitled to, — spreads into an upper and lower lake, above and below the town, though, from the distance between them, which is not less than four miles, they ought rather to be considered two distinct lakes.

This communication between the two lakes is not more than river breadth, and in one part, separates into two branches, encircling a tolerably elevated island; and upon this island, stands the town of Enniskillen. Two handsome bridges connect the town with the mainland, at each end of the island; and almost the whole of the island is covered by the town. On the opposite banks of the water, on both sides of the town, the scenery is of the most *riant* description. When I visited the neighbourhood, the corn harvest was just beginning, and the hay harvest was nearly over. On the sunny slopes that rise on all sides, the golden fields of ripe corn, were beautifully mingled with the brilliant green that follows the destruction of the meadow. Abundance of wood, and the broken surface of the country, gave sufficient shade to the landscape, which was, on all sides, imaged in the still, deep, broad waters that surround the town; and altogether, I shall long preserve in my memory, the recollection of this beautiful spot.

But this is not all I have to say in favour of Enniskillen. I found it *one of* the most respectable-looking towns I had seen in Ireland: and its population, by far *the most* respectable-looking, that I had anywhere yet seen. I speak of course of the lower classes; and I make no exception of either Dublin, or Cork, or Limerick, or any other place. I saw a population. — the first I had yet seen, — without rags; I saw scarcely a bare foot, even among the girls; there was a neat, tidy look among the women, who had not, as in other places, their uncombed hair hanging about their ears; and the men, appeared to me to have a decent farmer-like appearance.

Enniskillen is a busy, and a rising town; improvement is everywhere discernable. Many new buildings are seen; thatched houses, scarcely at all; and the suburbs even, are respectable. Enniskillen abounds in respectable shops; and I never saw shops better filled than they were on market day; I understood that many of the tradespeople were wealthy, and the retail trade is brisk and profitable. This, and the generally improving condition of the town, which possesses but little manufacture, are evidences of the prosperous condition of the surrounding agricultural population, — and by implication, speaks favourably also of the landlords. Lords Enniskillen, Ely, and Belmore, are the three great proprietors; but there are many resident gentlemen besides. The town belongs altogether, to Lord Enniskillen, who is generally well spoken of, and who, in letting his land, endeavours to ascertain its real value. I found the farmers of this neighbourhood enjoying some comforts, and not so ground down to the earth as in the south and west. Potatos are not the sole diet here: the country is a most fruitful one; and much of the wheat and oats, is consumed in the surrounding district. There is some export of grain to Derry, Armagh, &c., but the greater part is consumed. The export of live cattle and pigs, from Enniskillen to Derry, is also considerable. Most important advantages would accrue to Enniskillen, by opening an inland navigation to the sea: and nothing could be easier than this. From the town, there is already an uninterrupted navigation through Loch Erne, to the exit of the river, which, not eight miles distant from the lake, falls into the bay of Donegal: and half of this distance, the river is already navigable: so that it requires but a cut of four miles, to open a water communication, not only from Enniskillen, but from the upper lake to the sea, — a distance of not less than sixty miles. It is almost impossible to calculate the benefit which would be conferred upon the great extent of country bordering on the two Loch Ernes, by this very obvious, and unexpensive undertaking.

Enniskillen enjoys also, a considerable linen trade. From three to four hundred pieces are sold at each fortnight's market; and it speaks well for the prospects of the trade, that many merchants leave the market disappointed of purchases; and that three times the quantity actually sold, would find buyers if it were brought to market. It is a fact, that greatly more flax seed has been sown this year, than on any former year.

The population of Enniskillen, is about one-third Protestant: and the town and neighbourhood are Conservative in their politics. Three newspapers are published in the town, all Conservative. One is Toryish, a second Tory, and a third high Tory. It is singular, that in a town like this, there should be no circulating, or public library.

The price of provisions, in Enniskillen, is reasonable. When I visited it, potatos were 3½*d.* a stone; 120 lbs. of oatmeal were sold at 8*s.* 6*d.*; second quality of flour was 1*s.* 6*d.* per stone. Meat was from 5*d* to 6*d.* per lb.; fine fowls, 10*d.* a couple. Labour in town was at 1*s*; a day; but for constant employment, 10*d.*; and in the country did not exceed 8*d.* The provision, and retail trade of Enniskillen, is of course benefited by the town being military headquarters. During eight months in the year, there is pretty full employment for labour in Enniskillen. Just before the corn harvest began, and after the hay harvest had finished, I saw about eighty persons, in want of employment, and waiting for hire.

5) W. M. Thackeray

William Makepeace Thackeray (1811–63) first visited Ireland in

1842. He was accompanying his Irish wife, who was suffering from mental affliction, to her home in Cork, and kept a travel account of his experiences. According to the *D.N.B.* a preface to the journal in which Thackeray pronounced against the English government of Ireland was suppressed, perhaps to allay the publisher's anxiety.[13] Although Ireland figured as only a small item in Thackeray's global travel (which included visits to Paris, Athens, Constantinople, Jerusalem, Cairo and America), his experience there may have seemed more significant because of its personal connections. However, Thackeray's perception of Cork reinforces the English view of an imbalance in the Irish character, leading to big beginnings petering out in anti-climactic conclusions.

From *The Irish Sketch Book of 1842:*[14]

Amidst the bustle and gaieties of the Architectural meeting, the working-day aspect of the city was not to be judged of: but I passed a fortnight in the place afterwards, during which time it settled down to its calm and usual condition. The flashy French and plated goods' shops, which made a show for the occasion of the meeting, disappeared; you were no longer crowded and justled by smart male and female dandies in walking down Patrick Street or the Mall; the poor little theatre had scarcely a soul on its bare benches: I went once, but the dreadful brass-band of a dragoon regiment blew me out of doors. This music could be heard much more pleasantly at some distance off in the street.

One sees in this country many a grand and tall iron gate leading into a very shabby field covered with thistles; and the simile to the gate will in some degree apply to this famous city of Cork, — which is certainly not a city of palaces, but of which the outlets are magnificent. That towards Killarney leads by the Lee, the old Avenue of Mardyke, and the rich green pastures stretching down to the river; and as you pass by the portico of the county gaol, as fine and as glancing as a palace, you see the wooded heights on the other side of the fair stream, crowded with a thousand pretty villas and terraces, presenting every image of comfort and prosperity. The entrance from Cove has been mentioned before; nor is it easy to find anywhere a nobler, grander, and more cheerful scene.

Along the quays up to Saint Patrick's Bridge there is a certain bustle. Some forty ships may be lying at anchor along the walls of the quay, and its pavements are covered with goods of various merchandise: here a cargo of hides; yonder a company of soldiers, their kits, and their Dollies, who are taking leave of the red-coats at the steamer's side. Then you shall see a fine, squeaking, shrieking drove of pigs embarking by the same conveyance, and insinuated into the steamer by all sorts of coaxing, threatening, and wheedling. Seamen are singing and yeehoing on board; grimy colliers smoking at the liquor-shops along the quay; and as for the bridge — there is a crowd of idlers on that you may be sure, sprawling over the balustrade for ever and ever, with long ragged coats, steeple-hats, and stumpy doodeens.

Then along the Cool Quay you may see a clump of jingle-drivers, who have all a word for your honour;[15] and in Patrick Street, at three o'clock, when 'The Rakes of Mallow' gets under weigh (a cracked old coach with the paint rubbed off, some smart horses, and an exceedingly dingy harness) — at three o'clock, you will be sure to see at least forty persons waiting to witness the departure of the said coach: so that the neighbourhood of the inn has an air of some bustle.

At the other extremity of the town, if it be assize time, you will see some five hundred persons squatting by the court-house, or buzzing and talking within. The rest of the respectable quarter of the city is pretty free from anything like bustle: there is no more life in Patrick Street than in Russell Square of a sunshiny day; and as for the Mall, it is as lonely as the chief street of a German Residenz.

I have mentioned the respectable quarter of the city — for there are quarters in it swarming with life, but of such a frightful kind as no pen need care to describe: alleys where the odours and rags and darkness are so hideous, that one runs frightened away from them. In some of them, they say, not the policeman, only the priest, can penetrate. I asked a Roman Catholic clergyman of the city to take me into some of these haunts, but he refused very justly; and indeed a man may be quite satisfied with what he can see in the mere outskirts of the districts, without caring to penetrate further. Not far from the quays is an open space where the poor hold a market or bazaar. Here is liveliness and business enough: ragged women chattering and crying their beggarly wares; ragged boys gloating over dirty apple- and pie-stalls; fish frying, and raw and stinking; clothes-booths, where you might buy a wardrobe for scarecrows; old nails, hoops, bottles, and marine-wares; old battered furniture, that has been sold against starvation. In the streets round about this place, on a sunshiny day, all the black gaping windows and mouldy steps are covered with squatting lazy figures — women, with bare breasts, nursing babies, and leering a joke as you pass by — ragged children paddling everywhere. It is but two minutes' walk out of Patrick Street, where you come upon a fine flashy shop of plated goods, or a grand French emporium of dolls, walking-sticks, carpet-bags, and perfumery. The markets hard by have a rough, old-fashioned, cheerful look; it's a comfort after the misery to hear a red butcher's wife crying after you to buy an honest piece of meat.

The poor-house, newly established, cannot hold a fifth part of the poverty of this great town: the richer inhabitants are untiring in their charities, and the Catholic clergyman before mentioned took me to see a delivery of rice, at which he presides every day until the potatoes shall come in. This market, over which he presides so kindly, is held in an old bankrupt warehouse, and the rice is sold considerably under the prime cost to hundreds of struggling applicants who come when lucky enough to have wherewithal to pay.

That the city contains much wealth is evidenced by the number of handsome villas round about it, where the rich merchants dwell; but the warehouses of the wealthy provision-merchants make no show to the stranger walking the streets; and of the retail-shops, if some are spacious and handsome, most look as if too big for the business carried on within. The want of ready-money was quite curious. In three of the principal shops I purchased articles, and tendered a pound in exchange — not one of them had silver enough; and as for a five-pound note, which I presented at one of the topping book-seller's, his boy went round to various places in vain, and finally set forth to the Bank, where change was got. In another small shop I offered half-a-crown to pay for a sixpenny article — it was all the same.'Tim,' says the good woman, 'run out in a hurry and fetch the gentlemen change.' Two of the shopmen, seeing an Englishman, were very particular to tell me in what years they themselves had been in London. It seemed a merit in these gentlemen's eyes to have once dwelt in that city; and I see in the papers continually ladies advertising as governesses, and specifying particularly that they are 'English ladies.'

I received six 5*l.* post-office orders; I called four times on as many different days at the Post Office before the capital could be forthcoming, getting on the third application 20*l.* (after making a great clamour, and vowing that such things were unheard-of in England), and on the fourth call the remaining 10*l.* I saw poor people, who may have come from the country with their orders, refused payment of an order of some 40*s.*; and a gentleman who tendered a pound-note in payment of a foreign letter, was told to 'leave his letter and pay some other time.' Such things could not take place in the hundred-and-second city in England; and as I do not pretend to doctrinise at all, I leave the reader to draw his own deductions with regard to the commercial condition and prosperity of the second city in Ireland.

Half-a-dozen of the public buildings I saw were spacious and shabby beyond all cockney belief. Adjoining the 'Imperial Hotel' is a great, large, handsome, desolate reading-room, which was founded by a body of Cork merchants and tradesmen, and is the very picture of decay. Not Palmyra — not the Russell Institution in Great Coram Street — presents a more melancholy appearance of faded greatness. Opposite this is another institution, called the Cork Library, where there are plenty of books and plenty of kindness to the stranger; but the shabbiness and faded splendour of the place are quite painful. There are three handsome Catholic churches commenced of late years; not one of them is complete: two want their porticoes; the other is not more than thirty feet from the ground, and according to the architectural plan was to rise as high as a cathedral. There is an Institution, with a fair library of scientific work, a museum, and a drawing-school with a supply of casts. The place is in yet more dismal condition than the Library: the plasters are spoiled incurably for want of a sixpenny feather-brush; the dust lies on the walls, and nobody seems to heed it. Two shillings a year would have repaid much of the evil which has happened to this institution; and it is folly to talk of inward dissensions and political differences as causing the ruin of such institutions: kings or law don't cause or cure dust and cobwebs, but indolence leaves them to accumulate, and imprudence will not calculate its income, and vanity exaggerates its own powers, and the fault is laid upon that tyrant of a sister kingdom. The whole country is filled with such failures; swaggering beginnings that could not be carried through; grand enterprises begun dashingly, and ending in shabby compromises or downright ruin.

I have said something in praise of the manners of the Cork ladies: in regard of the gentlemen, a stranger too must remark the extraordinary degree of literary taste and talent amongst them, and the wit and vivacity of their conversation. The love for literature seems to an Englishman doubly curious. What, generally speaking, do a company of grave gentlemen and ladies in Baker Street know about it? Who ever reads books in the City, or how often does one hear them talked about at a Club? The Cork citizens are the most book-loving men I ever met. The town has sent to England a number of literary men, of reputation too, and is not a little proud of their fame. Everybody seemed to know what Maginn was doing, and that Father Prout had a third volume ready, and what was Mr. Croker's last article in the *Quarterly*.[16] The young clerks and shopmen seemed as much *au fait* as their employers, and many is the conversation I heard about the merits of this writer or that — Dickens, Ainsworth, Lover, Lever.[17]

I think, in walking the streets, and looking at the ragged urchins crowding there, every Englishman must remark that the superiority of intelligence is here, and not with us. I never saw such a collection of bright-eyes, wild, clever, eager faces. Mr. Maclise has carried away a number of them in his memory; and the lovers of his admirable pictures will find more than one Munster countenance under a helmet in company of Macbeth, or in a slashed doublet alongside of Prince Hamlet, or in the very midst of Spain in company with Señor Gil Blas. Gil Blas himself came from Cork, and not from Oviedo.[18]

I listened to two boys almost in rags: they were lolling over the quay balustrade, and talking about *one of the Ptolemys!* and talking very well too. One of them had been reading in 'Rollin,' and was detailing his information with a great deal of eloquence and fire. Another day, walking in the Mardyke, I followed three boys, not half so well dressed as London errand-boys: one was telling the other about Captain Ross's voyages, and spoke with as much brightness and intelligence as the best-read gentleman's son in England could do. He was as much of a gentlemen too, the ragged young student; his manner as good, though perhaps more eager and emphatic; his language was extremely rich, too, and eloquent. Does the reader remember his school-days, when half-a-dozen lads in the bedrooms took it by turns to tell stories? how poor the language generally was, and how exceedingly poor the imagination! Both of those ragged Irish lads had the making of gentlemen, scholars, orators, in them. Apropos of love of reading, let me mention here a Dublin story. Dr. Lever, the celebrated author of 'Harry Lorrequer,' went into Dycer's stables to buy a horse. The groom who brought the animal out, directly he heard who the gentleman was, came out and touched his cap, and pointed to a little book in his pocket in a pink cover. *'I can't do without it, sir,'* says the man. It was 'Harry Lorrequer.' I wonder does any one of Mr. Rymell's grooms take in 'Pickwick,' or would they have any curiosity to see Mr. Dickens, should he pass that way?

The Corkagians are eager for a Munster University; asking for, and having a very good right to, the same privilege which has been granted to the chief city of the North of Ireland. It would not fail of being a great benefit to the city and to the country too, which would have no need to go so far as Dublin for a school of letters and medicine; nor, Whig and Catholic for the most part, to attend a Tory and Protestant University. The establishing of an open college in Munster would bring much popularity to any Ministry that should accord such a boon. People would cry out, 'Popery and Infidelity,' doubtless, as they did when the London University was established; as the same party in Spain would cry out, 'Atheism and Heresy.'[19] But the time, thank God! is gone by in England when it was necessary to legislate for *them*: and Sir Robert Peel, in giving his adherence to the National Education scheme, has sanctioned the principle of which this so much longed-for college would only be a consequence.[20]

The medical charities and hospitals are said to be very well arranged, and the medical men of far more than ordinary skill. Other public institutions are no less excellent. I was taken over the Lunatic Asylum, where everything was conducted with admirable comfort, cleanliness, and kindness; and as for the county gaol, it is so neat, spacious, and comfortable, that we can only pray to see every cottager in the country as cleanly, well lodged, and well fed as the convicts are. They get a pound of bread and a pint of milk twice a day: there must be millions of people in this wretched country, to whom such food would be a luxury that their utmost labours can never by possibility procure for them; and in going over this admirable institution, where everybody is cleanly, healthy, and well-clad, I could not but think of the rags and filth of the horrid starvation market before mentioned; so that the prison seemed almost a sort of premium for vice. But the people like their freedom such as it is, and prefer to starve and be ragged as they list. They will not go to the poor-houses, except at the greatest extremity, and leave them on the slightest chance of existence elsewhere.

Walking away from this palace of a prison, you pass amidst all sorts of delightful verdure, cheerful gardens, and broad green luscious pastures, down to the beautiful River Lee. On one side, the river shines away towards the city with its towers and purple steeples; on the other it is broken by little waterfalls and bound in by blue hills, an old castle towering in the distance, and innumerable parks and villas lying along the pleasant wooded banks. How beautiful the scene is, how rich and how happy! Yonder, in the old Mardyke Avenue, you hear the voices of a score of children, and along the bright green meadows, where the cows are feeding, the gentle shadows of the clouds go playing over the grass. Who can look at such a charming scene but with a thankful swelling heart?

In the midst of your pleasure, three beggars have hobbled up and are howling supplications to the Lord. One is old and blind, and so diseased and hideous, that straightway all the pleasure of the sight round about vanishes from you — that livid ghastly face interposing between you and it. And so it is throughout the south and west of Ireland; the traveller is haunted by the face of the popular starvation. It is not the exception, it is the condition of the people. In this fairest and richest of countries, men are suffering and starving by millions. There are thousands of them at this minute stretched in the sunshine at their cabin doors with no work, scarcely any food, no hope seemingly. Strong countrymen are lying in bed *'for the hunger'* — because a man lying on his back does not need so much food as a person a-foot. Many of them have torn up the unripe potatoes from their little gardens, to exist now, and must look to winter, when they shall have to suffer starvation and cold too. The epicurean, and traveller for pleasure, had better travel anywhere than here: where there are miseries that one does not dare to think of; where one is always feeling how helpless pity is, and how hopeless relief, and is perpetually made ashamed of being happy.

I have just been strolling up a pretty little height called Gratten's Hill, that overlooks the town and the river, and where the artist that comes Cork-wards may find many subjects for his pencil. There is a kind of pleasure-ground at the top of this eminence — a broad walk that draggles up to a ruined wall, with a ruined niche in it, and a battered stone bench. On the side that shelves down to the water are some beeches, and opposite them a row of houses from which you see one of the prettiest prospects possible — the shining river with the craft along the quays, and the busy city in the distance, the active little steamers puffing away towards Cove, the farther bank crowded with rich woods, and pleasant-looking country-houses: perhaps they are tumbling, rickerty and ruinous, as those houses close by us, but you can't see the ruin from here.

What a strange air of forlorn gaiety there is about the place! — the sky itself seems as if it did not know whether to laugh or cry, so full is it of clouds and sunshine. Little fat, ragged, smiling children are clambering about the rocks, and sitting on mossy door-steps, tending other children yet smaller, fatter, and more dirty. 'Stop till I get you a posy' (pronounced *pawawawsee*), cries one urchin to another. 'Tell me who is it ye love, Jooly?' exclaims another, cuddling a red-faced infant with a very dirty nose. More of the same race are perched about the summer-house, and two wenches with large purple feet are flapping some carpets in the air.

It is a wonder the carpets will bear this kind of treatment at all, and do not be off at once to mingle with the elements: I never saw things that hung to life by such a frail thread.

This dismal pleasant place is a suburb of the second city in Ireland, and one of the most beautiful spots about the town. What a prim, bustling, active, green-railinged, tea-gardened, gravel-walked place would it have been in the five-hundreth town in England! — but you see the people can be quite as happy in the rags and without the paint, and I hear a great deal more heartiness and affection from these children than from their fat little brethren across the Channel.

17. PICTURESQUE AND ROMANTIC IRELAND

One of the earliest characterisations of Ireland offered by British writers had been that of a wild, unimproved country inhabited by a wild people, both land and people forming an unacceptable contrast to civilised England. Though not unchallenged, the theme never left English writing, and was still dominating attitudes towards Ireland throughout the seventeenth century. But in the eighteenth century a new emphasis took over as the perception of a threat to England in Irish difference receded. During the same years wild nature and scenic beauty claimed greater attention as the aesthetic of the picturesque began to make its way through English and European culture.

Writing in 1797, G. Holmes pointed out the anomaly of Ireland about to become unified with Britain yet being less well known to English readers than the most remote regions of the globe.[1] The political attention focussed on Ireland at this time combined with the taste for wild natural scenery (abundantly represented among Ireland's varied landscapes and seascapes) to attract admiring notice from the traveller, and continued to do so long after the Union controversy, even from a traveller like Thackeray, avowed foe of the Romantic style.[2]

Part of the appeal was that areas of Ireland continued to remain, if not inaccessible, difficult to negotiate in comfort; and though by the end of the eighteenth century the traveller was becoming a tourist (or because of the fact) this remoteness held a growing appeal. Publishers recognised the trend and began issuing special travellers' handbooks for Ireland similar to those on offer for tourists on the European grand tour. These directories increased in number after 1800. They included road maps, route advice between town and town, often detailing a variety of alternatives, summaries of places of interest along the way, a register of miles and sundry travel advice.[3] There were other reasons for the increased attention Ireland was now receiving. One was Napoleon's closure of the Continent to the English. Another was the rising awareness among

English writers of the poverty spread throughout the ordinary population of Ireland, and visibly on the increase. Thus Irish travel expanded vastly after the mid-eighteenth century. A sign of how established it had become might be recognised in the number of writers who point out how strange it is that English men and women know nothing of Ireland on their doorstep yet flock in their thousands to Italy and France and other remote Continental destinations. When this can be said Irish travel is catching on.

Of Ireland's beauty spots the Giant's Causeway and Killarney, which had always drawn attention, remained primary,[4] but Lough Erne, Dunluce, Clew Bay and other regions also drew admiring praise. There might be at work here some fashionable questioning of fashion. Lord John Manners, for instance, visiting Ireland in 1849, terms Dunluce castle on the north Antrim coast 'without any exception, the grandest, romanticest, awfullest sea-king's castle in broad Europe' and judged the Causeway, by comparison, tame and flat.[5] Usually in these descriptions of romantic Ireland tourists appear not to notice the people who live there. They are wiped from the scene. This is not the first time English writers have erased the Irish people from their conception of Ireland; see page 50 above; see also the Introduction where a similar technique operates in nineteenth-century travellers' accounts of Africa (p. 231 above).[6] There is, too, another affinity. English travellers of the nineteenth century perceived neither the Irish nor the Africans as noble savages. By 1800 the Irish were too poor and helpless. Possibly though in Dunton's account of Connaught a hundred years before (printed below in the first extract) there is just a touch of that feeling.

1) John Dunton

From *Teague Land* (1699):[7]

Ireconaught lyes west of Galway: on one side it is environ'd by the sea and on the other by the county of Mayo; it is a mountainous rough country: on the top of the mountains are boggy grounds, and in most of the vallies lye bogg, loughs and woods some of which have good timber among them, but of the less use because of the difficultye to carry it out of the country.

[. . .]

[T]he next morning earely after a large breakfast of six wodden bowls filled with hott flesh meate which I could not taste, and a drachm of theire bulcaan or worse sort of aqua vitae, Oflaghertie invited me to walk a small mile to view theire deer. I willingly consented because I did not expect to heare of Deer Park in so wild a place; we walked over mountains and through boggs, thro thick and thin, sometimes out and sometimes in untill I lost the heels of my shoos, which tyred me soe that I thought I should never come to the miles end, which was modestly speakeing as farr as half way from Whitehall to Barnet. At last we came to [a] pleasant vale called Glinglass, or the Green Vale, of an English miles breadth encompasst with lovely green mountaines which were tufted with pleasant groves and thickets of natures provideing, for none here imitate her in ought but her coarser draughts; on the sides of these hills I wonder'd to see some hundreds of stately red deer, the stags bigger than a large English yeareling calfe, with suitable antlers much bigger than I ever saw before.

It was the most pleasing scene that ever I met with in this kingdom, and the only thing worth my notice in these parts. We return'd before the heate of the day to our greate cabbin, where we had at dinner, no less then a whole, beef boyl'd and roasted, and what mutton I know not so profewsly did they lay it on the table. At the upper end where the lady sate was placed an heap of oaten cakes above a foot high, such another in the middle and the like at the lower end; at each side of the middle heap were placed two large vessells filled with Troander or the whey made with buttermilk and sweet milk, which being about two days old was wonderfull cold and pleaseing in that hott time of the day. We had ale (such as it was) and Bulcaan, and after dinner myn host ordered his doggs to be gotten ready to hunt the stagg. He had his horse saddled and one for me too, because the loss of my heels render'd me incapable of such a walk. Eighteen long greyhounds and above thirty footemen made up the company. We were not long before we arriv'd at Glinglass, our horses in a manner galloping over the boggs and hills, for I rode one of his, it being unpracticable to mine to goe fast on such ground. Our foote company kept close to our horses and the grey hounds did sometimes putt themselves into a trott which was noble and greate; the hills which before were cover'd with red deer were now quite empty and not one to be seen. It seems in the heat of the day they retire into covert and lye there untill towards evening. Oflaghertie gave the word and immediately the company with the doggs surrounded a large thicket, whilst he and I with two hunting poles enter'd it to rouze the game. The first we saw was a stately stagg who secure of daunger skipped forth of the bushes; he at first seem'd amazed at the cry which was raised looing the doggs, but he bravely endeavour'd to charge through them, and was seized by one of the dogs at the haunch, which threw him on his back. The whole kenel was not suffer'd to come in for feare of spoyleing the skin which the people most value, and never did I see a spanniell more subject to command than those mighty dogs are; I desir'd the next might have more play for his life; accordingly the doggs were all taken up, and the next proveing a stagg too broke through the men who did not let slip more than a brace of their doggs. It was indeed a noble course for a little way, but the stagg tooke a leap out of our sight from a prominent part of the hill into the valley where the doggs lost. After we had done beateing this thicket, where we rouzed two brace, three of which we kill'd, after the same manner, I went to view the leap which the stagg made that escapt. It seem'd to me as high as a steeple, and the deere was not kill'd by the fall. After this afternoones diversion we return'd home where to beef and mutton we had venison, boyld and roasted, and a fish call'd a Loggerhead by them. It was a firm white fish of good taste and as bigg as a salmon, but how to describe it they could not tell, and I saw not any but that one, which I could not observe to any purpose of description.

2) Arthur Young

From *Tour in Ireland*:[8]

Soon entered the wildest and most romantic country I had any where seen; a region of steep rocks and mountains, which continued for nine or ten miles, till I came in view of Mucruss. There is something magnificently wild in this stupendous scenery, formed to impress the mind with a species of terror. All this tract has a rude and savage air, but parts of it are strikingly interesting; the mountains are bare and rocky, and of a great magnitude; the vales are rocky glens, where a mountain-stream tumbles along the roughest bed imaginable, and receives many torrents, pouring from clefts, half overhung with shrubby wood; some of these streams are seen, and the roar of others heard, but hid by vast masses of rock. Immense fragments, torn from the precipices, by storms and torrents, are tumbled about in the wildest confusion, and seemed to hang rather than rest upon projecting precipices. Upon some of these fragments of rock, perfectly detached form the soil, except by the side on which they lie, are beds of black turf, with luxuriant crops of heath, &c. which appeared very curious to me, having no where seen the like; and I observed very high in the mountains, much higher than any cultivation is at present, on the right hand, flat and cleared spaces of good grass among the ridges of rock, which had probably been cultivated, and proved that these mountains were not incapable from climate of being applied to useful purposes.

From one of these heights, I looked forward to the lake of Killarney at a considerable distance, and backward to the river Kenmare; came in view of a small part of the upper lake, spotted with several islands, and surrounded by the most tremendous mountains, that can be imagined, of an aspect savage and dreadful. From this scene of wild magnificence, I broke at once upon all the glories of Killarney; from an elevated point of view I looked down on a considerable part of the lake, which gave me a specimen of what I might expect. The water you command (which, however, is only a part of the lake) appears a bason of two or three miles round; to the left it is inclosed by the mountains you have passed particularly by the Turk, whose outline is uncommonly noble, and joins a range of others, that form the most magnificent shore in the world: on the other side is a rising scenery of cultivated hills, and Lord Kenmare's park and woods; the end of the lake at your feet is formed by the root of Mangerton,[9] on whose side the road leads. From hence I looked down on a pretty range of inclosures joining the lake, and the woods and lawns of Mucruss, forming a large promontory of thick wood, shooting far into the lake. The most active fancy can sketch nothing in addition. Islands of wood beyond seem to join it, and reaches of the lake, breaking partly between, give the most lively intermixture of water: six or seven isles and islets form an accompanyment, some are rocky, but with a slight vegetation, others contain groups of trees, and the whole thrown into forms, which would furnish new ideas to a painter. Further is a chain of wooded islands, which also appear to join the main land, with an offspring of lesser ones scattered around.

[. . .]

Returned, took boat again towards Ross isle, and as Mucruss retires from us, nothing can be more beautiful than the spots of lawn in the terrace opening in the wood; above it, the green hills with clumps, and the whole finishing in the noble group of wood about the abbey, which here appears a deep shade, and so fine a finishing one, that not a tree should be touched. Rowed to the east point of Ross, which is well wooded, turn to the south coast.

Doubling the point, the most beautiful shore of that island appears; it is the well wooded environs of a bay, except a small opening to the castle; the woods are in deep shades, and rise on the regular slopes of a high range of rocky coast. The part in front of Filekilly point rises in the middle, and sinks towards each end. The woods of Tomys here appear uncommonly fine. Open Innisfallen, which is composed at this distance of various shades, within a broken outline, entirely different from the other islands. No pencil could mix a happier assemblage. Land near a miserable room, where travellers dine — Of the isle of Innisfallen, it is paying no great compliment to say, it is the most beautiful in the King's dominions, and perhaps in Europe. It contains 20 acres of land, and has every variety that the range of beauty, unmixed with the sublime, can give. The general feature is that of wood; the surface undulates into swelling hills, and sinks into little vales; the slopes are in every direction, the declivities die gently away, forming those slight inequalities which are the greatest beauty of dressed grounds. The little vallies let in views of the surrounding lake between the hills, while the swells break the regular outline of the water, and give to the whole an agreeable confusion. The wood has all the variety into which nature has thrown the surface; in some parts it is so thick as to appear impenetrable, and secludes all farther view; in others, it breaks into tufts of tall timber, under which cattle feed. Here they open, as if to offer to the spectator the view of the naked lawn; in others close, as if purposely to forbid a more prying examination. Trees of large size, and commanding figure, form in some places natural arches; the ivy mixing with the branches, and hanging across in festoons of foliage, while on one side the lake glitters among the trees, and on the other a thick gloom dwells in the recesses of the wood. The figure of the island renders one part a beautiful object to another; for the coast being broken and indented, forms bays surrounded either by rock or wood: slight promontories shoot into the lake, whose rocky edges are crowned with wood. These are the great features of Innisfallen; the slighter touches are full of beauties easily imagined by the reader. Every circumstance of the wood, the water, the rocks, and lawn are characteristic, and have a beauty in the assemblage from mere disposition. I must, however, observe, that this delicious retreat is not kept as one could wish.

Scenes, that are great and commanding from magnitude or wildness, should never be dressed; the *rugged*, and even the *horrible*, may add to the effect upon the mind: but in such as Innisfallen, a degree of dress, that is, cleanliness, is even necessary to beauty. I have spoken of lawn, but I should observe, that expression indicates what it ought to be, rather than what it is. It is very rich grass, poached by oxen and cows, the only inhabitants of the island. No spectator of taste but will regret the open grounds not being drained with hollow cuts; the ruggedness of the surface levelled, and the grass kept close shaven by many sheep instead of beasts. The bushes and briers where they have encroached on what ought to be lawn, cleared away; some parts of the isle more opened: in a word, no ornaments given, for the scene wants them not, but obstructions cleared, ruggedness smoothed, and the whole cleaned. This is what ought to be done; as to what might be made of the island, if its noble proprietor (Lord Kenmare) had an inclination, it admits of being converted into a terrestrial paradise, lawning with the intermixture of other shrubs and wood, and a *little* dress, would make it an example of what ornamented grounds might be, but which not one in a thousand is. Take the island, however, as it is, with its few imperfections, and where are we to find such another? What a delicious retreat! An emperor could not bestow such an one as Innisfallen; with a cottage, a few cows, and a swarm of poultry, is it possible that happiness should refuse to be a guest here?

3) Philip Luckombe

From *A Tour through Ireland in 1779*:[10]

From Passage to Cork the view is extremely pleasant, and exhibits a variety of beautiful landscapes, which the genius, fancy, and spirit of Poussin, or Claude Lorraine, could never exceed. The road is carried, for some distance, along the side of the river Lea, which is adorned with pleasant islands. One of these is called L'Isle, or the Little Island, which denomination it bears to distinguish it from Barrymore, or the Great Island; it contains about one thousand six hundred Irish acres, and is three miles distant from the city of Cork, etc.

4) G. Holmes

G. Holmes travelled through southern Ireland in 1797 and in his tour published four years later registers the strangeness encountered by an English tourist in the Irish landscape. He describes a journey from Kilkenny to Cashel, Limerick, Killarney, Cork and Clonmel. Though much of his account is a potted redaction of old histories the following appreciation of Ireland as place of scenic wonders, and as a place where you could get lost and frightened, is typical of late eighteenth century English travellers.

From *Sketches of Some of the Southern Counties* (1801):[11]

This morning, having consulted with our host, concerning the road, we adopted his advice, and determined on exploring Stack's mountains. Having crossed a fine bridge, of eleven arches over the Feale, and finding a kind of foot-path, we jogged on merrily, until the track became uncertain; by degrees we found ourselves environed by lofty hills, whose dreary summits broke the impendent clouds, and sent such a torrent from their watery store, as completely drenched us through; however, there was no alternative, so we were obliged to push on through this desolate tract.

We now had no guide, but the supposed situation of the country; all traces of a path were gone; cultivation seemed to have fled, or rather never appeared. Mountain rose above mountain, obtruding, each, its discouraging head; at last, by a sudden turning, we observed a cabin near us, which we joyfully approached; it looked like a speck in the boundless ocean, being the only solitary habitation, for many miles, through these mountains. Here we found only two children, one nursing the other; the youngest was about one year old, and the eldest seven; she could not speak English, but shewed a second room, wherein we lodged our horses. I never saw Nature in her native garb so truly marked, as in this child; she was rather handsome, with very intelligent eyes, which probably were rendered more speaking, from her inability to make herself understood by her tongue. Every object around us seemed indigenous to the soil; even the mountain cow and horse;[12] the aborigines of the county, gave a marked and peculiar character to the spot. We gave the little girl a few halfpence, but she seemed unacquainted with their uses. Shortly after, the father and mother returned, carrying fuel from the neighbouring bog; they both spoke a little English, and, as well as they could, directed us to the path, which it seems we had lost, by a considerable way.

The clouds having expended their ammunition, we again set forward, winding round one hill, rising another, anxiously looking for the wished for road; at length, we found what we conjectured to be it, a rugged path-way, interrupted by bogs and holes. Fatigued with past disappointments, and bewildered with doubts as to the true course we were taking, we still persevered, hoping, as we ascended each hill, that it might terminate our journey. The day again began to lower and threaten, which conjured up within us a thousand dismal ideas of being benighted in these unhospitable regions.

The path frequently sunk underneath our horses feet, against which, nothing but the most painful watchfulness could provide. About five o'clock, the setting sun became visible, and the clouds, gradually dispersing, gave no farther sign of molestation. Shortly after, between two opening hills, we descried, at a distance, a promontory running out into the Atlantic, which, by consulting my map, we found to be Tralee head and bay.

This gave us new life; so urging briskly to the rising of a hill, we had the pleasure of seeing before us the low country, stretching into a far extended fertile vale, with the village of Castle Island, cheering us with a thousand comforts, which the tired traveller never fails to anticipate. However, before we reached the village we encountered another torrent of rain.

5) Thomas Carlyle

From *Reminiscences of My Irish Journey in 1849* (1882):[13]

Lake clear, blue, — almost black; slaty precipitous islets rise frequent; rocky dark hills, somewhat fringed with native arbutus (very frequent all about Killarney), mount skyward on every hand. well enough; — but don't bother me with *audibly* admiring it: Oh! if you but wouldn't! Come once or twice aground with our boat, in muddy creeks seeking the picturesque too eagerly; otherwise a pleasant sail. 'Ornamental cottages,' deep shrouded in arbutus wood, with clearest cascades, and a depth of *silence* very inviting, abound on the shores of these lakes; but *something* of dilapidation, beggary, human fatuity in one or other form, is painfully visible in nearly all. 'Ornamental Cottage' first; woman had gone out to gain a halfpenny by opening a gate for us (but missed that somehow); within one window of the place, a grey fat *savant* is busy sticking dead beetles into his Natural History pocket-book with pins; rolls a big minatory eye on us as we pass; Kitchen next to him, where we enter, is squalling infant (mother out to gain halfpenny), rubbishy fireless floor with two other children; — ugly upon my honor! Stag-hunts have been; *yonder* (west side of the lake); most silent, solitary, with a wild beauty looking thro' the squalor of one's thoughts; that is the impression of the scene; moist, soft weather too harmonized.

6) An 'Oxonian'

From *A Little Tour in Ireland* (1859):[14]

The Englishman who desires a new sensation should pay a visit to the *Claddagh.* When we arrived, the men were at sea; but the women, in their bright red petticoats, descending half-way down the uncovered leg, their cloaks worn like the Spanish mantilla, and of divers colours, their headkerchiefs and hoods, were grouped among the old grey ruins where the fish market is held, and formed a tableau not to be forgotten. Though their garments are torn, and patched, and discoloured, there is a graceful simple dignity about them which might teach a lesson to Parisian milliners; and to my fancy the most becoming dress in all the world is that of a peasant girl of Connamara [sic]. Compare, it, reader, with our present mode, and judge. Look at the two, sculptor, and say which will you carve? Say, when 'Santa Philomena' is graved in marble, shall it be with flounces and hoops?

No, whatever may be the wrongs of Ireland no lover of the picturesque and beautiful would wish to see her *re-dressed* (so far as the ladies are concerned — the gentlemen might be improved); no one would desire to see the peasant girls in the tawdry bonnets and brass-eyed boots, which stultify the faces and cripple the feet of the daughters of our English labourers.

As to the origin of these Claddagh people, I am not sufficiently 'up' in ethnology, to state with analytical exactness the details of their descent; but I should imagine them to be one-third Irish, one-third Arabian, and the other Zingaro, or Spanish gypsy. I thought that I recognised in one old lady an Ojibbeway chief, who frightened me a good deal in my childhood, but she had lost the expression of ferocity, and I was, perhaps, mistaken.

7) Queen Victoria

When Queen Victoria landed in Cork on 2 August, 1849, on her first Irish tour, she decided that the muggy weather was 'the character of the Irish climate'.[15] She was seasick between Waterford and Wexford. She visited some of Dublin's main buildings, reviewed troops in Phoenix Park, witnessed some Irish dancing and embarked for an equally brief visit to Belfast. She visited Dublin again in 1861 and travelled to the Curragh and Killarney, where her appreciation of the fine scenery was spoiled for her by hot weather, midges, jungle-like vegetation and shrieking women.

From *Her letters from the journal of our life* (1858):[16]

Tuesday, August 27. — At eleven o'clock we all started in our own sociable, and another of our carriages, and on ponies, for Ross Castle, the old ruin which was a celebrated stronghold, and from which the Kenmare family take their name. Here there was an immense crowd and a great many boats. We got into a very handsome barge of eight oars — beautifully rowed. Lord Castlerosse steering. The four children, and Lady Churchill, Lady Castlerosse, and Lord Granville were with us.

We rowed first round Innisfallen Island and some way up the Lower Lake. The view was magnificent. We had a slight shower, which alarmed us all, from the mist which overhung the mountains; but it suddenly cleared away and became very fine and very hot. At a quarter to one we landed at the foot of the beautiful hill of Glena, where on a small sloping lawn there is a very pretty little cottage. We walked about, though it was overpoweringly hot, to see some of the splendid views. The trees are beautiful, — oak, birch, arbutus, holly, yew, — all growing down to the water's edge, intermixed with heather. The hills, rising abruptly from the lake, are completely wooded, which gives them a different character from those in Scotland, though they often reminded me of the dear Highlands. We returned to the little cottage, where the quantity of midges and the smell of peat made us think of Alt-na-Giuthasach. Upstairs, from Lady Castlerosse's little room, the view was towards a part of the Lower Lake, the outline of which is rather low. We lunched, and afterwards re-embarked, and then took that most beautiful row up the rapid, under the Old Weir Bridge, through the channel which connects the two lakes, and which is very intricate and narrow. Close to our right as we were going, we stopped under the splendid hill of the Eagle's Nest to hear the echo of a bugle; the sound of which, though blown near by, was not heard. We had to get out near the West Bridge to let the empty boats be pulled up by the men. The sun had come out and lit up the really magnificent scenery splendidly; but it was most oppressively hot. We wound along till we entered the Upper Lake, which opened upon us with all its high hills — the highest, The Reeks, 3,400 feet high — and its islands and points covered with splendid trees; such arbutus [sic] (quite large trees) with yews, making a beautiful foreground. We turned into a small bay or creek, where we got out and walked a short way in the shade, and up to where a tent was placed, just opposite a waterfall called Derricaunihy, a lovely spot, but terribly infested by midges. In this tent was tea, fruit, ice, cakes and everything was most tastefully arranged. We first took some tea, which was very refreshing in the great heat of this relaxing climate. The vegetation is quite that of a jungle — ferns of all kinds and shrubs and trees, — all springing up luxuriantly. We entered our boats and went back the same way we came, admiring greatly the beauty of the scenery; and this time went down the rapids in the boat. No boats, except our own, had followed us beyond the rapids. But below them there were a great many, and the scene was very animated and the people very noisy and enthusiastic. The Irish always give that peculiar shrill shriek — unlike anything one ever hears anywhere else.

Wednesday, August 28. — At a quarter-past eleven we started on a most beautiful drive. . . . We drove with Mrs Herbert and Bertie in our sociable, driven from the box of Wagland; and, though the highest mountains were unfortunately occasionally enveloped in mist, and we had slight showers, we were enchanted with the extreme beauty of the scenery. The peeps of the lake; the splendid woods full of the most magnificent arbutus, which in one place form, for a few yards, an avenue under which you drive, with the rocks, — which are very peculiar — all made it one of the finest drives we had ever taken. Turning up by the village and going round, the Torc mountain reminded us of Scotland — of the woods above Abergeldie, of Craig Daign and Craig Clunie. It was *so* fine. We got out at the top of the Torc Waterfall and walked down to the foot of it. We came home at half-past one. At four we started for the boats, quite close by. The Muckross Lake is extremely beautiful; at the beginning of our expedition it looked dark and severe in the mist and showers which kept coming on, just as it does in the Highlands. Mr Herbert steered. Our girls, Mrs Herbert, Lady Churchill, and Lord Granville were in the boat with us. The two boys went in a boat rowed by gentlemen, and the rest in two other boats. At Mr and Mrs Herbert's request I christened one of the points which runs into the lake with a bottle of wine, Albert holding my arm when we came close by, so that it was most successfully smashed.

When we emerged from under Brickeen Bridge, we had a fine view of the Lower Lake and of the scenery of yesterday, which rather puzzled me, seeing it from another *point de vue.* At Benson's Point we stopped for some time, merely rowing about backwards and forwards, or remaining stationary, watching for the deer (all this is a deer forest as well as at Glena), which we expected the dogs would find and bring down into the water. But in vain: we waited till past six and no deer came. The evening had completely cleared and became quite beautiful; and the effect of the numbers of boats full of people, many with little flags, rowing about in every direction and cheering and shouting, lit up by the evening light, was charming. At Darby's Garden, the shore was densely crowded, and many of the women in their blue cloaks waded into the water, holding their clothes up to their knees.

We were home by seven o'clcok, having again a slight sprinkling of rain.

18 POVERTY AND FAMINE

English visitors from the closing years of the eighteenth century begin to register the sharp increase in the visible signs of Ireland's poverty. These included undernourishment, squalid conditions, beggarly importunity, hopelessness. There had always been this theme in English writing about Ireland, of course; it figures in Spenser's famous description of the Munster Irish (see above, pp. 99–100). But Spenser's had been a time of war. Eighteenth-century and nineteenth-century Irish poverty (despite the 1798 rebellion) was a peacetime phenomenon. It seemed profound, and unattributed to a specific reason — a condition of wasting not easy to explain or correct, mysterious, depressing, almost as if the land was blighted. Arthur Young, travelling through Ireland in the 1770s, praised the community of cabin life — family and animals happily feeding off enough food. Philip Luckombe in the same decade recognised signs of poverty in the ill-constructed habitations of the people of the south west and west, which he describes as 'a collection of the vilest cribs',[1] but, he also notes, the dry stone buildings were 'interspersed with the antique towers of battered castles, and august remains of ruined monasteries, where fine paintings in fresco are yet visible on the walls, highly pleasing to those who have any taste for the polite arts' (p. 182). Luckombe, that is to say, saw poverty as a specific problem, not a general condition. Connections between Irish poverty and Anglo-Irish splendour are not wanting, as in the anonymous tourist of 1781 who contrasts one with the other.[2] The generalised awareness of poverty grows after 1800. Patricia Hodgart remarks on the shock felt by Keats, touring Ireland in 1818, at the living conditions to which the poor were reduced.[3] Having seen only a section of the eastern seaboard of Ireland, Keats cut short his journey and made for home. For Shelley too, Hodgart suggests, the spectacle of poor Ireland constituted 'probably his first sight of real distress and hopeless ignorance' (p. 51). Later in the century W. Bennett describes the inland roads of Ireland busy with wandering families on the search for food: in the modern term, 'refugees' from the starvation of their homelands. For a contrast, we may set Thomas Reid's observation, amidst the general gloom, of strangely cheerful beggars, undestroyed by their plight.[4] John Gough judged the insults imposed on the Irish people by their imperial masters harder to bear even than physical poverty; chief among the insults, he judged, was hiding from the Irish the beauty and blessings of England's 'glorious constitution'.[5] By the middle years of the nineteenth century, hopeless poverty was for English travellers Ireland's predominant image.

English travellers were repelled yet fascinated by the Irish cabin, perhaps because, next to the Irish language (which, however, they did not have to deal with), it was the most discernible evidence they were likely to encounter of the extreme poverty, to their way of thinking, of Irish life; though perhaps one should rather say it denoted the otherness of Irish culture. That is to say, the cabin's lack of windows and of a chimney and its makeshift nature challenged English assumptions about the permanence, comfort and strength required of a family house. Its inclusiveness and communality offended travellers' notions of decent, cleanly living. They saw it merely as a hovel. Descriptions tend, consequently, to be abusively contemptuous, like Farewell's satiric account, or horrified. It naturally followed that the people who lived in such conditions appeared to the average English traveller congenitally inferior, if not savage. Although occasional observers (such as Arthur Young) discerned the Irish domestic economy with more sympathetic insight, the characteristic view was that expressed by Ann Plumptre. She had, she confessed, frequently seen to her surprise 'troops of healthy-looking children issue forth' from them, but was sure they could not but be morally degraded.[6]

1) John Wesley

From *Journal* (1765):[7]

Before noon we were met by a violent shower, which drove us into a little cabin, where were a company of children, with their mother, grandmother, and great-grandmother. They seemed much frighted; but one of our company, who spoke Irish, soon took away their fears. We then sang a hymn, and went to prayer. They gaped and stared abundantly; and when we went away, after giving them a small piece of money, followed us with a thousand blessings.

2) Richard Twiss

From *A Tour in Ireland* (1776):[8]

The out-skirts of Dublin consist chiefly of huts, which are termed cabbins; they are made of mud dried, and mostly without either chimney or window; and in these miserable dwellings, far the greater part of the inhabitants of Ireland linger out a wretched existence. There is generally a small piece of ground annexed to each cabbin, which produces a few potatoes; and on these potatoes, and milk, the common Irish subsist all the year round, without tasting bread or meat, except perhaps at Christmas once or twice; what little the men can obtain by their labour, or the women by their spinning, is usually consumed in whisky, which is a spirituous liquor resembling gin. Shoes and stockings are seldom worn by these beings, who seem to form a distinct race from the rest of mankind; their poverty is much greater than that of the Spanish, Portuguese, or even Scotch peasants; notwithstanding which they appear to exist contentedly.

3) J. Hall

From *A Tour through Ireland in 1807* (1813):[9]

From Blarney to Mill-Street, which is more than twenty miles, there is neither town nor village, nor any thing but marks of poverty. The greater part of the country is in grass; the people, on account of the tithes, being averse from improving it; to be freed from which, many of them would give more than ten *per* cent. on their whole rent. Those who have sense, however, drive culm from Cork, and make lime for the improvement of their fields.

The itch is not unfrequent in the cabins in this part of the country; and so poor are many, that there is neither chair, nor stool, nor table in the houses, but round stones about the fire for seats. The crook, as it is called, or hook, on which they hang the pot over the fire, is of wood, tied by a straw rope to something at the top, and the pot, for boiling potatoes, &c. is not unfrequently found mouth downwards, and used as a seat about the fire. Having gone into a variety of cabins, on various pretences, my boy jogging on with the poney, and hovering about till I appeared, in some places, thinking me a new tithe-proctor, they were afraid; others thought me a person appointed to lay on new taxes, or one sent by the landlord to see if a few more shillings could be got for the cabin; and therefore hated me. Some actually fell down on their knees, thinking me a priest and father-confessor; while others, again, thought me one sent to contrive some scheme to rescue them from the hands of their oppressors, the middlemen, tithe-proctors, and the Protestant clergy. In short, the poverty and oppression of many hereabouts can scarcely be imagined.

The kraals of the Hottentots, the huts of the Laplanders, and the caves and holes of the natives of New Holland, seem preferable, in many points of view, to the hovels of the poor Irish. If they be happy, it proceeds from their ignorance, and not being habituated to other conveniences. What a contrast, when one considers the rooms in our great houses, furnished after the Grecian, the Italian, Egyptian, Turkish and other styles! In a word, when we view the carpets, hangings, splendid carriages, and numerous conveniences of the rich in this and other countries, as well at the present as in ancient times, we are led to conclude that, if it were not for the prospect beyond the grave, of all men the situation of the poor cabin-people in Ireland would be the most miserble. The accommodation of these poor people called up to my mind the splendour of a Solomon, and of the antients; many of whom had tables, cupboards, chariots. &c. &c. of solid silver intermixed with gold. It brought to my mind the splendour of Artaxerxes on his throne; of Pompey in triumph, blazing with diamond pearls; of Alexander the Great, who, at one time, entertained three hundred commanders on seats of solid silver; and of Poppaea; Nero the Emperor's wife, whose horses were shod with gold. On the authority of Seneca and Vitruvius we may assert, that, at Rome, the man was accounted poor and mean whose bath did not shine with precious stones and mosaic-work, the vaults arched with crystal, and the cocks of silver to spout out water; nay, so great was the Roman vanity and luxury, that, in some, the whole side-seats and pavements were of pure silver.

4) Thomas Cromwell

Thomas Cromwell (1792–1870) was employed by the publishers Longmans at an early age. He wrote poetry and drama, plus a book on Oliver Cromwell which Carlyle termed vaporous.[10] In later life he contributed to a number of magazines and periodicals. His *Excursions*, published in numbers, lacks direction; it begins as topographical description but degenerates into pretty views. Cromwell also wrote descriptive accounts of Clerkenwell and Islington.

From *Excursions through Ireland* (1818–22):[11]

The eye of the traveller, however familiar with the generally wretched hovels of the poor in this country, must be immediately struck with the singular construction of those he will meet with in the Bog of Allen. To a moderate distance on each side of the canal, the bog is let in small lots to turf-cutters; who, for convenience, and the facility of guarding their property from theft, take up their residence on the spot, however dreary or uncomfortable. The first care of one of these is, to seek a dry bank above the influence of the floods; and here he *excavates* his future habitation, to such a depth that little more than the roof is visible: this is sometimes covered with scanty thatch, but oftener with turf pared from the bog; which, as the herbage is upwards, so perfectly assimilates with the surrounding scenery, that the eye would pass over it as an undulation of the surface, were it not undeceived by seeing an occasional sally of children, accompanied by the pig or the goat — or by the issue of a volume of smoke — from a hole on one side: while, to his yet greater surprise, the latter, rising from the endless crannies in the roof, sometimes presents the momentary idea of its being caused by subterranean fires. It is properly remarked, that the wretched manner in which the lower class of the inhabitants of Ireland is lodged, may be traced to other sources than to rack-rents, unfeeling landlords, &c. in this scene; the proprietors of these hovels earning an easy subsistence; and one of them in particular having been known to have accumulated the sum of £100; and yet his habitation, the only one he possessed, was perfectly similar to those of his neighbours. To what, it is asked, must we impute this seeming inconsistency? — not, surely, to any peculiar attachment in the Irish peasant to inconvenience and dirt; but, to the neglected state of his mind, (and still more to that depressed state of ideas and feelings, which, as to himself, mainly induces that neglect) and to the want of an education, which, raising him above the semi-barbarism that now marks his character, would give him a taste for, and a pride in the possession of, the comforts and conveniences of life.

5) T. Reid

From *Travels in Ireland* (1823):[12]

Many of their hovels were constructed by placing long sticks in a slanting position against a high bank, and covering them with scraws; these were afterwards thatched with heath, and as they did not project above the level of the heathy bank, they could not be easily discovered or distinguished by a stranger, until he came close upon them. The doors of these huts, if doors they can be called, are formed by two perpendicular sticks, and five cross ones, somewhat resembling a gate of rude workmanship, having the interstices filled with ropes made of straw, worked in after the manner of a basket.

Persons desirous of *extra* comfort plaster these doors with a substance composed of tenacious clay and cow-dung, which renders them impermeable to the severe winds of winter, or rather helps to make their hut a little less wretched, for the word *comfort* cannot with propriety be in any way applied to such places. Their bed (they seldom have more than one) is generally formed of straw, frequently of green heath, spread on the ground: a blanket or horse-rug is commonly used for a covering, but very often they have nothing but their ordinary ragged garments, and these they seldom divest themselves of, even for repose, as long as they can be made to stick together. These nests are used as dormitories, not *only* for the father, mother, and all the children, — the pigs, goats, or cows, if they are fortunate enough to possess such inmates, all inhabit the same mansion, and partake of the same bed if possible.

I happened to pass near a place where five young men and a young female were regaling over a bottle of whisky, for the purpose, as they said, of 'christening Donald's castle.' This Donald had been married the day before, but having no house to live in, four good-natured neighbours volunteered their services to assist him and his bride to construct one. They accordingly had assembled at day-light this morning, and in thirteen hours they completed their task: the 'castle' was finished, and the newly married couple were to sleep in it that very night! Green heath composed the bed, a row of sods was to serve for a pillow, and Donald's 'big coat' with Sally's cloak had to answer for bed-clothes.

In the summer months it is difficult to ascertain, with any degree of correctness, the number of persons belonging to a house; for, during June, July, and August, it will frequently be without a single inhabitant at all. It is customary here, and in many other parts of Ireland, when a bit of ground is sown with oats, and another spot is planted with potatoes, for the cabin to be closed, and the family to 'take the country,' that is, to travel into distant counties, and beg along until their potatoes and corn are nearly ripe. When the family is large, it is usual for the father and mother, after making a division of the children, to take different roads, and each to tell a woful [sic] tale of having been lately left a widow, or widower, as the case may be; to deplore the loss of an affectionate partner, which reduces the survivor to the heart-rending necessity of soliciting alms to save a helpless family from starving.

As far as I can collect from private friends, and other persons well acquainted with the country, the number of children in a cabin is seldom less than four, and that it would average *above five*, which, with the parents, would give at least seven to every cottage or house. Taking them at five and a half, as I have done, I am quite sure that every estimate of the total population is considerably under, rather than above the truth. From the first moment I was capable of making observations, I have invariably found the increase of children in Ireland to be in an inverse proportion to the means possessed by their parents to support them, namely, that the poorest persons in the country have always been the most prolific; and the more I see of the country, the more decided is my conviction of that remarkable fact. I have often seen nine, ten, and eleven children, all of one family, — some ragged others quite naked, existing, rather than living, in places that would shock the humanity of an English gentleman to see his dogs or his swine driven into.

In my excursion today I entered a cabin while the family were at dinner; the repast consisted of dry potatoes only, which were contained in a basket set upon the pot in which they had been boiled; this was placed on the floor in the middle of the cabin. The father was sitting on a stool, and the mother on a kreel of turf; one of the children had a straw boss; the youngest was sprawling on the floor, and five others were standing round the potato-basket. On seeing me enter, the man rose up, and offering me his stool, made a confused apology for his homely fare, and expressed his regret that he had neither whiskey nor milk to give me. He said to his wife, in a sort of loud whisper, 'May be the gentleman will taste the *bull's milk*:' she signified her fear that it was too sour, 'but such as it is,' said she, smiling, 'the gentleman is welcome to it, and if it was *cream* or wine, he would be welcome too.' I declined this civility, but knowing how much these poor people are gratified by a stranger's eating or drinking with them, I took a potato, which not being boiled enough, I put down, and took up another, and another, but all were equally hard. The man instantly put one into the hot turf-ashes to have it better cooked for me. He said, 'We always have our praties hard, they stick to our ribs, and we can fast longer that way.'

The term 'bull's milk' will be unintelligible to most English readers, and, I regret to say, there are thousands of Irish whose ears are too finely attuned to bear the rude shock of such vulgar sounds, — whose eyes are too delicate to look for an instant on the afflictions of their desponding countrymen, and whose hearts are made of materials by far too *genteel* to relieve or pity the agonies of a starving family. I assure myself of the humane reader's indulgence for this digression. There is a wide difference between the feelings that will be elicited by witnessing distress in real life, and seeing an imperfect account of it on paper: if any man can contemplate such scenes without feeling as much indignant concern as I do, I will patiently endure his censure and his scorn. With regard to the peasant's beverage just mentioned, it is thus prepared: — A quantity of unsifted ground oats, called seed-meal, the same materials from which flummery, or sowins, is made, is left to ferment in a very large proportion of water. When fully acidulated by the action of the atmosphere, it is poured off and reserved for use, and may not unaptly be compared to diluted vinegar. Even this, 'such as it is,' is in general sparingly used to kitchen the scanty meal of potatoes, which are not unfrequently eaten in a half-boiled state, from motives of pitiable economy, such as has been noticed in the instance of this poor family.

23d. Early this morning left Ballygawley for Omagh, a distance of fourteen miles; the road is good, but the country is exceedingly dreary. A great many of the cabins are not much better than those I had seen the two preceding days; the roofs are often irregularly covered by nature with a green sward, which at a little distance strongly resembles a long-neglected dunghill. On a nearer approach, the neck of a broken bottle, an old tea-cup, and sometimes a *brogue*, (an old shoe,) fixed on the end of a stick, and placed over the door, apprizes the traveller that what at first he, perhaps, mistook for a dunghill, is a house of entertainment! — a place where smuggled whiskey is publicly vended in defiance of the numerous absurd and oppressive measures which the Board of Excise has adopted for its prevention, but which, in stead of effecting this, have proved a curse to the country and a greater scourge to the innocent than the guilty.

6) William Cobbett

From *Cobbett in Ireland* (1834):[13]

At the town of CLONMELL, I went to see one of the places full where they kill every year for this purpose, about *sixty thousand hogs,* weighing from *eight score,* to *twenty score.* Every ounce of this meat is sent out of Ireland, while the poor half-naked creatures, who raise it with such care, are compelled to live on the *lumpers,* which are such bad potatoes, that the hogs will not thrive on them, and will not touch them, if they can get other potatoes. The *rooks,* which eat the good potatoes, will not eat these, though they be starving. And, yet, this is the stuff that the working people are fed on. There are about *eighty thousand firkins of butter,* and, perhaps, *a hundred thousand quarters of wheat,* and more of oat sent away out of this one town; while those who raise it all by their labour, live upon *lumpers*! 'How,' you will ask, 'are the millions of working people made to submit to this?' I will tell you, when I get back to the Parliament House, or to a county meeting at Guildford. It will be better to say it *there,* than here!

From CLONMELL, we came to FERMOY, on Saturday, the 11. instant. Fine land; a fine country; flocks of turkeys all along the way; cattle, sheep, hogs, as before; and the people, the working people, equally miserable as before. Here is a fine view, and beautiful meadows, compared to which the meadows at Farnham are not worth naming. From one side of this valley there rises up a long and most beautiful chain (miles in length) of gently sloping hills, and on those hills and on their sides, corn-fields and grass-fields are interspersed with woods and groves. But, standing on the bridge, and reviewing this scene, my *eyes were blasted* by the sight of three BARRACKS for *foot, horse,* and *artillery*; buildings surpassing in extent all the palaces that I ever saw; elegant and costly as palaces; buildings containing, they say three thousand windows; and capable of lodging forty thousand men! 'Good God!' say you; 'what can all this BE FOR?' I will tell you, MARSHALL, when I get to the county meeting at GUILDFORD, to which you must all come. 'But,' you will say, 'do these *soldiers* live upon *lumpers* too?' MARSHALL, do not ask *me* any more questions about this matter. Ask Mr DEAN: he can tell you about it.

But, now, MARSHALL, I am coming *nearer home*; and I beg you all to pay great attention to what I am going to say. You will think it strange, that all this food should be sent out of the country, and that the people should *get nothing back* for it. You will think, that we must send them *clothes* and *household goods* and *tea* and *sugar* and *soap* in return for the hogs and other things. To the *rich* we do; and to the *barracks*; but, the millions of working people have only rags for parts of their bodies, and they have neither goods nor tea nor sugar nor plate nor knife nor fork nor tea-kettle nor cup nor saucer.

The case is this: the owners of all the great estates *live in England or in France or in Italy.* The *rents are sent to them*; and, as there are no *poor-rates*, they get all the produce of the land from the miserable farmer, except just enough to keep him alive. They *spend these rents out of Ireland*; so that the working people here, who might eat meat three times a day, are compelled to live upon *lumpers*! And, be you assured, that this would be the lot of the English working people if the Scotch vagabonds could succeed in their projects for sweeping away our poor-laws. If that were done, the English farmers would be a set of beggarly slaves, the landlords would take so much from them, that they would be able to give the labourers not more than 6d. a day, and you would all be living in hovels without chimneys, and be eating with the pigs, that you would be rearing and fatting for somebody else to eat! I would rather see you all perish, and perish along with you!

But, MARSHALL, mind me well. You know, that, at PEPPER-HARROW (only about four miles from your cottage) there lives LORD MIDDLETON. You know that he was a long while Lord-Lieutenant of our county. Now, MARSHALL, HE is one of the GREAT LANDOWNERS OF IRELAND. His real name is BRODERICK. He is the owner of a *town*, called *Middleton*, half as big as Guildford. He is the owner of the lands for many miles round, and, it is supposed, that he draws *yearly, from twenty-five to thirty thousand pounds from this estate*!

I came here to see things with my own eyes; and, I have, *today*, been to see this BRODERICK'S estate, which begins at about sixteen miles from this City of Cork; and the land of this sixteen miles, taking in two miles on each side of the road, the finest that you can possibly imagine. Ah! but, how did I find the *working people* upon the land of this BRODERICK? That is the question for you to ask, and for me to answer.

I went to a sort of HAMLET near to the town of Middleton. It contained about 40 or 50 hovels. I went into several of them, and took down the names of the occupiers. They all consisted of mud-walls, with a covering of rafters and straw. None of them so good as the place where you keep your little horse. I took a particular account of the first I went into. It was 21 feet long and 9 feet wide. The floor, the bare ground. No fire-place, no chimney, the fire (made of potato-haulm) made on one side against the wall, and the smoke going out of a hole in the roof. No table, no chair; I sat to write upon a block of wood. Some stones for seats. No goods but *a pot*, and a shallow tub, for the pig and the family both to eat out of. There was one window, 9 inches by 5, and the glass broken half out. There was a mud-wall about 4 feet high to separate off the end of the shed for the family to sleep, lest the hog should kill and eat the little children when the father and mother were both out, and when the hog was shut in; and it happened some time ago that a poor mother, being ill on her straw, unable to move, and having her baby dead beside her, *had its head eaten off by a hog before her own eyes*! No bed; no mattress: some large flat stones, to keep the bodies from the damp ground; some dirty straw and a bundle of rags were all the bedding. The man's name was OWEN GUMBLETON. *Five small children*; the mother, about thirty, naturally handsome, but worn into half-ugliness by hunger and filth; she had no shoes or stockings, no shift, a mere rag over her body and down to her knees. The man BUILT THIS PLACE HIMSELF, and yet he has to pay *a pound a year* for it with perhaps a rod of ground! Others, 25s a year. *All built their own hovels,* and yet have to pay their rent. All the hogs were in the hovels today, it being coldish and squally; and then, you know, hogs like cover. GUMBLETON's hog was lying in the room and in another hovel there was a fine large hog that had taken his bed close by the fire. There is a nasty dunghill (no privy) to each hovel. The dung that the hog makes *in the hovel* is carefully put into a heap by itself, as being the most precious. This dung and the pig are the main things to raise the rent and get fuel with. The poor creatures sometimes *keep the dung in the hovel,* when their hard-hearted tyrants will not suffer them to let it be at the door! So there they are, in a far worse state, MARSHALL.

LORD MIDDLETON may say, that HE is not the *landlord* of these wretched people. Ah! but his *tenant*, his *middleman,* is their landlord, and LORD MIDDLETON gets the *more rent from him,* by enabling him to let these holes in this manner. If I were to give Mr DEAN a shilling a week to squeeze you down to twelve shillings a week, who would you think was most to blame, me or Mr Dean?

7) Henry Inglis

From *A Journey throughout Ireland* (1835):[14]

To the antiquarian, there are many interesting vestiges in the old towns of Limerick. The Limerick reader will understand why I say towns; to the English reader it requires to be told, that there is an English and an Irish town. Remnants of walls, and isolated bastions, are here and there discovered; and the stone, on which the treaty of Limerick was signed, is pointed out to the stranger.

But there are objects of a far different nature, in the old towns of Limerick; — objects of a deeper, and more melancholy interest. The reader will recollect, that in Cork, Waterford, Kilkenny, and in other towns which I have visited, I have made it a part of my duty to inquire into the condition of the poor; and having been informed by those upon whom I thought some reliance was to be placed, that I should find more and deeper destitution in Limerick, than in any place which I had yet visited, my inquiries in Limerick were prosecuted with all the care which I was capable of bestowing; and I regret to say, that I found too dreadful confirmation of the very worst reports. I spent a day visiting those parts of the city, where the greatest destitution and misery were said to exist. I entered upwards of forty of the abodes of poverty; and to the latest hour of my existence, I can never forget the scenes of utter and hopeless wretchedness that presented themselves that day. I shall endeavour to convey to the reader some general idea of what I saw.

Some of the abodes I visited were garrets, some were cellars; some were holes on the ground-floor, situated in narrow yards, or alleys. I will not speak of the filth of the places; *that* could not be exceeded in places meant to be its receptacles. Let the worst be imagined, and it will not be beyond the truth. In at least three-fourths of the hovels which I entered, there was no furniture of any description, save an iron pot, — no table, no chair, no bench, no bedstead; — two, three, or four little bundles of straw, with, perhaps, one or two scanty and ragged mats, were rolled up in the corners, unless where these beds were found occupied. The inmates, were some of them old, crooked, and diseased; some younger, but emaciated, and surrounded by starving children; some were sitting on the damp ground, some standing, and many were unable to rise from their little straw heaps. In scarcely one hovel, could I find even a potato. In one which I entered, I noticed a small opening, leading into an inner room. I lighted a bit of paper, at the embers of a turf which lay in the chimney, and looked in. It was a cellar wholly dark; and about twelve feet square: two bundles of straw lay in two corners; on one, sat a bed-ridden woman; on another, lay two naked children, — literally naked, with a torn rag of some kind thrown over them both. But I saw worse even than this. In a cellar which I entered, and which was almost quite dark, and slippery with damp, I found a man sitting on a little sawdust. He was naked: he had not even a shirt: a filthy and ragged mat was round him: this man was a living skeleton; the bones all but protruded through the skin: he was literally starving.

In place of forty hovels, I might have visited hundreds. In place of seeing, as I did, hundreds of men, women, and children, in the last state of destitution, I might have seen thousands. I entered the alleys, and visited the hovels, and climbed the stairs at a venture; I did not select; and I have no reason to believe that the forty which I visited, were the abodes of greater wretchedness than the hundreds which I passed by.

8) William Bennett

In the following extract William Bennett describes his recollections of Belmullet during the 1847 Famine. The passage is included as an example of the speechlessness to which English visitors were reduced by what they saw. Bennett and his companions were, he explains, 'too much overcome to note specifically' the inside of the cabins visited. He adds that 'language utterly fails' him when he attempts to describe on paper the condition of their inhabitants. Modern famine analogies do not need to be laboured here.

From *Narrative of a recent journey* (1847):[15]

Many of the cabins were holes in the bog, covered with a layer of turves, and not distinguishable as human habitations from the surrounding moor, until close down upon them. The bare sod was about the best material of which any of them were constructed. Doorways, not doors, were usually provided at both sides of the bettermost — back and front — to take advantage of the way of the wind. Windows and chimneys, I think, had no existence. A second apartment or division of any kind within was exceedingly rare. Furniture, properly so called, I believe may be stated at *nil.* I would not speak with certainty, and wish not to with exaggeration, — we were too much overcome to note specifically; but as far as memory serves, we saw neither bed, chair, nor table, at all. A chest, a few iron or earthen vessels, a stool or two, the dirty rags and night-coverings, formed about the sum total of the best furnished. Outside many were all but unapproachable, from the mud and filth surrounding them; the same inside, or worse if possible, from the added closeness, darkness, and smoke. We spent the whole morning in visiting these hovels indiscriminately, or swayed by the representations and entreaties of the dense retinue of wretched creatures, continually augmenting, which gathered round, and followed us from place to place, — avoiding only such as were known to be badly infected with fever, which was sometimes sufficiently perceptible from without, by the almost intolerable stench. And now language utterly fails me in attempting to depict the state of the wretched inmates. I would not willingly add another to the harrowing details that have been told; but still they are the FACTS of actual experience, for the knowledge of which we stand accountable. I have certainly sought out one of the most remote and destitute corners; but still it is within the bounds of our Christian land, under our Christian Government, and entailing upon us — both as individuals and as members of a human community — a Christian responsibility from which no one of us can escape. My hand trembles while I write. The scenes of human misery and degradation we witnessed still haunt my imagination, with the vividness and power of some horrid and tyrannous delusion, rather than the features of a sober reality. We entered a cabin. Stretched in one dark corner, scarcely visible, from the smoke and rags that covered them, were three children huddled together, lying there *because they were too weak to rise,* pale and ghastly, their little limbs — on removing a portion of the filthy covering — perfectly emaciated, eyes sunk, voice gone, and evidently in the last stage of actual starvation. Crouched over the turf embers was another form, wild and all but naked, scarcely human in appearance. It stirred not, nor noticed us. On some straw, soddened upon the ground, moaning piteously, was a shrivelled old woman, imploring us to give her something, — baring her limbs partly, to show how the skin hung loose from the bones, as soon as she attracted our attention. Above her, on something like a ledge, was a young woman, with sunken cheeks, — a moother I have no doubt, — who scarcely raised her eyes in answer to our enquiries, but pressed her hand upon her forehead, with a look of unutterable anguish and despair. Many cases were widows, whose husbands had recently been taken off by the fever, and thus their only pittance, obtained from the public works, entirely cut off. In many the husbands or sons were prostrate, under that horrid disease, — the results of long-continued famine and low living, — in which first the limbs, tand then the body, swell most frightfully, and finally burst. We entered upwards of fifty of these tenements. The scene was one and invariable, differing in little but the number of the sufferers, or of the groups, occupying the several corners within. The whole number was often not to be distinguished, until — the eye having adapted itself to the darkness — they were pointed out, or were *heard,* or some filthy bundle of rags and straw *was perceived to move.* Perhaps the poor children presented the most piteous and heart-rending spectacle. Many were too weak to stand, their little limbs attenuated, —

except where the frightful swellings had taken the place of previous emaciation, — beyond the *power of volition when moved.* Every infantile expression entirely departed; and in some, reason and intelligence had evidently flown. Many were *remnants of families,* crowded together in one cabin; orphaned little relatives taken in by the equally destitute, and even strangers, for these poor people are kind to one another to the end. In one cabin was a sister, just dying, lying by the side of her little brother, just dead. I have worse than this to relate, but it is useless to multiply details, and they are, in fact, unfit. They did but rarely complain. When inquired of, what was the matter, the answer was alike in all — *'Tha shein ukrosh,'* — *indeed the hunger.* We truly learned the terrible meaning of that sad word *'ukrosh'*. There were many touching incidents. We should have gone on, but the pitiless storm had now arisen, beating us back with a force and violence against which it was difficult to stand; and a cutting rain, that drove us for shelter beneath a bank, fell on the crowd of poor creatures who continued to follow us unmitigatedly. My friend the clergyman had distributed the tickets for meal to the extent he thought prudent; and he assured me wherever we went it would be a repetition of the same all over the country, *and even worse* in the far off mountain districts, as this was near the town, where some relief could reach. It was my full impression that *one-fourth* of those we saw were in a *dying state,* beyond the reach of any relief that could now be afforded; and many more would follow. The lines of this day can never be effaced from my memory. These were our fellow-creatures, — children of the same Parent, — born with our common feelings and affections, — with an equal right to live as any one of us, — with the same purposes of existence, — the same spiritual and immortal natures, — the same work to be done, — the same judgment-seat to be summoned to, — and the same eternal goal.

NOTES

INTRODUCTION

1 G. Bennington, 'Postal Politics and the Institution of the Nation, in *Nation and Narration*, ed. by H. Bhabha (London: Routledge & Kegan Paul, 1990), pp. 121–37.
2 Bennington, p. 123.
3 Benedict Anderson, *Imagined Communities: reflections on the origin and spread of nationalism* (London: Verso, 1983).
4 See A. J. Polan, *Lenin and the End of Politics* (London: Methuen, 1984), Ch. 1.
5 See M. Hamer, 'Putting Ireland on the Map', *Textual Practice*, 3 (1989), pp. 184–201.
6 R. McHugh and M. Harmon, *A Short History of Anglo-Irish Literature from its origins to the present day* (Dublin: Wolfhound, 1982), pp. 1–2.
7 S. Gwynn, *Irish Literature and Drama in the English Language: a short history* (London: Nelson, 1936), pp. 7–11.
8 A. Norman Jeffares, *Anglo-Irish Literature* (London: Macmillan, 1982), p. 1.
9 See T. Brennan, 'The National Longing for Form' in Bhabha, pp. 44–70.
10 T. McDonagh, *Literature in Ireland: Studies Irish and Anglo-Irish* (New York: Kennikat, 1916; repr. 1970), p. 28.
11 P. Bishop and E. Mallie, *The Provisional I.R.A.* (London: Heinemann, 1987), p. 104.
12 T. D. Kendrick, *British Antiquity* (London: Methuen, 1950), Chs. 1, 3.
13 W. J. McCormack, *The Battle of the Books* (Dublin: Lilliput, 1986), p. 52.
14 Author not named, 'Dr Paisley refers to lessons of history at Independent Demonstration in Ballycastle', *The Coleraine Chronicle*, 16 July 1988, p. 12.
15 R. Wallis, S. Bruce and D. Taylor, 'No Surrender': *Paisleyism and the Politics of Ethnic Identity in Northern Ireland* (Belfast: Queen's University of Belfast, 1986), p. 7.
16 On nationalism, see E. Gellner, *Nations and Nationalism* (Oxford: Blackwell, 1983). On ethnicity, see W. Sollers, 'Ethnicity', in *Critical Terms for Literary Study*, ed. by F. Lentricchia and T. McLaughlin, (Chicago: Chicago University Press, 1990), pp. 288–305.

17 See Conor Cruise O'Brien, *States of Ireland* (London: Hutchinson, 1972) and Tom Paulin's critique of O'Brien's arguments, 'The Making of a Loyalist', in *Ireland and the English Crisis* (Newcastle: Bloodaxe, 1984), pp. 23–38.
18 B. Fitzpatrick, 'Interview with Andy Tyrie', *Crane Bag*, 4 (1980), pp. 652–59; 652.
19 Reginald Maudling, quoted in Tim Pat Coogan, *The I.R.A.* (London: Pall Mall, 1970, revised edition Fontana, 1987), p. 438.
20 A. F. N. Clarke, *Contact* (London: Pan, 1984), p. 134.
21 *The Daily Express*, 24 December 1977; cited in Liz Curtis, *Ireland: The Propaganda War* (London: Pluto, 1984), p. 61.
22 Mary Louise Pratt, 'Scratches on the Face of the Country; or, What Mr. Barrow Saw in the Land of the Bushmen', *'Race', Writing, and Difference*, ed. by Henry Louis Gates, Jr. (Chicago and London: University of Chicago Press, 1985; repr. 1986), pp. 138–162. See also *English Literature and the Wider World. Volume 1 1660–1780 All Before Them*, ed. by John McVeagh (London and Atlantic Highlands, N.J.: The Ashfield Press, 1990), 'Introduction' and passim; John P. Harrington, *The English Traveller in Ireland: Accounts of Ireland and the Irish through five centuries* (Dublin: Wolfhound Press, 1991).
23 Homi BhaBha, 'Of Mimicry and Man: The Ambivalence of Colonial Discourse', *October* 28 (1984), pp. 125–133.
24 *The Prose Works of Jonathan Swift*, ed. by Herbert Davis and Irvin Ehrenpreis, 14 vols (Oxford: Basil Blackwell, 1968) XII, pp. 109–118.
25 See N. P. Canny, *The Formation of the 'Old' English Elite In Ireland* (O'Donnell Lecture, Dublin, 1975); T. C. Barnard, 'Crises of Identity among Irish Protestants, 1641–1685', *Past and Present*, 127 (1990), pp. 39–83.
26 B. Bradshaw, *The Irish Constitutional Revolution of the Sixteenth Century* (Cambridge: Cambridge University Press, 1979); C. Lennon, 'Richard Stanihurst and "Old" English Identity', *Irish Historical Studies*, 82 (1978), pp. 121–43; N. P. Canny, 'Identity Formation in Ireland: the emergence of the Anglo-Irish', in *Colonial Identity in the Atlantic World*, ed. by N. P. Canny and A. Pagden (New Haven: Yale University Press, 1987), pp. 159–212.
27 R. Holinshed, *Chronicles of England, Scotland and Ireland*, 6 vols (London: Johnson, 1807–8), VI, p. 109.
28 On Keating's sense of identity in his history, see B. Cunningham, 'Seventeenth Century Interpretations of the Past: the case of Geoffrey Keating', *Irish Historical Studies*, 98 (1986), pp. 116–28; see also, N. P. Canny, 'The Permissive Frontier: the problem of social control in 'English settlements in Ireland and Virginia, 1550–1650', in *The Westward Enterprise: English activities in Ireland, the Atlantic and America, 1480–1650*, ed. by K. R. Andrews and others (Liverpool: Liverpool University Press, 1978), pp. 17–44.
29 In Keating's terms, 'Gall' and to be carefully distinguished from 'Sean-Ghaill', the Anglo-Normans or 'Old foreigners'.

30 Geoffrey Keating, *The History of Ireland*, ed. and trans. by D. Comyn and R. S. Dineen, 4 vols (London: Early Irish Text Society, 1902–8), I, p. 153.
31 For the use of this Gramscian term in an Irish context, see D. Cairns and S. Richards, *Writing Ireland: Colonialism, Nationalism and Culture* (Manchester: Manchester University Press, 1988), Ch. 1 et passim.
32 M. Richter, *Giraldus Cambrensis* (Aberystwyth: National Library of Wales, 1976), Pt. 2.
33 M. Richter, 'The Interpretation of Medieval Irish History', *Irish Historical Studies*, 24 (1985), pp. 289–98; J. Gillingham, 'Images of Ireland, 1170–1600: the origins of English Imperialism', *History Today* 37 (1987), pp. 16–22; R. Frame, *English Lordship in Ireland, 1318–61* (Oxford: Clarendon Press, 1982).
34 Richter, 'The Interpretation of Medieval Irish History', p. 298.
35 S. Ellis, *Tudor Ireland: crown, community and the conflict of cultures, 1470–1503* (London: Longman, 1985), pp. 139–40.
36 Reprinted in *State Papers, Vol. II, Henry VIII, Pt. 3 — Correspondence between the governments of England and Ireland, 1515–38* (London: H.M. Stationary Office, 1831), pp. 1–31.
37 Ellis, *Tudor Ireland*, Ch. 2.
38 N. P. Canny, *From Reformation to Restoration: Ireland, 1534–1660* (Dublin: Helicon, 1987), p. 41.
39 F. Le Van Baumer, *The Early Tudor Theory of Kingship* (New Haven: Yale University Press, 1940).
40 Text in *Giraldus Cambrensis, Expugnatio Hibernica*, ed. and trans. by A. B. Scott and F. X. Martin (Dublin: Royal Irish Academy, 1978), pp. 144–6; see also F. X. Martin, 'Dairmat MacMurchada and the coming of the Anglo-Normans', in *A New History of Ireland, 1169–1534*, ed. by A. Cosgrove (Oxford: Clarendon Press, 1987), pp. 43–97; pp. 57–9.
41 A. D. Hadfield, 'Briton and Scythian: the representation of the origins of Tudor Ireland' *Irish Historical Studies* (forthcoming, 1993).
42 P. Corish, *The Irish Catholic Experience, a historical survey* (Dublin: Gill and MacMillan, 1985), Chs. 2, 3.
43 Bradshaw, *Constitutional Revolution*, Chs. 4–8.
44 K. Bottigheimer, 'Kingdom and Colony: Ireland in the Westward Enterprise, 1536–1660', in *The Westward Enterprise*, ed. by Andrews et al, pp. 45–64, p. 55. On the Henrican Reformation in Ireland, see Bradshaw, *Constitutional Revolution*, Chs. 1–8; Ellis, *Tudor Ireland*, Ch. 5.
45 Bradshaw, *Constitutional Revolution*, Ch. 6; S. Ellis, 'The Kildare Rebellion and the early Henrican Reformation', *Historical Journal* 19 (1976), pp. 807–30.
46 A. Cosgrove, *Late Medieval Ireland, 1370–1541* (Dublin: Helicon, 1981), Ch. 7.
47 See *The Mid-Tudor Polity, c. 1540–1560*, ed. by J. Loach and K. Tittler (London: Macmillan, 1980).

48 R. Dudley Edwards, *Church and State in Tudor Ireland: a history of penal laws against Irish Catholics, 1534–1603* (Dublin: Talbot Press, 1935), Ch. 7; but for a different explanation see also S. Ellis, 'Economic Problems of the Church: why the Reformation failed in Ireland', *Journal of Ecclesiastical History*, 41 (1990), pp. 239–65.
49 Ellis, *Tudor Ireland*, Chs. 6, 8.
50 R. Dunlop, 'The Plantation of Leix and Offaly', *English Historical Review*, 6 (1891), pp. 61–96.
51 H. Morgan, 'The end of Gaelic Ulster: a thematic interpretation of events between 1534 and 1610', *Irish Historical Studies*, 26 (1990), pp. 8–32.
52 See R. Dudley Edwards, *Ireland in the Age of the Tudors: the destruction of Anglo-Norman Civilization* (London: Croom Helm, 1977).
53 C. Brady, 'The Killing of Shane O'Neill: some new evidence', *Irish Sword*, 15 (1982–3), pp. 116–28.
54 J. E. A. Dawson, 'Two Kingdoms or Three? Ireland in Anglo-Scottish Relations in the middle of the Sixteenth Century', in *Scotland and England, 1286–1815*, ed. by R. A. Mason (Edinburgh: John Donald, 1987), pp. 113–38.
55 J. J. Silke, *Ireland and Europe, 1559–1607* (Dundalk: Dundalgan Press, 1966): C. Z. Wiener, 'The Beleagured Isle: a study of Elizabethan and early Jacobean anti-Catholicism', *Past and Present*, 51 (1971), pp. 27–62.
56 C. Brady, 'Court, Castle and Country: the framework of government in Tudor Ireland', in *Natives and Newcomers: the making of Irish colonial society*, ed. by C. Brady and R. Gillespie (Dublin: Irish Academic Press, 1986), pp. 22–49; E. Hardy, *Survivors of the Armada* (London: Constable, 1966).
57 Finglas's 'Breviat of the getting of Ireland and the decaie of the same' is conveniently reprinted in *Hibernica*, ed. by W. Harris (Dublin: printed for the editor, 1747), pp. 39–52.
58 N. P. Canny, 'The Flight of the Earls, 1607', *Irish Historical Studies*, 17 (1970–1), pp. 380–99.
59 J. C. Beckett, *The Making of Modern Ireland, 1603–1923* (London: Faber, 2nd. edition 1981), Ch. 2.
60 N. P. Canny, *The Elizabethan Conquest of Ireland: a pattern established, 1565–76* (Hassocks: Harvester, 1976); C. Brady, 'Court, Castle and Country'.
61 H. Morgan, 'The Colonial Venture of Sir Thomas Smith in Ulster, 1571–5', *The Historical Journal*, 28 (1985), pp. 261–78; M. McCarthy-Morrogh, *The Munster Plantation: English Migration to Southern Ireland, 1583–1641* (Oxford: Clarendon Press, 1986).
62 R. Foster, *Modern Ireland, 1600–1972* (Harmondsworth: Penguin, 1988), Ch. 3.
63 M. Dewar, *Sir Thomas Smith, a Tudor intellectual in office* (London: Athlone, 1964), Ch. 14.
64 Dewar, *Sir Thomas Smith*, pp. 164–7.

65 T. W. Moody, *The Londonderry Plantation, 1609–41: the City of London and the plantation of Ulster* (Belfast: W. Mullen, 1939).

66 M. Hechter, *Internal Colonialism: the Celtic Fringe in British National Development* (London: Routledge & Kegan Paul, 1975).

67 ' "My mission is to pacify Ireland" was his first comment on receiving the expected summons from the queen'; quoted in J. C. Beckett, *The Making of Modern Ireland*, p. 266. On Gladstone's Irish policy see P. Magnus, *Gladstone, a biography* (London: Murray, 1954), Ch. 13 et passim. See also Ellis, *Tudor Ireland*, Ch. 9; Sir Thomas Stafford, *Pacata Hibernica* (Dublin: Hibernica Press, 1810).

68 Sir James Ware, *Ancient Irish Histories* (Dublin: Hibernica Press, 1809), preface.

69 For a list of Ware's excisions, see *The Works of Edmund Spenser: A Variorum Edition*, ed. by E. Greenlaw and others, 10 vols (Baltimore: Johns Hopkins Press, 1932–49), Appendix 3, pp. 516–24.

70 S.T.C. 6348. Sir John Davies, *Discovery* (Shannon: Irish University Press, 1969). Facsimile reprint of 1612 London edition. Davies did not abandon any plans of plantation, though, often preferring that method of keeping Ireland quiet to cultivating Irish loyalty.

71 See P. Coughlan, ' "Cheap and common animals": the English anatomy of Ireland in the Seventeenth Century', in *Literature and the English Civil War*, ed. by T. Healy and J. Sawday (Cambridge: Cambridge University Press, 1990), pp. 205–23. For two contrasting assessments of the controversial evidence, see A. T. Q. Stewart, *The Narrow Ground: Patterns of Ulster History* (Belfast: Pretani, 1986), pp. 45–52; and T. Fitzpatrick, *The Bloody Bridge and other papers related to the Insurrection of 1641* (Dublin: Sealy, Bryers and Walker, 1903).

72 Foster, *Modern Ireland*, Ch. 4, p. 99. Foster's comments in this chapter give a succinct account of a notoriously complex series of events.

73 B. Worden, 'Andrew Marvell, Oliver Cromwell and the Horatian Ode', in *The Politics of Discourse: the literature and history of seventeenth century England*, ed. by K. Sharpe and S. Zwicker (Berkeley: California University Press, 1987), pp. 147–80.

74 T. C. Barnard, 'Planters and Policies in Cromwellian Ireland', *Past and Present*, 61 (1973), pp. 31–69; 39–44; S. R. Gardiner, 'The Transplantation to Connaught', *English Historical Review*, 14 (1899), pp. 700–34.

75 K. S. Bottigheimer, *English Money and Irish land: the adventurers in the Cromwellian settlement of Ireland* (Oxford: Clarendon Press, 1971).

76 See F. Braudel, *The Perspective of the World*, trans. S. Reynolds, (London: Collins, 1984), Conclusion.

77 C. Russell, 'The British Background to the Irish Rebellion of 1641', *Historical Research*, 61 (1988), pp. 166–82, 169.

78 A. Clarke, *The Old English in Ireland, 1625–42* (London: MacGibbon and Kee, 1966), Chs. 7–9.

79 C. Russell, 'The British Problem and the English Civil War', *History*, 73 (1988), pp. 395–415, 404.
80 T. C. Barnard, 'Crises of Identity among Irish Protestants, 1641–1685', *Past and Present*, 127 (1990), pp. 39–83, 48.
81 See, for example, T. Brown, *Ireland, a Social and Cultural History, 1922–79* (London: Fontana, 1985).
82 C. Buci-Glucksmann, *Gramsci and the State*, trans. D. Fernbach (London: Lawrence and Wishart, 1980), pp. 273–90.
83 Barnard, 'Crises of Identity', p. 81.
84 Barnard, 'Crises of Identity', p. 54.
85 C. Hill, *The Century of Revolution, 1603–1714* (London: Cardinal, 1974).
86 D. Defoe, *A Tour thro' the Whole Island* (London: 1724–7). On a possible Defoe visit to Ireland see F. Bastian, *Defoe's Early life* (London: Macmillan, 1981), pp. 68–80, 326.
87 Margaret T. Hodgen, *Early Anthropology in the Sixteenth and Seventeenth Centuries* (Philadelphia: University of Pennsylvania Press, 1964), p. 410.
88 Quoted in Hodgen, *Early Anthropology*, p. 408.
89 See D. W. Hayton, 'From Barbarian to Burlesque: English Images of the Irish c. 1660–1750', *Irish Economic and Social History* 15 (1988), pp. 5–31.
90 For Petty and Gookin, see below, chapters 14 and 11. For Clarendon see his *Settlement and Sale of Ireland* (London, 1688; repr. Dublin, 1846). For the Civil Survey of the 1650s see *Civil Survey (1654–56)*, ed. by R. C. Simington (Dublin: The Stationery Office, 1931–1945).
91 Luke Gernon, *A Description of Ireland. Anno 1620*. See below pp. 81–83.
92 *The Poems and Letters of Andrew Marvell*, ed. H. M. Margouliouth, 3rd edition revised by Pierre Legouis with the colaboration of E. E. Duncan-Jones, 2 vols (Oxford: Clarendon Press, 1971), 1, pp. 100–103.
93 See R. Selden, 'Roughness in Satire from Horace to Dryden', *Modern Language Review*, 66 (1971), pp. 264–272.
94 On Dineley's Irish travels see Constantia Maxwell, *The Stranger in Ireland* (London: Jonathan Cape, 1954), pp. 101–6.
95 John Dunton, *Teague Land, or A Merry Ramble to the Wild Irish*, ed. by E. MacLysaght (Dublin: Irish Academic Press, 1982), p. 9.
96 For a modern account of these land changes see the essays by J. G. Simms in *A New History of Ireland. Volume 3. Early Modern Ireland 1534–1691*, ed. by T. W. Moody, F. X. Martin and F. J. Byrne (Oxford: Clarendon Press, 1976), Chs. 18 and 19. See also James McGuire's essay on 'Richard Talbot, earl of Tyrconnell (1603–91) and the Catholic Counter-Revolution', in *Worsted in the Game. Losers in Irish History*, ed. by Ciaran Brady (Dublin: Lilliput, 1989), Ch. 6.
97 Constantia Maxwell, *The Stranger in Ireland*, p. 81.
98 See Rev. Robert H. Murray, *Revolutionary Ireland and Its Settlement* (London: Macmillan, 1911), Chs. 7, 8, 9; Maureen Wall, *The Penal*

Laws, 1691–1760 (Dundalk: Dublin Historical Association, 1961). Irish History series, no. 1.

99 J. C. Beckett, *A Short History of Ireland* (London: Hutchinson, 1952; repr. 1979), p. 105.

100 R. F. Foster, *Modern Ireland*, p. 177.

101 E. M. Johnston, *Ireland in the Eighteenth Century* (Dublin: Gill and Macmillan, 1974, repr. 1980), p. 164.

102 *Boswell's Life of Johnson*, ed. by George Birkbeck Hill, revised and enlarged by L. F. Powell, 6 vols (Oxford: Clarendon Press, 1934; repr. 1979), 3, p. 410.

103 *The Letters of Joseph Addison*, ed. by W. Graham (Oxford: Clarendon Press, 1941), p. 149.

104 *The Journal of the Rev. John Wesley, A. M.*, ed. by Nehemiah Curnock, 8 vols (London: Culley, 1909–16), 5, p. 516.

105 Mark Elstob, *A Trip to Kilkenny from Durham by Way of Whitehaven and Dublin in the year MDCCLXXVI* (Stockton: R. Christopher, 1778), pp. 116–120.

106 Philip Luckombe, *A Tour through Ireland in 1779* (London: T. Lowndes, 1780), p. 25.

107 *Arthur Young's Tour in Ireland in the years 1776, 1777 and 1778*, ed. by A. W. Hutton, 2 vols (London: George Bell & Sons and New York, 1892), 2, p. 45.

108 Sir John Carr, *The Stranger in Ireland: or A Tour in the Southern and Western Parts of that Country in the year 1805* (London: 1806), p. 529.

109 J. A. Froude, *Thomas Carlyle. A History of his Life in London 1834–1881*, 2 vols (London: Longmans, Green and Co, 1884, republished Westmead, England: Gregg International Publishers, 1969) 1, p. 398.

110 See J. C. Beckett, *A Short History of Ireland* (London: Hutchinson University Library, 1952; repr. 1973), Ch. 5.

111 Patricia Hodgart, *A Preface to Shelley* (London and New York: Longman, 1985), pp. 49–51.

112 E. Wayne Marjarum, 'Wordsworth's View of the State of Ireland', *P.M.L.A.*, 55 (1940), pp. 608–11.

113 See D. J. O'Donoghue, *Sir Walter Scott's Tour in Ireland in 1825* (Glasgow: Gowans and Gray, 1905), Ch. 3.

114 See P. J. Keating, 'Arnold's Social and Political Thought', in *Writers and their Background. Matthew Arnold*, ed. by Kenneth Allott (Athens, Ohio: Ohio University Press, 1976), pp. 207–235.

115 See *Cobbett in Ireland: A Warning to England*, ed. by Denis Knight (London: Lawrence and Wishart, 1984), p. 11.

116 *Marx Engels, Ireland and the Irish Question*, ed. by R. Dixon (Moscow: Progress Publishers 1971; repr. 1978), pp. 388, 167.

117 *The Works of John Ruskin*, ed. by E. T. Cook and Alexander Wedderburn, 38 vols (London: George Allen and New York: Longmans, Green and Co., 1904), 4, pp. 19–20.

118 Thomas Carlyle, *Reminiscences of My Irish Journey in 1849* (London: Sampson, Low Marston, Searle, & Rivington, 1882), p. 135.
119 *The Works of W. M. Thackeray*, editor not named, 22 vols (London: Smith, Elder & Co., 1869), 14, pp. 126–7.
120 On the 'simian' Irishman, see L. P. Curtis, Jr., *Apes and Angels: The Irishman in Victorian Caricature* (Newton Abbott: David and Charles, 1971).
121 T. W. Freeman gives a brief account of the Ordnance Survey in 'Land and People in 1841', in *A New History of Ireland. 5 Ireland Under the Union I 1801–1870*, ed. by W. E. Vaughan (Oxford: Clarendon Press, 1989), pp. 242–265. See also J. H. Andrews, *A paper landscape: the Ordnance Survey in nineteenth-century Ireland* (Oxford: Clarendon Press, 1975).
122 *Marx Engels*, pp. 93–5.
123 *Marx Engels*, p. 94.
124 *Marx Engels*, p. 94.

1. GIRALDUS CAMBRENSIS AND ENGLISH WRITING ABOUT IRELAND

1 A. Pagden, *The Fall of Natural Man: the American Indian and the origins of comparative ethnology* (Cambridge: Cambridge University Press, 1982), p. 2.
2 See A. D. Hadfield, 'Briton and Scythian'.
3 On Giraldus, see M. Richter, *Giraldus Cambrensis and the Welsh Nation* (Aberystwyth: National Library of Wales, 1972; repr. 1976); R. Bartlett, *Gerald of Wales, 1146–1223* (Oxford: Clarendon Press, 1988).
4 Text taken from *Expugnatio Hibernica, The Conquest of Ireland*, ed. and trans. by A. B. Scott and F. X. Martin (Dublin: Royal Irish Academy, 1978), p. 149.
5 See *Topography*, Ch. 92.
6 Geoffrey of Monmouth, *The History of the Kings of Britain*, ed. and trans., by L. Thorpe (Harmondsworth: Penguin, 1966; repr. 1980), pp. 100–1.
7 Monmouth, *History*, p. 227.
8 See *Topography*, Ch. 92.
9 See *Expugnatio*, Bk. 1, Chs. 31–3.
10 A reference to the 'Donation of Constantine'; see W. Ullmann, 'Donation of Constantine' in *New Catholic Encyclopedia* 4 (1966), pp. 1000–1.
11 Text taken from *The Topography of Ireland*, trans. by Thomas Forester, in *The Historical Works of Giraldus Cambrensis*, ed. by T. Wright (London: M. G. Bohn, 1863), pp. 1–164.
12 The Basques, who were often perceived as a primitive and uncouth people in the Middle Ages; see J. Gillingham, *Richard the Lionheart* (London: Weidenfeld and Nicolson, 1978), p. 50.

13 On the Norse invasions of Ireland, see L. de Paor, 'The age of the Viking Wars' in *The Course of Irish History*, ed. by F. X. Martin and T. W. Moody (Dublin: Mercier, 1967; repr. 1968); G. Jones, *A History of the Vikings* (Oxford: Oxford University Press, 1973), Pt. 3, Ch. 3.
14 Lucan, *Pharsalia*, 1, 29.
15 See P. Corish, *The Irish Catholic Experience*, Ch. 1, on the origins of Irish Christianity.
16 Local ecclesiastical taxation — see, for example, D. Pill, *The English Reformation, 1529–38* (London: University of London Press, 1973), Pt. 1.

2. JOHN BALE AND THE REFORMATION IN IRELAND

1 L. P. Fairfield, *John Bale: Mythmaker for the English Reformation* (Indiana: Purdue University Press, 1976), Chs. 3–5; J. N. King, *English Reformation Literature: the Tudor Origins of the Protestant Tradition* (Princeton: Princeton University Press, 1982), passim.
2 W. Haller, *Foxe's Book of Martyrs and the Elect Nation* (London: Jonathan Cape, 1963), pp. 58–9 et passim.
3 *Scriptorum Illustrium Majoris Brytanniae Catalogus*, 2 vols. (Basel, 1557–9; repr. Gregg International, 1971).
4 His first exile occurred after Cromwell's fall: see Haller, *Foxe's Book of Martyrs*, p. 59; Fairfield, *John Bale*, pp. 71–2.
5 See L. P. Fairfield, 'The Vocacyon of Johan Bale and early English autobiography', *Renaissance Quarterly* 14 (1971), pp. 327–39. Text taken from *The Vocacyon of Johan Bale to the Bishopricke of Ossorie* (Rome, i.e., Wesel?, 1553), S.T.C. 1307, ff. 18, 22–4 and 45–6. The text is reprinted in *The Harleian Miscellany* (1813), pp. 437–64.
6 See B. Bradshaw, 'The Edwardian Reformation in Ireland: 1547–53', *Archivium Hibernicum* 14 (1977), pp. 83–99. On Irish reactions to Bale's preaching see S. G. Ellis, 'John Bale, Bishop of Ossory, 1552–3', *Journal of the Butler Society* 3, ii (1984), pp. 283–93.
7 See H. Pawlisch, *Sir John Davies and the conquest of Ireland: a study in legal imperialism* (Cambridge: Cambridge University Press, 1985), Ch. 7.
8 For example, in his autograph notebook, the *Index Britannaie Scriptorum*, ed. by R. L. Poole and M. Bateson (Oxford: Clarendon Press, 1902) Bale separates the different nations of Britain, as he does in the *Scriptorum*.
9 On the question of obedience to secular powers after the Reformation, see Q. Skinner, *The Foundations of Modern Political Thought, Vol. 2, The Age of Reformation* (Cambridge: Cambridge University Press, 1978).
10 See King, *English Reformation Literature*, p. 293.
11 See B. Bradshaw, 'George Browne, First Reformation Archbishop of Dublin, 1536–54', *Journal of Ecclesiastical History* 21, 4 (1970), pp. 301–26; 'Edwardian Reformation in Ireland', for an analysis of the

reluctance of Irish ecclesiastics to preach according to Edwardian decrees.

12 Aqua Vitae is any high alcohol spirit, e.g., whiskey, brandy, etc. Rob davye is 'Metheglin', spiced mead.

13 Let us rejoice in grief.

14 Bale's trilogy, *God's Promises, Johan Baptistes Preachynge* and *The Temptation of Our Lord.* See *The Complete Plays of John Bale*, ed. by P. Happé (Cambridge: Brewer, 1986), 2.

15 Free services and entertainment for himself and his followers which an Irish lord was entitled to demand from his people, often adopted by English marcher lords in Ireland. See Ellis, *Tudor Ireland*, p. 41.

16 The comparison of Irish and Turks was often made; see, for example, *Shakespeare's Europe, being unpublished chapters of Fynes Moryson's 'Itinerary'*, ed. by C. Hughes, (London: Sherrat and Hughes, 1903), pp. 8–10.

17 One of these is probably Giraldus, whom Bale includes in the *Index* (pp. 419, 421–3 et passim). Bale possessed a copy of Giraldus's works; see H. McCusker, 'Books and manuscripts formerly in the possession of John Bale', *The Library*, 4th Series, 16 (1935), pp. 144–65, p. 151.

18 Mercenaries from the Scottish islands employed by Irish chiefs to bolster their military strength; see G. A. Hayes-McCoy, *Scots Mercenary Forces in Ireland, 1565–1603* (Dublin: Burns, Oates and Co., 1937).

3. THE NATURE OF THE IRISH

1 See *Expugnatio*, preface, p. xxxi et passim; Giraldus, *The Description of Wales* in *The Journey through Wales/The Description of Wales*, ed. and trans. by L. Thorpe (Harmondsworth: Penguin, 1978; repr. 1988), pp. 211–74; 271.

2 *Expugnatio*, Bk. II, Ch. 39.

3 N. Canny, 'The ideology of English Colonization: from Ireland to America', *William and Mary Quarterly* 30 (1973), pp. 575–98; D. B. Quinn, *The Elizabethans and the Irish* (Ithaca: Cornell University Press, 1966).

4 B. Bradshaw, 'Sword, word and strategy in the Reformation in Ireland', *Historical Journal* 21, 3 (1978), pp. 475–98; A. Ford, *The Protestant Reformation in Ireland* (Frankfurt: Peter Lang, 1985).

5 See D. McDonell, *Theories of Discourse: an introduction* (Oxford: Blackwell, 1986).

6 Ironically, both were closely connected to Henry Sidney; see E. Campion, *Two Bokes of the Histories of Ireland*, ed. by A. F. Vossen (Assen: Van Gorcum, 1963), introduction; Bk. 2, Ch. 10 et passim; J. Derricke, *The Image of Irelande* (London, 1581); especially the woodcuts.

7 'Mere' was not a term of abuse, but meant 'pure' or 'unmixed'.

8 A concept which has caused considerable debate amongst colonial

theorists; see H. Bhabha, 'Of Mimicry and Men: the Ambivialence of Colonial Discourse', repr. in *Modern Literary Theory: A Reader*, ed. by P. Rice and P. Waugh (London: Arnold, 1989), pp. 234–41; 'The Other Question: The Stereotype and Colonial Discourse', *Screen* 24, 6 (1983), pp. 18–36; Abdul Jan Mohamed, 'The Economy of Manichaen Allegory: The Function of Racial Difference in Colonialist Literature' in *'Race', Writing and Difference*, ed. by H. L. Gates (Chicago: Chicago University Press, 1985; repr. 1986), pp. 78–106.

9 *Two Bokes*, ed. by Vossen, introd., Chs. 1, 5.

10 *Two Bokes*, ed. by Vossen, Ch. 3. See also, E. Waugh, *Edmund Campion: Scholar, Priest, Hero, Martyr* (Oxford: Oxford University Press, 1935; repr. 1980).

11 Text used, *Two Bokes*, ed. by Vossen, pp. 19–20.

12 Cess, also known as purveyance, was a tax 'levied for the provisioning not only of the governor's household but of his retinue too'; Ellis, *Tudor Ireland*, p. 197. It was designed to replace government reliance on 'coyne and livery' in the Pale (see Ch. 2, note 18).

13 See C. Brady, 'The Road to the View: On the Decline of Reform Thought in Tudor Ireland' in *Spenser and Ireland: an interdisciplinary perspective*, ed. by P. Coughlin (Cork: Cork University Press, 1989), pp. 25–45. On Gerard's life, see *D.N.B.* entry.

14 Text from Gerard, 'Notes of his report on Ireland — May, 1578', *Analecta Hibernica* 2 (1931), pp. 93–291; 95–6, 122.

15 'Nacion' could mean either country or people in sixteenth century English.

16 Broadly speaking, a synonym for 'coyne and livery' (see Ch. 2, note 18).

17 (Braghan) Brehon Laws were those of the native Irish legal system, frequently condemned by English observers; see below, pp. 77–80.

18 In other words, cattle raids and hostage taking; see Quinn, *The Elizabethans and the Irish*, pp. 46–7 et passim.

19 M. W. Wallace, *The Life of Sir Philip Sidney* (Cambridge: Cambridge University Press, 1915), Chs. 5, 15 et passim.

20 'A light-armed Irish foot-soldier' (*O.E.D.*).

21 On Derricke's life, see *D.N.B.* entry.

22 Text from *The Image of Irelande* (London, 1581); S.T.C. 6734.

23 Cf. Giraldus, *Topographia*, 1, 21–2. The legend was that St. Patrick had banished poisonous reptiles from Ireland. Derricke rewrites the myth in order to claim that snakes were removed from Ireland because the Gods declared that it was the land where those who wanted to invade heaven were put. Mars persuaded the Gods that unless the snakes went, Ireland would become too evil (Pt. 1).

24 J. Hooker, *The Lyffe of Sir Peter Carew*, ed. by J. MacLean (London: Bell and Daldy, 1857).

25 On Hooker's life, see *D.N.B.* entry.

26 R. Holinshed, *Chronicles of England, Scotland and Ireland*, 6 Vols., ed. by V. Snow (New York: AMS Press, 1807; repr. 1976), 6, pp. 233–460.

27 A common image of rebellion; see C. Hill, 'The Many-headed

Monster in late Tudor and early Stuart Political Thinking' in *From the Renaissance to the Counter-Reformation: essays in honour of Garrett Mattingly*, ed. by C. H. Carter (London: Cape, 1966), pp. 296–324.

28 'Hooker may be referring to a fable of Aesop, wherein a feline creature is transformed by Aphrodite rather than Jupiter' (note supplied by Ken Rowe); see also E. Spenser, *Mother Hubberds Tale*, 659ff.

29 On Rich's life, see T. M. Cranfill and D. H. Bruce, *Barnaby Rich, A Short Biography* (Austin: Texas University Press, 1953); E. M. Hinton, 'Rich's Anatomy of Ireland, with an account of the author', *PMLA* 55 (1940), pp. 73–101; C. Lennon, *The Lords of Dublin*, Ch. 6.

30 Hinton, 'Rich's Anatomy', p. 81.

31 For theological arguments about the nature of the Irish, see B. Bradshaw, 'Sword, word and strategy'; on savagery, see Pagden, *The Fall of Natural Man*, B. Sheehan, *Savagism and Civility: Indians and Englishmen in Colonial Virginia* (Cambridge: Cambridge University Press, 1980).

32 Text from B. Rich, *A New Description of Ireland* (London, 1610) S.T.C. 20992, pp. 13–7; Hinton, 'Rich's Anatomy', pp. 82–3.

33 Trews or trousers.

34 Phylautus might mean 'A member of a tribe or nation'; I can find no relevant etymology for Antodonus.

35 *Croftus, sive de Hibernica Liber*, ed. by W. E. Buckley (London: Roxburghe Club, 1887) and those reprinted in *Calendar of State Papers for Ireland, 1586–8*, ed. by H. C. Hamilton (London: Longman, 1877), pp. 527–47.

36 On Herbert's life, see *D.N.B.* entry.

37 Reproduced in *C.S.P.I., 1586–8*, pp. 527–39; pp. 532–3.

38 H. Arendt, *Eichmann in Jerusalem: A Report on the Banality of Evil* (Harmondsworth: Penguin, 1963; repr. 1987).

39 'Not even the Cromwellian settlement envisaged such a drastic liquidation of the Irish nation' (D. B. Quinn). Text taken from Quinn's ' "A Discourse of Ireland" (Circa 1599): A sidelight on English colonial policy' in *Proceedings of the Royal Irish Academy* 47 (1941–2), section C, pp. 151–66.

40 See S. Greenblatt, 'Learning to curse: Aspects of Linguistic Colonialism in the Sixteenth Century' in *First Images of America: the impact of the New World on the Old*, ed. by F. Chiapelli, 2 vols (Berkeley: California University Press, 1976), 2, pp. 561–81.

41 See P. Ramsey, *Tudor Economic Problems* (London: Gollancz, 1972), pp. 14–16, 22–3. Excessive population was often cited as a reason for establishing colonies; see K. R. Andrews, *Trade, Plunder and Settlement: Maritime Enterprise and the Genesis of the British Empire* (Cambridge: Cambridge University Press, 1984), p. 34; H. Morgan, 'The Colonial Venture of Sir Thomas Smith', pp. 269–70.

42 'The number was nearer 10,000 than 20,000' (Quinn's note).

43 The estates of rebels were usually confiscated as were the Earl of Desmond's lands which formed the basis for the Munster Plantation. See M. MacCarthy-Murrough, *The Munster Plantation*, Ch. 1.

4. THREE TRAVELLERS' OBSERVATIONS OF IRISH LIFE

1 See Hodgen, *Early Anthropology*; C. Lévi-Strauss, 'A Writing Lesson', *Tristes Tropiques*, trans. by J. and D. Weightman (Harmondsworth: Penguin, 1973; repr. 1978), pp. 385–99; 'Race and History', *Structural Anthropology*, trans. by C. C. Jacobson and B. Grundfest Schoepf, 2 vols (Harmondsworth: Penguin, 1973; repr. 1986), 2, pp. 323–62. Obviously, ethnology did not come about exclusively because of the discovery of the 'New' World; there were also the Far East, Russia and Africa to be considered as exotic. But it is at least arguable that the science of ethnology originated as a response to European desires to exploit the Americas.

2 See J. W. Stoye, *English Travellers Abroad, 1604–67* (New Haven: Yale University Press, 1952); *All Before Them*, ed. by John McVeagh.

3 *Natives and Newcomers*, ed. by Brady and Gillespie, p. 17.

4 The current incumbent, George Cranmer, was killed on the same day that Moryson arrived in Dundalk.

5 It has often been reprinted; see *Ireland under Elizabeth and James 1*, ed. by H. Morley (London: Routledge & Kegan Paul, 1890), pp. 413–30; C. Maxwell, *Irish History from Contemporary Sources* (London: Allen & Unwin, 1923), pp. 316–8 et passim.

6 C. Lévi-Strauss, *The Raw and the Cooked: Introduction to a Science of Mythology*, trans. by J. and D. Weightman (London: Cape, 1970); 'The Cullinary Triangle', *New Society* 8 (1966), pp. 137–40.

7 Text from Fynes Moryson, *An Itinerary containing his Ten Yeers Travell through the Twelve Dominions*, 4 vols (Glasgow: MacLehose, 1907), vol. 4, pp. 196–203. Some of Moryson's uncollected writings are to be found in *Shakespeare's Europe*, ed. by C. Hughes; 'The Commonwealth of Ireland', in C. Litton-Falkiner, *Illustrations of Irish history and Topography, mainly of the Seventeenth Century* (London: Longman, 1904), pp. 310–25.

8 A common allegation. See *Calendar of State Papers for Ireland, 1598–9* ed. by E. G. Atkinson, (London: Eyre and Spottiswode, 1895), pp. 149, 206–7.

9 The Irish were often said to be descended from the Scythians, most famously in Edmund Spenser's *A View of the Present State of Ireland* (see above, p. 75).

10 After a love affair with a local girl, her brothers abducted Lithgow and cut off his ears; hence his nickname, 'lugless Willie'.

11 Both covered roughly the same areas, but Lithgow also went to Greece, Cyprus, the Middle East and rather more of North Africa.

12 Lithgow had lost the use of his left arm after his treatment in Malaga.

13 On Lithgow's life, see *D.N.B.* entry; Stoye, *English Travellers Abroad*, pp. 382–9; introduction to *The Total discourse of his Rare Adventures* (London: 1632; repr. Glasgow: MacLehose 1906). Text from this edition, pp. 373–4, 377–8.

14 William Brereton, *Travels in Holland, the United provinces, England, Scotland and Ireland: 1634–5*, ed. by E. Hawkins (London: Chetham Society, 1844). Text from pp. 132–5, 137, 144–5.
15 On Brereton's life, see Stoye, *English Travellers Abroad*, pp. 242–5; J. Morrill, *Cheshire, 1630–1660: County Government and Society during the 'English Revolution'* (Oxford: Clarendon Press, 1974), passim; *D.N.B.* entry.
16 Arthur, son of Henry Bagenal (see below, p. 88).
17 Teringham became joint commander in chief of Antrim after the 1641 rebellion; Fortesque pursued a dangerous career, oscillating between Royalists and Parliamentarians, before fleeing with (the future) Charles II to become a gentleman of the privy chamber after the Restoration.
18 A recurrent theme in subsequent travel writing. Along these routes the old Irish mile of 2240 yards vied with the statute mile of 1760 yards.

5. LAND AND LANDSCAPE

1 See, for example, N. P. Canny, 'The Permissive Frontier: social control in English settlements in Ireland and Virginia, 1550–1650' in *The Westward Enterprise*, pp. 17–44.
2 See J. W. Bennett, 'Britain among the Fortunate Isles', *Studies in Philology* 53 (1956), pp 114–40.
3 See R. A. Butlin, 'Land and people, c. 1600' in *A New History of Ireland, Vol. 3, Early Modern Ireland, 1534–1691*, ed. by T. W. Moody and others (Oxford: Clarendon Press, 1976), pp. 142–67; 142–5.
4 See Sean McBride's contribution to *Ireland After Britain*, ed. by M. Collins (London: Pluto, 1985), pp. 26–35.
5 W. B. Devereux, *Lives and Letters of the Devereux, Earls of Essex*, 2 vols (London: Murray, 1853), 2, pp. 73–5 et passim.
6 Text from 'A Treatise of Ireland' (c. 1600)' in *Tracts Relating to Ireland* (Dublin: Irish Archaeological Society, 1842), 2, pp. 1–90. The work is dedicated to Edward Carye, but I have not been able to find any trace of him.
7 According to the will of the lord.
8 'Jennett': a small, Spanish breed of horse.
9 Luke Gernon, 'A Discourse of Ireland, anno 1620', in C. Litton Falkiner, *Illustrations of Irish history and Topography*, pp. 345–62; 346.
10 *The Lismore Papers, Autobiographical Notes, remembrances and Diaries of Sir Richard Boyle, first and 'great' Earl of Cork*, ed. by A. B. Grosart, 1st series, 5 vols (privately printed, 1886), 2, p. 302; 3, p. 72; 4, p. 4, 83, 93–4 et passim.
11 James Ussher, 1581–1656; scholar, controversialist and Archbishop of Armagh, 1624–56.
12 Strictly speaking, a poem describing a woman's body, from the head downwards, much used by Renaissance poets.
13 For example, in Yeats's play *Cathleen Ni Houlihan* (1902).
14 For example, in Pearse's poems 'I am Ireland' and 'The Mother' (both 1916).

15 See the 'Punch' cartoon reproduced in L. Curtis, *Nothing But The Same Old Story: the roots of anti-Irish Racism* (London: G.L.C., 1984), p. 56.

16 See R Strong, *Portraits of Elizabeth 1* (Oxford: Clarendon Press, 1963).

17 See W. Raleigh, 'The Discovery of Guiana' in R. Hakluyt, *Voyages and Discoveries*, ed. by J. Beeching (Harmondsworth: Penguin, 1972; repr. 1985), pp. 386–410; 408. More generally, see C. Herr's provocative and absorbing, 'The Erotics of Irishness', *Critical Inquiry* 17 (1990), pp. 1–34 and E. B. Cullingford, ' "Thinking of her . . . as . . . Ireland": Yeats, Pearse And Heaney', *Textual Practice*, 4 (1990), pp. 1–21.

18 Text from Falkiner, *Illustrations*, pp. 349–50.

19 'Foliage on the trees'.

20 See W. S. Maltby, *The Black Legend: the development of anti-Spanish sentiment, 1558–1660* (Durham, N. C.: Duke University Press, 1971). On Payne's life, see *D.N.B.* entry.

21 Text from R. Payne, *A Briefe Description of Ireland*, ed. by A. Smith (Dublin: Irish Archaelogical Society, 1841), pp. 3–4, 6–7.

22 See Thomas Hariot's attack on those returning settlers who complained about conditions in Virginia colony in 'A Briefe and True Report of the new found land of Virginia' in R. Hakluyt, *The Principal Navigations, Voyages and Discoveries of the English Nation*, 12 vols. (Glasgow: MacLehose, 1904), 8, pp. 348–86; pp. 350–2.

23 See Quinn, *The Elizabethans and the Irish*, p. 35.

24 W. Camden, *Britannia*, ed. by E. Gibson (Newton Abbot: David and Charles, 1971); J. Speed, *The Theatre of great Britain, presenting an exact Geography of the Kingdomes of England, Scotland and Ireland* (London, 1611), S.T.C 23041.

25 On Gainsford's life, see *D.N.B.* entry.

26 T. Gainsford, *The Glory of England* (London, 1618), S.T.C. 11517, p. 144.

27 *A Treatise of Ireland* (Sept. 1644), Thomason Tract E. 1190 (1).

28 See the tract (1572) endorsed by Burghley, which suggested that extreme Protestants emigrate to Ireland, *Calendar of State Papers, Domestic Series, 1566–79, Addenda*, ed. by M. A. Everett Green (London: Longman, 1871), p. 439.

29 The comparison/contrast of Wales and Ireland was often made; see H. Sidney, 'Memoir addressed to Sir Francis Walsingham, 1583', ed. by J. Hoare, *Ulster Journal of Archaeology* 3 (1855), pp. 37–52, 91–109, 336–53; 5 (1857), pp. 299–323; 8 (1860), pp. 179–95; 8, (1860), p. 191ff.

30 *Lismore Papers*, 2nd series, Vol. 3, p. 4. For details on Boyle, see below pp. 120–1.

6. IRISH SOCIETY

1 See A. B. Ferguson, 'Circumstances and the sense of History in Tudor England: the coming of the Historical Revolution', *Medieval and*

Renaissance Studies 3 (1967), pp. 170–205. For a contemporary view of Elizabethan society, see Sir Thomas Smith, *De Republica Anglorum*, ed. by L. Alston (Shannon: Irish Academic Press, 1906; repr. 1972). For a recent historical overview, see K. Wrightson, *English Society, 1580–1680* (London: Hutchinson, 1982).

2 See Canny, *Elizabethan Conquest*, Ch. 6; P. Coughlan, ' "Cheap and Common Animals" '.

3 See T. Elyot, *The Boke Named the Gouvernour*, ed. by S. Lehmberg (London: Dent, 1966), p. 38; K. Bottigheimer, 'Kingdom and Colony: Ireland in the Westward Enterprise, 1536–1660' in *The Westward Enterprise*, pp. 45–64.

4 See A. Laurence, 'The Cradle to the Grave: English observations of Irish social customs in the Seventeenth Century', *The Seventeenth Century* 3, i (1988), pp. 63–84.

5 See T. Smith, *De Republica*, Bk. 3. The standard historical work is L. Stone, *The Family, Sex and Marriage in England, 1500–1800* (London: Weidenfeld and Nicolson, 1977).

6 See K. Nicholls, *Land, Law and Society in Sixteenth Century Ireland* (O'Donnell lecture, Cork, 1976); G. A. Hayes-McCoy, 'Gaelic Society in the Sixteenth Century', *Historical Studies* 4 (1963), pp. 45–61.

7 Quinn, *The Elizabethans and the Irish*, Ch. 5.

8 See, for example, Castiglione, *The Book of the Courtier*, trans. by G. Bull (Harmondsworth: Penguin, 1967; repr. 1980), pp. 134–6 et passim.

9 Text from Litton Falkiner, *Illustrations*, pp. 318–9.

10 See L. Jardine, ' "Mastering the Uncouth": Gabriel Harvey, Edmund Spenser and the English experience of Ireland', in *New Perspectives on Renaissance Thought: Essays in the History of Science, Education and Philosophy in Memory of Charles Schmitt*, ed. by J. Henry and H. Sutton (London: Duckworth, 1988), pp. 68–82.

11 As the fictionalised account of this visit, 'Colin Clout's Come home Againe' implies.

12 See A. C. Judson, *The Life of Spenser* (Baltimore: Johns Hopkins, 1945), Chs. 12, pp. 16–7. This is still the standard life.

13 *Lismore Papers*, 1st series, Vol. 1, introduction.

14 Assuming that it is by Spenser; see *Variorum*, Vol. 10, Appendix 4, pp. 533–8; C. Brady, 'Spenser's Irish Crisis': pp. 48–9.

15 See E. Arber, *A Manuscript of the Stationer's Register, 1554–1640* 5 vols. (privately printed, 1876), Vol. 3, p. 34. The *View* was first printed in James Ware, *Ancient Irish Histories*, 2 Vols. (Dublin, 1633; repr. 1809), Vol. 1, pp. 1–266.

16 See Select Bibliography, p. 298.

17 On the Scythians, see M. Hodgen, *Early Anthropology*, Chs. 1, 11; J. Bodin, *Method for the Easy Comprehension of History*, trans. by B. Reynolds (New York: Columbia University Press, 1945), Ch. 5.

18 P. Sidney, *An Apologie for Poetry*, ed. by G. Shepherd (Manchester: Manchester University Press, 1965; repr. 1973), p. 96.

19 Text from *A View of the Present State of Ireland,* ed. by W. L. Renwick (Oxford: Clarendon Press, 1935; repr. 1970), pp. 48–50.
20 'Booleys', or 'builes': summer encampments set up by societies practising transhumance. See Quinn, *Elizabethans and the Irish,* pp. 14–5, 53–4 et passim.
21 See *Variorum* note, Vol. 10, p. 327, for details.
22 See R. Bagwell, *Ireland under the Stuarts and during the Interregnum* 3 vols (London: Longmans, 1909), Vol. 1, pp, 112–5.
23 On Davies's life, see *D.N.B.* entry; H. Pawlisch, *Sir John Davies;* J. L. Sanderson, *Sir John Davies* (New York: Twayne, 1975).
24 Text from *A Discoverie of the True Causes why Ireland was never entirely subdued until his magesties raigne* (London, 1612), S.T.C. 6348.
25 Lord Deputy, 1571–5, 1588–94.
26 In other words, Vikings; see Ch. 1, note 14.
27 'In the chain of blood'.
28 'A tax or tribute formerly levied by Irish chiefs for the maintenance of soldiers' (*O.E.D.*).
29 'The voice of the oppressed'.
30 'The labour of a long year perishes, fruitless'.
31 'Did we for these barbarians plant and sow?
On these, on these, our happy fields bestow?
Good heaven, what dire effects from civil discord flow!'
Vergil, *Eclogue* 1, 11. 97–9, trans. by J. Dryden.
32 Text from *Itinerary,* Vol. 1, p. 330.
33 Mountjoy tells the same story; Mountjoy to Robert Cecil, *Calendar of State Papers for Ireland, 1600,* ed. by E. G. Atkinson (London: Eyre and Spottiswoode, 1903), pp. 337–9.
34 Text from Falkiner, *Illustrations,* pp. 356–9.
35 Text from *View,* ed. by Renwick, pp. 50–3.
36 On the etymology, see *Variorum,* Vol. 10, pp. 331–2.
37 Text from *The Irish Hubbub, or the English Hue and Cry* (London, 1617), S.T.C. 20989, pp. 2–3.
38 See R. Stanihurst, 'Chronicle of Ireland' in Holinshed, *Chronicles,* 6, pp. 1–94, Ch. 8.
39 Marginal Note: 'The old Proverbe. Its no more pity to see a woman weep, then to see a Goose goe barefoot'.
40 Text from *View,* ed. by Renwick, pp. 72–5.
41 See Sidney, *Apologie,* p. 142.

7. HUGH O'NEILL, SECOND EARL OF TYRONE (1540–1616)

1 See H. Morgan, 'The end of Gaelic Ulster'; Bagwell, *Ireland Under the Tudors,* Vol. 3; Ellis, *Tudor Ireland,* Ch. 9. See also Brian Friel's play, *Making History* (London: Faber, 1989).
2 See N. Canny, 'The Flight of the Earls (1607)'.
3 On Lee's life, see *D.N.B.* entry; text from 'A Brief Declaration of the

Government of Ireland' in J. Lodge, ed., *Desiderata Curiosa Hibernica* (Dublin, 1772), pp. 87–150; 113–4.

4 S.T.C. 11524. Text from p. 16.

5 J. Harington, *A New Discourse of a Stale Subject Called the Metamorphosis of Ajax*, ed. by E. S. Donno (New York: Columbia University Press, 1962).

6 G. B. Harrison, *The Life and Death of Robert Devereux, Earl of Essex* (London: Cassell, 1937), pp. 265–6.

7 See J. Harington, *A Short View of the State of Ireland* (1605) in *Anecdota Bodleiana*, ed. by W. D. Macray (Oxford, 1879).

8 Harington left for London on October 29, 1599.

9 Text from *The Letters and Epigrams of Sir John Harington*, ed. by N. E. McClure (Philadelphia: Pennsylvania University Press, 1930), pp. 76–9.

10 William Warren, previously used in negotiations with Tyrone. See his account of the incident; *Calendar of Carew Manuscripts, 1589–1600*, ed. by J. S. Brewer and W. Bullen (London: Longman, 1869), p. 341.

11 A relation of Sir John's, also in Ireland at the time.

12 See *Calendar of State Papers for Ireland, 1599–1600*, ed. by E. G. Atkinson (London: Eyre and Spottiswoode, 1899), pp. 58–9.

13 BL. Add. Ms. 34, 313, ff 84–121. Typescript generously lent by Dr. William Maley of Strathclyde University. Text from ff 88–9.

14 Internal evidence.

15 See below, pp. 115. Ben Jonson alleged that 'the Irish. . . robbed Spenser's goods and burnt his house and a little child new-born'; 'Conversations with William Drummond of Hawthornden', section 12, *Ben Jonson: The Oxford Authors*, ed. by I. Donaldson (Oxford: Oxford University Press, 1985), p. 599. This event is contemporary with the 'Supplication'.

16 Text from pp. 40–41.

8. WAR AND REBELLION

1 Sidney, 'Memoir', 3, p. 94.

2 See A. O'Rahilly, *The Massacre at Smerwick* (1580) (Cork: Cork University Press, 1938).

3 See A. Fletcher, *Tudor Rebellions* (London: Longman 1968; repr. 1983); P. Williams, *The Tudor Regime* (Oxford: Oxford University Press, 1979; repr. 1985), Chs. 7, 10.

4 See L. B. Campbell, *Tudor Conceptions of History and Tragedy in 'A Mirror for Magistrates'* (Berkeley: California University Press, 1936).

5 See F. L. Van Baumer, *Early Tudor Theory of Kingship*; D. M. Loades, *Politics and the Nation, 1450–1660: obedience, resistance and public order* (London: Fontana, 1973), Ch. 6.

6 P. Williams, *Tudor Regime*, pp. 273, 352.

7 See P. Hulme, *Colonial Encounters: Europe and the Native Caribbean, 1492–1797* (London: Methuen, 1986).

8 Text from Holinshed, *Chronicles*, 6, pp. 382–3. Richard Burke

(1527–82), second Earl of Clanrickard. The Earldom of Clanrickard was created in 1544. The incident described here took place in 1576. One of the sons, Ulick, became third Earl of Clanrickard when his father died.

9 His best poem is often said to be 'Shore's Wife' in *A Mirror for Magistrates*, ed. by L. B. Campbell (Cambridge: Cambridge University Press, 1938), pp. 373–87.

10 See R. Helgerson, *Self-Crowned Laureates: Spenser, Jonson, Milton and the Literary System* (Berkeley: California University Press, 1983); M. Brennan, *Literary Patronage in the English Renaissance: The Pembroke Family* (London: Routledge & Kegan Paul, 1988).

11 For example, *A Scourge for Rebels* (1584), S.T.C. 5255; *The Most True Reporte of James Fitz Morice Death* (1579), S.T.C. 5244.

12 T. Churchyard, *A Generall Rehersall of Warres (Churchyard's Choice)* (London, 1579), S.T.C. 5235.

13 On the fate of Smith's son, see Morgan, 'Sir Thomas Smith'.

14 Text from *View*, p. 104.

15 See Canny's argument; *Elizabethan Conquest*, and his reply to his critics in *From Reformation to Restoration*, Ch. 3.

16 On Shane's death, see C. Brady, 'The killing of Shane O'Neill: some new evidence'.

17 The object of Sir Philip Sidney's 'Discourse on Irish affairs' is a defence of his father's attempt to establish the use of this tax. See *Miscellaneous Prose of Philip Sidney*, ed. by K. Duncan-Jones and J. Van Dorsten (Oxford: Clarendon Press, 1973), pp. 3–12.

18 On Sidney's life, see *D.N.B.* entry.

19 From 'Memoir', 3, pp. 349–50.

20 Vaughan's Beauty?

21 'Chronicles of Ireland from 1594 to 1613', *English Historical Review* 22 (1907), pp. 104–30, 527–52 (text from here, pp. 129–30); 'A Chronicle of Lord Chichester's Government of Ireland; containing certain chroniculary discourses for the years of our lord 1612, 13, 14, and 15, collected and gathered by William Farmer Chiurgeon', in *Desiderata Curiosa Hibernica*, ed. by Lodge.

22 'Garron': a small inferior horse.

23 See A. Lord Grey de Wilton, *A Commentary of the Services and Charges of William Lord Grey de Wilton, k.g., by his son*, ed. by Sir Philip de Malpas Grey Egerton (London: Camden Society, 1847).

24 See O'Rahilly, *The Massacre of Smerwick*, R. McCabe, 'The Fate of Irena: Spenser and Political Violence', in *Spenser and Ireland*, pp. 109–25.

25 In addition to sources cited, see *D.N.B.* entry.

26 Text from *Calendar of State Papers for Ireland, 1586–8*, ed. by H. C. Hamilton, (London: Longman, 1867), preface, pp. lxix–lxxiii.

27 *View*, pp. 106, 107–9.

28 Edmund Ludlow, *The Memoirs of Edmund Ludlow . . . 1625–1672*, ed. by C. H. Firth 2 vols (Oxford: Clarendon Press, 1894), 1, pp. 326–8.

9. COLONISATION

1 K. R. Andrews, *Trade, Plunder and Settlement*, introduction et passim.
2 'A Discourse of the necessities and commoditie of planting English colonies upon the North parte of America' in Hakluyt, *Voyages*, vol. 6. pp. 42–78.
3 Hakluyt, *Voyages*, 6, pp. 52–4.
4 See T. W. Moody, *The Londonderry Plantation, 1609–41.*
5 Muriel Bradbrook, 'No room at the Top: Spenser's pursuit of fame' in *The Artist and Society in Shakespeare's England: The Collected Papers of Muriel Bradbrook*, vol. 1 (Hassocks: Harvester, 1982), pp. 19–36. On the problem of younger sons, see above, pp. 108.
6 See Andrews, *Trade, Plunder and Settlement*, pp. 31–8; J. Parker, *Books to Build an Empire* (Amsterdam: New Israel, 1965).
7 Jardine, 'Mastering the Uncouth'.
8 Unlike Spenser's *View*, it was never entered into the Stationer's Register. See above, p. 75.
9 See A. C. Spearing, *Medieval Dream Poetry* (Cambridge: Cambridge University Press, 1976). In the early modern period 'dream visions' were sometimes used for political purposes; see W. Holme, *The Fall and Evil Successe of Rebellion* (London, 1572), S.T.C. 13602.
10 Solon (fl. 600 B.C.), the Athenian statesman and poet, famous for his legal and constitutional reforms.
11 As references to Hugh O'Neill, Garrett Fitzgerald and others make clear.
12 See C. Brady, 'Spenser's Irish Crisis', pp. 23–4; B. Bradshaw, 'Robe and Sword in the Conquest of Ireland' in C. Cross *et al*, eds., *Law and Government under the Tudors: Essays Presented to Sir Geoffrey Elton on his Retirement* (Cambridge, Cambridge University Press, 1988), pp. 139–62.
13 See S. Anglo, 'A Machiavellian Solution to the Irish Problem: Richard Beacon's *Solon his Follie* (1594)' in *England and the Continental Renaissance: Essays in Honour of J. P. Trapp*, ed. by E. Chent and P. Mack (Woodbridge: Boydell, 1990), pp. 153–64.
14 On Beacon, see A. Judson, 'Spenser and the Munster officials', *Studies in Philology* 44 (1947), pp. 157–73; McCarthy-Murrogh, *Munster Plantation*, Ch. 2 et passim; *D.N.B.* entry.
15 *Solon his Follie* (Oxford, 1594), S.T.C. 1653, pp. 107–10.
16 On the Act of Absentees, see Ellis, *Tudor Ireland*, p. 131.
17 On the Acts of Attainder, see McCarthy-Murrogh, *Munster Plantation*, pp. 7, 12, 14–17.
18 Pericles (c. 495–429 B.C.), Athenian statesman, under whose guidance Athens adopted an imperialistic policy. Beacon's source is undoubtedly, Plutarch: see 'Life of Persius' in *Lives*, trans. by B. Perrin, 11 vols (New York: Putnam, 1914–26), 3, pp. 1–115; 35, 59.
19 An obvious pun.

20 See L. B. Campbell, *Parts Added to 'The Mirror for Magistrates by John Higgens and Thomas Blenerhasset* (Cambridge: Cambridge University Press, 1946).
21 See R. Strong, *Henry, Prince of Wales, and England's Lost Renaissance* (London: Thames and Hudson, 1986).
22 See Geoffrey of Monmouth, *History of the Kings of Britain*, pt. 1.
23 Text from *A Direction for the Plantation of Ulster* (London, 1610), S.T.C. 3130.
24 A key theme of Blenerhasset's verses in *The Mirror for Magistrates.*
25 'Fee-simple' means that the land is to be held by the occupier and his heirs for ever; 'Free-farm' provides for the same on condition of a perpetual rent.
26 'A linen fabric, originally called, from the province of Holland in the Netherlands' (*O.E.D.*).

10. THE REBELLION OF 1641

1 M. Perceval-Maxwell, 'The Ulster Rising of 1641 and the Depositions', *Irish Historical Studies* 21 (1978–9), pp. 144–67; P. Coughlan, ' "Cheap and Common Animals" '.
2 See J. A. Froude, *The English in Ireland in the Eighteenth Century*, 1, Ch. 2; T. FitzPatrick, *The Bloody Bridge*; M. Hickson, *Ireland in the Seventeenth Century.*
3 A. T. Q. Stewart, *The Narrow Ground*, pp. 48–52.
4 FitzPatrick, *Bloody Bridge*; Perceval-Maxwell, 'Ulster Rising'.
5 A. Clarke, *The Old English in Ireland*; C. Russell, 'The British background to the Irish Rebellion of 1641', pp. 166–82.
6 See Introduction above, p. 13; R. Foster, *Modern Ireland*, Ch. 4.
7 Foster, *Modern Ireland*, p. 86.
8 H. Jones, *A Remonstrance of Divers Remarkable Passages concerning the Church and Kingdom of Ireland* (London, 1642), Wing 943; Sir John Temple, *The Irish Rebellion or an History* (London, 1646), Wing 627. Both are by second generation English immigrants, so extracts have not been included here.
9 Cited in Foster, *Modern Ireland*, p. 86.
10 See, N. P. Canny, 'Edmund Spenser and the Development of an Anglo-Irish identity', *Yearbook of English Studies* 13 (1983), pp. 1–19.
11 Coughlan, "Cheap and Common Animals", p. 210.
12 Wing 2800. I have been unable to find any information about Thomas Morley.
13 Early on in the rebellion the Irish leaders tried to persuade their followers to leave the Scots alone and attack only the English, but to little effect; see Clarke, *Old English in Ireland*, Ch. 12.
14 Wing 2427.
15 See H. Kearney, *Strafford in Ireland, 1633–41: a study in absolutism* (Manchester: Manchester University Press, 1959), Ch. 10.
16 On Boyle's life, see N. P. Canny, *The Upstart Earl: a study of the*

social and mental world of Richard Boyle, first Earl of Cork, 1566–1642 (Cambridge: Cambridge University Press, 1982); *The Lismore Papers*, ed. by A. B. Grosart, 10 vols. (Privately printed, 1886–8).

17 Text from *Lismore Papers*, 2nd Series, vol. 5, pp. 100–1.

11. THE TRANSPLANTATION TO CONNAUGHT, 1655–9

1 K. Bottigheimer, *English Money and Irish Land*; T. C. Barnard, *Cromwellian Ireland: English government and reform in Ireland* (Oxford: Clarendon Press, 1975).

2 Foster, *Modern Ireland*, p. 107. See also N. P. Canny, 'Dominant Minorities: English settlers in Ireland and Virginia, 1550–1650' in *Minorities in History*, ed. by A. C. Hepburn (London: Arnold, 1978), pp. 51–69; 54–5, for the use of this metaphor in relation to Ireland more generally.

3 See Spenser, *View*, pp. 123–5; Moody, *Londonderry Plantation*; 'A Discourse on Ireland', above, pp. 50–2.

4 Bottigheimer, *English Money and Irish Land*, p. 134; Foster, *Modern Ireland*, p. 110.

5 Bottigheimer, *English Money and Irish Land*, pp. 127–8.

6 Eventually it was decided that only a substantial number of landlords should be transplanted. Who should go and who had gone was one of the serious points of disagreement between Gookin and Lawrence (see below).

7 Bottigheimer, *English Money and Irish Land*; 'The Restoration Land Settlement: a structural view', *Irish Historical Studies* 69 (1972), pp. 1–21.

8 Foster, *Modern Ireland*, p. 110.

9 Foster, *Modern Ireland*, pp. 112–6.

10 On Henry Cromwell's role in Ireland, see Barnard, *Cromwellian Ireland*, passim.

11 On Gookin's life, see *D.N.B.* entry; Barnard, 'Crises of Identity', pp. 58–71.

12 Wing 1273.

13 That is, the Wars of the Roses. The idea that the English in Ireland degenerated when military forces were recalled is common; see Davies, *Discovery*, pp. 90–2, Spenser, *View*, p. 14.

14 'In the seventeenth century, one of the dispossessed Irish, who became outlaws, subsisting by plundering and killing the English settlers and soldiers'(*O.E.D.*).

15 Henry Ireton (1611–51), soldier and politician who led the Parliamentary forces in Ireland, becoming Lord Deputy in 1650.

16 On Lawrence see *D.N.B.* entry; Barnard, 'Crises of Identity', pp. 58–68.

17 Wing 677.

18 On millenarianism in the seventeenth century, see N. Cohn, *The*

Pursuit of the Millenium (London: Paladin, 1957; repr. 1972), Appendix; M. Waltzer, *The Revolution of the Saints: a study in the origins of radical politics* (London: Weidenfeld and Nicolson, 1966).

19 Lawrence does acknowledge that there were a few Irish gentry 'that did really use their endeavours and interest to preserve English lives'.

20 Text from *The Memoirs of Edmund Ludlow*, 1, pp. 338–40.

12. PASSAGE AND TRAVEL

1 See *Travels of Sir William Brereton in Ireland*, 1635 in *Illustrations of Irish History and Topography*, ed. Falkiner, pp. 363–407. Falkiner selects the Irish passages out of Brereton's wider travels in Europe, and omits the rest.

2 See *The Journal of John Stevens Containing a Brief Account of the War in Ireland 1689–1691*, (Oxford: Clarendon Press, 1912), pp. 43–49.

3 [W. R. Chetwood], *A Tour through Ireland by Two English Gentlemen* (London: J. Roberts, 1748), pp. 115–17.

4 See *Arthur Young's Tour in Ireland in the years 1776, 1777 and 1778*, ed. by A. W. Hutton, 2 vols (London: George Bell & Sons, 1892), 1, p. 17.

5 Thomas De Quincey, *Autobiography from 1785 to 1803* in *Collected Writings*, ed. by David Masson (Edinburgh: Adam and Charles Black, 1889), 1, pp. 208–210.

6 G.F.G. M., *Journal of a Tour in Ireland* (London: Privately printed, 1836), pp. 1–2.

7 See chapter one of Thackeray's *The Irish Sketch Book of 1842* in *The Works of W. M. Thackeray* 22 vols, editor not named (London: Smith, Elder and Co., 1869), 14, pp. 1–5.

8 Sir John Carr, *The Stranger in Ireland: or A Tour in the Southern and Western Parts of that Country in the year 1805*, (London: Printed for Samuel F. Bradford, and others, 1806), p. 27.

9 Pococke mentions that his observations on the Giant's Causeway were published in *Philosophical Transactions* for 1753. See *Pococke's Tour in Ireland in 1752*, ed. by George T. Stokes (Dublin: Hodges, Figgis, and Co. and London: Simpkin, Marshall, Hamilton, Kent, and Co., 1891), p. 38.

10 See *Pococke's Tour in Ireland in 1752*, ed. by George T. Stokes (Dublin: Hodges, Figgis & Co. and London: Simpkin, Marshall, Hamilton, and Kent and Co., 1891), p. 66.

11 See the entry on Pococke in *D.N.B.*, and for further biographical details the essays in George Stokes, *Pococke's Tour in Ireland in 1752* (Dublin: Hodges, Figgis and Co, and London: Simpkin, Marshall, Hamilton, and Kent and Co, 1891); D. W. Kemp, *Tours in Scotland 1747, 1750, 1760 by Richard Pococke* (Edinburgh: Publications of the Scottish History Society 1, 1887); and J. J. Cartwright, *The Travels*

through England of Dr Richard Pococke (London: The Camden Society, 1888).

12 Richard Pococke, 'A Copy of Bp. Pococke's tour in South and South-West Ireland, in a series of twenty letters, in July-Sept., 1758', Bodleian Library, Oxford (Ms Top. Ireland d.1 (30, 722)); letter of 24 July, 1758.

13 See Adam Smith, *The Wealth of Nations*, ed. by Andrew Skinner (Harmondsworth: Penguin, 1970), Bk. 1, Ch. 4. See also Albert O. Hirschman, *The Passions and the Interests, Political Arguments for Capitalism before its Triumph* (Princeton: Princeton University Press, 1977).

14 *Arthur Young's Tour in Ireland*, ed. by A. W. Hutton (London: George Bell & Sons, 1892), 2, pp. 77–8, 79.

15 Anne Plumptre, *Narrative of a Residence in Ireland* (London: Printed for H. Colburn, 1817), pp. 119–120.

16 Thomas Carlyle, 'The Nigger Question' (1849), in *Thomas Carlyle. English and other Critical Essays* (London: Dent and New York: Dutton, 1905; repr. 1967), pp. 303–333.

17 Thomas Carlyle, *Reminiscences of My Irish Journey in 1849*, ed. by J. A. Froude (London: Sampson, Low, Marston, Searle, & Rivington, 1882), Preface, p. v.

18 See, for an example, Lady Chatterton's *Rambles in the South of Ireland*, 2 vols (London, 1839), particularly her sugary words on the charming Irish chambermaid (2, pp. 198–201).

19 Carlyle, T., *Reminiscences of My Irish Journey*, pp. 15–17.

20 Lord John Robert Manners, *Notes of an Irish Tour* (London: J. Ollivier, 1849), pp. 79–83.

21 Harriet Martineau, *Letters from Ireland* (London: J. Chapman, 1853), pp. 73–77.

22 See *The Oxford Dictionary of Proverbs*, compiled by William George Smith, with an Introduction by Janet E. Heseltine (Oxford: Clarendon Press, 1935, second edition revised throughout by Sir Paul Harvey, 1948; repr. 1966), p. 290.

13. THE SENSE OF DIFFERENCE

1 A. P. Curtis, *Apes and Angels: The Irishman in Victorian Caricature* (Newton Abbott: David and Charles, 1971).

2 J. Gough, *A Tour in Ireland in 1813 and 1814* (Dublin, 1817), p. 4.

3 *Cobbett in Ireland: A Warning to England*, ed. by Denis Knight (London: Lawrence and Wishart, 1984), p. 70.

4 See the passage from William Bennett above, pp. 156–7, objecting against analogy between Ireland and savage cultures — in Bennett's opinion, a cliché.

5 See Introduction, pp. 23–4 and chapter 15 below, p. 187.

6 *Arthur Young's Tour in Ireland*, ed. by A. W. Hutton, 2 vols (London: George Bell & Co., 1892), 2, pp. 100–101.

7 R. Bell, *A Description of the Condition and Manners as well as of the Moral and Political Character of the Peasantry of Ireland such as they were between the Years 1780 and 1790* (London: Printed for the Author, 1804), pp. 14–15.
8 R. C. Hoare, *Journal of a Tour in Ireland in 1806* (London: W. Miller, 1807), pp. xviii-xxi.
9 Footnote: 'Harris's Hibernica, 8vo, edit. p. 274.'
10 Anne Plumptre, *Narrative of a Residence in Ireland* (London: Printed for H. Colburn, 1817), pp. 324–7; pp. 344–6.
11 Properly 'côute-que-côute': cost what it may.
12 See above, chapter 15, note 22.
13 Bennett, W., *Narrative of a recent journey of six weeks in Ireland* (London: C. Gilpin, 1847), pp. 137–47.
14 *Victoria Travels. Journeys of Queen Victoria between 1830 and 1900, with Extracts from Her Journal*, ed. by David Duff (London: Frederick Muller, 1970), p. 13.
15 *Victoria Travels*, pp. 120–22.

14. FROM WAR TO UNION

1 Arthur Capel, *Letters Written . . . in the Year 1675* (London, 1770), pp. 321–3.
2 Samuel Mullenaux, *A Journal of the Three Months Royal Campain of His Majesty in Ireland* (London, 1690), pp. 12–13. Mullenaux also includes a journal of the Limerick siege.
3 John Stevens, *The Journal of John Stevens Containing a Brief Account of the War in Ireland 1689–1691*, ed. by Rev. R. H. Murray (Oxford: Clarendon Press, 1912), pp. 119–130.
4 Claude Lévi Strauss, 'The Quest for Power' in *Tristes Tropiques*, pp. 42–52.
5 For a comparison between Petty's work and earlier Irish map-making see Rev. P. J. McLaughlin, 'Surveys of Ireland in the seventeenth century', *The Irish Ecclesiastical Record* 73 (1950), pp. 129–39.
6 Petty, Sir W., *The Political Anatomy of Ireland*, ed. by John O'Donovan (Shannon: Irish University Press, 1970), pp. 25–9.
7 John Stevens, *The Journal of John Stevens Containing a Brief Account of the War in Ireland 1689–1691*, ed. by Rev. R. H. Murray, (Oxford: Clarendon Press, 1912).
8 Text from *The Journal of John Stevens*, ed. by Rev. R. H. Murray, pp. 166–183.
9 For information on Story's life see the *D.N.B.*
10 George Story, *An Impartial History of the Wars of Ireland* (London: Printed for R. Chiswell, 1693), pp. 151–3.
11 See *The Journal of the Rev. John Wesley. A. M.*, ed. by Nehemiah Curnock, 8 vols (London: Culley, 1909–16), 5, pp. 507–9. Text taken from this source.
12 See *D.N.B.* article on De Quincey (5, 839–40).
13 Thomas De Quincey, *Autobiography from 1785 to 1803* in *Collected*

Writings, ed. by David Masson, 14 vols (Edinburgh: Adam and Charles Black, 1889), 1, pp. 217–23.

14 The king wants it: let it be done as it is wished.

15 Sons of the earth.

16 Thomas Reid, *Travels in Ireland, in the year 1822* (London: Printed for Longman, Hurst, Rees, Orme, and Brown, 1823), pp. 162–3. The extract that follows is taken from this edition.

17 Thomas Reid, *Travels in Ireland*, p. 335.

18 Thomas Reid, *Travels in Ireland*, pp. 187–92.

19 Hoemoptysis or haemoptysis: spitting of blood.

20 *Cobbett in Ireland: A Warning to England*, ed. by Denis Knight (London: Lawrence and Wishart, 1984), pp. 59–61.

21 That is, philosopher. Cobbett attacks the new science of political economy, whose major practitioners included David Hume, Adam Smith, Sir James Steuart and James Mill — all Scotsmen.

22 Sir John Forbes, *Memorandums made in Ireland in the Autumn of 1852*, 2 vols (London: Smith, Elder and Co., 1853), 1, pp. 201–05.

15. IRISH LIFE AND CUSTOMS

1 See *The Collected Works of Oliver Goldsmith*, ed. by Arthur Friedman 5 vols (Oxford: Clarendon Press, 1966), 3, p. 84.

2 See Thomas Campbell's *Life of Mrs Siddons* (London: Effingham Wilson, 1834), 1, pp. 261–8, recalling the magnificent entertainments at Shane's Castle.

3 John Dunton, *Teague Land, or A Merry Ramble to the Wild Irish* edited by E. MacLysaght (Blackrock: Irish Academic Press, 1982), p. 51.

4 R. Pococke, 'A Copy of Bp. Pococke's tour in South and South-West Ireland, in a series of twenty letters, in July-Sept., 1758', Bodleian Library, Oxford: Ms Top. Ireland d. 1 (30, 722); letter of 24 July, 1758. See 'Pococke's tour of south and south-west Ireland in 1758', ed. by Padraig O Maidin, *Journal of the Cork Archaeological and Historical Society*, 63 (1958), pp. 73–94, 64 (1959), pp. 35–56, 65 (1960), pp. 130–141. The reference to drink is to be found in vol. 63, p. 82; see also Pococke's reference to a typical 'Milesian feast' in vol. 64, p. 37.

5 Henry D. Inglis, *A Journey throughout Ireland, during the spring, summer, and autumn of 1834*, 2 vols (London: Whittaker & Co., 1835), 2, pp. 194–5.

6 J. Gough, *A Tour in Ireland in 1813 and 1814* (Dublin, 1817), p. 68.

7 William Petty, *The Political Anatomy of Ireland*, introduced by John O'Donovan (Shannon: Irish University Press, 1970), pp. 25–9, 93–102.

8 James Farewell, *The Irish Hudibras or Fingallian Prince* (London, 1689), pp. 32–6.

9 Marginal note: 'Songs'.

10 Marginal note: 'A Game at Cards'.

11 Laurence Echard, *An Exact Description of Ireland* (London, 1691). Echard was a compiler who wrote about Ireland because, as he says, it 'is a Place of very Considerable Action' (unpaged). There seems to be no evidence that he visited Ireland personally.

12 John Dunton, *Teague Land, or a Merry Ramble to the Wild Irish*, ed. by E. MacLysaght (Dublin: Irish Academic Press, 1982), pp. 41–3.

13 It seems to be mostly English, but 'ribin a ruin' could mean 'little ribbon, my darling', and 'ribin muirnin' means 'little ribbon, my dear'; alternatively 'ribin a ruin' could mean 'little dear thing' and 'ribin muirnin' could mean 'little darling'. 'Bairneach' means 'limpet'.

14 *Pococke's Tour in Ireland in 1752*, ed. by George T. Stokes (Dublin: Hodges, Figgis, and Co. and London: Simpkin, Marshall, Hamilton, Kent, and Co., 1891), p. 60.

15 *Arthur Young's Tour in Ireland in the years 1776, 1777 and 1778*, 2 vols, ed. by A. W. Hutton (London: George Bell & Sons, 1892), 1, pp. 446–7.

16 *Arthur Young's Tour*, ed. by A. W. Hutton, 2, pp. 43–5.

17 Cobbett was against tea and in favour of beer, as was Coleridge, on the grounds that whereas tea was a deleterious beverage, traditional English beer was nutritious and wholesome. See *The Collected Works of Samuel Taylor Coleridge*, ed. by Lewis Patton and Peter Mann. Bollingen Series number 25. (Princeton: Routledge and Kegan Paul), 1, p. 223.

18 Philip Luckombe, *A Tour through Ireland in 1779* (London: T. Lowndes, 1780), pp. 102–3.

19 Miled was the legendary leader of the Scythian invaders of Ireland. He sought Inis Fail (the land of destiny) and after sojouring in Spain eventually arrived in Ireland.

20 John Edwin, *The Eccentricities of John Edwin, Comedian*, 2 vols (London, 1791), pp. 61–5.

21 Thomas De Quincey, *Autobiography from 1785 to 1803* in *Collected Writings* edited by David Masson, 14 vols (Edinburgh: Adam and Charles Black, 1889), 1, pp. 224–6.

22 Gaius Suetonius Tranquillus (fl. 117–38), Roman biographer and historian.

23 On the O'Donnells, and on James Butler, Duke of Ormonde, see J. C. Beckett, *The Making of Modern Ireland 1603–1923* Chs. 3–4 et passim. On the O'Neills see above, chapter 7. On Ulick de Burgh, fifth Earl of Clanricarde (1604–1657), and on Murrough O'Brien, first Earl of Inchiquin (1614–1674), see *D.N.B.*

24 'Green Erin's knight and Europe's wandering star', is how Byron referred to Carr in a cancelled section of canto two of *Childe Harold*; for further details see *D.N.B.* Maria Edgeworth reviewed Carr's *The Stranger in Ireland* in the *Edinburgh Review* for 1807.

25 Sir John Carr, *The Stranger in Ireland: or A Tour in the Southern and Western Parts of that Country in the year 1805* (London: Printed for Samuel F. Bradford, and others, 1806) Carr, p. 187.

26 Carr, pp. 329, 406.

27 Richard Cumberland, *Memoirs written by himself* 2 vols (London: Lackington, Allen, 1807), pp. 212–14, 206–210.

28 Ulic, fifth Earl of Clanricarde, fortified Portumna castle when war broke out in 1641, and made the castle his main residence after 1650. Supporters of James II garrisoned the castle when Revolutionary war broke out but surrendered to the Williamite general Eppinger. The castle was probably built during the Elizabethan era. It was destroyed by fire in 1826.

29 Robert Bell, *A Description of the Condition and Manners as well as of the Moral and Political Character of the Peasantry of Ireland* (London: Printed for the Author, 1804), pp. 18–21.

30 John Gough, *A Tour in Ireland in 1813 and 1814; with an Appendix, Written in 1816, on another Visit to that Island. By an Englishman* (Dublin, 1817), pp. 239–41.

31 Maria Edgeworth (1768–1849) published *The Absentee* in 1812, and *Ennui* (one of the *Tales of Fashionable Life*) in 1809.

32 See James Johnson, *A Tour in Ireland; with Meditations and Reflections* (London, 1844), p. 1.

33 Henry D. Inglis, *A Journey throughout Ireland*, 2 vols (London: Whittaker & Co., 1835), 2, pp. 46–52.

34 Gerald Griffin (1803–40) published his novel *The Collegians* in 1829. It became the basis of Dion Boucicault's popular play *The Colleen Bawn* (1860). See John Cronin, *Gerald Griffin (1803–1840): a critical biography* (Cambridge: Cambridge University Press, 1978).

16. IRISH TOWNS

1 See T. Reid, *Travels in Ireland, in the year 1822* (London: Printed for Longman, Hurst, Rees, Orme, and Brown, 1823), particularly pp. 163–7; and James Glassford, *Notes on three tours in Ireland in 1824 and 1826* (Bristol: W. Strong and J. Chilcott, 1832). Glassford, a commissioner into the state of education in Ireland, describes a typical good school at Lisnaskea on pages 96–9 and a typical bad school at Youghall on pages 170–3.

2 See Thackeray, *Irish Sketch Book*, p. 146. Thackeray repeats the theme of scrappy and impoverished markets in provincial Irish towns when he describes Carlow (p. 35) and Cork (p. 73).

3 Richard Cumberland, *Memoirs written by himself*, 2 vols (London: Lackington, Allen, 1807), 1, pp. 172–6.

4 George Stone (1708?–1764), archbishop of Armagh from 1747. See *D.N.B.* for an account of the political struggles to which Cumberland refers in the text.

5 George Faulkner (1699?–1775), Dublin bookseller. For some details on Faulkner's brushes with the political authorities (including being reprimanded on his knees in 1733 by the Irish House of Lords), see *D.N.B.*

6 See W. Jackson Bate, *Samuel Johnson* (London: Chatto and Windus, 1978), pp. 428–9 for details.

7 Richard Bentley (1708–1782), *The Wishes, or Harlequin's Mouth opened* (Drury Lane, 1761), was acted for three nights. It ridiculed the notion of the unities and the moralising chorus in Greek drama; for example, Bentley's chorus, instead of escaping to safety, laments the human condition when informed that a lunatic is about to set fire to a nearby powder keg. The play was never printed.

8 John Gough, *A Tour in Ireland in 1813 and 1814; with an Appendix, Written in 1816, on another visit to that Island. By an Englishman* (Dublin, 1817), pp. 160–165.

9 Anne Plumptre, *Narrative of a Residence in Ireland during the Summer of 1814, and that of 1815* (London, 1817), pp. 95–7.

10 Downhill Castle on the northern coast of County Derry was built by Frederick Augustus Hervey, Bishop of Derry and Earl of Bristol from 1775 onwards. He employed a number of architects on the project, including John Soane, Robert Adam, possibly James Wyatt, and the Cork architect Michael Shanahan. Shanahan also built the Mussenden Temple on the cliff edge, which still exists. The mansion was gutted by fire in 1851, then restored in 1876, and is once more a ruin.

11 For illustrations of eighteenth-century and modern bleaching grounds and a general discussion of the Belfast linen and cotton industry, see Conrad Gill, *The Rise of the Irish Linen Industry* (Oxford: Clarendon Press, 1925; repr., 1964), pp. 227, 232–3, 238–9 and passim.

12 Henry Inglis, *A Journey throughout Ireland, during the spring, summer, and autumn of 1834*, 2 vols (London: Whittaker & Co., 1835), 2, pp. 151–6).

13 See *D.N.B.* (London, 1898) 56, 96. For a critical assessment of Thackeray's attitude to Ireland see B. G. MacCarthy, 'Thackeray in Ireland', *Studies. An Irish Quarterly Review* 40 (1951), pp. 55–68. More sympathetic is J. S. C[rone], 'Thackeray and Ireland', in *Irish Book Lover* 3 (1912), pp. 3–4.

14 Thackeray, W. M., *The Irish Sketch Book of 1842* in *The Works of W. M. Thackeray*, 22 vols, editor not named (London: Smith, Elder and Co., 1869), 14, pp. 72–9.

15 On jingles see Constantia Maxwell, *County and Town in Ireland under the Georges* (Dundalk: Dundalgan Press, 1949), p. 293 and Ch. 6 passim.

16 John Wilson Croker (1780–1857) was a lawyer, politician and essayist. Thomas Crofton Croker (1798–1854) was an Irish antiquary and littérateur. Probably the reference is to the latter.

17 Charles Lever (1806–1872) trained as a medical doctor but achieved widespread poularity as a novelist of military and Irish life. Samuel Lover (1797–1868), Irish painter and novelist, was the founder of the influential *Dublin University Magazine*. William Harrison Ainsworth (1805–1882) was a popular novelist who specialised in historical and so-called 'Newgate' fiction.

18 Gil Blas is the hero of a picaresque romance published in 1715–35 by the French novelist and dramatist Alain René Le Sage (1668–1747).

19 In 1826 Lord Brougham, Thomas Campbell (the poet) and others set up the University of London in Gower Street in protest at the denominational tests which excluded dissenters and others from Oxford and Cambridge. Theology was not included in its syllabus. In response the Archbishop of Canterbury, the Prime Minister Wellington, Peel and others spearheaded a movement to set up King's College, London in the Strand on a strictly Anglican basis. See Sir James Mountford, *British Universities* (London: Oxford University Press, 1966), pp. 14–17.

20 On the background to Thackeray's educational remarks here see John Lawson & Harold Silver, *A Social History of Education in England* (London: Methuen & Co., 1973), pp. 267–313; and Brian Simon, *Studies in the History of Education 1780–1870* (London: Lawrence and Wishart, 1960), Chs. 5, 6, 7.

17. PICTURESQUE AND ROMANTIC IRELAND

1 G. Holmes, *Sketches of Some of the Southern Counties of Ireland during a Tour in the Autumn, 1797* (London, 1801), pp. v-vii.

2 See Thackeray on Westport in *The Irish Sketch Book of 1842* in *The Works of W. M. Thackeray* 14, pp. 1–344, 214.

3 See for example J. S. Dodd, *The Traveller's Director through Ireland* (Dublin, 1801). This work includes a digest of information on distances, the ownership of buildings, history of places, trade and manufacture, and political importance. D. A. Beaufort's *Memoir of a Map of Ireland* (London: W. Faden, 1792) is an earlier example. William Wilson claims that his *Post-Chaise Companion* (London, 1784) is the first of its kind attempted in Ireland (preface). But G. Taylor and A. Skinner's *Maps of the Roads of Ireland Surveyed 1777* (London and Dublin, 1778) was a foundation work. However the genre goes back long before this. More than a century earlier, John Woodhouse had published a similar *Guide for Strangers in the Kingdom of Ireland* (London, 1647).

4 See an early account of the Killarney 'season' in J. Bush, *Hibernia Curiosa* (London: Printed for W. Flexney, 1764), pp. 113–15. William Ockenden, *Letters describing the Lake of Killarney* (Dublin, 1770) allies Killarney with classical landscapes, nymphs and the poetry of Milton in his first letter, second series.

5 Lord John Robert Manners, *Notes of an Irish Tour* (London: J. Ollivier, 1849), p. 136.

6 See Mary Louise Pratt, 'Scratches on the Face of the Country'.

7 John Dunton, *Teague Land, or a Merry Ramble to the Wild Irish*, ed. by E. MacLysaght (Dublin: Irish Academic Press, 1982), pp. 17–27.

8 *Arthur Young's Tour in Ireland*, ed. by A. W. Hutton, 2 vols (London: George Bell & Co., 1892), 1, pp. 348–49, 367–59.

9 Presumably Lake Guitane.

10 P. Luckombe, *A Tour through Ireland in 1779* (London: T. Lowndes, 1780), p. 113.

11 G. Holmes, *Sketches of Some of the Southern Counties of Ireland during a Tour in the Autumn, 1797* (London, 1801), pp. 104–8.

12 Footnote in text: 'These small horses are the properest to travel through this county with; a man must entirely abandon himself to their guidance, which will answer much better than if one should strive to manage and direct their footsteps. They are naturally sure-footed, and though small, an excellent breed; they climb over the most rugged rocks, and both ascend and descend the steepest precipices with great facility and safety; are so light, as to skim over waving bogs and morasses without sinking, and where heavier would certainly perish. They are strong and durable, easily supported, and not ill-shaped; so hardy as to stand abroad all winter, and will brouze upon heath, furze, and other shrubs; add to this, their gait is ambling, which is extremely easy. SMITH'S HISTORY OF KERRY, P 109'

Sir James Ware observes, that these kind of horses were formerly called austuriones; as having been originally imported from the Austurias in Spain, into this kingdom, where they are now become rare, except in these mountainous parts; a large breed of cattle being more useful in the plain champain parts of it.'

13 Thomas Carlyle, *Reminiscences of My Irish Journey in 1849* (London: Sampson Low, Marston, Searle, & Rivington, 1882), pp. 139–40.

14 An Oxonian, *A Little Tour in Ireland. . . . With Illustrations by John Leech* (London: Bradbury and Evans, 1859), pp. 38–40.

15 Queen Victoria, *Her letters from the journal*, p. 120. The text is taken from this edition.

16 Queen Victoria, *Her letters from the journal*, pp. 313–15.

18. POVERTY AND FAMINE

1 Philip Luckombe, *A Tour through Ireland in 1779* (London: T. Lowndes, 1780), p. 182.

2 *A Month's Tour in North Wales, Dublin, and its Environs* (London, 1781), pp. 70–94.

3 Patricia Hodgart, *A Preface to Shelley* (London: and New York: Longman, 1985), pp. 49ff.

4 W. Bennett, *Narrative of a recent journey of six weeks in Ireland* (London: C. Gilpin, 1847), pp. 5–6; T. Reid, *Travels in Ireland, in the year 1822* (London: Printed for Longman, Hurst, Rees, Orme, and Brown, 1823), pp. 236–8.

5 J. Gough, *A Tour in Ireland in 1813 and 1814* (Dublin, 1817), p. 251.

6 Anne Plumptre, *Narrative of a Residence in Ireland during the Summer of 1814, and that of 1815* (London: Printed for H. Colburn, 1817), p. 339.

7 John Wesley, *Journal*, ed. by Nehemiah Curnock, 8 vols (London: Culley, 1909–16), 5, p. 131.

8 Richard Twiss, *A Tour in Ireland in 1775* (London, 1776), pp. 29–30.

9 Rev. J. Hall, *A Tour through Ireland in 1807*, 2 vols (London, 1813, pp. 199–202.
10 Quoted in *D.N.B.* article on Thomas Cromwell (5, p. 202).
11 T. K. Cromwell, *Excursions through Ireland. Province of Leinster*, 3 vols (London: Printed for Longman, Hurst, Rees, Orme, and Brown, 1818[–22], 2, pp. 176–7.
12 T. Reid, *Travels in Ireland*, pp. 201–05.
13 William Cobbett, *Cobbett in Ireland: A Warning to England*, pp. 122–24.
14 Henry D. Inglis, *A Journey throughout Ireland*, 1, pp. 301–4.
15 Bennett, W., *Narrative of a recent journey of six weeks in Ireland* (London: C. Gilpin, 1847), pp. 25–9.

SELECT BIBLIOGRAPHY: A GUIDE TO FURTHER READING

1 Primary sources

Ancient Irish Histories, ed. by J. Ware (Dublin, 1633).

Bale, J., *The Vocacyon of Bishop Johan Bale to the Bishopricke of Ossorie in Irelande* (1553); repr. in *Harleian Miscellany* (1813), pp. 437–64.

Barrow, John, *A tour Round Ireland, through the sea-coast counties, in the autumn of 1835* (London, 1836).

Beacon, R., *Solon His Follie* (Oxford, 1594).

Bell, R., *A Description of the Condition and Manners as well as of the Moral and Political Character of the Peasantry of Ireland such as they were between the Years 1780 and 1790* (London: Printed for the Author, 1804).

Bennett, William, *Narrative of a recent journey of six weeks in Ireland* (London: C. Gilpin, 1847).

Blenerhasset, T., *A Direction for the Plantation of Ulster* (London, 1610).

Boate, G., *Ireland's Natural History* (London, 1652).

Bowden, C. T., *A Tour through Ireland in 1790* (Dublin: Printed by W. Corbet, 1791).

Bush, J., *Hibernia Curiosa. A letter from a Gentleman in Dublin to his Friend at Dover in Kent . . . Giving a general view of the manners, customs, dispositions, &c. of the inhabitants of Ireland* (London: Printed for W. Flexney, [1768]). Campion, E., *Two Bokes of the History of Ireland*, ed. by A. F. Vossen (Assen, Netherlands: Van Gorcum, 1963).

Carlyle, Thomas, *Reminiscences of My Irish Journey in 1849* (London: Sampson, Low, Marston, Searle, & Rivington, 1882).

Carr, Sir John, *The Stranger in Ireland: or A Tour in the Southern and Western Parts of that Country in the year 1805* (Philadelphia: Printed for Samuel F. Bradford, and others, 1806).

Chatterton, Lady Henrietta, *Rambles in the South of Ireland during the year 1838*, 2 vols (London: Saunders and Otley, 1839).

[Chetwood, W. R.?], *A Tour through Ireland by Two English Gentlemen* (London: J. Roberts, 1748).

'A Discourse between two Councillors of State, the one of England, and the other of Ireland (1642)', ed. by A. Clarke, *Analecta Hibernica* 26 (1976), pp. 159–76.

Cobbett, William, *Cobbett in Ireland: A Warning to England*, ed. by Denis Knight (London: Lawrence and Wishart, 1984).

Cromwell, T. K., *Excursions through Ireland. Province of Leinster*, 3 vols (London: Printed for Longman, Hurst, Rees, Orme, and Brown, 1818[–221]).

Cumberland, Richard, *Memoirs written by himself*, 2 vols (London: Lackington, Allen, 1807).

Davies, J., *A Discoverie of the True Causes why Irelande was never entirely subdued* (London, 1612).

De Quincey, Thomas, *Autobiography from 1785 to 1803* in *Collected Writings*, 1, ed. by David Masson (Edinburgh: Adam and Charles Black, 1889).

Derricke, J. *The Image of Irelande, with a discourse of woodkerne* (London, 1581).

The Description of Ireland and the state thereof, as it is at this present in anno 1598, ed. by E. Hogan (Dublin, 1878).

Dineley, Thomas,'Extracts from the Journal of Thomas Dinely, giving some Account of his Visit to Ireland in the Reign of Charles II', ed. by E. P. Shirley, *Journal of the Royal Society of Antiquaries of Ireland*, 4 (1856–57), pp. 143–6, 170–88; 5 (1858), pp. 22–32, 55–6; 7 (1862–3), pp. 38–52, 103–9, 320–38; 8 (1864–6), pp. 40–48, 268–90, 425–46; 9 (1867), pp. 73–91, 176–202; ed. by F. E. Ball, 43 (1913), pp. 275–309.

Dodd, J. S., *The Travellers' Director through Ireland* (Dublin, 1801).

Dunton, John, *Teague Land, or A Merry Ramble to the Wild Irish*, ed. by E. MacLysaght (Dublin: Irish Academic Press, 1982).

Edmundson, William, *A Journal of the Life . . . of William Edmundson*, second edition (London: Printed and sold by M. Hinde, 1774).

Edwin, John, *The Eccentricities of John Edwin, Comedian*, 2 vols (London, 1791).

Elstob, Mark, *A Trip to Kilkenny from Durham by Way of Whitehaven and Dublin in the Year MDCCLXXVI* (Stockton: R. Christopher, 1778).

Falkiner, C. L., *Illustrations of Irish history and topography* (London, New York, etc.: Longman, Green & Co., 1904).

Farewell, J., *The Irish Hudibras or Fingallian Prince* (London, 1689).

Gerald of Wales (Giraldus Cambrensis), *The History and*

Topography of Ireland, trans. by J. J. O'Meara (Harmondsworth: Penguin, and Mountrath, Portlaois: Dolmen, 1982).

Glassford, James, *Notes on three tours in Ireland in 1824 and 1826* (Bristol: W. Strong and J. Chilcott, 1832).

Gookin, V., *The Great Case of Transplantation in Ireland Discussed* (London, 1655).

Gough, John, *A Tour in Ireland in 1813 and 1814; with an Appendix, Written in 1816, on another Visit to that Island. By an Englishman* (Dublin, 1817).

Holinshed, R., *Cronicles of England, Scotland and Ireland*, ed. by V. Snow, 6 vols (New York: A.M.S. Press, 1976), vol 6.

Holmes, G., *Sketches of Some of the Southern Counties of Ireland during a Tour in the Autumn, 1797* (London, 1801).

Inglis, Henry D., *A Journey throughout Ireland, during the spring, summer, and autumn of 1834*, 2 vols (London: Whittaker & Co., 1835).

Jones, H., *A Remonstrance of Divers Remarkable Passages concerning the Church and Kingdom of Ireland* (London, 1642).

Laurence, R., *The Interest of England in the Irish Transplantation Stated* (London, 1655).

Luckombe, P., *A Tour through Ireland in 1779* (London: T. Lowndes, 1780).

Martineau, Harriet, *Letters from Ireland* (London: J. Chapman, 1853).

Marx, K. and F. Engels, *Marx Engels, Ireland and the Irish Question*, ed. by R. Dixon (Moscow: Progress Publishers, 1971; repr. 1978).

Moryson, F., *An Itinerary of his travels* (Glasgow: MacLehose, 1907).

Payne, R., *A Brief Description of Ireland*, ed. by A. Smith (Dublin: Irish Archaeological Society, 1841).

Perrot, J., *The Chronicles of Ireland*, ed. by H. Wood (Dublin, Irish Manuscripts Commission, 1933).

Petty, Sir W., *The History of the Survey of Ireland Commonly Called the Down Survey*, ed. by T. A. Larcom (Dublin, 1851).

Petty, Sir W., *The Political Anatomy of Ireland*, ed. by John O'Donovan (Shannon: Irish University Press, 1970).

Plumptre, Anne, *Narrative of a Residence in Ireland during the Summer of 1814, and that of 1815* (London: Printed for H. Colburn, 1817).

Pococke, R., *Pococke's tour in Ireland in 1752*, ed. by George T. Stokes (Dublin: Hodges, Figgis, and Co. and London: Simpkin, Marshall, Hamilton, Kent, and Co., 1891).

Quinn, D. B., ' "A Discourse on Ireland (circa 1599)": a sidelight on English colonial policy', *Proceedings of the Royal Irish Academy* 47, Sec. C, 3 (1942), pp. 151–66.

Reid, T., *Travels in Ireland, in the year 1822* (London: Printed for Longman, Hurst, Rees, Orme, and Brown, 1823).

Rich, B., *A New History of Ireland* (London, 1610).

Shakespeare's Europe, ed. by C. Hughes (London: Sherrat and Hughes, 1903).

Spenser, E., *A View of the Present State of Ireland*, ed. by W. L. Renwick (Oxford: Clarendon Press, 1970).

Stevens, John, *The Journal of John Stevens Containing a Brief Account of the War in Ireland 1689–1691* edited by Rev. R. H. Murray (Oxford: Clarendon Press, 1912).

Story, George Warter, *An Impartial History* (London: Printed for R. Chiswell, 1693).

Story, George Warter, *A Continuation of an Impartial History* (London, 1691).

Temple, J., *The Irish rebellion, or an History* (London, 1646).

Thackeray, William Makepeace, *The Irish Sketch Book of 1842* in *The Works of W. M. Thackeray*, editor not named (London: Smith, Elder & Co., 1869), 14, 1–344.

Victoria Travels, ed. by David Duff (London: Frederick Muller, 1970).

Wesley, John, *The Journal of the Rev. John Wesley. A. M.*, ed. by Nehemiah Curnock, 8 vols (London: Culley, 1909–16).

Young, Arthur, *Arthur Young's Tour in Ireland in the years 1776, 1777 and 1778*, ed. by A. W. Hutton, 2 vols (London: George Bell & Sons and New York, 1892).

2 **Secondary sources**

Anderson, John P., *The Book of British Topography. A Classified Catalogue of the Topographical Works in the Library of the British Museum relating to Great Britain and Ireland* (London: W. Satchell and Co., 1881; republished with a new introduction by Jack Simmons, East Ardsley: E. P. Publishing, 1976).

Anglo, S., 'A Machiavellian Solution to the Irish Problem: Richard Beacon's *Solon His Follie* (1594)', in *England and the Continental Renaissance: Essays in Honour of J. B. Trapp*, ed. by E. Cheney and P. Mack (Woodbridge: Boydell, 1990), pp. 153–64.

Avery, B., 'Mapping the Irish Other: Spenser's *A View of the Present State of Ireland*', *English Literary History*, 57 (1990), pp. 263–79.

Barnard, T. C., 'Crises of Identity among Irish Protestants, 1641–85', *Past and Present*, 127 (1990), pp. 39–83.

Barnard, T. C., *Cromwellian Ireland: English Government and Reform in Ireland, 1649–1660* (Oxford: Clarendon Press, 1975).

Bartlett, R., *Gerald of Wales, 1146–1223* (Oxford: Clarendon Press, 1982).

Beckett, J. C., *A Short History of Ireland* (London, New York: Hutchinson's University Library, 1952).

Bottigheimer, K., *English Money and Irish Land: the Adventurers in the Cromwellian Settlement of Ireland* (Oxford: Clarendon Press, 1971).

Bradshaw, B., *The Irish Constitutional Revolution of the Sixteenth Century* (Cambridge: Cambridge University Press, 1979).

Brady, C., 'Spenser's Irish Crisis: Humanism and Experience in the 1590s', *Past and Present*, 111 (1986), pp. 17–49.

Canny, N. P., *The Elizabethan Conquest of Ireland: a pattern established, 1565–76* (Hassocks: Harvester, 1976).

Canny, N. P., 'Identity formation in Ireland: the emergence of the Anglo-Irish', in *Colonial Identity in the Atlantic World, 1500–1800*, ed. by N. P. Canny and A. Pagden (Princeton: Princeton University Press, 1987), pp. 159–212.

Clarke, A., *The Old English in Ireland, 1625–42* (London: McGibbon and Kee, 1966).

Cox, E. G., *A Reference Guide to the Literature of Travel*, 3 vols (Seattle: University of Washington, 1935).

Coughlan, P., ' "Cheap and Common Animals": the English anatomy of Ireland in the Seventeenth Century', in *Literature and the English Civl War*, ed. by T. Healy and J. Sawday (Cambridge: Cambridge University Press, 1990), pp. 205–23.

Crone, J. S., 'Thackeray in Ireland', *Irish Book Lover*, 3 (1912), pp. 3–5.

Curtis, L. P., Jr., *Apes and Angels: The Irishman in Victorian Caricature* (Newton Abbott: David and Charles, 1971).

Dawson, J., 'Two Kingdoms or Three? Ireland in Anglo-Scottish Relations in the Middle of the Sixteenth Century', in *Scotland and England, 1286–1815*, ed. by R. A. Mason (Edinburgh: John Donald, 1987), pp. 113–138.

Eager, Alan R., *A Guide to Irish Bibliographical Material* (London: The Library Association, 1980).

Edwards, P., *Threshold of a Nation* (Cambridge: Cambridge University Press, 1979).

Edwards, R. D. and Mary O'Dowd, *Sources for Early Modern Irish History, 1534–1641* (Cambridge: Cambridge University Press, 1985).

Ellis, S. G., *Tudor Ireland, Crown, Community and the Conflict of Cultures, 1470–1603* (London: Longman, 1985).

Ellison, C. C., *The Hopeful Traveller. The Life and Times of Daniel Augustus Beaufort LL.D. 1739–1821* (Kilkenny: Boethius Press, 1987).

Fackler, H. V., 'Wordsworth in Ireland 1829: a survey of his tour', *Eire-Ireland*, 6 (1971), pp. 53–64.

Foster, R., *Modern Ireland, 1600–1972* (Harmondsworth: Penguin, 1988).

Frantz, Ray. W., *The English Traveller and the Movement of Ideas, 1660–1732* (Lincoln, NE: The University, 1934).

Freeman, T. W., 'John Wesley in Ireland', *Irish Geography*, 8 (1975), pp. 86–96.

Gillingham, J., 'Images of Ireland, 1170–1600: the origins of English imperialism', *History Today*, 37 (1987), pp. 16–22.

Grenfell, M., *Elizabethan Ireland* (London: Longman, 1971).

Haire, R., *Wesley's One-and-Twenty Visits to Ireland. A Short Survey* (London: Epworth Press, 1947).

Harrington, John P., *The English Traveller in Ireland: Accounts of Ireland and the Irish through five centuries* (Dublin: Wolfhound Press, 1991).

Hayes-McCoy, G. A., 'Sir Walter Scott and Ireland', *Historical Studies*, 10 (1976), pp. 91–108.

Hayman, J. G., 'Notions on National Characters in the Eighteenth Century', *Huntington Library Quarterly*, 35 (1971–72), pp. 1–17.

Heaney, H., *Tourists in Ireland, 1800–1850; evaluative bibliography.* Typescript submitted to Library Association for Fellowship, 1968.

Hechter, M., *Internal Colonialism; the Celtic fringe in British national development, 1536–1966* (London: University of California Press, 1974).

Hodgart, Margaret, *A Preface to Shelley* (London and New York: Longman, 1985).

Hodgen, Margaret T., *Early Anthropology in the Sixteenth and Seventeenth Centuries* (Philadelphia: University of Pennsylvania Press, 1971).

Laurence, A., 'The Cradle to the Grave: English Observations of Irish Social Customs in the Seventeenth Century', *The Seventeenth Century*, 3 (1988), pp. 63–84.

Leersen, J. Th., *Mere Irish and Fior-Ghael: studies in the idea of Irish nationality, its development and literary expression prior to the nineteenth century* (Amsterdam: Benjamens, 1986).

Lennon, C., *Richard Stanihurst, Dubliner* (Dublin: Irish Academic Press, 1981).

Lévi-Strauss, Claude, 'An End to Journeying', in *Tristes Tropiques*, trans. by John and Doreen Weightman (Harmondsworth: Penguin, 1976; repr. Peregrine, 1984).

MacCarthy, B. G., 'Thackeray in Ireland', in *Studies. An Irish Quarterly Review*, 40 (1951), pp. 55–68.

MacCarthy-Morrogh, M., *The Munster Plantation: English Migration to Southern Ireland, 1583–1641* (Oxford: Clarendon Press, 1986).

Marjarum, E. Wayne, 'Wordsworth's View of the State of Ireland', *P.M.L.A.*, 55 (1940), pp. 608–11.

Marshall, P. J. and Glyndwr Williams, *The Great Map of Mankind* (London: Dent, 1982).

Maxwell, C., *Country and Town in Ireland under Georges* (London: Harrap, 1940; repr. Dundalk: Dundalgan Press, 1949).

Maxwell, C., *Irish History from Contemporary Sources, 1509–1610* (London: Allen and Unwin, 1923).

Maxwell, C., *The Stranger in Ireland* (London: Cape, 1954).

McKerrow, R. E., 'The Legend of Bonnie Prince Charlie's travels in Donegal in 1746', *Eire-Ireland*, 10 (1975), pp. 48–61.

McLaughlin, Patrick, 'Surveys of Ireland in the seventeenth century', *Irish Ecclesiastical Record*, 73 (1950), pp. 129–39.

Moody, T. W., *The Londonderry Plantation, 1609–41: the City of London and the Plantation of Ulster* (Belfast: William Mullen, 1939).

Natives and Newcomers: the making of Irish Colonial Society, 1534–1641, ed. by C. Brady and R. Gillespie (Dublin: Irish Academic Press, 1986).

A New History of Ireland, Vol. 3, Early Modern Ireland, 1534–1691, ed. by T. W. Moody, F. X. Martin and F. J. Byrne (Oxford: Clarendon Press, 1976).

O'Cillin, S. P., *Travellers in Co. Clare, 1459–1843* (Galway, 1977).

O'Donoghue, D. J., *Sir Walter Scott's Tour in Ireland in 1825* (Glasgow: Gowans and Gray, 1905).

O Muirithe, Diarmaid, *A Seat Behind the Coachman. Travellers in Ireland 1800–1900* (Dublin: Gill and Macmillan, 1972).

Page, E., *Michael Hechter's Internal Colonial thesis* (Glasgow: University of Strathclyde Centre for the Study of Public Policy, 1977).

Panter, G. W., *Bibliography of Irish tours, with remarks on those before 1700*. Paper read before Bibliographical Society of Ireland, 29 January 1923.

Parkes, G. B., 'The Turn to the Romantic in Travel Literature of the Eighteenth Century', *Modern Language Quarterly*, 25 (1964), pp. 22–33.

Pawlisch, H., *Sir John Davies and the Conquest of Ireland: a study in legal imperialism* (Cambridge: Cambridge University Press, 1985).

Quinn, D. B., *The Elizabethans and the Irish* (Ithaca: Cornell University Press, 1966).

'Race', Writing, and Difference, ed. by Henry Gates, Jr., (Chicago and London: University of Chicago Press, 1985; repr. 1986).

Spenser and Ireland: an interdisciplinary perspective, ed. by P. Coughlan (Cork: Cork University Press, 1989).

Spivak, G., *In Other Worlds* (London: Methuen, 1987).

Stafford, Barbara Maria, 'Toward Romantic Landscape Perception: Illustrated Travel Accounts and the Rise of "Singularity" as an Aesthetic Category', *Art Quarterly*, ns 1 (1977), pp. 89–124.

INDEX

Addison, Joseph, on life in Ireland, 19, 20
'Address to the Lord Deputy' (1621), on Irish woodland, 72
Adrian IV, grants Ireland to Henry II, 9
Africa, travellers' accounts ignore inhabitants, 239; inhabitants compared with Irish, 239
America, civil war displaces Ireland in English minds, 22; descriptions of, 36
Amerindians, compared to Irish, 73
Anderson, Benedict, on nationhood, 3, 5
Andrews, K. R., on colonisation, 108
Anglo-Irish literature, its nature discussed, 3, 4
Anglo-Irish, the 7, 14; Engels describes, 24; travellers visit, 135; travellers praise their houses, 160; splendour of, 251; changing attitudes to, 149; precariousness of their power, 187; Oliver Goldsmith on, 187; Maria Edgeworth on, 187
Antrim, admired by travellers, 19
Armagh, South, judged barbaric, 6
Arnold, Matthew, not a visitor to Ireland, 1
Ascendancy, the, 19
Athlone, falls to William III, 18

Bagenal, Mabel, marries Hugh O'Neill, 88
Bagenal, Henry, on Ireland, 63
Bale, John, 30; his *Image of Both Churches*, 30; his *Scriptorum Illustrium Majoris Brytanniae Catalogus*, 30; Irish connections, 30; his *Vocacyon of Johan Bale to the Bishopperycke of Ossorie*, 30; his plays, 31; compared with Giraldus, 30–1; advocates Irish language, 30–1; quoted on popery in Ireland, 31–5; compared with Barnaby Rich, 45
Ballycastle, Orange meeting at, 5
Barnard, T. C., on Protestant divisions, 14; on class, 14
Barrow, John, on African travel, 6
Beacon, Richard, 108; his Irish career, 108–9; his *Solon his Follie* discussed, 109; quoted from on ways of subduing Ireland, 109–11; influence of Machiavelli on, 109
Beckett, J. C., on English unawareness of Ireland, 21–22
Belfast, its growing prosperity, 219; Anne Plumptre describes, 225–7; Queen's College, 21
Bell, Robert, on racial stereotypes, 148; criticises British accounts of Ireland, 150–1; quoted on, 151–2; his *Description* quoted on Irish wedding, wake, pattern 210–13
Belmullet, William Bennett quoted on Famine conditions, 263–5
Bennett, William, his Irish travels, 155–6; his mixed assessment, 156; his *Narrative* quoted on Irish character, 156–7; describes wandering Irish poor, 251–2; on Famine in Belmullet, 263–5
Bennington, Geoffrey, on national identity, 3
Berkeley, Bishop, 18
BhaBha, Homi, on John Locke and colonial writing, 6
Bishop, P., on the I.R.A., 4
Blenerhasset, Thomas, his Irish career, 111; his involvement in Plantation, 111; his *Direction for the Planting of Ulster* discussed, 111–12; quoted from, 112–14
Boate, Gerard, not an Irish traveller, 1
Boethius, Hector, 25
Bottigheimer, Karl, on transplantation, 123
Boyle, Elizabeth, marries Edmund Spenser, 75
Boyle, Richard, his Irish wealth, 63;

friendship with Luke Gernon, 65; connected with Edmund Spenser, 75; his Irish career discussed, 120–1; connections with Earl of Essex, 120; his feud with Wentworth, 120–1; his correspondence quoted on 1641 rebellion, 121–2; his relations with Vincent Gookin, 124
Boyne, Battle of the, 160
Brady, C., on Ireland's anomalous position, 53
Brereton, Sir William, his travels, 60; compared with Fynes Moryson and William Lithgow, 60; admires Dublin, 60; is critical of Ireland, 60; his *Travels* quoted on Newry, Dundalk, Drogheda, Dublin, 60–2; his journey from Scotland to Ireland, 134
Britishness, concept of, 1
Britons, ancient, on Roman civilisers of, 73
Bruce, S., on Ulster Protestants, 5
Buchanan, 25
Burghley, Lord, praises William Herbert, 48
Byron, and Alpine travel, 135; satirises Sir John Carr on Ireland, 205
Caesar, Julius, 25, 53
Campion, Edmund, on educating Irish, 37; *History of Ireland*, 37–8; in Dublin, 37–8; flees to Douai, 38; compared with William Herbert, 48; his *Histories* quoted on Irish character, 38–9
Canada, self-determination in, 22
Capel, Arthur, on military conflict, 160
Carew, Sir Peter, his claims in Ireland, 43; employs John Hooker, 43
Carlyle, Thomas, compares Ireland with Dahomey, 15; linked with Cobbett, 23; his *Reminiscences*, 23; attacks sentimentality, 23; his involvement with Ireland, 141; illness while travelling, 141; his *Reminiscences* quoted on Irish characteristics, 141–2; on Killarney, 246
Carr, Sir John, his travels, 204–5; his writing satirised by Edward Dubois, 205; by Byron, 205; his view of Grattan, 21; his impressions of Dublin, 135; his *The Stranger in Ireland* quoted on Irish speech, 205–6
Castlereagh, Lord, Cobbett on, 23
Charles I, his Irish policy criticised, 70
Churchyard, Thomas, his writings discussed, 45, 97; influenced by *The Mirror for Magistrates*, 97; his Irish career, 98–9; associated with Lord Grey, 99; with Sir William Drury, 99; his *Choise* quoted on Irish conflict, 99
Civil Survey, The, 17
Claddagh, the, described in 1859, 247
Clanricarde, Earl of, defeated by Edmund Ludlow, 105
Clare, transplantation to, 123
Claredon, Earl of, on Irish economics, 17
Claude Lorraine, and Irish scenery, 244
Clew Bay, admired by travellers, 239
Clonmel, its market described by William Cobbett, 258–61
Cobbett, William, 180–1; visits Ireland, 22; attacks exploitation, 22, 161; attacks absenteeism, 181; on Kilkenny horse fair, 23; linked with Carlyle, 23; with Swift, 23; Karl Marx on, 23; rebuts conventional attitudes to Ireland, 149; writes on Ireland with England in mind, 181; quoted on a Mendicity dinner, 181–3; on Clonmel market, 258–61
Colonisation, 108
Comical Pilgrim, The, satire, 19
Compleat Irish Traveller, The, 20
Confederates, the, 13
Connaught, transplantation to, discussed, 123–4
Cook, John, on transplantation, 123
Cork, its shabby appearance, 134; Queen's College, 21
Coughlan, Patricia, on English view of 'inhuman' Irish, 115
Crane Bag, The, on Ireland's 'fifth' province, 4
Crimea, displaces Ireland in English politics, 22
Croker, J. W., writings excluded, 1
Cromwell, Henry, supported by Vincent Gookin, 124
Cromwell, Oliver, invades Ireland, 13; massacres at Drogheda, Wexford, 13; his transplantation policy, 161
Cromwell, Thomas, his Irish travels, 254; criticised by Thomas Carlyle, 254; his *Excursions* quoted on Irish cabins, 255
Cruthain, its genealogy, 5
Cumberland, Richard, his Irish experiences,

206; becomes connection with Lord Halifax, 206; is replaced, 206; criticises Anglo-Irish, 149; his *Memoirs* quoted on Irish manners, 206–10; on Dublin society, 219–21
Curtis, L. P., on English hostility to Ireland, 148; on Irish stereotypes, 23

Davies, Sir John, *Discovery of the True Causes*, 12; travels to Scottish court, 76; his Irish career, 76–7; recommends suppression of Irish Catholics, 76; his Irish travels, 77; becomes Solicitor-General, 76; becomes Lord chancellor, 77; is opposed by Sir John Everard, 77; his *Discovery* discussed, 77; quoted on Irish customs, 77–80
De Quincey, Thomas, his visits to Ireland, 134, 173–4; witnesses Union, 21; his view of it, 21, 161; criticises Anglo-Irish, 149, 151; his *Autobiography* quoted on Union, 174–7; on Anglo-Irish manners, 203–4
Defoe, Daniel, work attributed to, 19; did not visit Ireland, 15
Denny, Edward, attacks William Herbert, 48
Derricke, John, on wild Irish, 37; praises Sidney, 41; his *The Image of Irelande*, 41; describes native Irish, 41–3
Deschamps, Eustache, 53
Desmond, Earl of, opposed by Hugh O'Neill, 88
Devereux, Walter, Earl of Essex, and plantation, 11; helped by Hugh O'Neill, 88
Dineley, Thomas, his travels in Ireland, 17
Diodorus Sicilius, 25
'Discourse of Ireland, A', (*c*1599), advocates extermination of Irish race; 37; aim discussed, 49–50; contrasted with William Herbert, 50; describes Ireland's resources, 50–2, 63; quoted on Irish woodland, 72
Dodds, J., 20–1; *Traveller's Director through Ireland*, 20–1
Donegal, fashionable among tourists, 22
'Down Survey', the, 161
Drogheda, Sir William Brereton describes, 61–2
Drury, Sir William, commander of Thomas Churchyard, 99
Dublin, admired by travellers, 19, 219; Campion in, 37; Sir William Brereton on, 60; Sir John Carr on, 135; compared with Naples, 135; Sir John Gough on markets, 221–4
Dubois, Edward, satirises Sir John Carr on Ireland, 205
Dundalk, Sir William Brereton describes, 61
Dunluce Castle, admired by travellers, 239
Dunton, John, 194; his travels in Ireland, 17, 194; on prejudice, 187; corrects Lawrence Echard on Ireland, 194; his 'The Dublin Scuffle', 194; *Teague Land* quoted on Irish pastimes, 195–6; on west Connaught, 239–41
Dymmok, John; possibly accompanied Earl of Essex, 63–4; his 'Treatise' quoted on Irish geography, 64–5

Eachard, Lawrence, not an Irish traveller, 1
Earls, Flight of the, 45
Edgeworth, Maria, *Castle Rackrent*, 187; on Anglo-Irish, 187
Edwin, John, 200–1; his removal to Dublin, 200; *The Eccentricities* quoted on Irish funeral celebrations, 201–3
Elizabeth, Queen, and English rule in Ireland, 10; her policy criticised, 70
Ellis, Stephen, on Henrican politics, 8
Engels, Friedrich, on Irish ruins, 23–4; on homelessness, 24; criticises Anglo-Irish, 148
English, 'Old' versus 'New' in Ireland, 7, 13, 14, 37; 'degenerate', 9; Giraldus on, 25ff.
Enniskillen, praised by Henry Inglis, 227–9
Essex, Earl of, his expedition to Ireland, 45; accompanied by Barnaby Rich, 45
Everard, Sir John, opposes Sir John Davies for Lord Chancellorship, 77

Farewell, James, 17; on his burlesque satire, 192; *The Irish Hudibras* quoted on an Irish funeral, 192–4; on the Irish cabin, 252
Farmer, William, friend of Sir Arthur Chichester, 101; his Irish career, 101;

his 'Chronicles of Ireland' quoted on Irish famine conditions, 101–2
Finglas, his *Breviat* and English plans for Ireland, 11
Forbes, John, his Irish travels, 183–4; on emigration, 184; his *Memorandums* quoted on emigration, 184–6
Foster, R. F., on Anglo-Irish differentiation, 18
Fox, George, on rough Ireland, 219

Gainsford, Thomas, *History of Tyrone*, 17; on Ireland, 63; his Irish career, 69; served with Mountjoy, 69; bought land in Ulster, 69; his 'Description of Ireland' quoted on Irish landscape, 69–70; his *History of . . . Tirone* quoted on O'Neill's submission, 90–1
Galway, falls to William III, 18; Queen's College, 21; region a desert, 24
Gerard, William, on Irish speech, 37; Irish career, 39; 'Notes of his Report', 39; his recommendations for Ireland, 39–41
Gernon, Luke, approves of Irishman, 17; his Irish career, 65; friendship with Richard Boyle, 65; acquainted with Archbishop Ussher, 65; his description of Ireland, 65; his 'Discourse' quoted on Irish geography, 66–7; on Irish dress, 81–3
Giant's Causeway, becomes fashionable, 22, 239; approached by sea, 135; Richard Pococke examines, 135; Lord John Manners unimpressed by, 239
Gillespie, R., on Ireland's anomalous position, 53
Giraldus Cambrensis, Welsh historian, 7, 8; on cultural change, 25; Bale compared with, 30–1; on Irish people, 36; on the Welsh, 36; his *Expugnatio* quoted on the English claim to Ireland, 25–6; his *Topography* quoted on the Irish character, 26–8; on Irish ignorance, 29; on newcomers in Ireland, 29
Gladstone, W. E., and 'pacification', 12
Glassford, James, his Irish travel, 219
Goldsmith, Oliver, on English in Ireland, 187
Gookin, Vincent, his clash with Richard Lawrence, 15, 124, 127; compared with Spenser, 124; his Irish career discussed, 124; his relations with Richard Boyle, 124; his support for Henry Cromwell, 124; his collaboration with Sir William Petty, 124; his *Great Case of Transplantation*, 17; quoted from on English interests in Ireland, 124–7
Gough, John, his servant's prejudices, 148; on the Irish howl, 188; his Irish travels, 213; his criticism of Priscilla Wakefield, Richard Twiss, 213; his *Tour in Ireland* quoted on Irish speech, 213–15; on Dublin markets, 221–4; on English insults 252
Grand Tour, the, 53, 239
Grattan, Henry, on Irish freedom, 18
Greece, self-determination in, 22
Grey de Wilton, Lord Arthus, defends massacre at Smerwick, 97; commander of Thomas Churchyard, 99; his Irish career, 102; his reputation, 102; opposed by Turlough O'Neill, 102; disagreements with Queen Elizabeth, 102; his letters quoted on the Smerwick massacre, 102–4

Hall, J., his *Tour* quoted on Irish cabins, 253–4
Harington, Sir John, his writings, 91; accompanies Essex to Ireland, 91; his Irish career, 91; visits Hugh O'Neill, 91
Harvey, Gabriel, on ancient colonisation, 108
Hayton, D. W., on Irish stereotypes, 16
Henry II, his authority over Ireland, 9
Henry VIII, self-declared king, 8; death, 10
Herbert, William, on Irish language, 37; his Irish career, 47–8; praised by Burghley and Walsingham, 48; by Meyler Magrath, 48; criticised by Edward Denny, 48; compared with Campion, 48; his *Description* quoted on the Irish nation, 48–9
Herodotus, 53
Hidden Ireland, 18
Hoare, Richard Colt, his Irish travels, 152; on paucity of information on Ireland, 152; his *Journal* quoted on Irish conditions, 152–4

Hodgart, Patricia, on Shelley and Keats in Ireland, 22, 251
Hodgen, Margaret, on travellers' reports, 16
Holinshed, Irish section added to *Chronicles* by Hooker, 7
Holmes, George, his Irish travels, 244–5; his *Sketches* quoted on wild scenery, 245–6
Holmes, George, on English ignorance of Ireland, 238
Hooker, John, translates Giraldus, 7, 43; adds to Holinshed, 7, 43; on Irish character, 37; his career in Ireland, 43; connections with Sir Peter Carew, 43; writings on Irish affairs, 43–4; 97; influenced by *The Mirror for Magistrates*, 97; his 'The sons of Clanricard' quoted on Irish rebels, 97–8

Indian mutiny, displaces Ireland in English politics, 22
Inglis, Henry, 215; his Irish travels, 215; on mashed potatoes, 187; his *Journey* quoted on Ennis lawsuits, 215–18; on attractive Enniskillen, 227–9; on poor Limerick, 261–3
Italy, displaces Ireland in English politics, 22
James I, his Irish policy criticised, 70
James II, overturns Protestant confiscations, 18
Jardine, Lisa, on Gabriel Harvey, 108
Johnson, Samuel, on Irish travel, 19
Johnston, E. M., on eighteenth-century Ireland, 19
Jones, General, defeats Ormond, 13
Jones, Henry, his writings excluded, 1; on 1641 rebellion, 115; used as propaganda, 123
Jones, Thomas, Bishop of Meath, 45; attacks Barnaby Rich, 45
Jonson, Ben, 192; his *On the Famous Voyage*, 192
Juvenal, his influence on anti-Irish satire, 17

Keating, Geoffrey, critic of Giraldus, 7
Keats, John, his visit to Ireland, 22; shocked by poverty, 251; his visit cut short, 22
Kerry, admired by travellers, 19; becomes fashionable, 22
Kilkenny, centre of 1641 rebellion, 115; Bishop Henry Jones on, 115; Sir John Temple on, 115; horse fair described by Cobbett, 23; Richard Lawrence at, 127
Killarney, admired by travellers, 19; becomes fashionable, 22, 239; Thomas Carlyle describes, 246; Queen Victoria describes, 248–50
King's County, its naming, 10
Kingsborough, Lord, his connection with Arthur Young, 137
Kinsale, battle of, establishes English rule in Ireland, 10
Knight, Denis, on Cobbett in Ireland, 22
Kötzebue, translated by Anne Plumptre, 139
Kupperman, K. O., on settlers' attitudes to American Indians, 2
Laudabiliter, the, 9; its influence in 1641, 15
Lawrence, Richard, and Calvanist theory, 15; on transplantation, 124; his clash with Vincent Gookin, 124, 127, 124; his Irish career discussed, 127–8; his connection with Cromwell, 127; negotiates at Kilkenny, 127; his conflict with Sir William Petty, 127–8; his *The Interest of England* quoted on transplantation, 128–31
Lee, Sir Thomas, accompanies Walter Devereux to Ireland, 89; his Irish career, 89; negotiates with Hugh O'Neill, 89; defends him, 89; his 'Brief Declaration' quoted in defence of the Earl of Tyrone, 89–90
Leix, renamed King's County, 10
Lévi-Strauss, Claude, 54; *The Raw and the Cooked*, 54; on cultural fabrication, 161
Limerick, falls to William III, 18; its poverty described by Henry Inglis, 261–3
Lithgow, William, his travels, 58; compared with Fynes Moryson, 58; compared with William Lithgow, 60; his involvement with the Spanish Inquisition, 58; with the Spanish ambassador, 58; his Irish experiences, 59; his criticism of Irish women, 59; his *Total Discourse* quoted on Irish customs, 59–60

Liuneach, Turlough, opposed by Hugh O'Neill, 88
Locke, John, *Two Treatises* as colonial text, 6
Loftus, Adam, Lord Chancellor, 45; attacks Barnaby Rich, 45
Lough Erne, admired by travellers, 239
Luckombe, Philip, his Irish travels, 199; his praise of Dublin, 199; his *Tour* quoted on an old proprietor, 199–200; on Ireland and Poussin, Claude Lorraine, 244; on Irish poverty, 251
Ludlow, Edmund regicide, 105; his associations with Cromwell, 105; his Irish career, 105; defeats Lord Muskerry, 105; defeats Earl of Clanricarde, 105; his *Memoirs* quoted on military conflict, 105–7; on the allocation of land, 131–3; discussed, 131

MacDonnells, enemies of Shane O'Neill, 11
Machiavelli, influence on Richard Beacon, 109
Magrath, Meyler, praises William Herbert on Ireland, 48
Mallie, E., on the I.R.A., 4
Mandeville, travel writer, 53
Manners, Lord John, his Irish travel described, 142; his view of Dunluce Castle, 142, 239; of the Giant's Causeway, 239; his *Notes* quoted on the south west islands, 142–4
Martineau, Harriet, her Irish travels, 144; her *Letters* quoted on rail travel, 144–7; her sympathy, 161
Marvell, Andrew, his *Ode to Cromwell*, 13
Marx, Karl, on Cobbett, 23
Mary, Queen, and Catholic reinstatement in Ireland, 10
Maxwell, Constantia, on landlord and tenant clashes in Ireland, 18
McClure, James, on anti-Republican war, 5
McCormack, W. J., on Irish Utopianism, 4
McDonagh, Thomas, on Anglo-Irish literature, 4
Mirror for Magistrates, The, its influence on John Hooker, 97; on Thomas Churchyard, 97
Molyneux, William, 18
Morley, Thomas, his *Remonstrance* quoted on Irish atrocities, 116–18
Moryson, Fynes, 54; his travels, 54; compared with William Lithgow, 59; with Sir William Brereton, 60; his connection with Lord Mountjoy, 54; his opposition to Tyrone, 54; his criticism of Turks, 54; of the 'meere' Irish, 54; his *Itinerary* quoted on Irish habits, 54–8; on Irish childbirth, 73–4; on Irish agriculture, 80–1; as Henrican propagandist, 97
Mountjoy, his defeat of Hugh O'Neill, 11, 88; his connection with Barnaby Rich, 45; with Fynes Moryson, 54
Mullenaux, Samuel, on Protestant fears, 160
Munster, praised by English writers, 63
Muskerry, Lord, defeated by Edmund Ludlow, 105

Napoleon, threat to Ireland, 21; closure of Continent, 22, 238
Newry, Sir William Brereton describes, 60
Nine Years' War, its origin, 88

O'Brien, Conor Cruise, on tribalism, 5
O'Connell, Daniel, and Catholic Emancipation, 21; and Irish people, 21; Carlyle scoffs at, 21
O'Neill, Hugh, Earl of Tyrone, his associations with Sir Philip Sidney, 88; his life, 88–9; his connection with Walter Devereux, 88; his opposition to the Earl of Desmond, 88; his marriage to Mabel Bagenal, 88; his appeal to Spain, 88; his military campaign, 88–9; his defeat by Mountjoy, 10, 88; his death in Italy, 89; his significance, 89; his dealings with Sir Thomas Lee, 89; Lee quoted on, 89–90; Thomas Gainsford quoted on, 90–91, 95–6; Sir John Harington visits, 91; is quoted on, 91–3
O'Neill, Shane, and English opposition, 11; his defeat by Sir Henry Sidney, 100; his death, 88
Offaly, renamed Queen's County, 10
Ordnance Survey, its establishment, 23
Ormond, Duke of, leader of royalist forces, 13; his surrender, 13

'Oxonian, An', his *Little Tour* quoted on the Claddagh, 247

Parnell, and Home Rule, 21
Payne, Robert, his career in Ireland, 67; his favourable account of Ireland, 67; his *Brief Description* quoted on Ireland's advantages, 67–9
Peckham, George, on colonisation, 108; on discovery of Newfoundland, 108
Petty, Sir William, his collaboration with Vincent Gookin, 124; his conflict with Sir Richard Lawrence, 127–8; his anthropological theories, 16; his Irish work, 16; his *Scale of Creatures*, 16; his analysis of Ireland, 17; his plans for re-allocation, 161; his Irish career, 161; his criticism of Benjamin Worsley, 161; his 'Down Survey', 161; influenced by Strafford, 162; his advocacy of ethnic union, 162; his *Political Anatomy* quoted on subduing the Irish, 162–5; on the Irish character, 188–92
Pigot, J., 21; his *Commercial Directory of Ireland*, 21
Plantation, in Elizabethan period, 11; in Jacobean period, 11; in Munster, 12; its varied aims, 12; in Ulster, 108
Plumptre, Anne, 21; her visit to Rathlin Island, 135; her career, 139; compared with Sheridan, 139; her journey to Ireland, 139; on racial stereotypes, 148; on prosperous Belfast, 219; on Irish cabins, 252; her *Narrative* quoted on sailing to Rathlin, 139–40; on the people of Ireland, 154–5; on pre-industrial Belfast, 225–7
Pococke, Richard, his adventurous travel, 20, 135; his visit to the Giant's Causeway, 135; to the offshore islands, 135; his Irish career, 135; his travels, 135; his approval of the Anglo-Irish, 149; on Irish feasts, 187; on drinking, 187; his 'Tour of 1758' quoted on Cape Clear, 136–7; his 'Tour of 1752' on open-air Mass, 196
Poussin, and Irish scenery, 244
Pratt, Mary Louise, on travel writing, 6
Protestant Ireland, its emergence, 14
Provisional I.R.A., its origin, 4

Queen's Colleges, 21
Queen's County, its naming, 10

Raleigh, Sir Walter, his influence on Edmund Spenser, 75
Rathlin Island, visited by boat, 135
Rebellion, of 1641, 12; its context, 13; issue discussed, 115; its focus in Kilkenny, 115
Reid, Thomas, his travels in Ireland, 21, 177; 219; his view of Ireland as anomaly, 177; his *Travels* quoted on Orange riots, 177–80; on cheerful beggars, 252; on Irish cabins, 255–8
Renaissance, travel in, 53; significance of clothes in, 73
Rich, Barnaby, on 'wilful' Irish, 37; his attack on English recusants, 37; his military career, 45; his friendship with Thomas Churchyard, 45; his Irish connections, 45; his connection with the Earl of Essex, 45; his opposition to Thomas Jones and Adam Loftus, 45; his connection with Lord Mountjoy, 45; his *A New Description of Ireland*, 45; his 'The Anatomy of Ireland', 45; compared with John Bale, 45; his *New Description* quoted on Irish resistance, 45–7; his *Irish Hubbub* quoted on Irish weeping, 85–6
Richter, Michael, on Giraldus's allegiances, 8; on political terminology, 8
Roche, Lord, his dispute with Edmund Spenser, 75
Romans, as civilisers of ancient Britons, 73
Russell Conrad, on Wentworth in Ireland, 13; on 'British' context of English civil war, 14

Scott, Sir Walter, his tour of Ireland, 22
Serbia, self-determination in, 22
Shelley, and Alpine travel, 135
Shelley, Percy Bysshe, his visit to Dublin, 22; its impact, 251
Sheridan, Richard Brinsley, compared with Anne Plumptre, 139
Sidney, Sir Henry, and Irish struggles, 11; his reforms, 39; his connection with Sir William Gerard, 39; with John Derricke, 41; with the court, 97; on Irish war, 97; his Irish career, 100; his advocacy on colonisation, 100; his

defeat of Shane O'Neill, 100; his 'Memoir' quoted on military campaigns, 100–101
Silken Thomas, his revolt, 10
Smerwick, massacre of, 88
Smith, Adam, influences Arthur Young, 138
Smith, Sir Thomas, and Ulster plantation, 11; his change of plan, 12; his Ards project, 108
Solinus, 25
South Africa, self-determination in, 22
Spain, and Irish invasion, 11; Hugh O'Neill appeals to for help, 88
Spenser, Edmund, on Ireland's influence, 2; his Irish career, 74–5; his connection with Lord Grey, 74; his defence of the massacre at Smerwick, 97; on Munster famine, 97; his Munster estate, 74; the influence of Sir Walter Raleigh on, 75; his dispute with Lord Roche, 75; his marriage to Elizabeth Boyle, 75; his travel to London, 75; his *View* discussed, 75, 124; his *View* quoted on Irish customs, 75–6; on Irish clothing, 83–5; on Irish bards, 86–7; on the starving Irish, 99–100; on the massacre at Smerwick, 104–5
St Leger, his 'surrender and regrant' policy, 9
Stanihurst, James, his patronage of Edmund Campion, 37
Stanihurst, Richard, 1; his relationship with Edmund Campion, 37, 38
Starkey, Thomas, as Henrican propagandist, 97
Stevens, John, Jacobite officer, 17; his arrival at Cork, 134; his description of the Battle of the Boyne, 160; of the siege of Limerick, 165; his Irish career, 165; his *Journal* quoted on the siege of Limerick, 165–70
Stewart, A. T. Q., on 1641 rebellion, 115
Story, George, his Irish experience, 170; his *History* quoted on Irish rapparees, 170–1
Strabo, 25
'Supplication of the Blood of English' (1599), discussed, 94; quoted on Irish atrocities, 94–5
Swift, Jonathan, *A Modest Proposal*, 6; his influence on William Cobbett, 23

Tacitus, 25, 53
Taylor, D., on Ulster Protestants, 5
Taylor, G., and A. Skinner, *Maps of the Roads of Ireland*, 20
Temple, Sir John, 1; on Irish rebellion, 15
Temple, Sir John, on the 1641 rebellion, 115
Thackeray, William Makepeace, compares Irish with Hottentots, 15; debunks travel writing, 23; his hostility to Romantic writing, 238; on Ireland, 23; his Irish travel, 229–30; his first impressions, 134; his view of Cork and Galway, 219; his *Irish Sketch Book* quoted on Cork city, 230–7
Tour through Ireland by Two English Gentlemen, A, 20
Tourism, beginning of, 19
Transplantation, 13
'Treatise of Ireland, A', critical of Irish policy of English monarchs, 70; on opportunities in Ireland, 70; quoted on Ireland's advantages to English, 70–2
Trotter, J. B., 21; his *Walks through Ireland*, 21
True and Credible Relation, A (1642), quoted on Irish atrocities, 118–20
Twiss, Richard, criticised on Ireland by John Gough, 213; on Irish cabins, 253
Tyrone, 54

Ulster, and Irish resistance, 63; and the Famine, 21; its poverty in 1650s, 123
Ussher, Archbishop, his acquaintance with Luke Gernon, 65

Victoria, Queen, her visits to Ireland, 157, 247; her attitude, 157; feels response to Cork, 157; on Irish weather, 247; her journal quoted on arriving in Ireland, 157–9; on Killarney, 248–50

Wakefield, Priscilla, criticised on Ireland by John Gough, 213
Wallis, R., on Ulster Protestants, 5
Walsingham Sir Francis, his praise of William Herbert, 48
Ware, Sir James, *Ancient Irish Histories*, 38; his edition of Edmund Spenser, 12; of Edmund Campion, 38; his assessment of war, 115
Waterford, admired by travellers, 219
Welsh, judged barbarous by Giraldus, 36

Wentworth, his Irish policies, 13; his fate, 13; his feud with Sir Richard Boyle, 120–1

Wesley, John, unappreciative of Ireland, 20; his criticism of the Anglo-Irish, 149, 160; his travels in Ireland, 171, 219; his attitude to Ireland, 171–2; his *Journal* quoted on Irish rioting, 172–3; on an Irish cabin, 252

Westward Enterprise, the, 36

Wicklow, admired by travellers, 19

Wordsworth, William, his tour of Ireland, 22

Young Ireland, and Daniel O'Connell, 21

Young, Arthur, his career, 137–8; his journey to Ireland, 134; his Irish travel, 15, 137; his sympathy, 20; his work for Lord Kingsborough, 137; his belief in self-interest, 137; his *Tour* quoted on Irish road-making, 138–9; on Irish bogs, 149–50; on Irish customs, 196–9; on Killarney, 241–244; on Irish community, 251–2